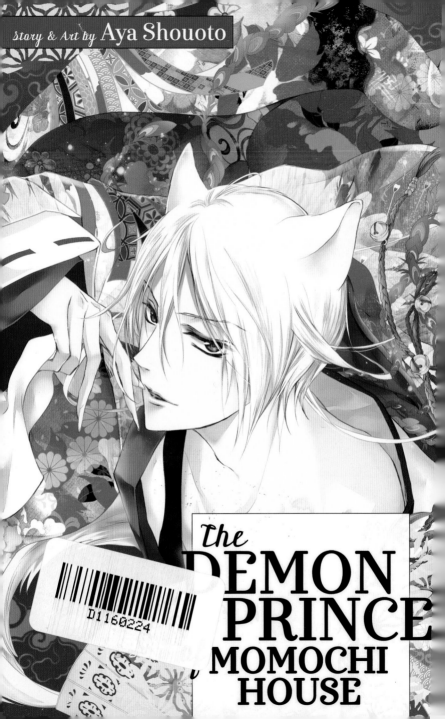

Story & Art by Aya Shouoto

The
DEMON
PRINCE
MOMOCHI
HOUSE

D1160224

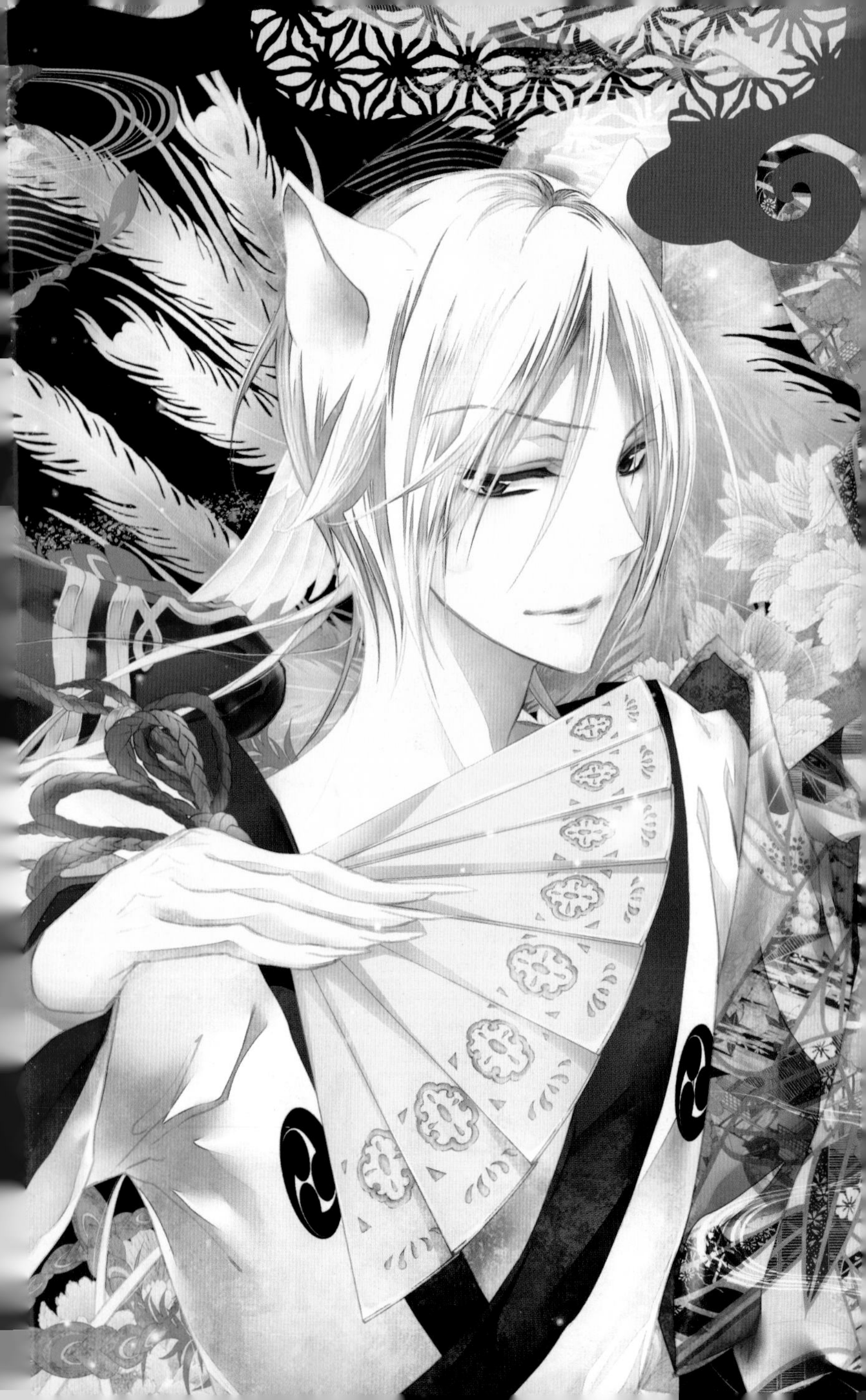

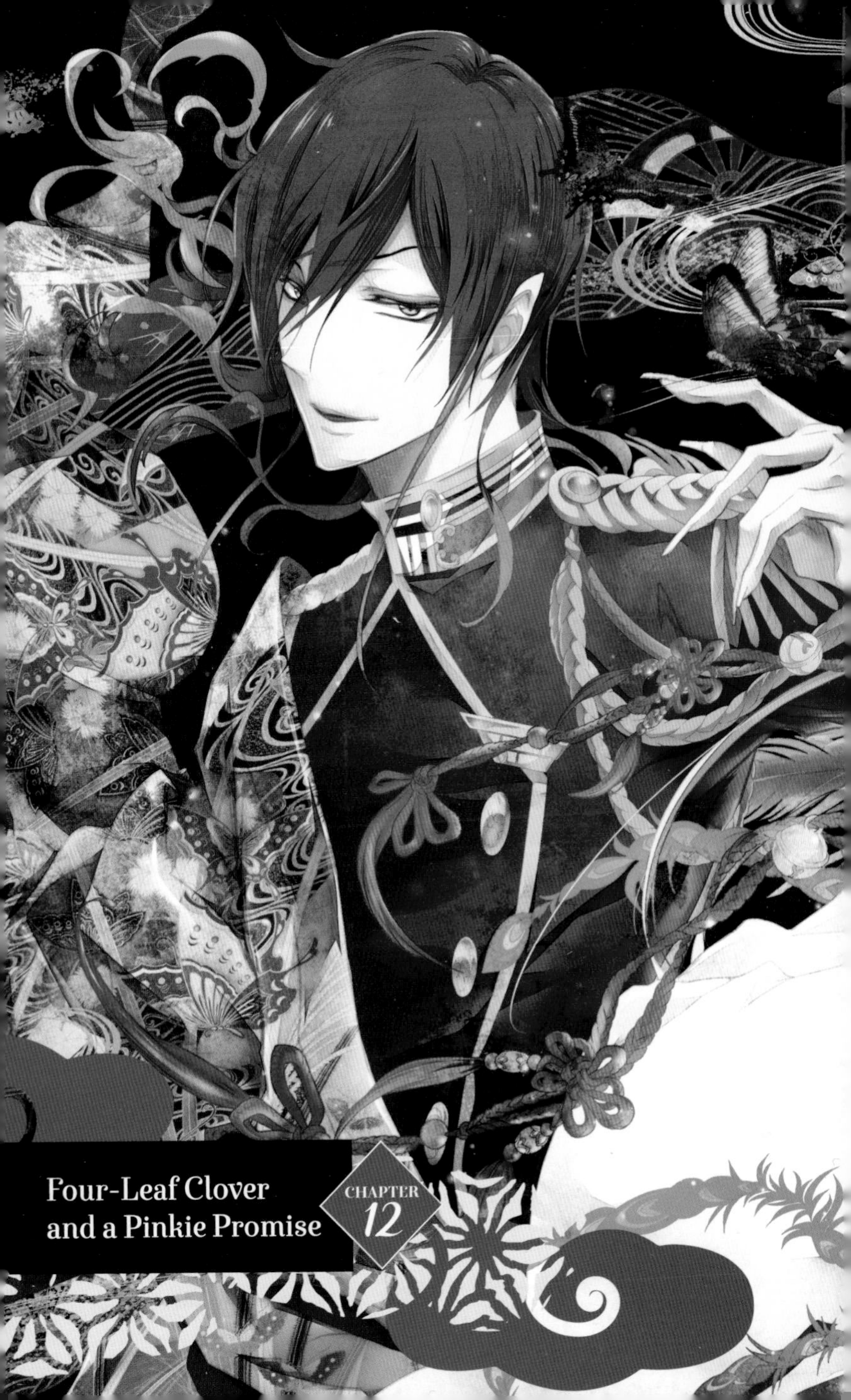
Four-Leaf Clover
and a Pinkie Promise
CHAPTER
12

The DEMON PRINCE of MOMOCHI HOUSE

④

Contents

The Mysterious Residents of Momochi House

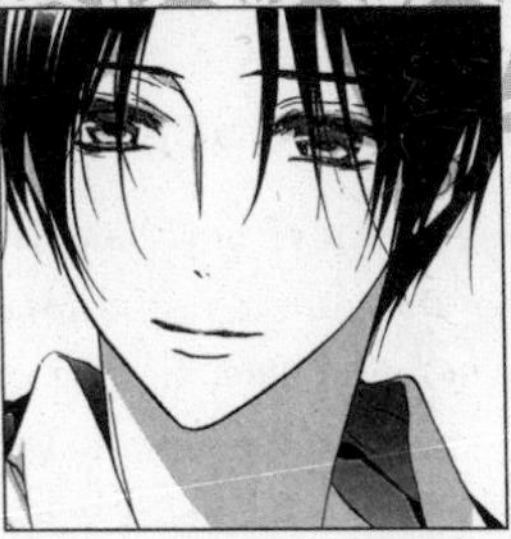

Aoi Nanamori

When he was 7 years old, he wandered into Momochi House and was chosen as the Omamori-sama. He transforms into a nue to perform his duties, but it seems this role was meant for Himari.

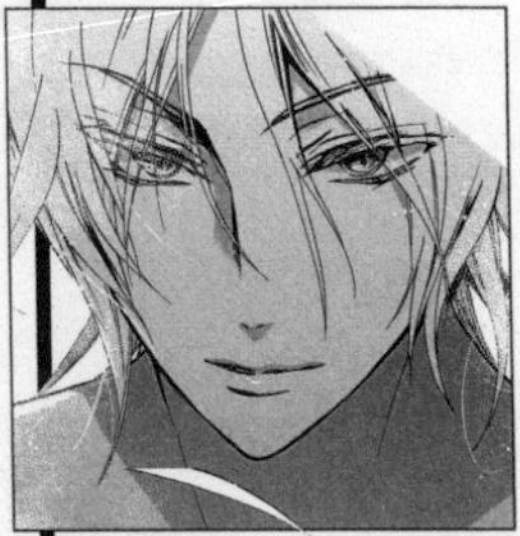

Omamori-sama (Nue)

An ayakashi, or demon, with the ears of a cat, the wings of a bird, and the tail of a fox. As the Omamori-sama, the nue protects Momochi House and eliminates demons who make their way in from the spiritual realm.

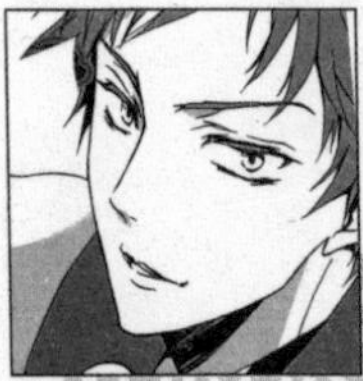

Ise

One of Omamori-sama's shikigami. He's an orangutan.

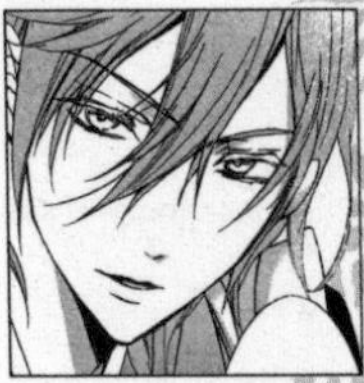

Yukari

One of Omamori-sama's shikigami. He's a water serpent.

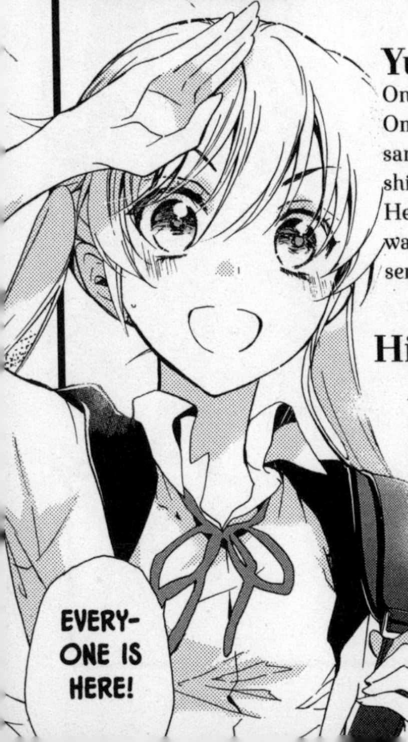
EVERY-ONE IS HERE!

Himari Momochi

A 16-year-old orphan who, according to a certain will, has inherited Momochi House. As rightful owner, she has the ability to expel beings from the house.

Lesser Yokai

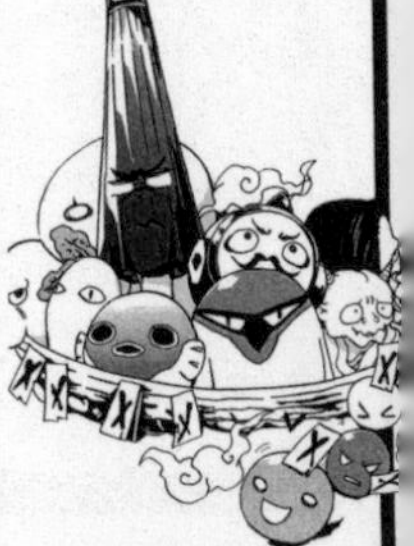

Momochi House: Story Thus Far

Four of Himari's friends from school visit Momochi House. But a great demon by the name of Kasha has entered the house by pretending to be one of them. Kasha's appearance forces Aoi to the brink of becoming a true demon... Later, Aoi invites Himari to an area deep within Momochi House that she has never before seen. A great number of ayakashi are celebrating the Nue's Resealing Rite. The rite is successful and Himari and her friends go back to their normal lives. Aoi makes Himari a four-leaf clover ring as a token of thanks for aiding him. Himari happily wears the ring to school, but one boy has a strong reaction the instant he sees it...

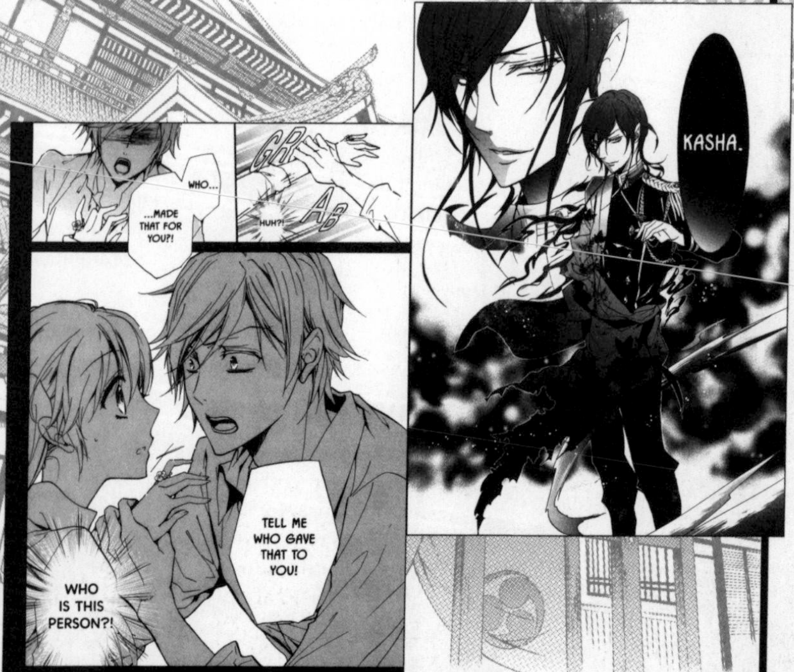
KASHA.
GR
AB
HUH?!
WHO...
...MADE THAT FOR YOU?!
TELL ME WHO GAVE THAT TO YOU!
WHO IS THIS PERSON?!

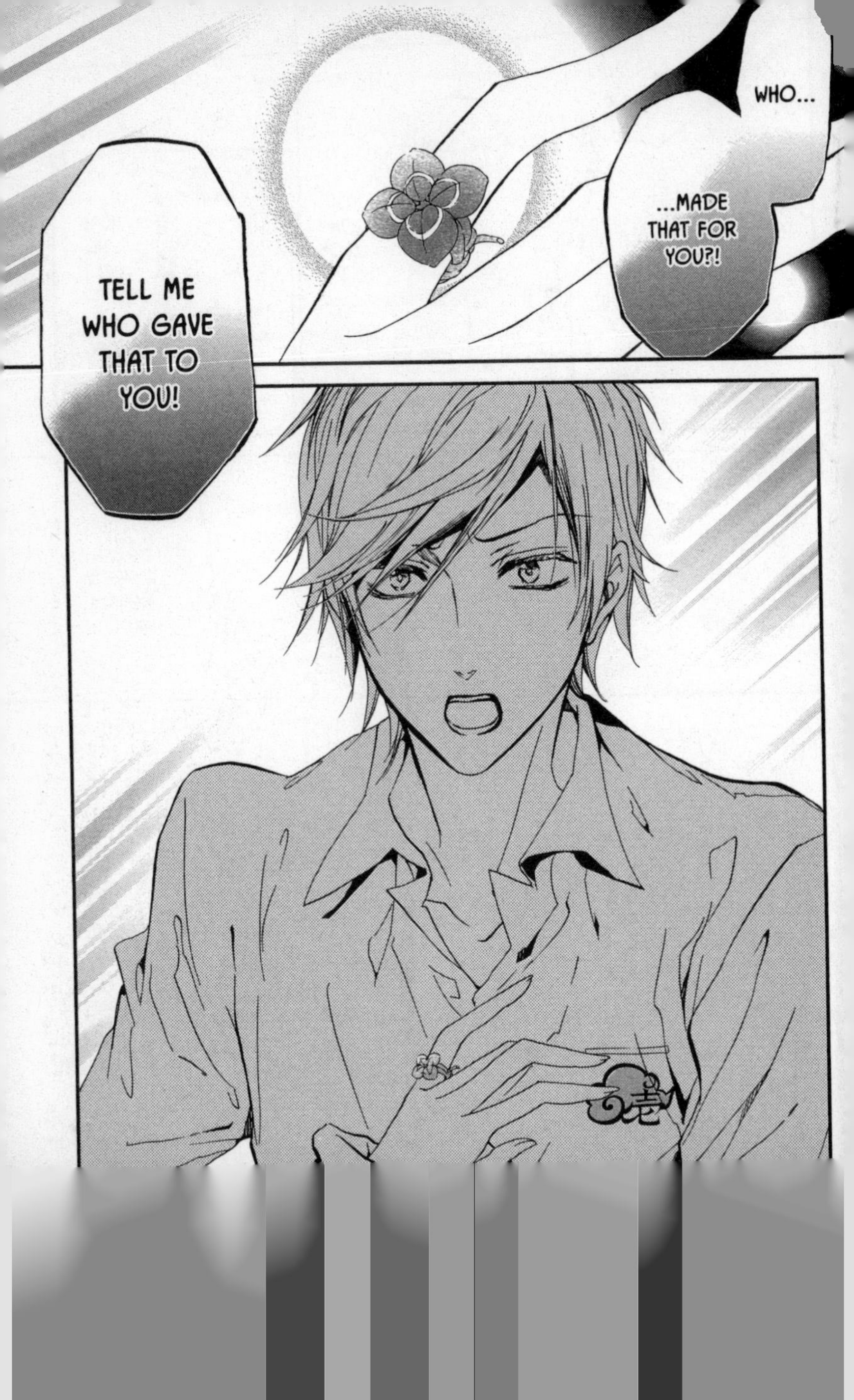
WHO...
...MADE THAT FOR YOU?!
TELL ME WHO GAVE THAT TO YOU!

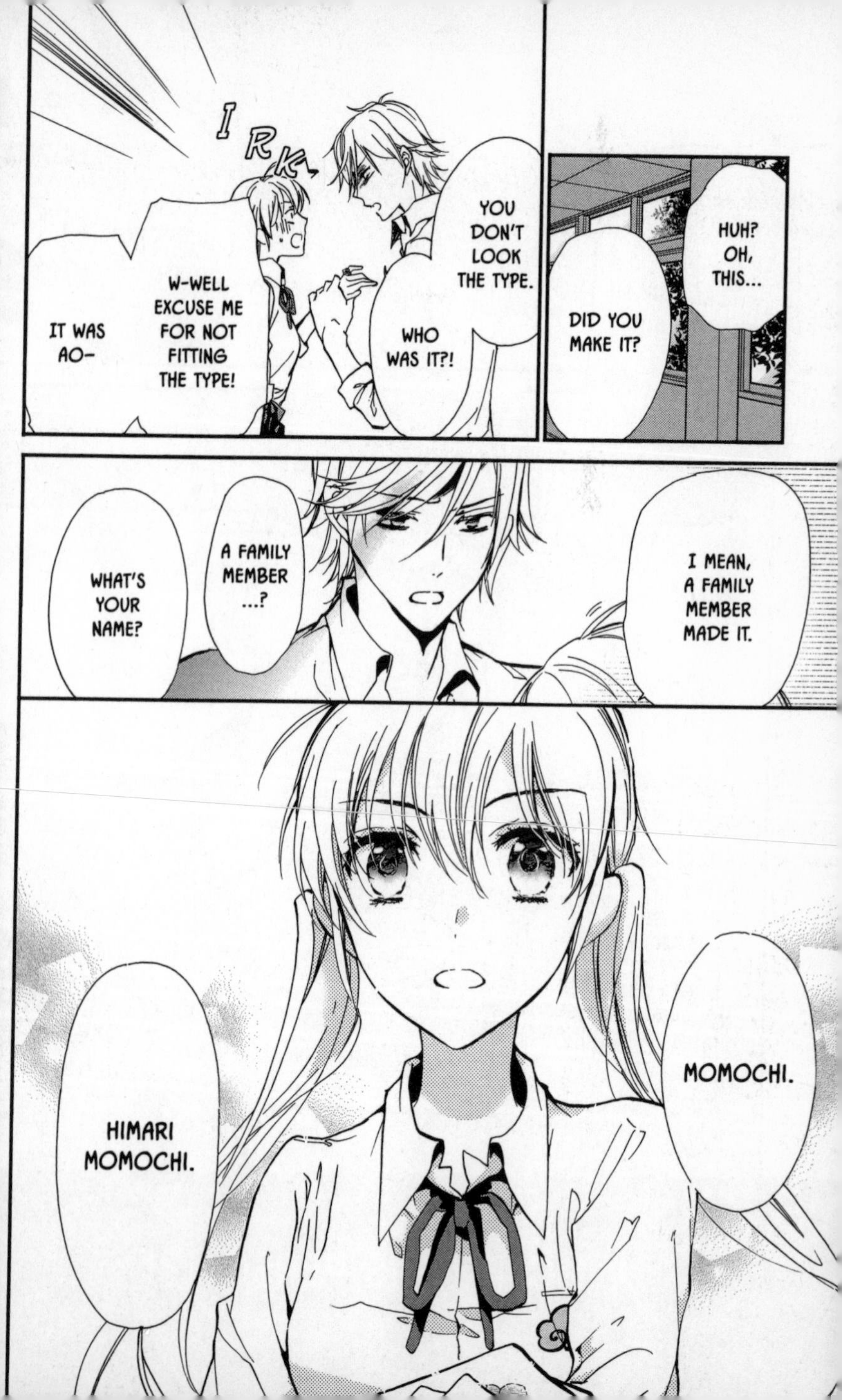
HUH? OH, THIS...
DID YOU MAKE IT?
YOU DON'T LOOK THE TYPE.
IRK
WHO WAS IT?!
W-WELL EXCUSE ME FOR NOT FITTING THE TYPE!
IT WAS AO-
I MEAN, A FAMILY MEMBER MADE IT.
A FAMILY MEMBER ...?
WHAT'S YOUR NAME?
MOMOCHI.
HIMARI MOMOCHI.

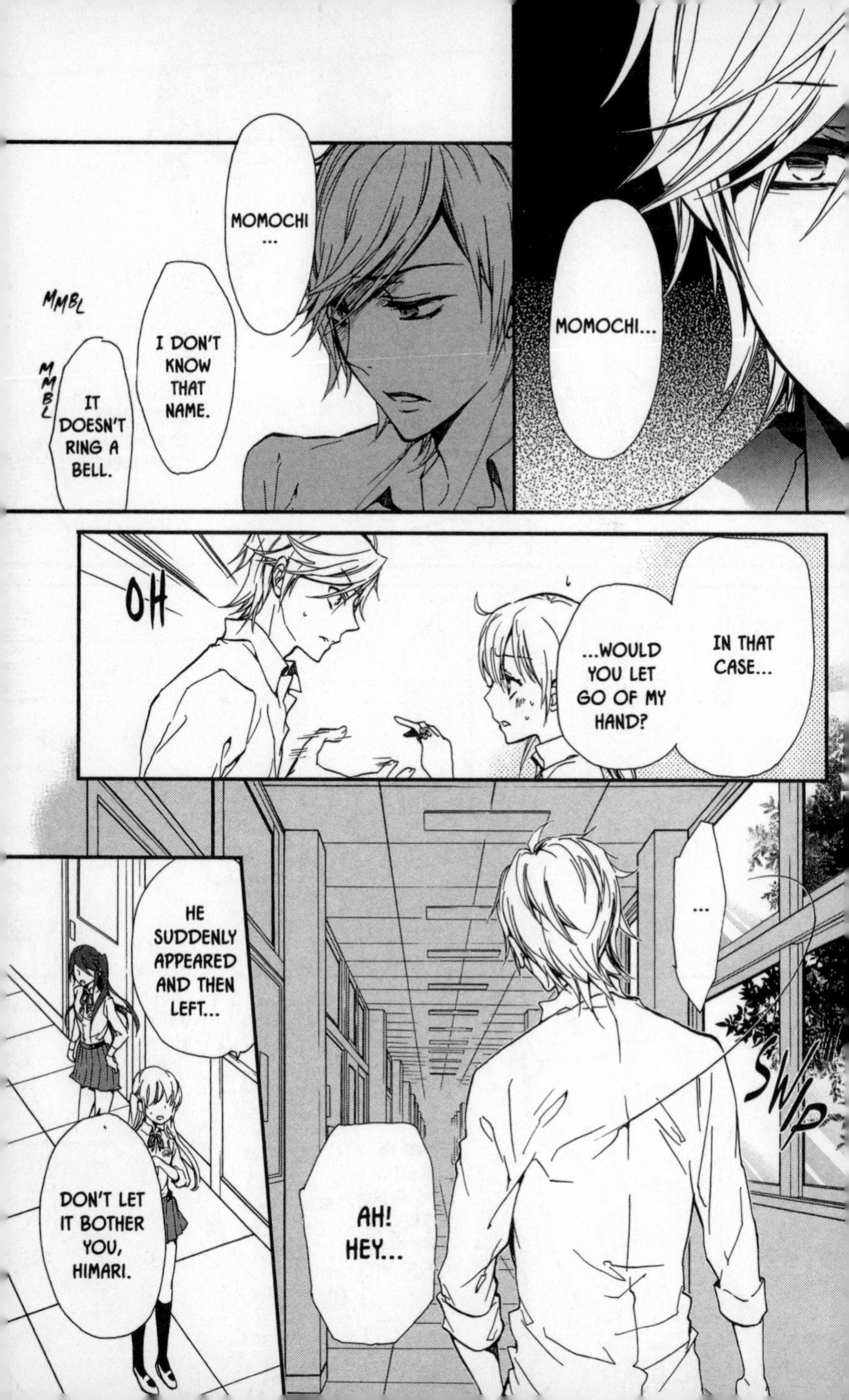
MOMOCHI...
MOMOCHI
...
I DON'T KNOW THAT NAME.
MMBL
MMBL
IT DOESN'T RING A BELL.
IN THAT CASE...
...WOULD YOU LET GO OF MY HAND?
OH
...
SWIP
AH! HEY...
HE SUDDENLY APPEARED AND THEN LEFT...
DON'T LET IT BOTHER YOU, HIMARI.

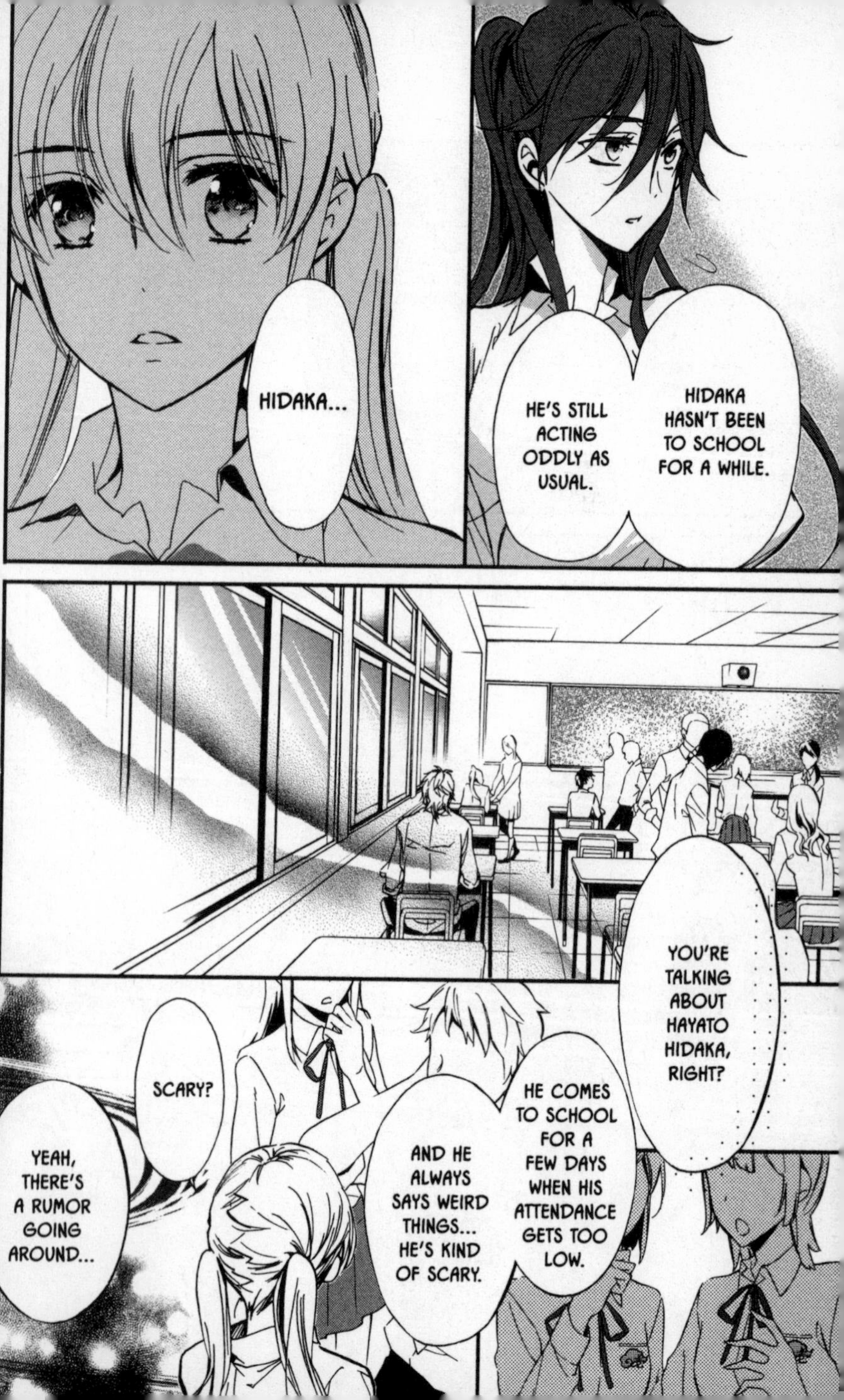
HIDAKA HASN'T BEEN TO SCHOOL FOR A WHILE.
HE'S STILL ACTING ODDLY AS USUAL.
HIDAKA...
YOU'RE TALKING ABOUT HAYATO HIDAKA, RIGHT?
HE COMES TO SCHOOL FOR A FEW DAYS WHEN HIS ATTENDANCE GETS TOO LOW.
AND HE ALWAYS SAYS WEIRD THINGS... HE'S KIND OF SCARY.
SCARY?
YEAH, THERE'S A RUMOR GOING AROUND...

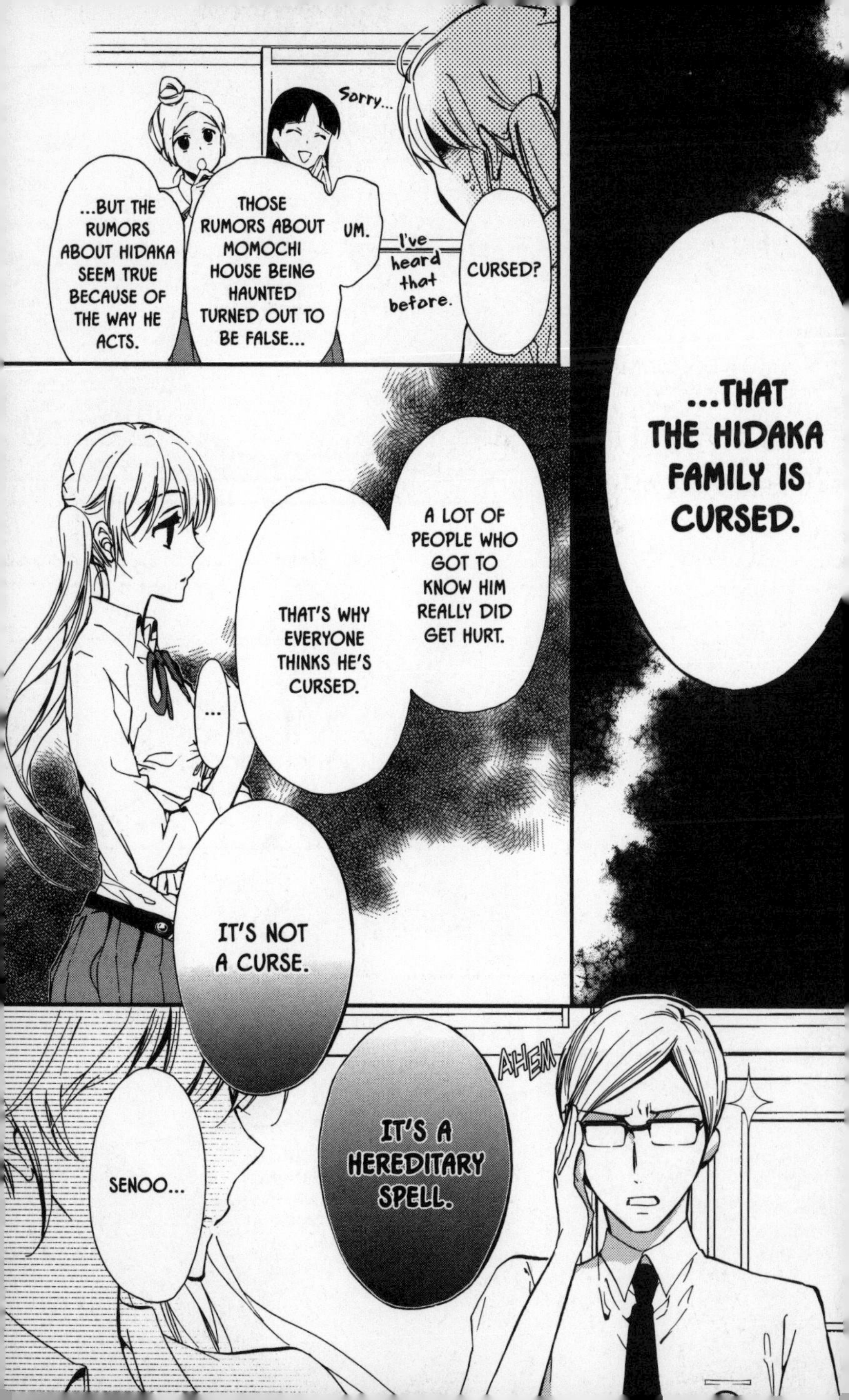
Sorry...
CURSED?
I've heard that before.
UM.
THOSE RUMORS ABOUT MOMOCHI HOUSE BEING HAUNTED TURNED OUT TO BE FALSE...
...BUT THE RUMORS ABOUT HIDAKA SEEM TRUE BECAUSE OF THE WAY HE ACTS.
...THAT THE HIDAKA FAMILY IS CURSED.
A LOT OF PEOPLE WHO GOT TO KNOW HIM REALLY DID GET HURT.
THAT'S WHY EVERYONE THINKS HE'S CURSED.
...
IT'S NOT A CURSE.
AHEM
IT'S A HEREDITARY SPELL.
SENOO...

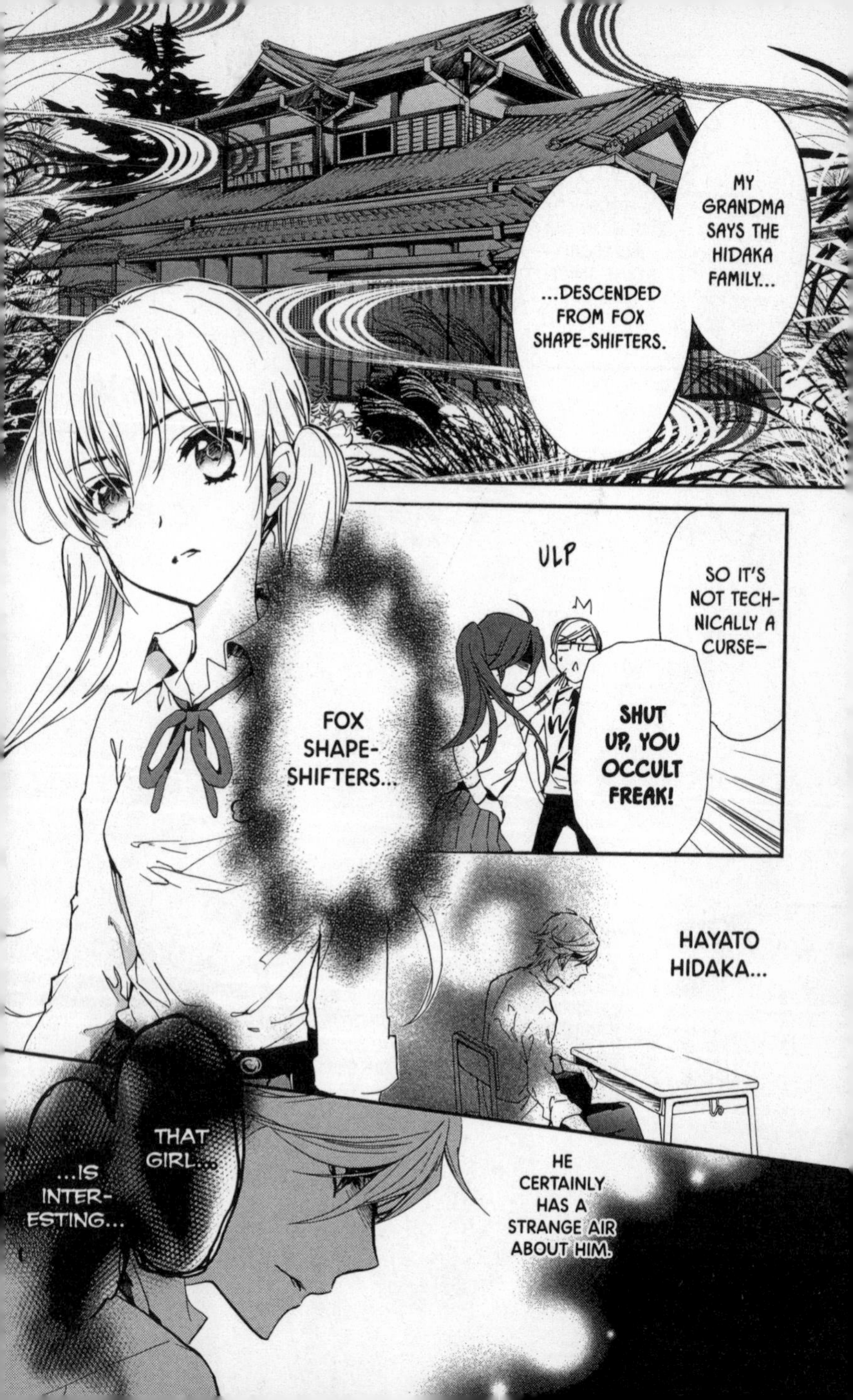
MY GRANDMA SAYS THE HIDAKA FAMILY...
...DESCENDED FROM FOX SHAPE-SHIFTERS.
SO IT'S NOT TECHNICALLY A CURSE—
SHUT UP, YOU OCCULT FREAK!
ULP
FOX SHAPE-SHIFTERS...
HAYATO HIDAKA...
HE CERTAINLY HAS A STRANGE AIR ABOUT HIM.
THAT GIRL...
...IS INTERESTING...

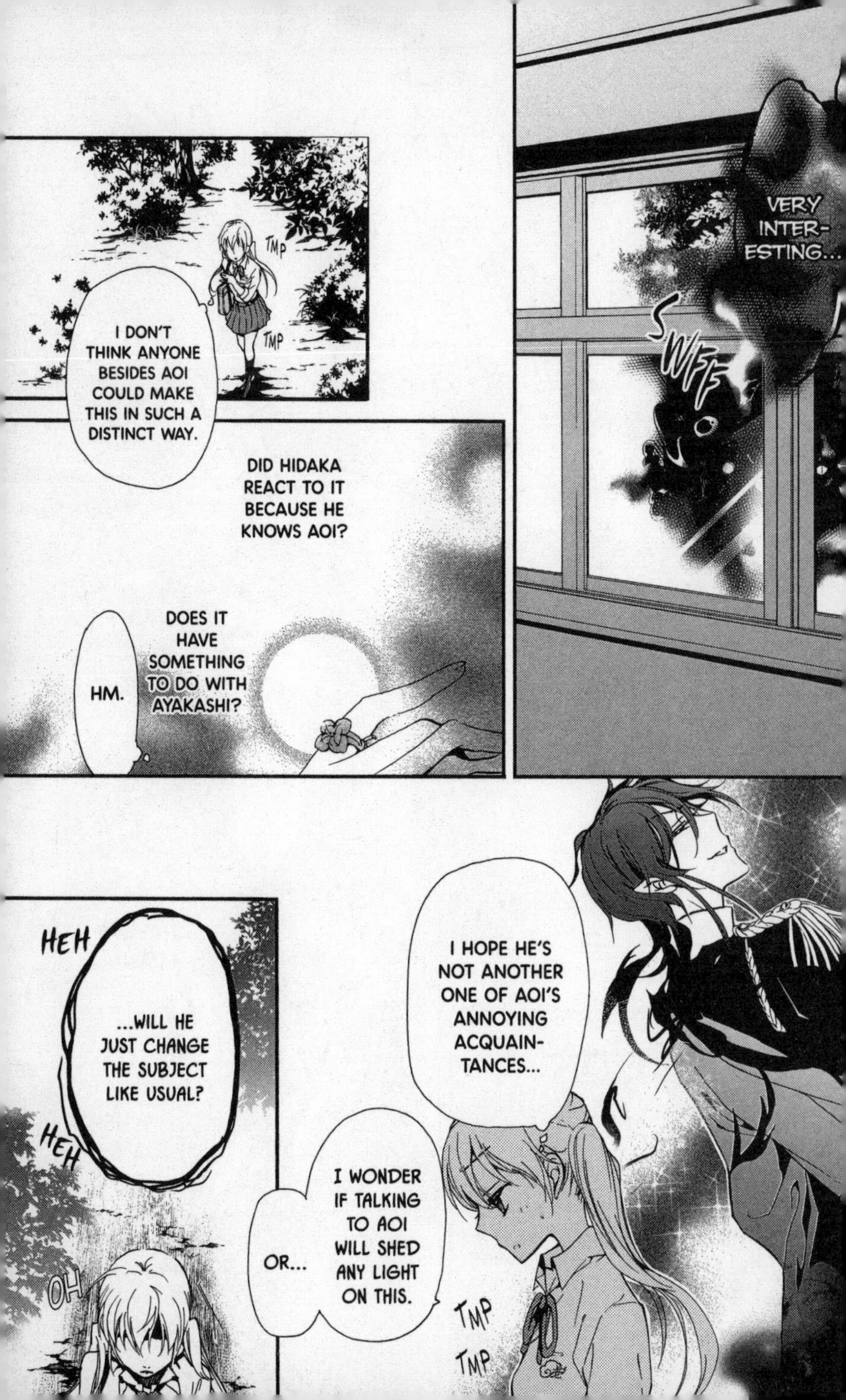
VERY INTER-ESTING...
SNIFF
TMP
TMP
I DON'T THINK ANYONE BESIDES AOI COULD MAKE THIS IN SUCH A DISTINCT WAY.
DID HIDAKA REACT TO IT BECAUSE HE KNOWS AOI?
DOES IT HAVE SOMETHING TO DO WITH AYAKASHI?
HM.
I HOPE HE'S NOT ANOTHER ONE OF AOI'S ANNOYING ACQUAIN-TANCES...
I WONDER IF TALKING TO AOI WILL SHED ANY LIGHT ON THIS.
OR...
TMP
TMP
HEH
...WILL HE JUST CHANGE THE SUBJECT LIKE USUAL?
HEH
OH

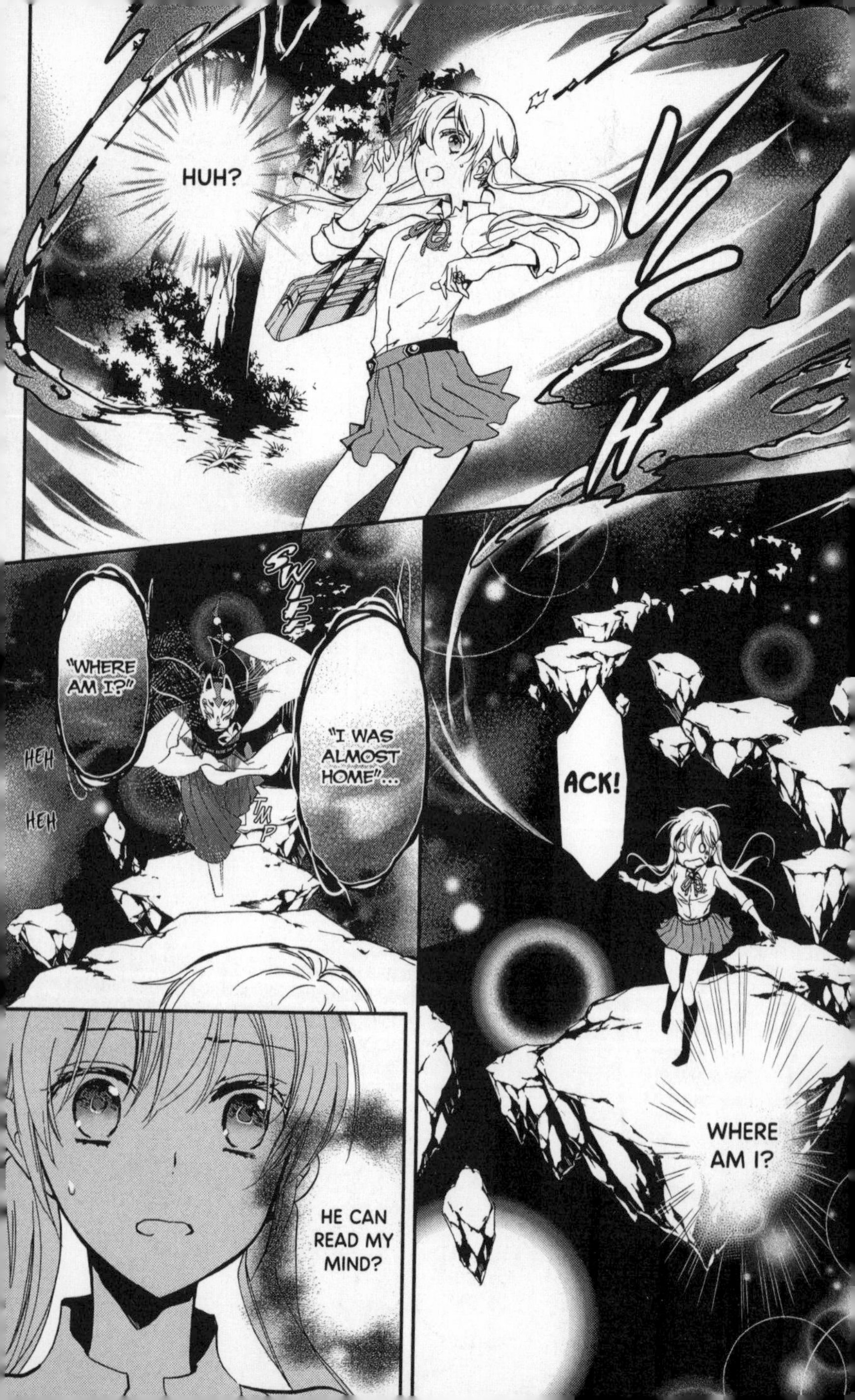
HUH?
VWSH
ACK!
WHERE AM I?
SWFF
"I WAS ALMOST HOME"...
"WHERE AM I?"
HEH
HEH
TMP
HE CAN READ MY MIND?

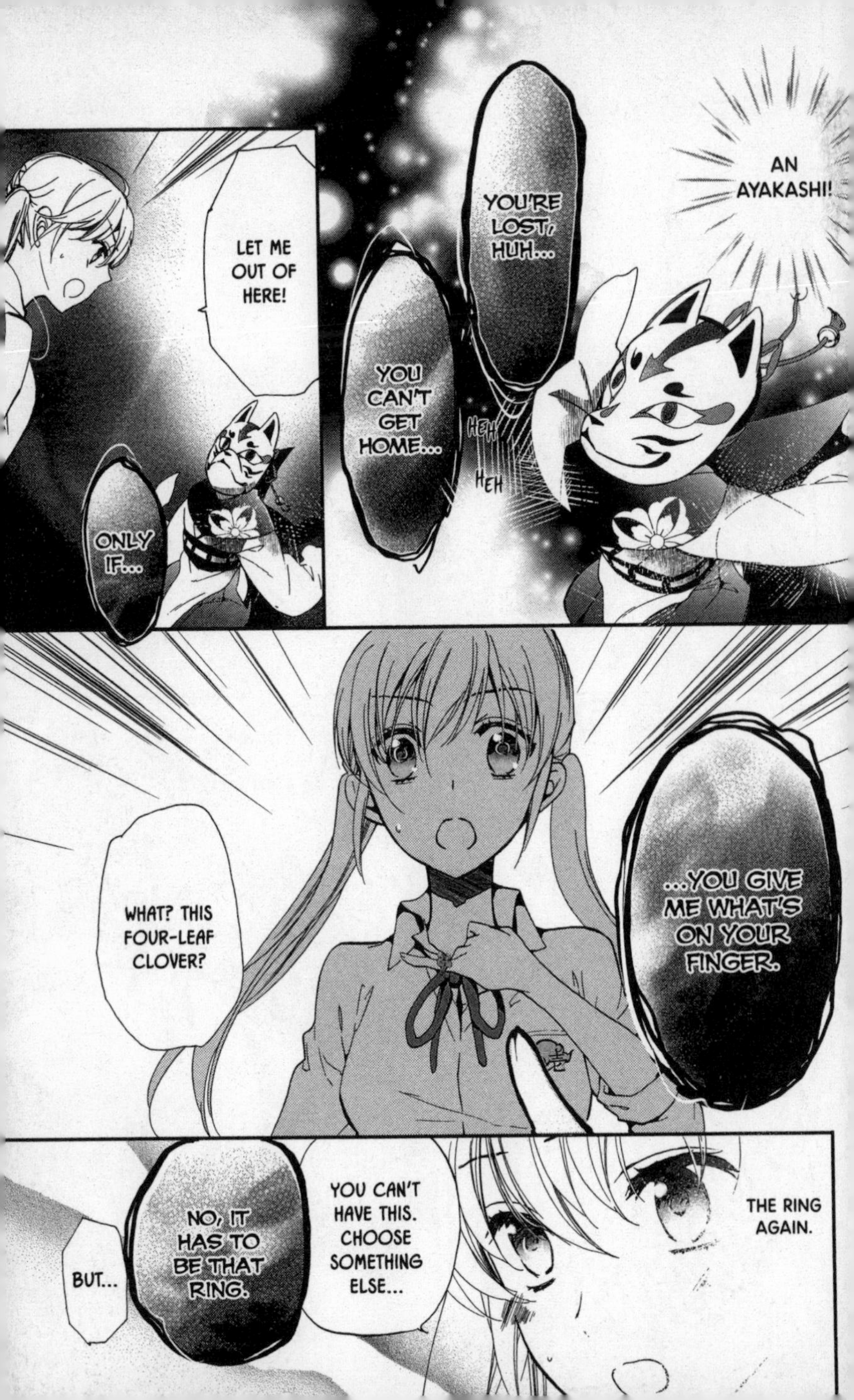
AN AYAKASHI!
YOU'RE LOST, HUH...
YOU CAN'T GET HOME...
HEH HEH
LET ME OUT OF HERE!
ONLY IF...
...YOU GIVE ME WHAT'S ON YOUR FINGER.
WHAT? THIS FOUR-LEAF CLOVER?
THE RING AGAIN.
YOU CAN'T HAVE THIS. CHOOSE SOMETHING ELSE...
NO, IT HAS TO BE THAT RING.
BUT...

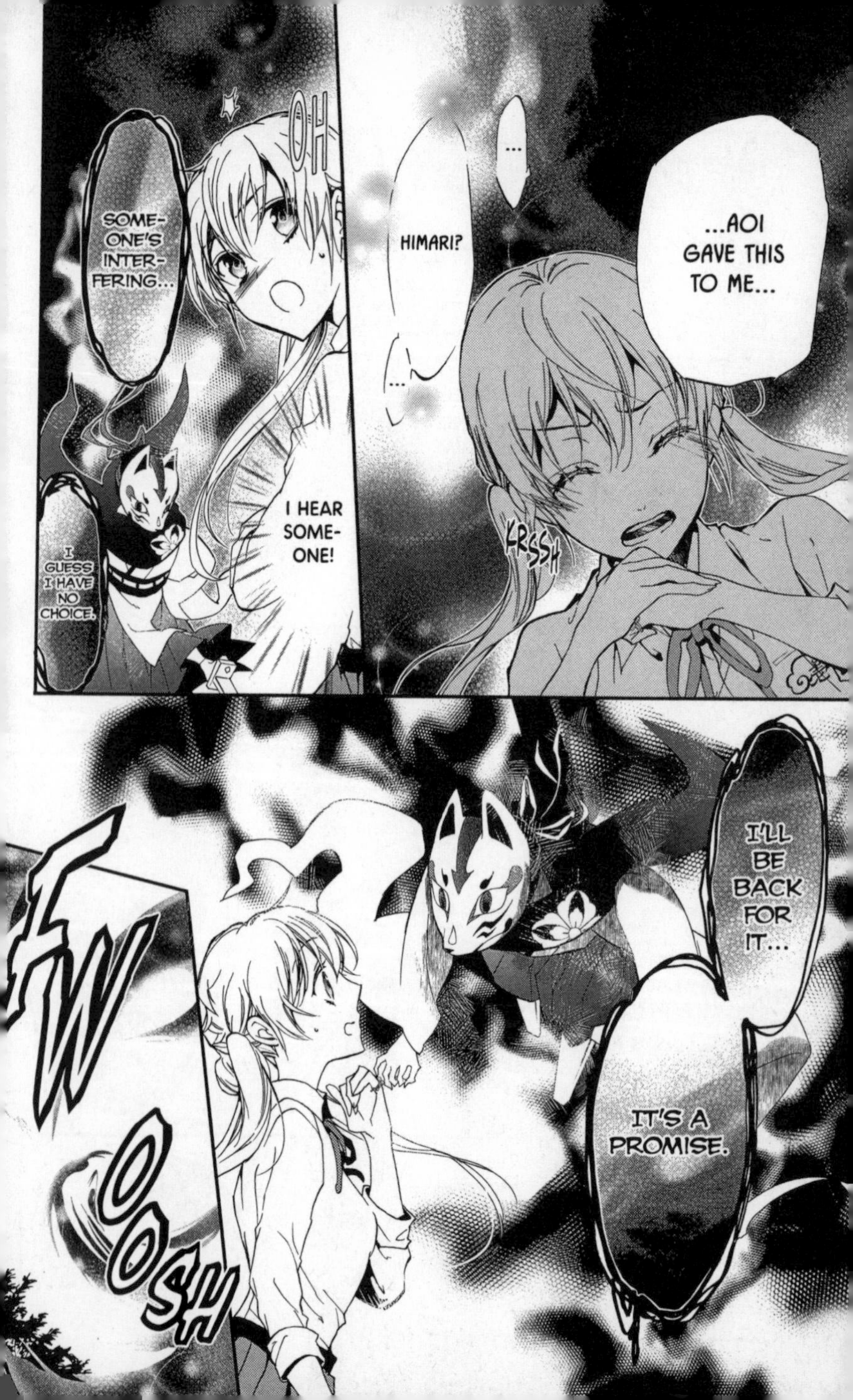

...AOI GAVE THIS TO ME...
...
HIMARI?
...
KRSSH
OH
SOME-ONE'S INTER-FERING...
I HEAR SOME-ONE!
I GUESS I HAVE NO CHOICE.
I'LL BE BACK FOR IT...
IT'S A PROMISE.
FWOOOSH

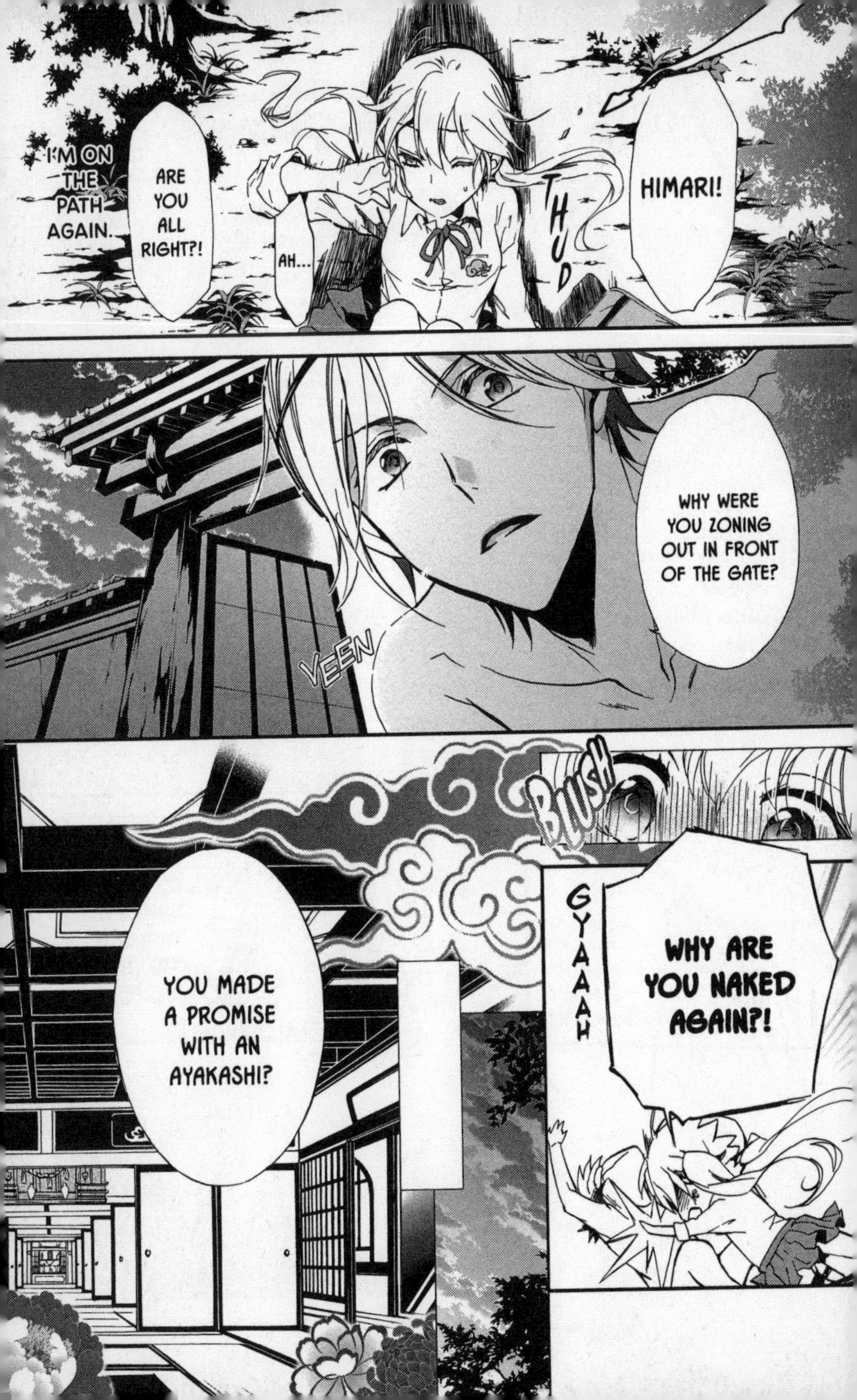
HIMARI!
THUD
AH...
ARE YOU ALL RIGHT?!
I'M ON THE PATH AGAIN.
WHY WERE YOU ZONING OUT IN FRONT OF THE GATE?
YEEN
BLUSH
WHY ARE YOU NAKED AGAIN?!
GYAAAH
YOU MADE A PROMISE WITH AN AYAKASHI?

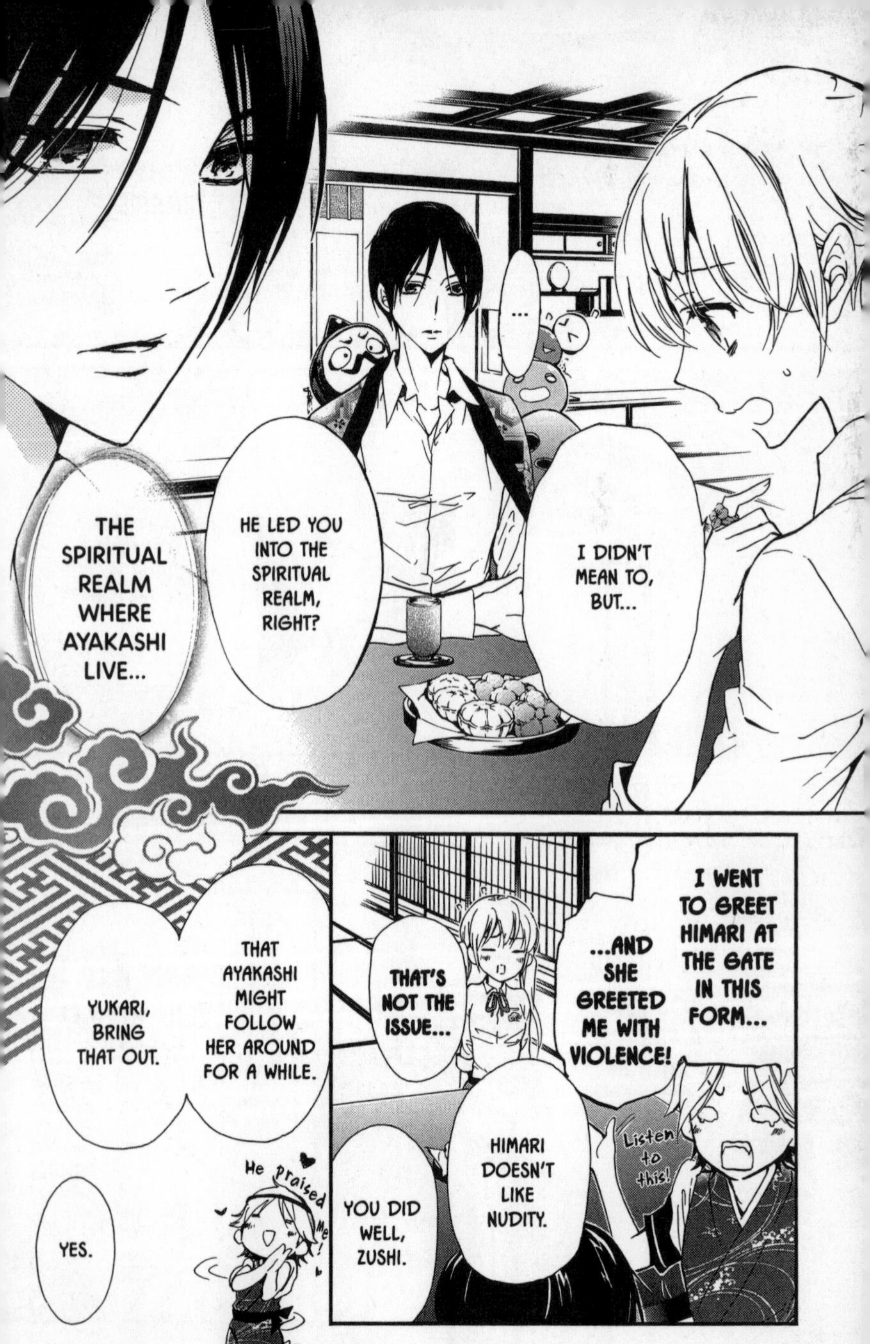
...
I DIDN'T MEAN TO, BUT...
HE LED YOU INTO THE SPIRITUAL REALM, RIGHT?
THE SPIRITUAL REALM WHERE AYAKASHI LIVE...
I WENT TO GREET HIMARI AT THE GATE IN THIS FORM...
...AND SHE GREETED ME WITH VIOLENCE!
THAT'S NOT THE ISSUE...
Listen to this!
HIMARI DOESN'T LIKE NUDITY.
YOU DID WELL, ZUSHI.
THAT AYAKASHI MIGHT FOLLOW HER AROUND FOR A WHILE.
YUKARI, BRING THAT OUT.
He praised me!
YES.

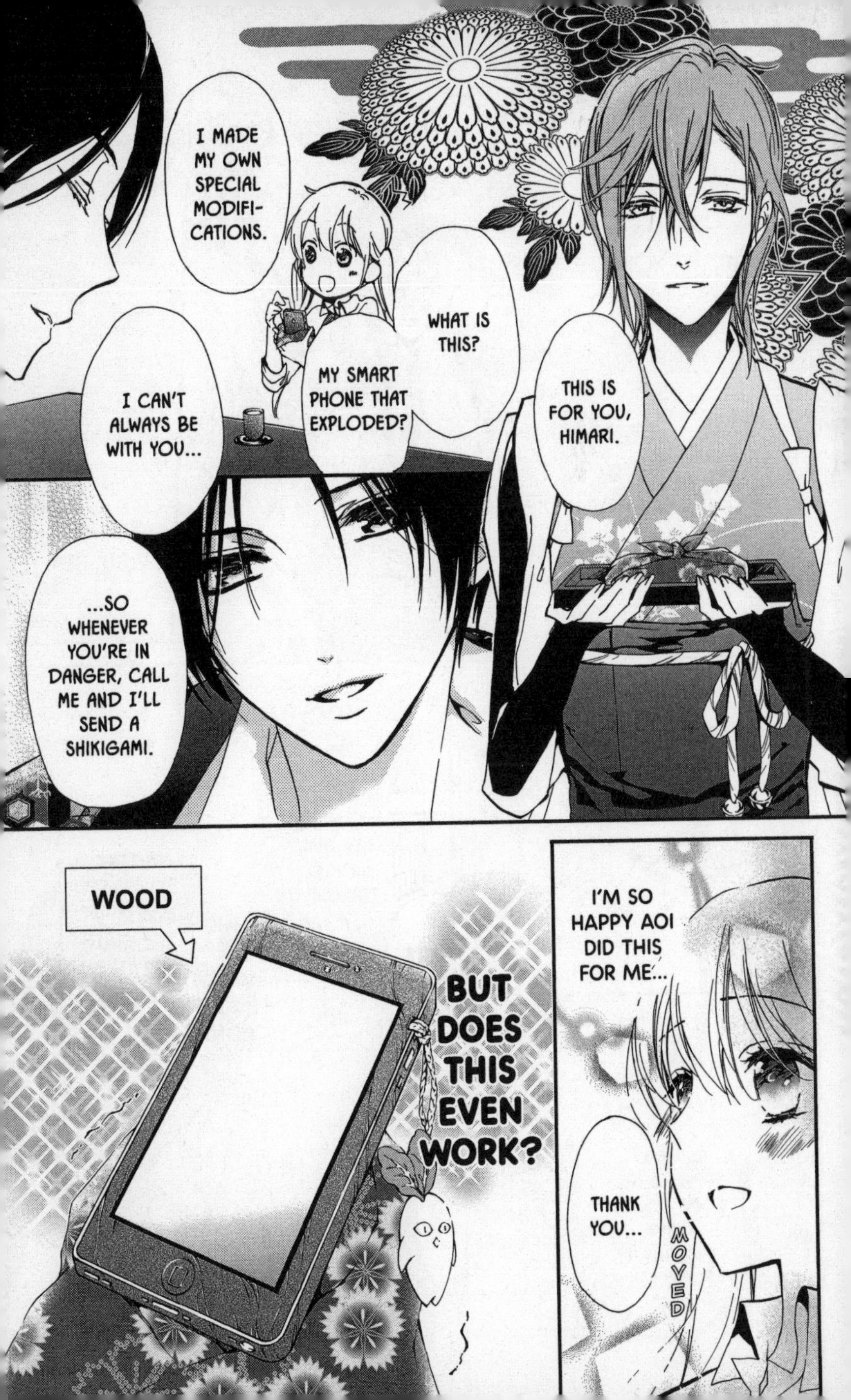
THIS IS FOR YOU, HIMARI.
WHAT IS THIS?
MY SMART PHONE THAT EXPLODED?
I MADE MY OWN SPECIAL MODIFICATIONS.
I CAN'T ALWAYS BE WITH YOU...
...SO WHENEVER YOU'RE IN DANGER, CALL ME AND I'LL SEND A SHIKIGAMI.
I'M SO HAPPY AOI DID THIS FOR ME...
THANK YOU...
MOVED
WOOD
BUT DOES THIS EVEN WORK?

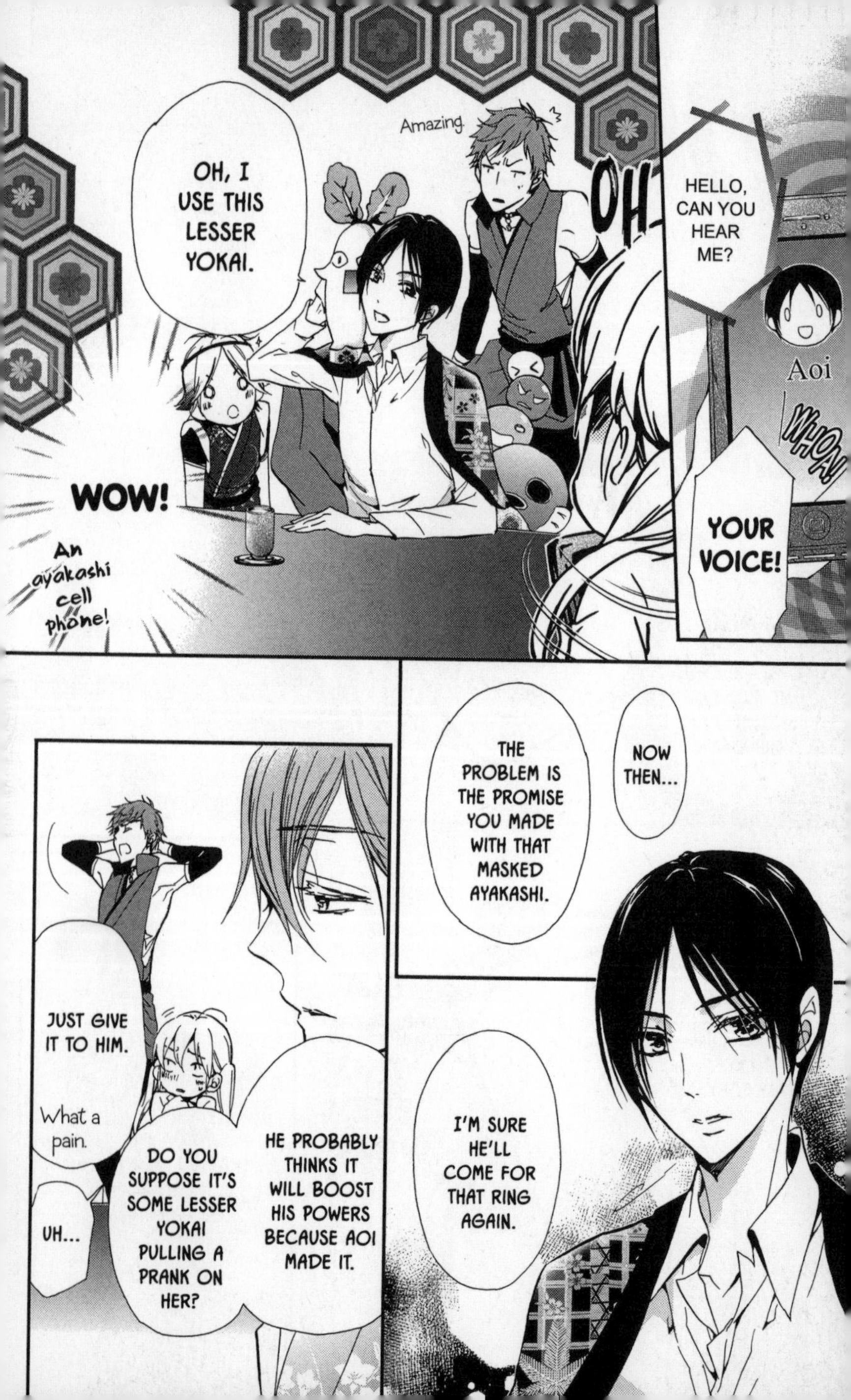
HELLO, CAN YOU HEAR ME?
Aoi
WHOA!
YOUR VOICE!
OH!
Amazing.
OH, I USE THIS LESSER YOKAI.
WOW!
An ayakashi cell phone!
NOW THEN...
THE PROBLEM IS THE PROMISE YOU MADE WITH THAT MASKED AYAKASHI.
I'M SURE HE'LL COME FOR THAT RING AGAIN.
HE PROBABLY THINKS IT WILL BOOST HIS POWERS BECAUSE AOI MADE IT.
DO YOU SUPPOSE IT'S SOME LESSER YOKAI PULLING A PRANK ON HER?
UH...
What a pain.
JUST GIVE IT TO HIM.

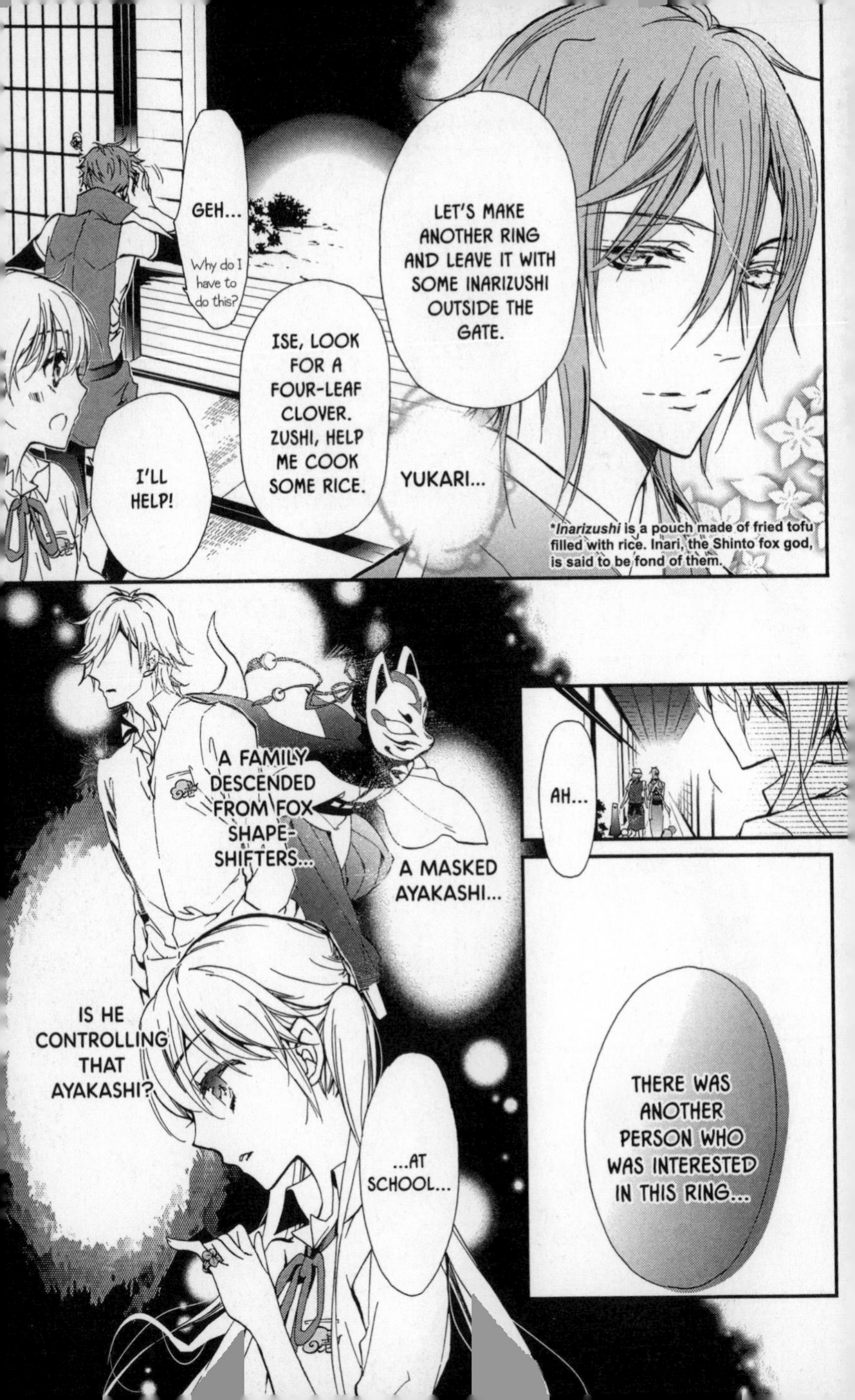
LET'S MAKE ANOTHER RING AND LEAVE IT WITH SOME INARIZUSHI OUTSIDE THE GATE.
YUKARI...
ISE, LOOK FOR A FOUR-LEAF CLOVER. ZUSHI, HELP ME COOK SOME RICE.
GEH...
Why do I have to do this?
I'LL HELP!
AH...
THERE WAS ANOTHER PERSON WHO WAS INTERESTED IN THIS RING...
A MASKED AYAKASHI...
A FAMILY DESCENDED FROM FOX SHAPE-SHIFTERS...
...AT SCHOOL...
IS HE CONTROLLING THAT AYAKASHI?

**Inarizushi* is a pouch made of fried tofu filled with rice. Inari, the Shinto fox god, is said to be fond of them.

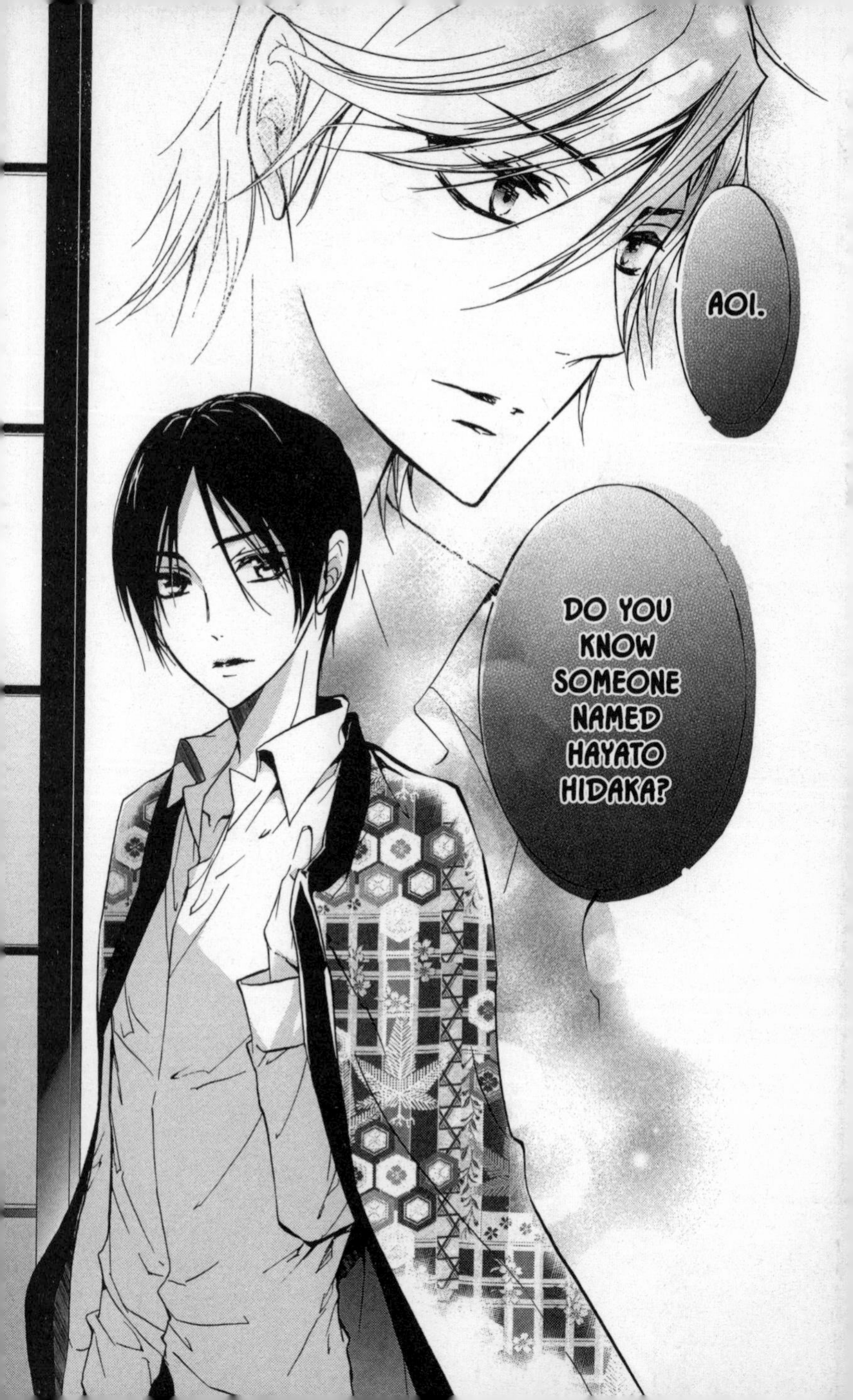
AOI.
DO YOU KNOW SOMEONE NAMED HAYATO HIDAKA?

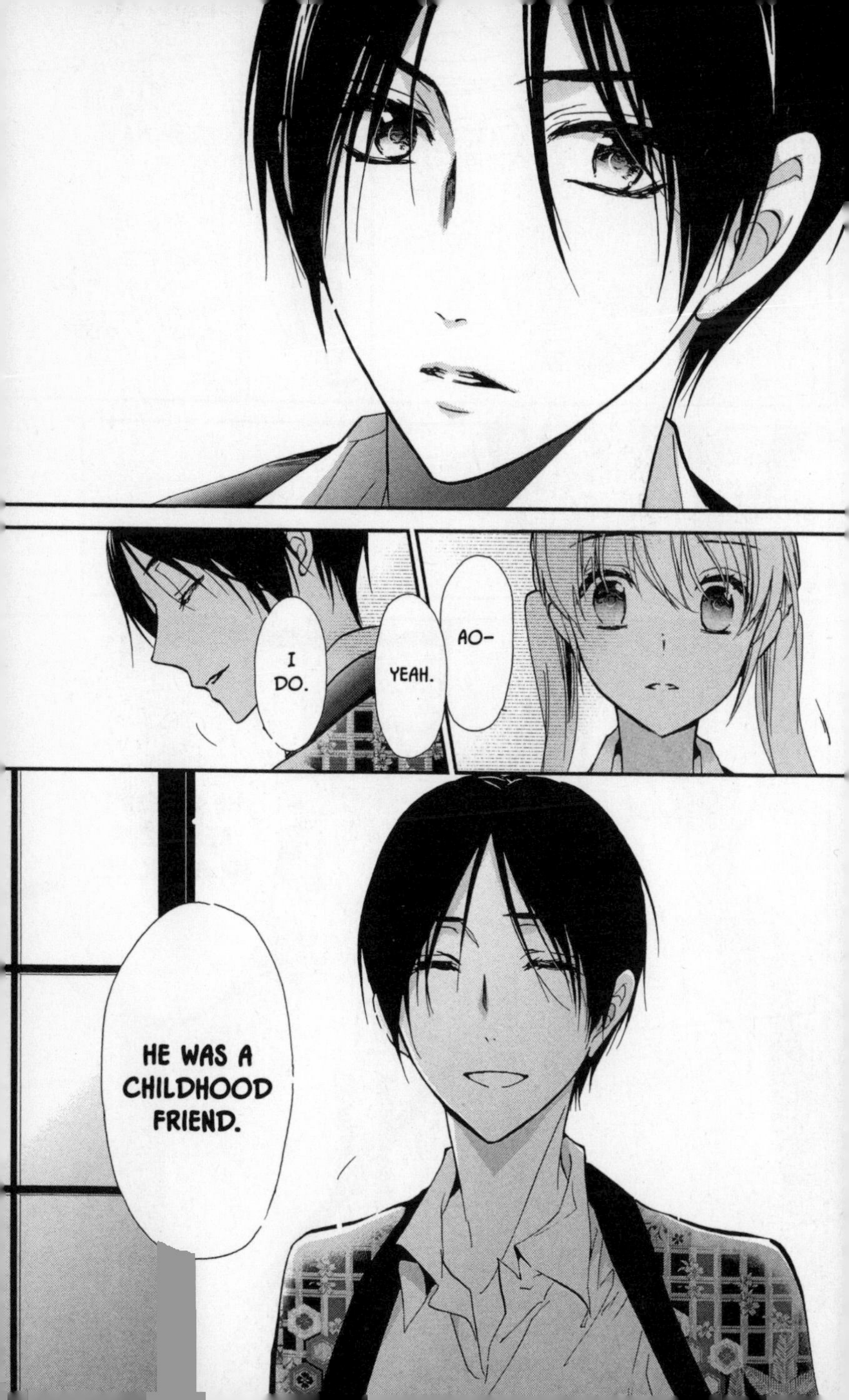
AO-
YEAH.
I DO.
HE WAS A CHILDHOOD FRIEND.

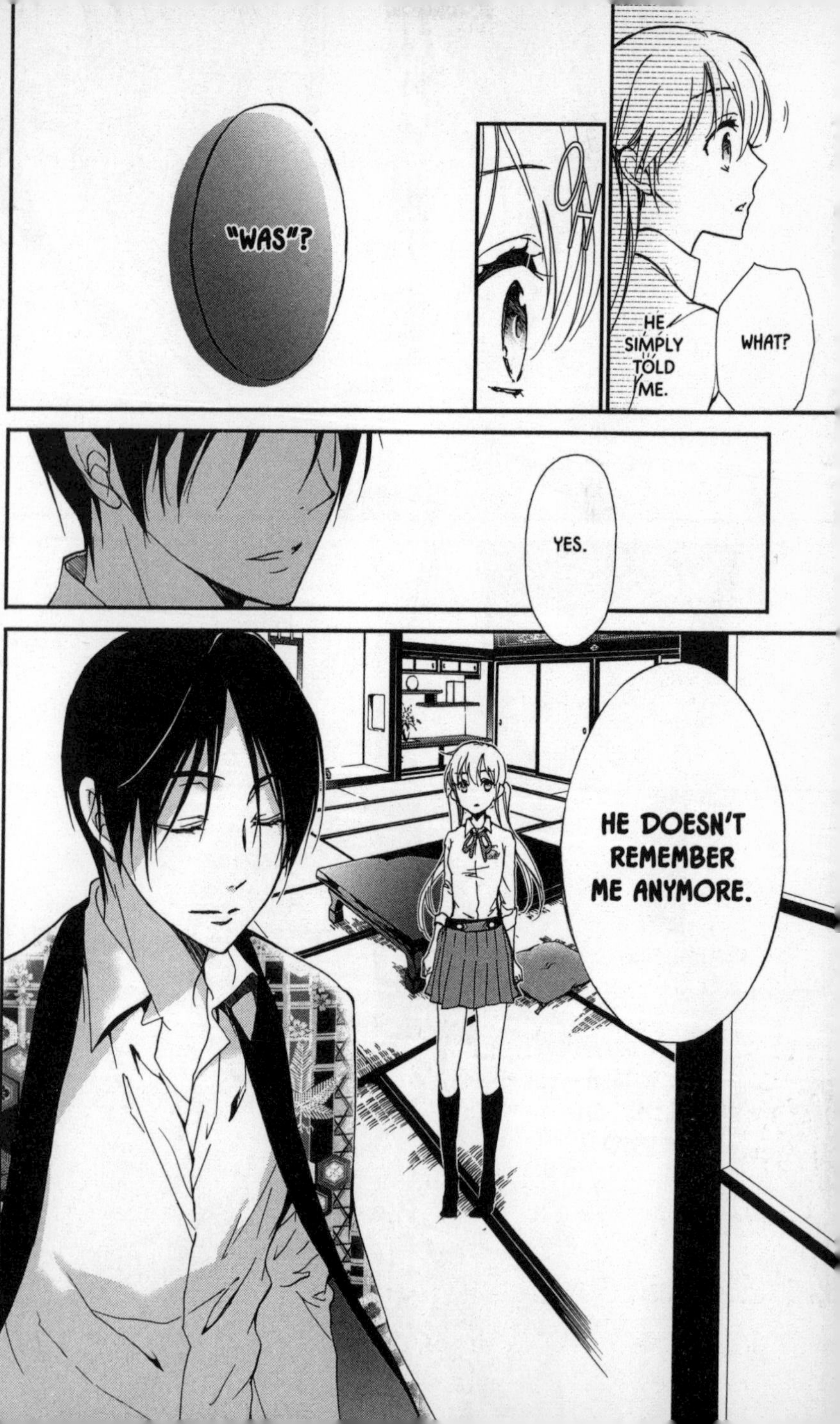
WHAT?
HE SIMPLY TOLD ME.
"WAS"?
YES.
HE DOESN'T REMEMBER ME ANYMORE.

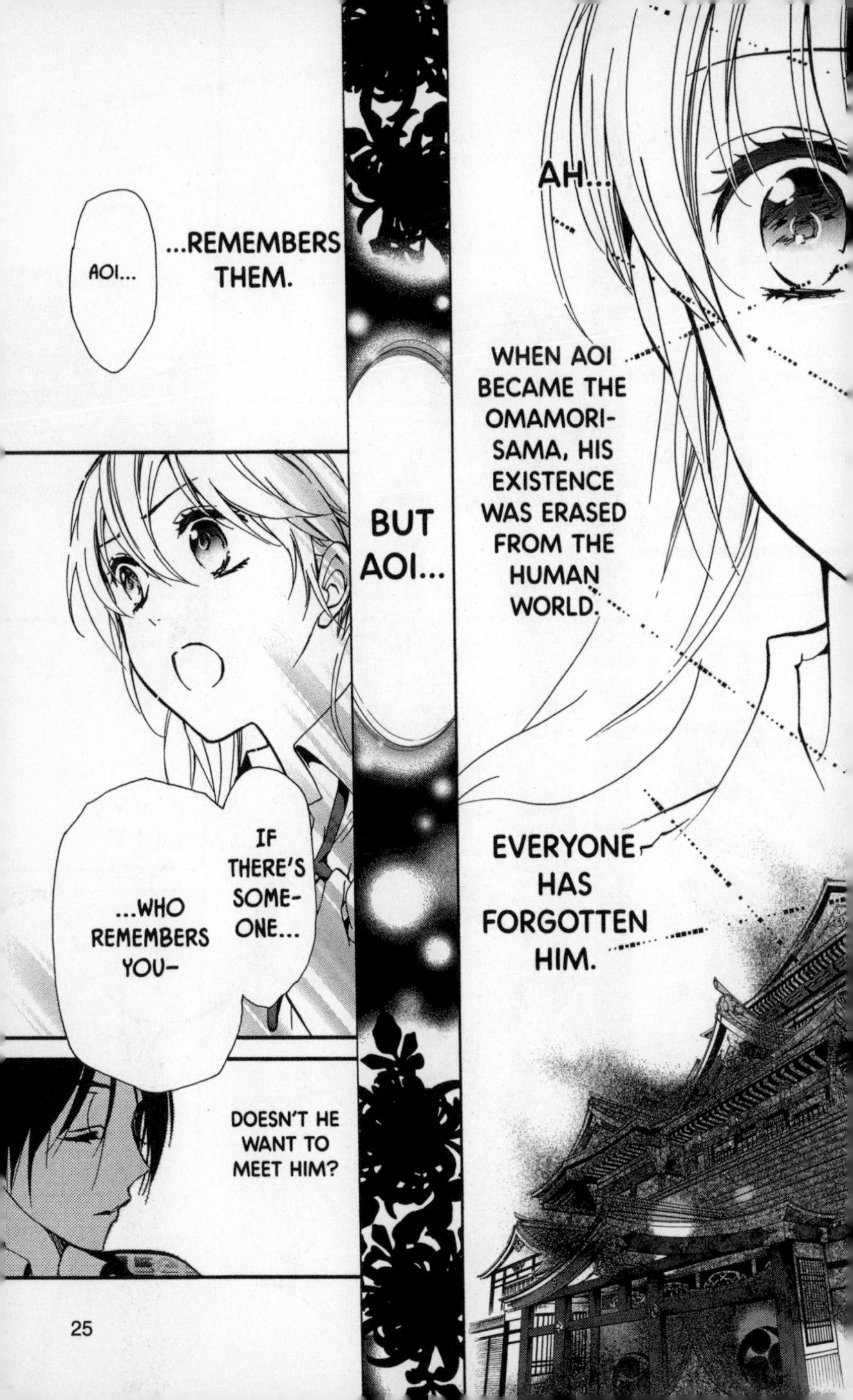
AH...
WHEN AOI BECAME THE OMAMORI-SAMA, HIS EXISTENCE WAS ERASED FROM THE HUMAN WORLD.
EVERYONE HAS FORGOTTEN HIM.
BUT AOI...
AOI...
...REMEMBERS THEM.
IF THERE'S SOME-ONE...
...WHO REMEMBERS YOU-
DOESN'T HE WANT TO MEET HIM?

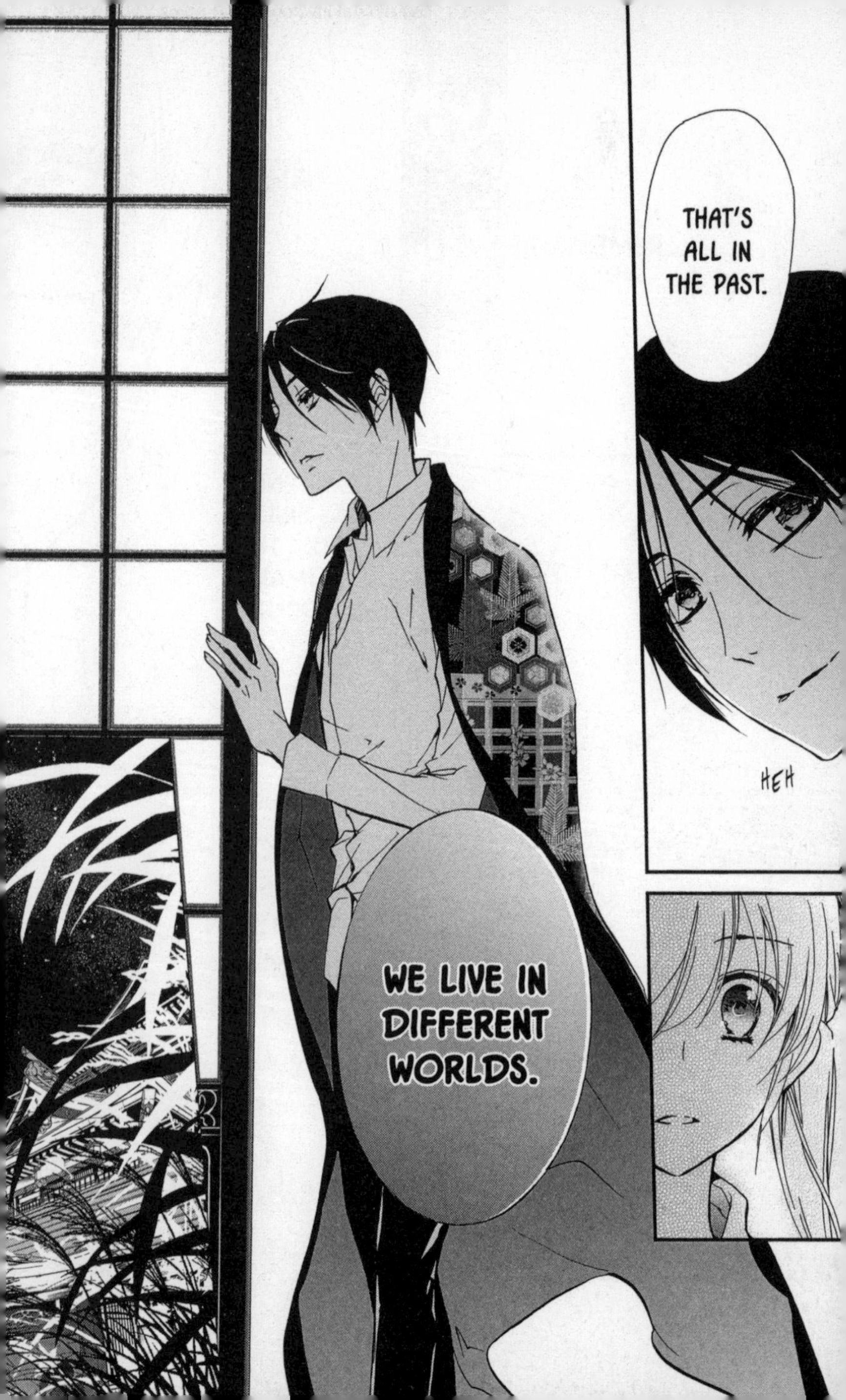
THAT'S ALL IN THE PAST.
HEH
WE LIVE IN DIFFERENT WORLDS.

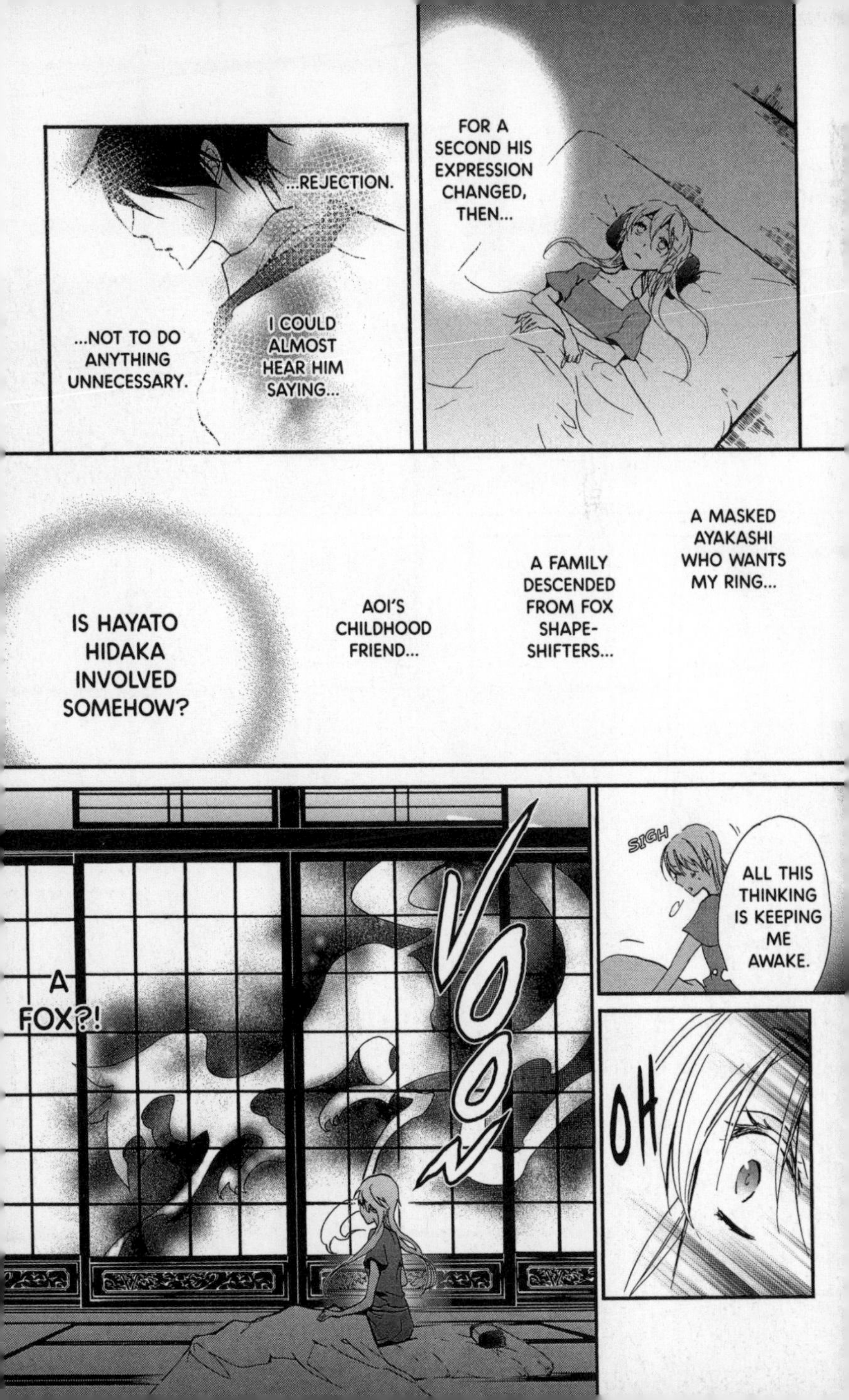

FOR A SECOND HIS EXPRESSION CHANGED, THEN...
...REJECTION.
I COULD ALMOST HEAR HIM SAYING...
...NOT TO DO ANYTHING UNNECESSARY.
A MASKED AYAKASHI WHO WANTS MY RING...
A FAMILY DESCENDED FROM FOX SHAPE-SHIFTERS...
AOI'S CHILDHOOD FRIEND...
IS HAYATO HIDAKA INVOLVED SOMEHOW?
SIGH
ALL THIS THINKING IS KEEPING ME AWAKE.
OH
VOOON
A FOX?!

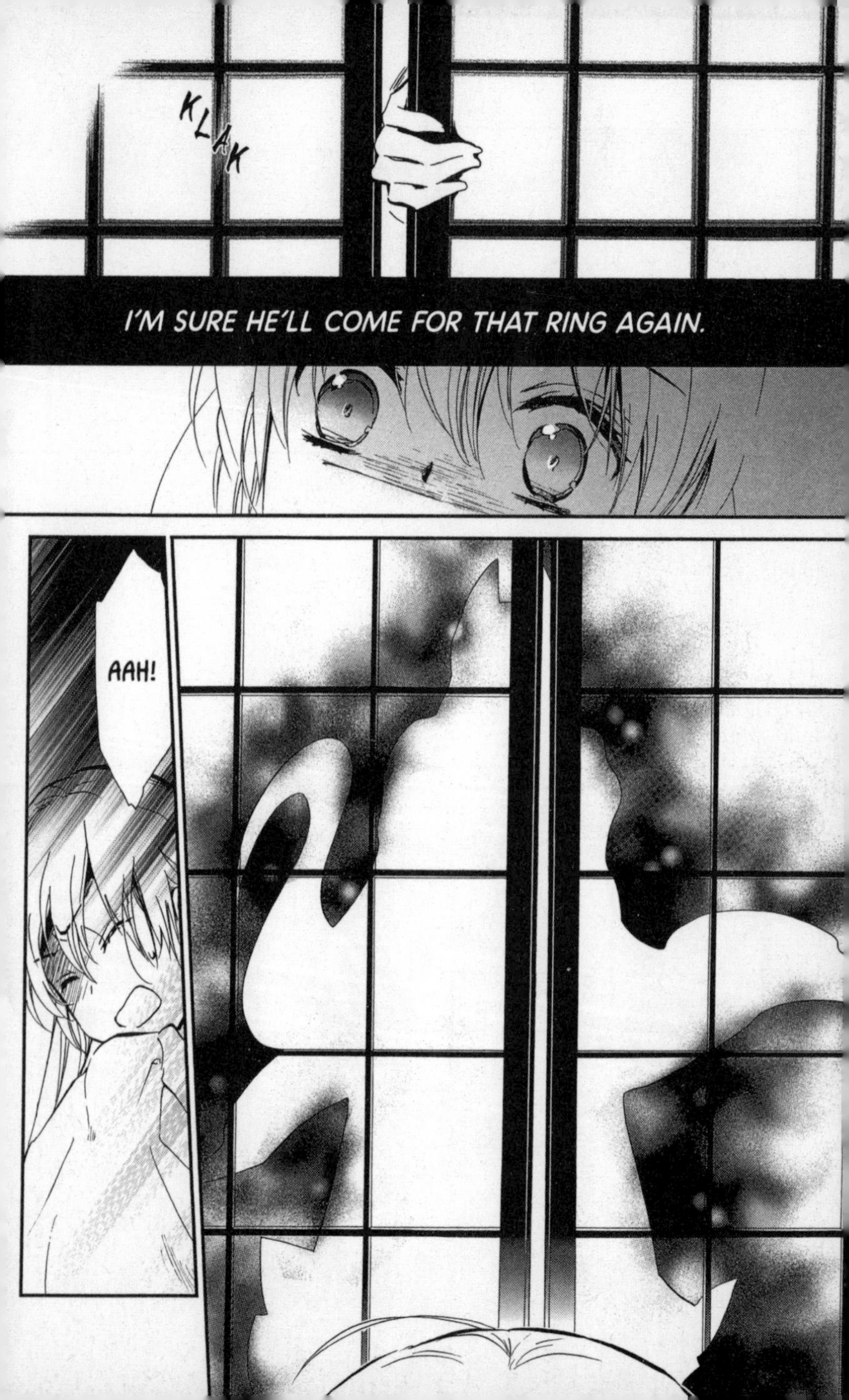
KLAK
I'M SURE HE'LL COME FOR THAT RING AGAIN.
AAH!

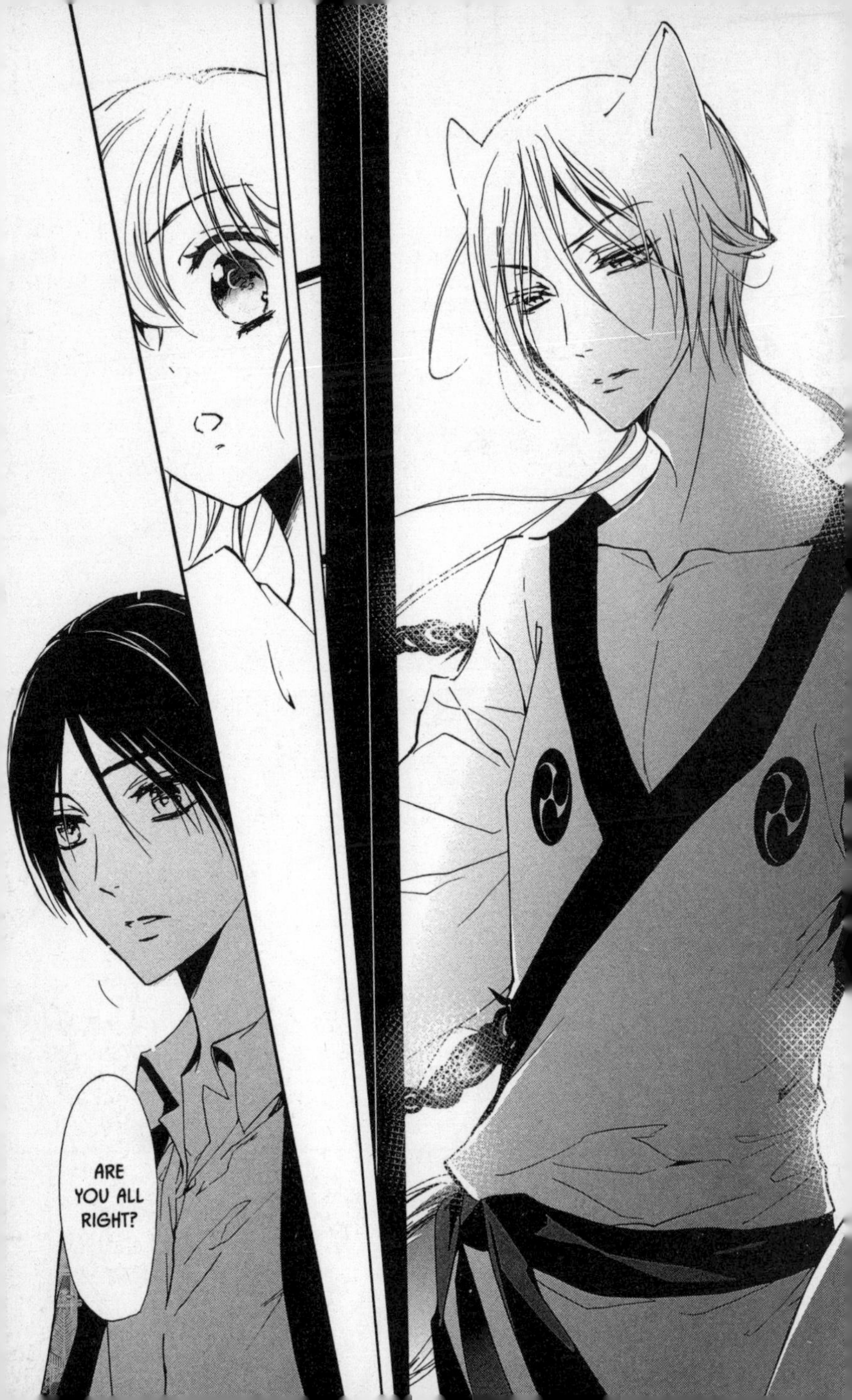
ARE YOU ALL RIGHT?

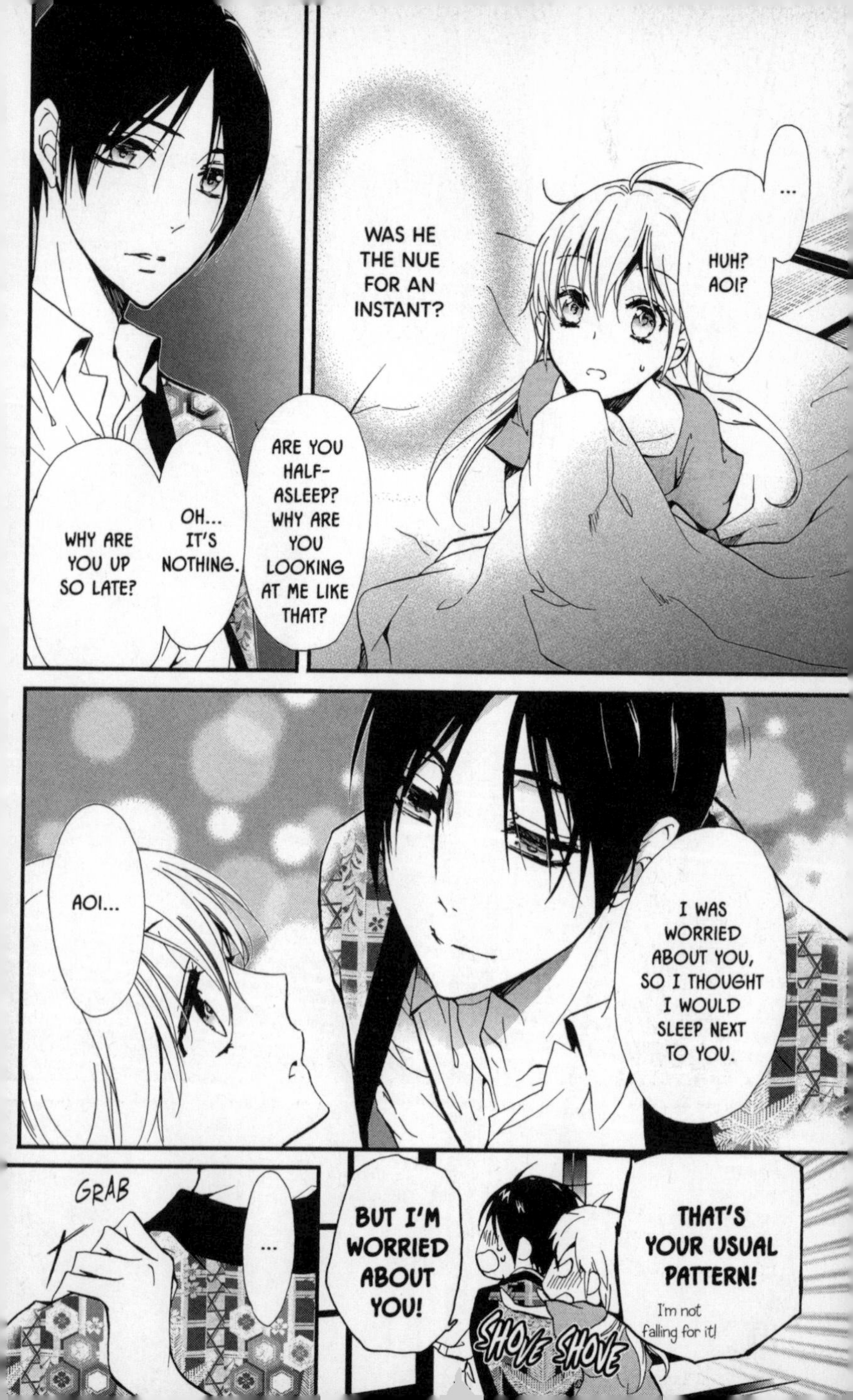
...
HUH? AOI?
WAS HE THE NUE FOR AN INSTANT?
ARE YOU HALF-ASLEEP? WHY ARE YOU LOOKING AT ME LIKE THAT?
OH... IT'S NOTHING.
WHY ARE YOU UP SO LATE?
I WAS WORRIED ABOUT YOU, SO I THOUGHT I WOULD SLEEP NEXT TO YOU.
AOI...
THAT'S YOUR USUAL PATTERN!
I'm not falling for it!
SHOVE SHOVE
BUT I'M WORRIED ABOUT YOU!
...
GRAB

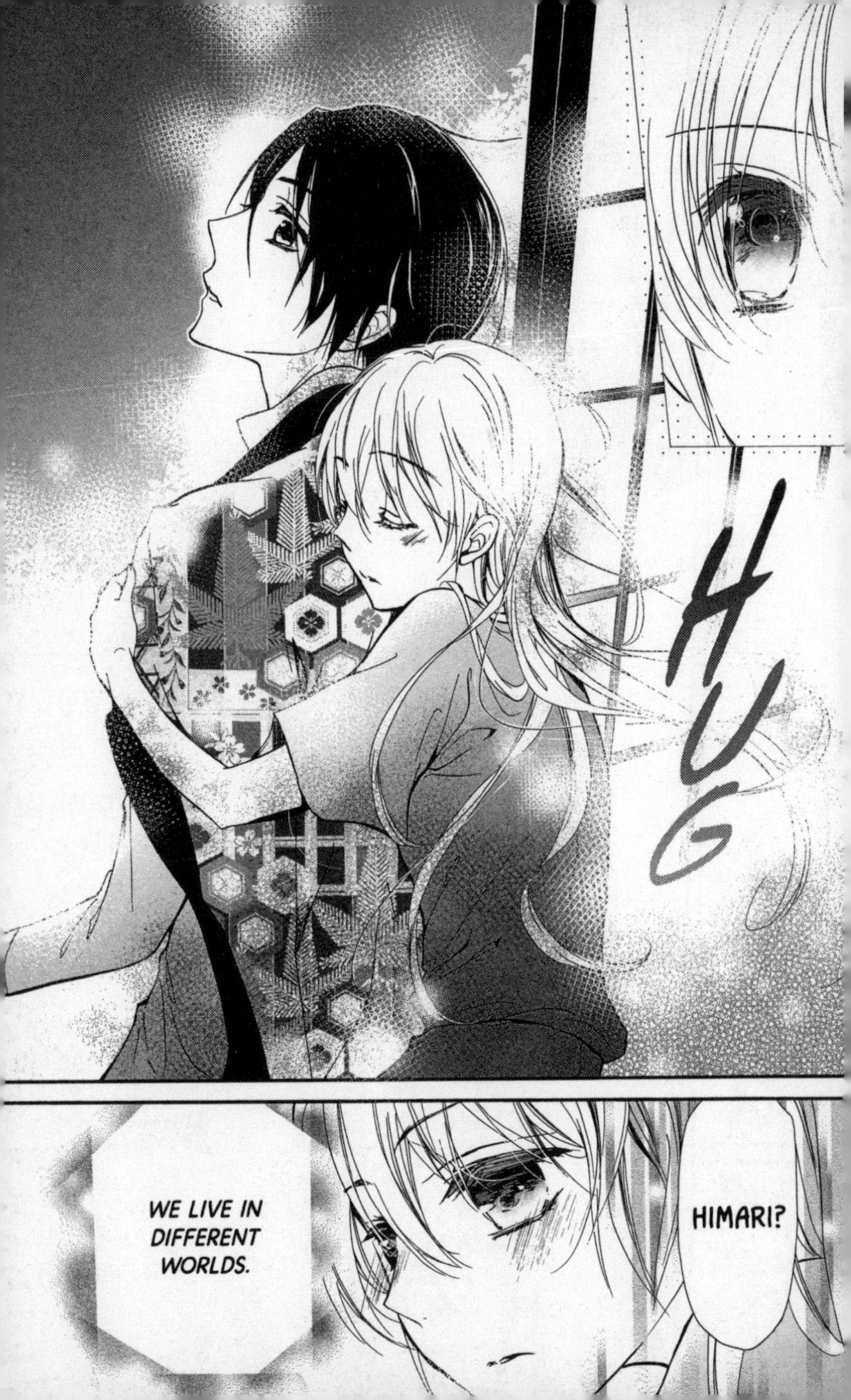
HUG
HIMARI?
WE LIVE IN DIFFERENT WORLDS.

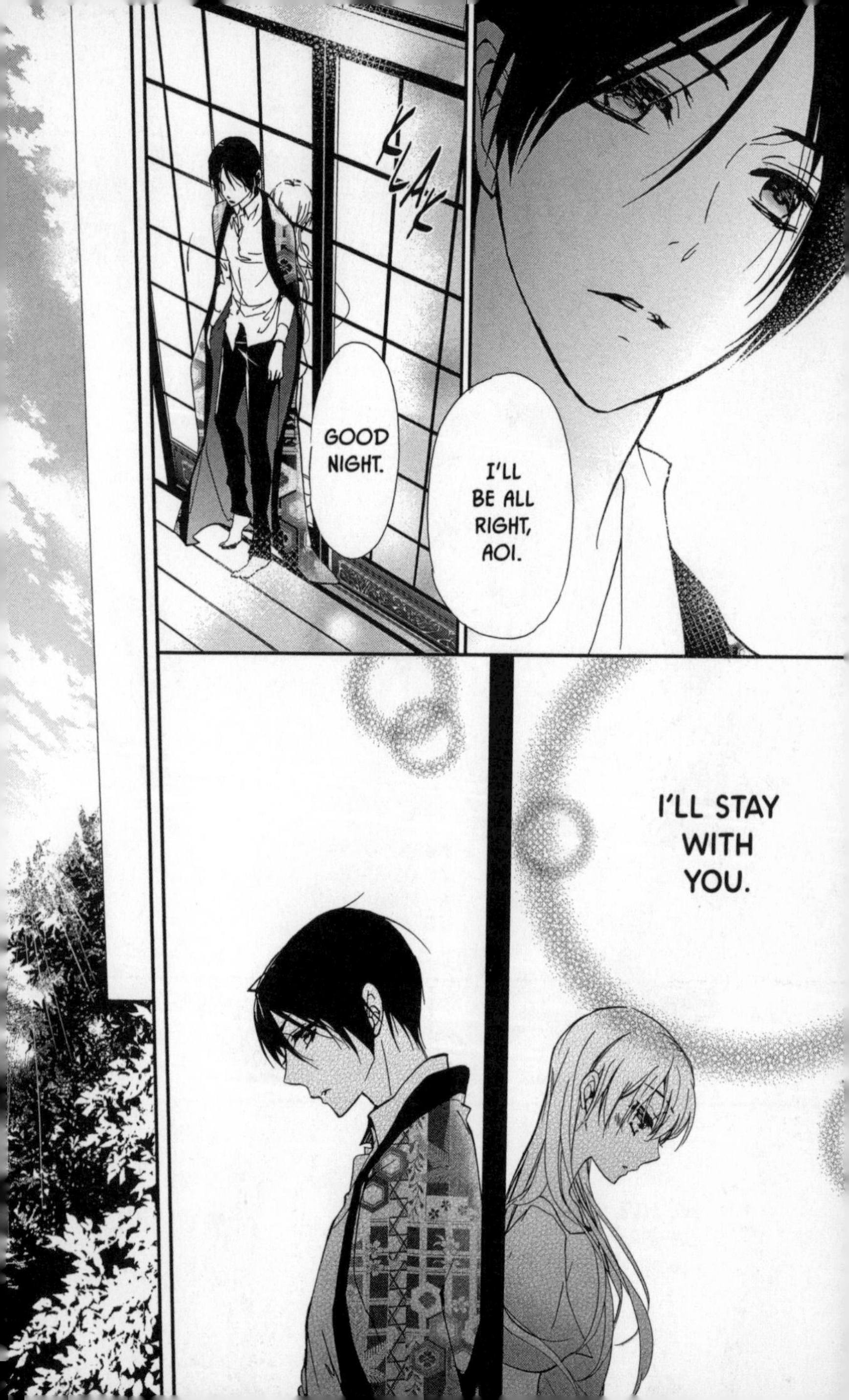
I'LL BE ALL RIGHT, AOI.
KLACK
GOOD NIGHT.
I'LL STAY WITH YOU.

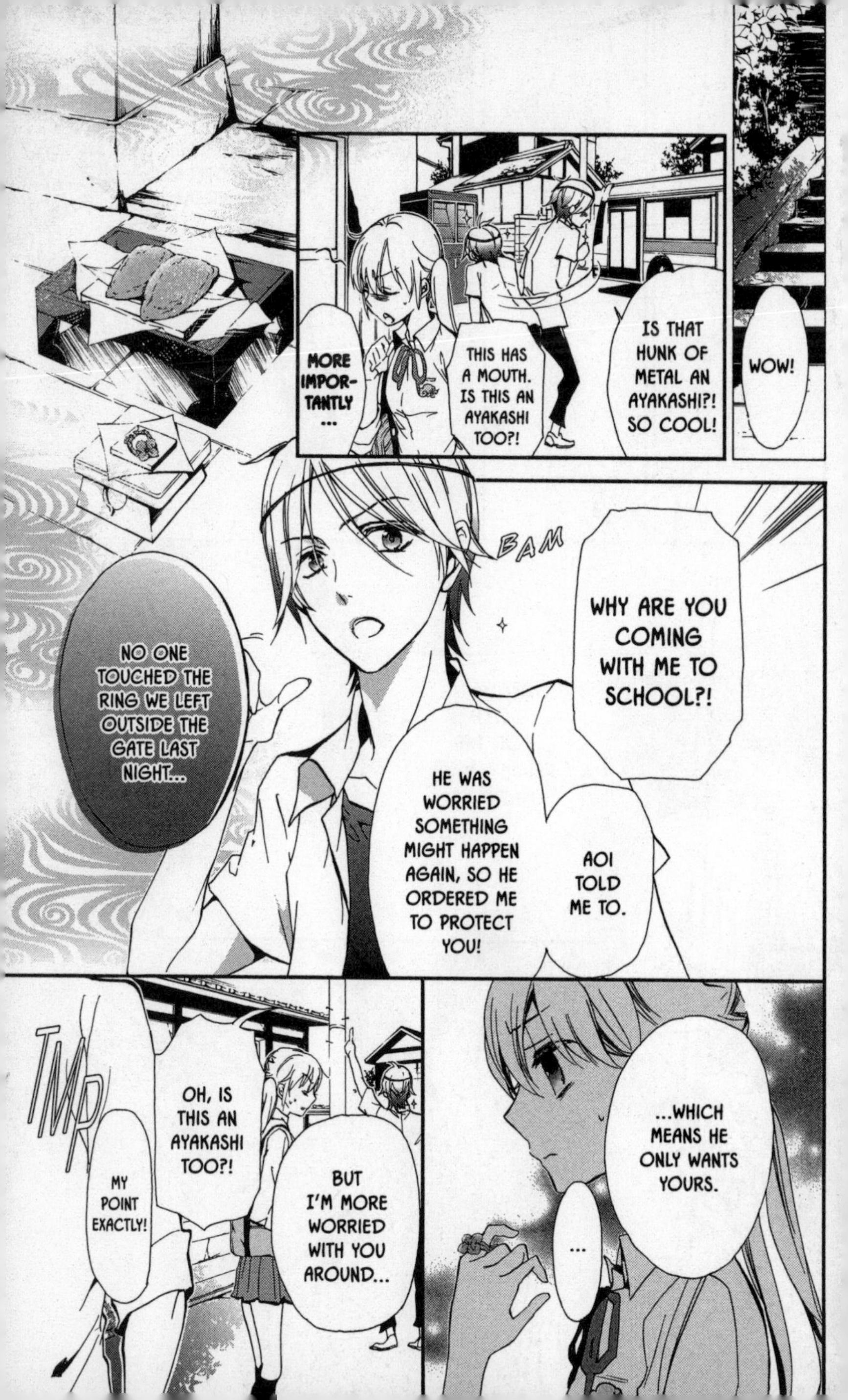
WOW!
IS THAT HUNK OF METAL AN AYAKASHI?! SO COOL!
THIS HAS A MOUTH. IS THIS AN AYAKASHI TOO?!
MORE IMPORTANTLY ...
BAM
WHY ARE YOU COMING WITH ME TO SCHOOL?!
AOI TOLD ME TO.
HE WAS WORRIED SOMETHING MIGHT HAPPEN AGAIN, SO HE ORDERED ME TO PROTECT YOU!
NO ONE TOUCHED THE RING WE LEFT OUTSIDE THE GATE LAST NIGHT...
...WHICH MEANS HE ONLY WANTS YOURS.
...
BUT I'M MORE WORRIED WITH YOU AROUND...
OH, IS THIS AN AYAKASHI TOO?!
TMP
MY POINT EXACTLY!

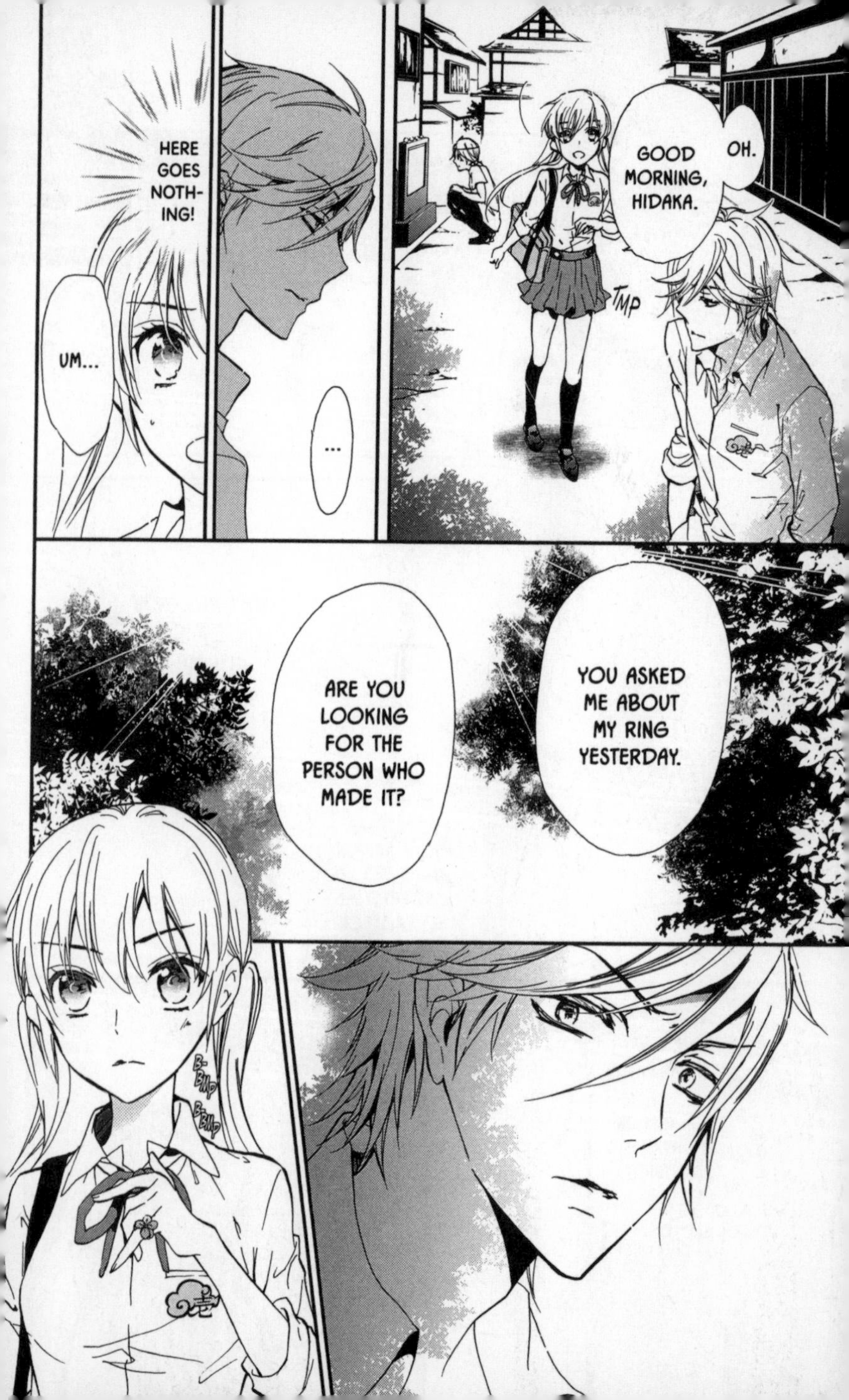
OH.
GOOD MORNING, HIDAKA.
TMP
...
HERE GOES NOTH-ING!
UM...
YOU ASKED ME ABOUT MY RING YESTERDAY.
ARE YOU LOOKING FOR THE PERSON WHO MADE IT?
B-BMP B-BMP

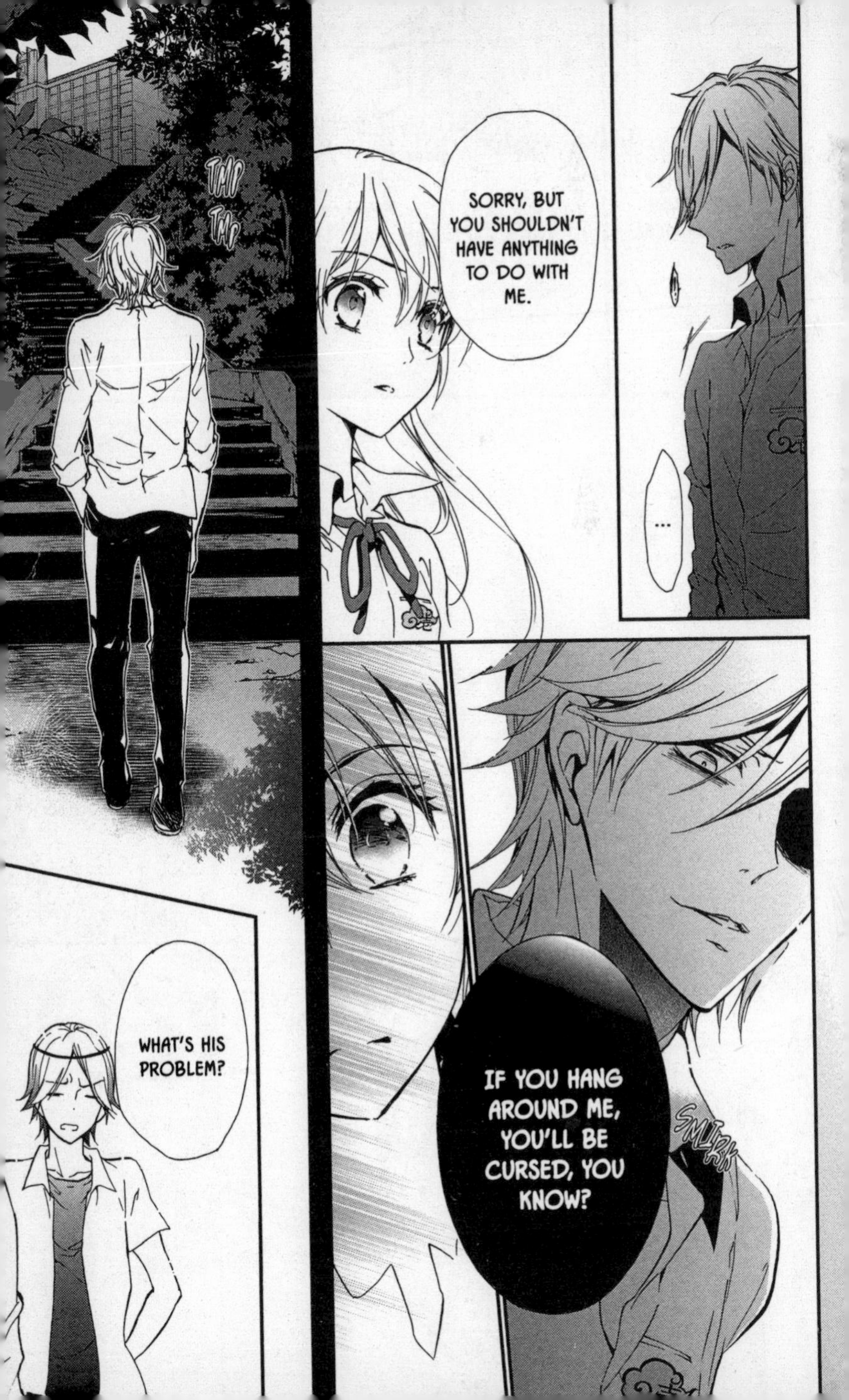
...
SORRY, BUT YOU SHOULDN'T HAVE ANYTHING TO DO WITH ME.
IF YOU HANG AROUND ME, YOU'LL BE CURSED, YOU KNOW?
SMIRK
TMP TMP
WHAT'S HIS PROBLEM?

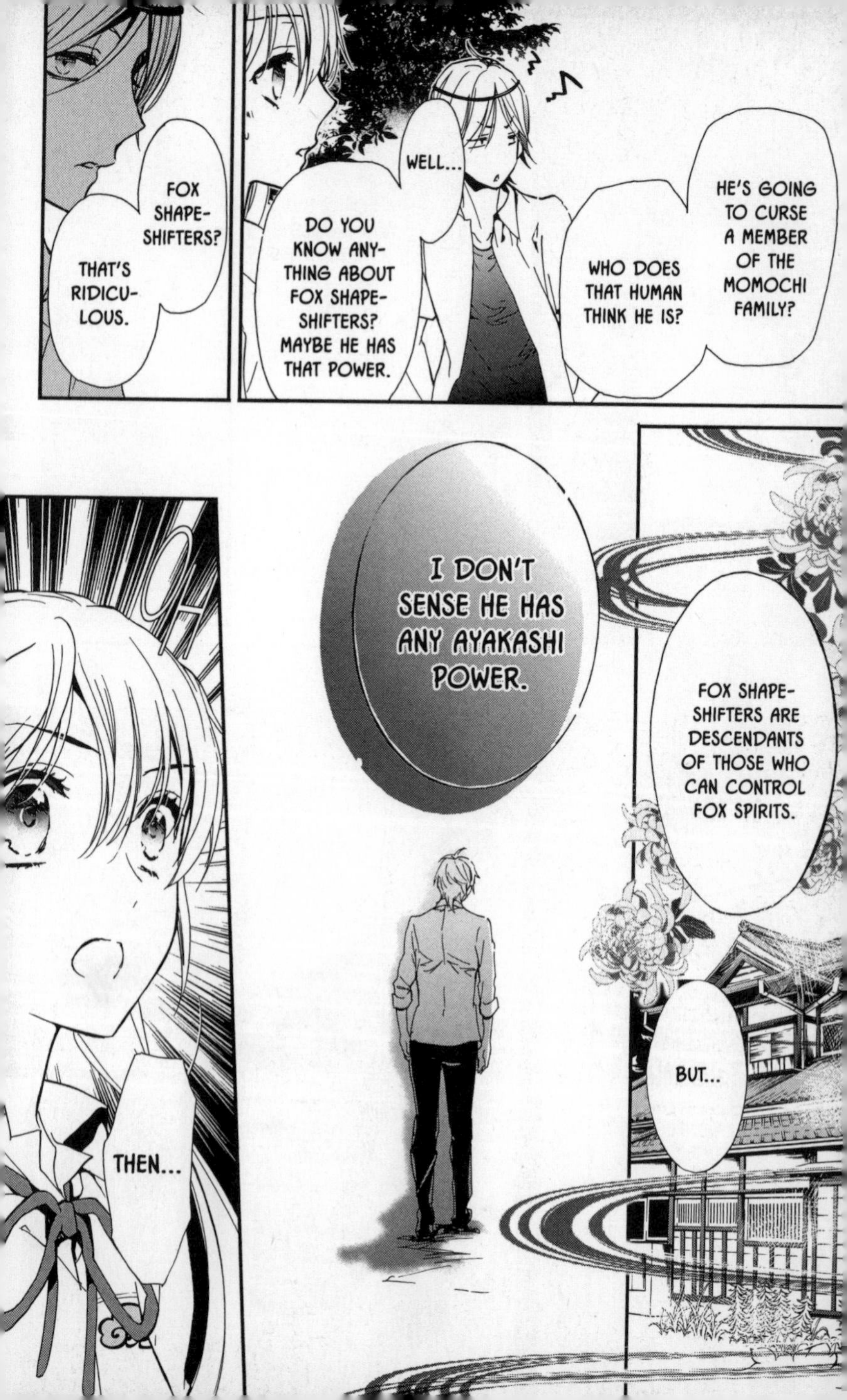
HE'S GOING TO CURSE A MEMBER OF THE MOMOCHI FAMILY?
WHO DOES THAT HUMAN THINK HE IS?
WELL...
DO YOU KNOW ANYTHING ABOUT FOX SHAPE-SHIFTERS? MAYBE HE HAS THAT POWER.
FOX SHAPE-SHIFTERS?
THAT'S RIDICULOUS.
FOX SHAPE-SHIFTERS ARE DESCENDANTS OF THOSE WHO CAN CONTROL FOX SPIRITS.
BUT...
I DON'T SENSE HE HAS ANY AYAKASHI POWER.
THEN...

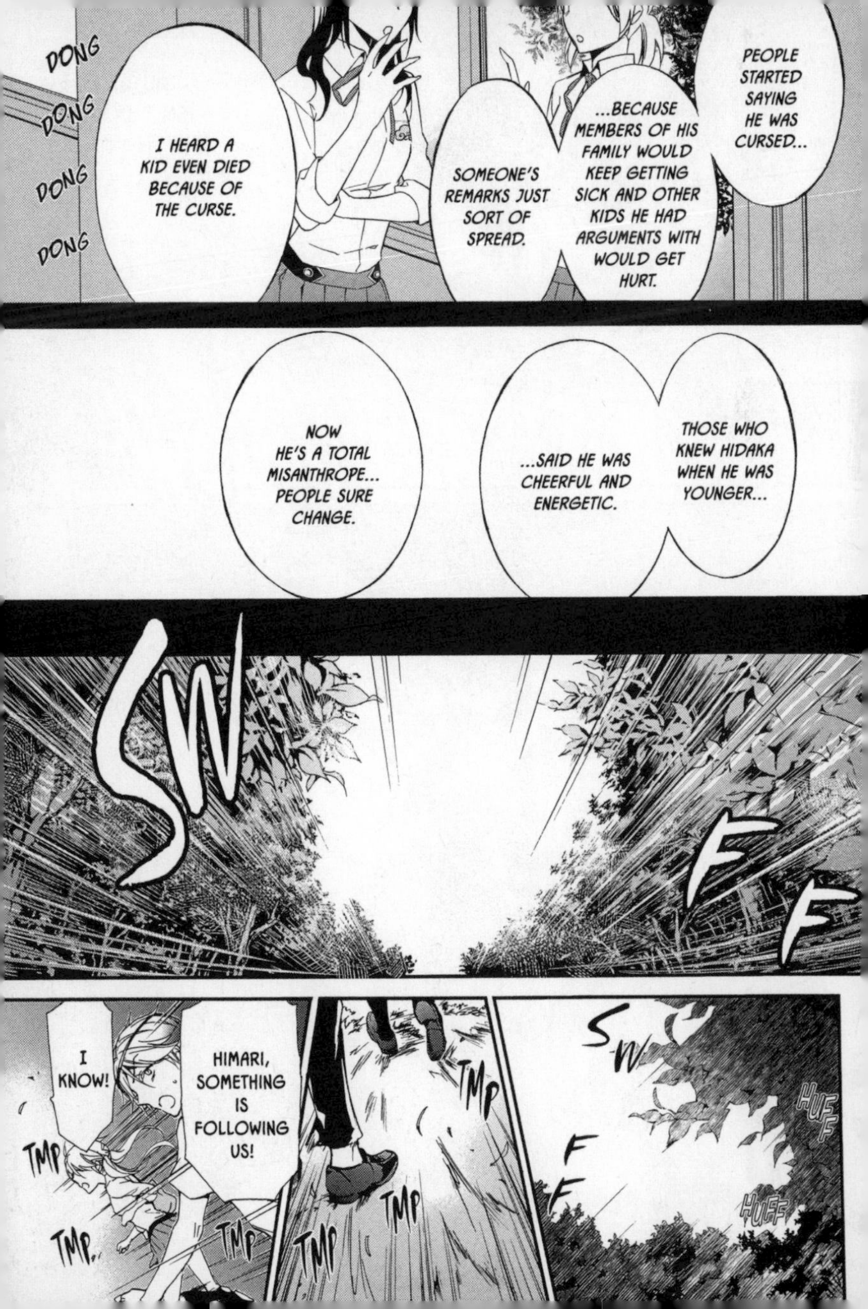
PEOPLE STARTED SAYING HE WAS CURSED...
...BECAUSE MEMBERS OF HIS FAMILY WOULD KEEP GETTING SICK AND OTHER KIDS HE HAD ARGUMENTS WITH WOULD GET HURT.
SOMEONE'S REMARKS JUST SORT OF SPREAD.
I HEARD A KID EVEN DIED BECAUSE OF THE CURSE.
DONG
DONG
DONG
DONG
THOSE WHO KNEW HIDAKA WHEN HE WAS YOUNGER...
...SAID HE WAS CHEERFUL AND ENERGETIC.
NOW HE'S A TOTAL MISANTHROPE... PEOPLE SURE CHANGE.
SWFF
SWFF
HUFF
HUFF
TMP
TMP
TMP
TMP
HIMARI, SOMETHING IS FOLLOWING US!
I KNOW!
TMP
TMP

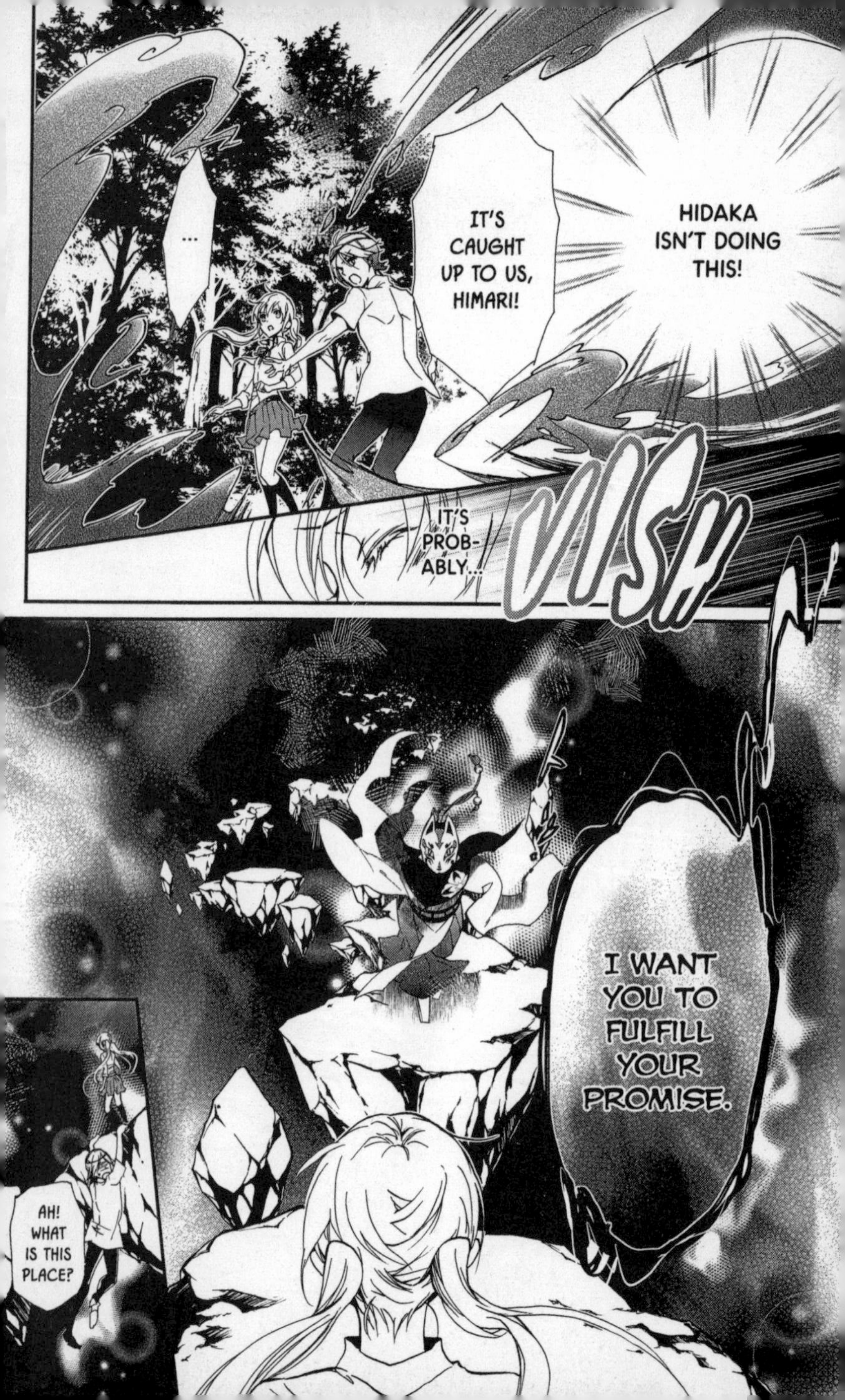
HIDAKA ISN'T DOING THIS!
IT'S CAUGHT UP TO US, HIMARI!
...
IT'S PROBABLY...
VASH
I WANT YOU TO FULFILL YOUR PROMISE.
AH! WHAT IS THIS PLACE?

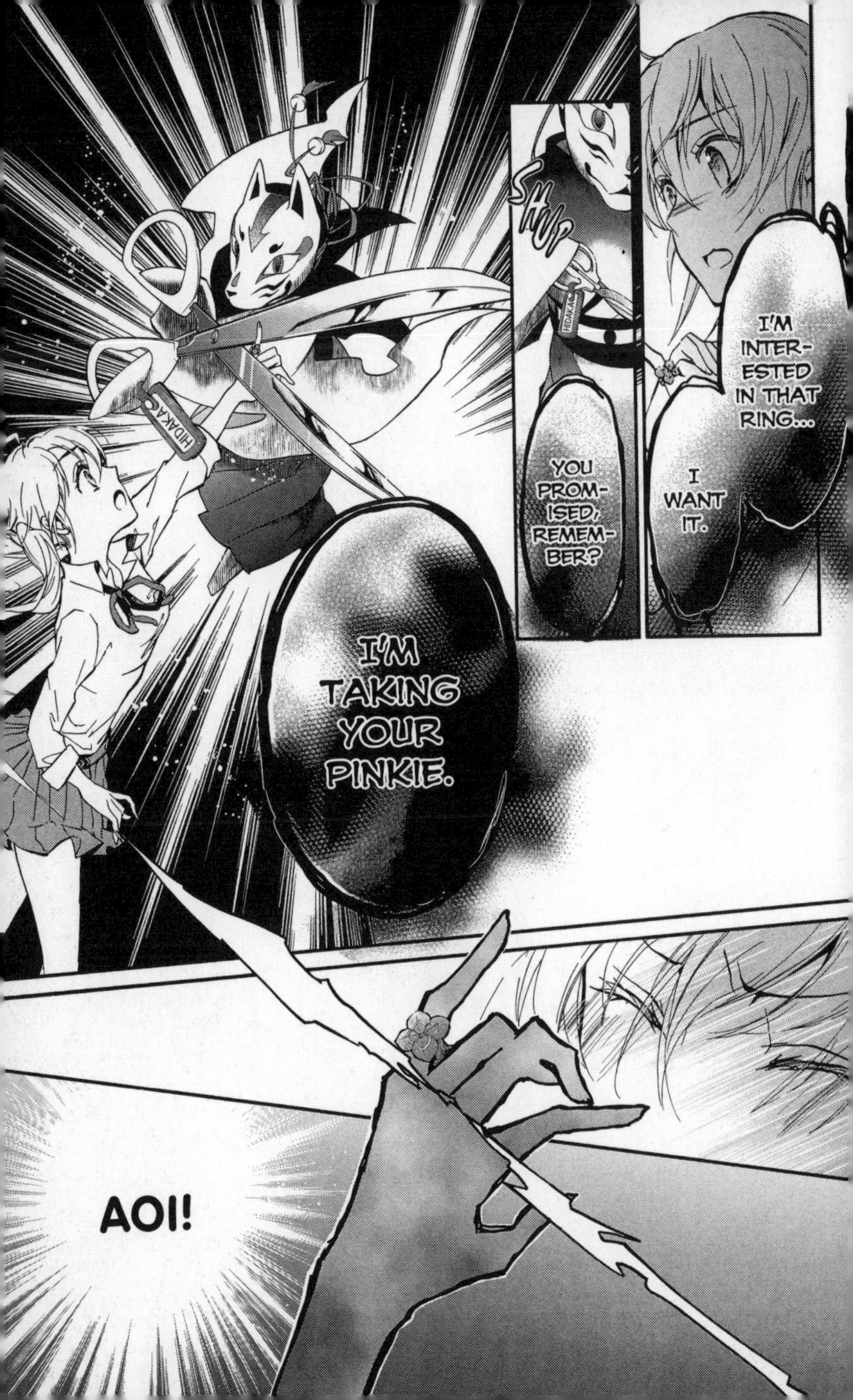
I'M INTER-ESTED IN THAT RING...
I WANT IT.
SHUP
YOU PROMISED, REMEMBER?
I'M TAKING YOUR PINKIE.
AOI!

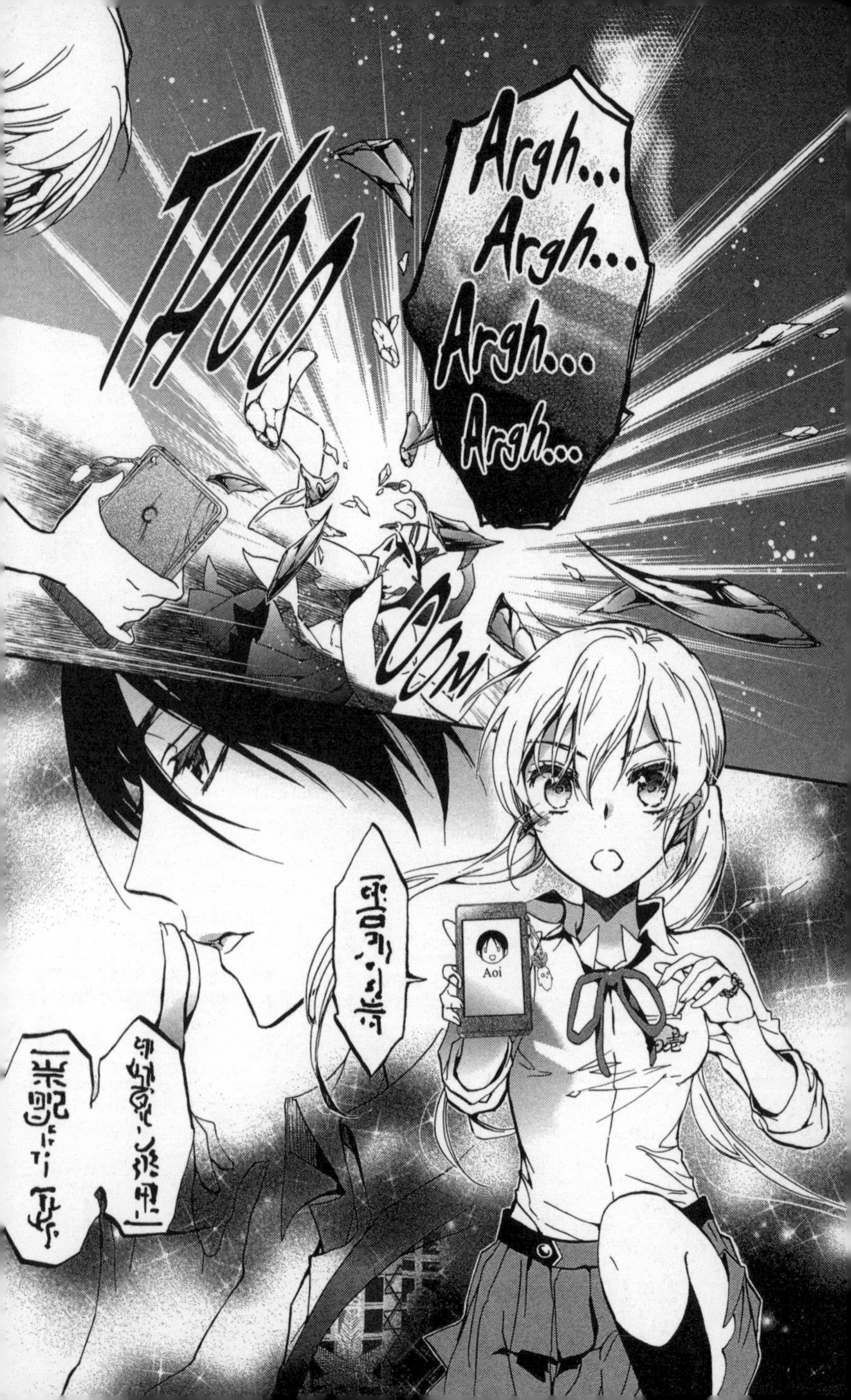
THOO
Argh...
Argh...
Argh...
Argh...
OOM
Aoi

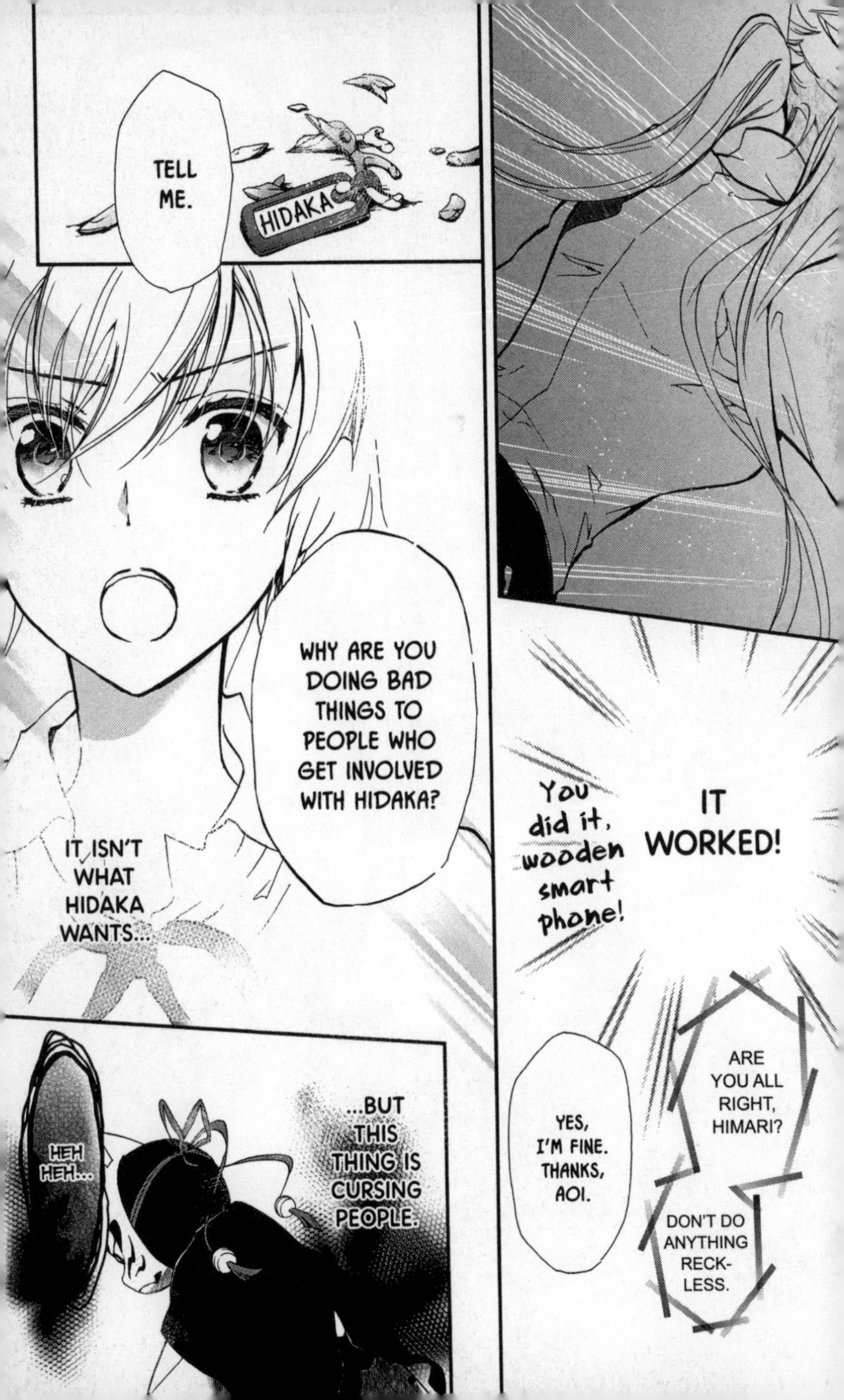
IT WORKED!
You did it, wooden smart phone!
ARE YOU ALL RIGHT, HIMARI?
DON'T DO ANYTHING RECKLESS.
YES, I'M FINE. THANKS, AOI.
TELL ME.
HIDAKA
WHY ARE YOU DOING BAD THINGS TO PEOPLE WHO GET INVOLVED WITH HIDAKA?
IT ISN'T WHAT HIDAKA WANTS...
...BUT THIS THING IS CURSING PEOPLE.
HEH HEH...

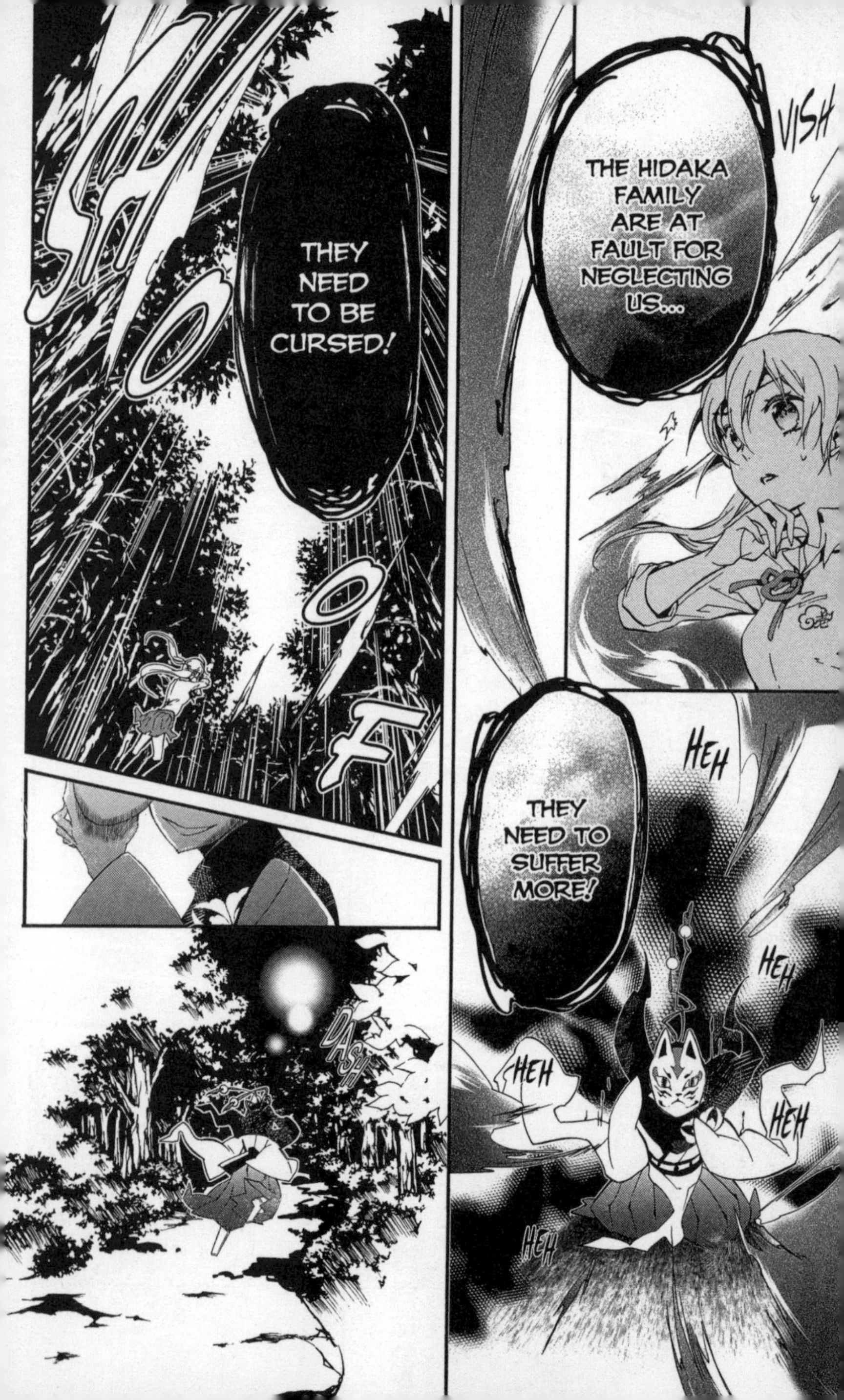
VISH
THE HIDAKA FAMILY ARE AT FAULT FOR NEGLECTING US...
THEY NEED TO BE CURSED!
THEY NEED TO SUFFER MORE!
HEH
HEH
HEH
HEH
HEH
DASH

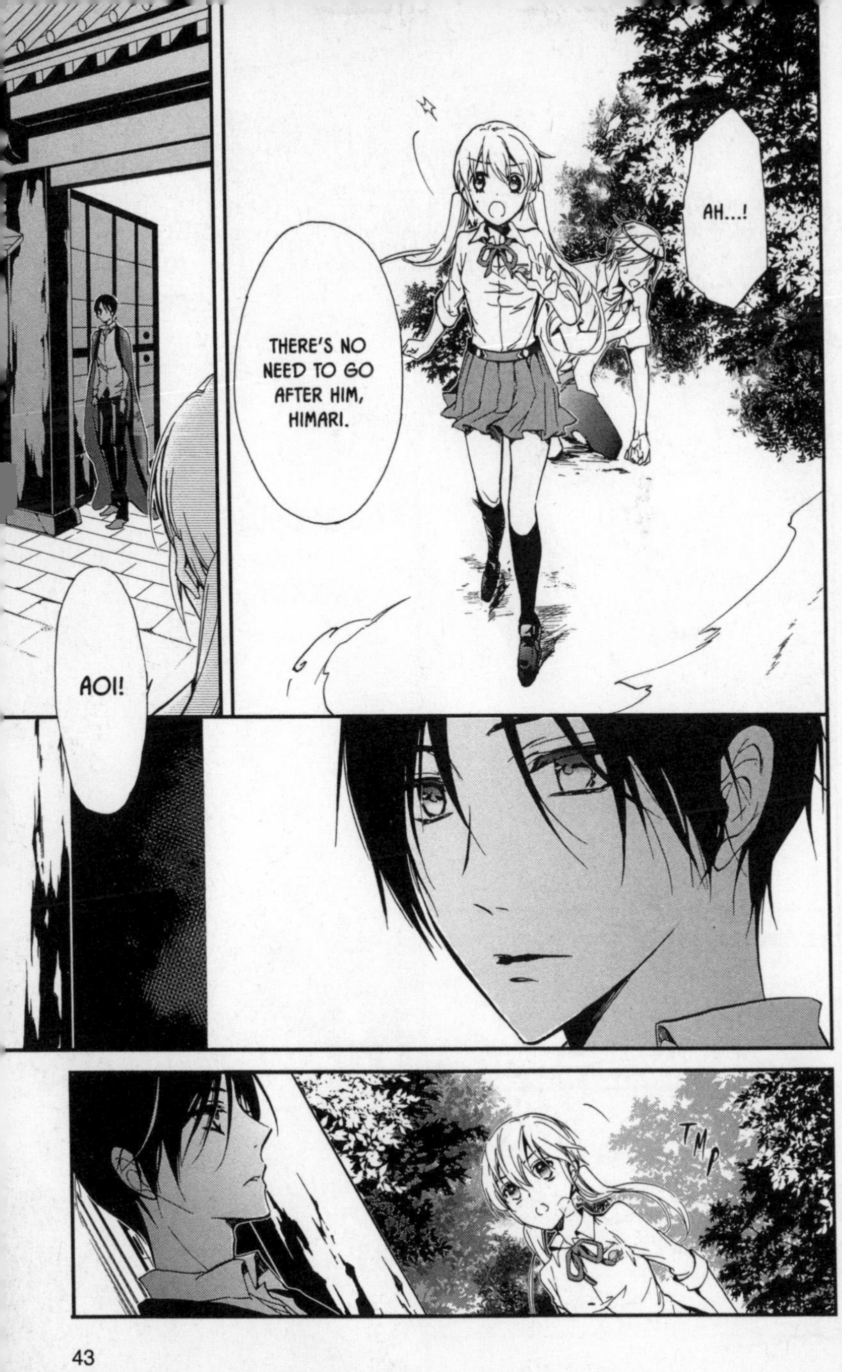
AH...!
THERE'S NO NEED TO GO AFTER HIM, HIMARI.
AOI!
TMP

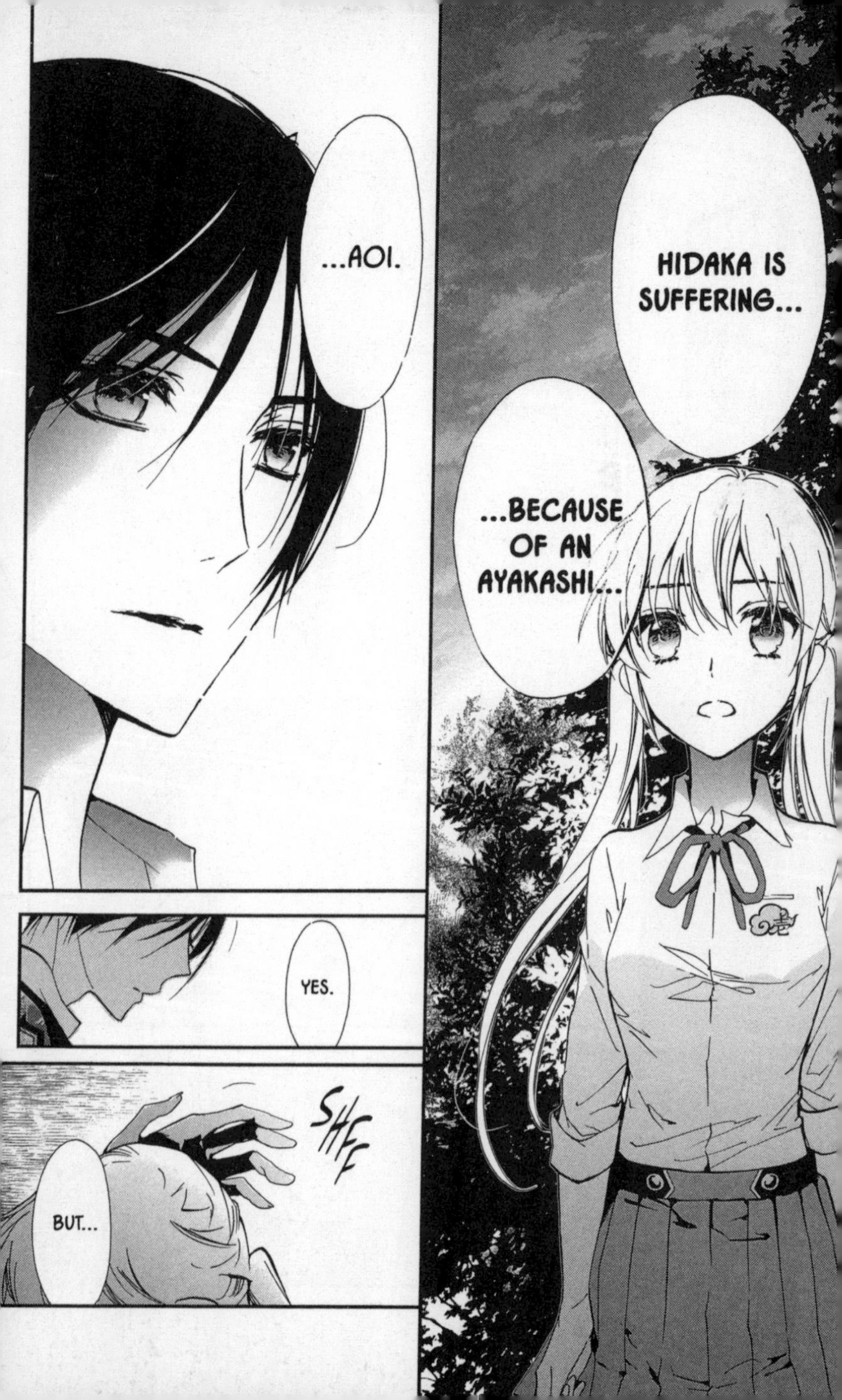
HIDAKA IS SUFFERING...
...BECAUSE OF AN AYAKASHI...
...AOI.
YES.
SHFF
BUT...

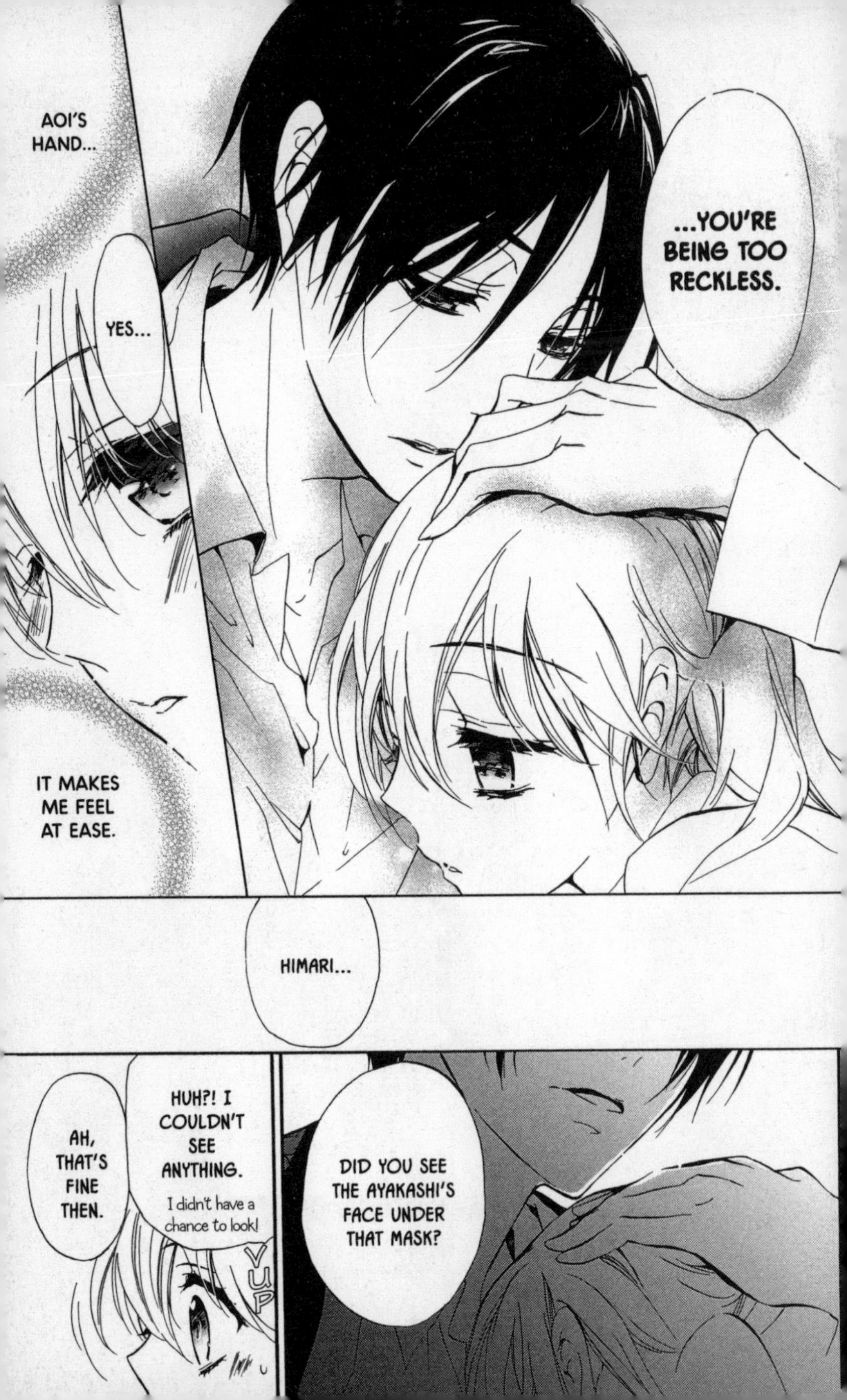
...YOU'RE BEING TOO RECKLESS.
AOI'S HAND...
YES...
IT MAKES ME FEEL AT EASE.
HIMARI...
DID YOU SEE THE AYAKASHI'S FACE UNDER THAT MASK?
HUH?! I COULDN'T SEE ANYTHING.
I didn't have a chance to look!
YUP
AH, THAT'S FINE THEN.

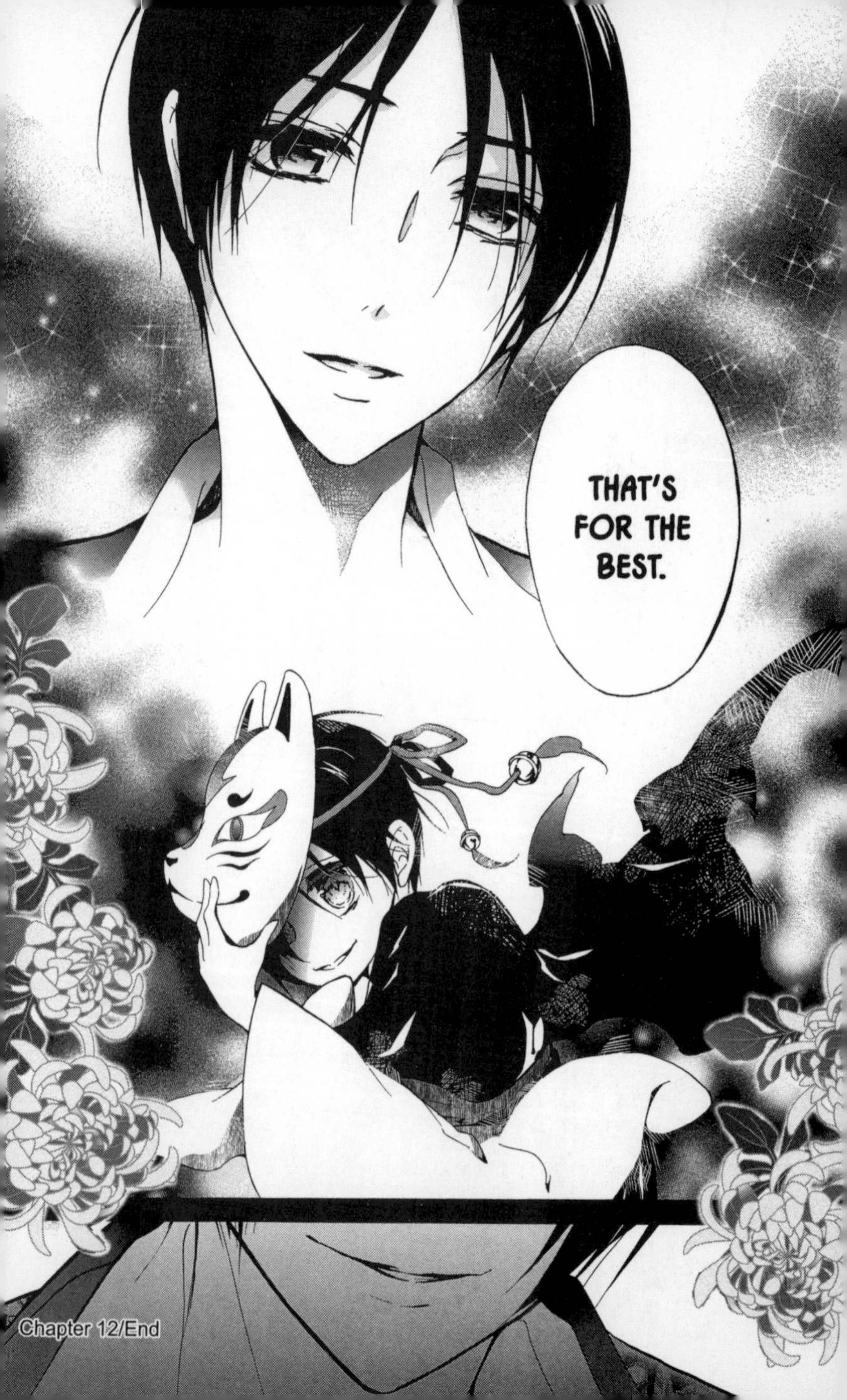
THAT'S FOR THE BEST.
Chapter 12/End

the
DEMON
PRINCE
of MOMOCHI
HOUSE

the
DEMON
PRINCE
of MOMOCHI
HOUSE

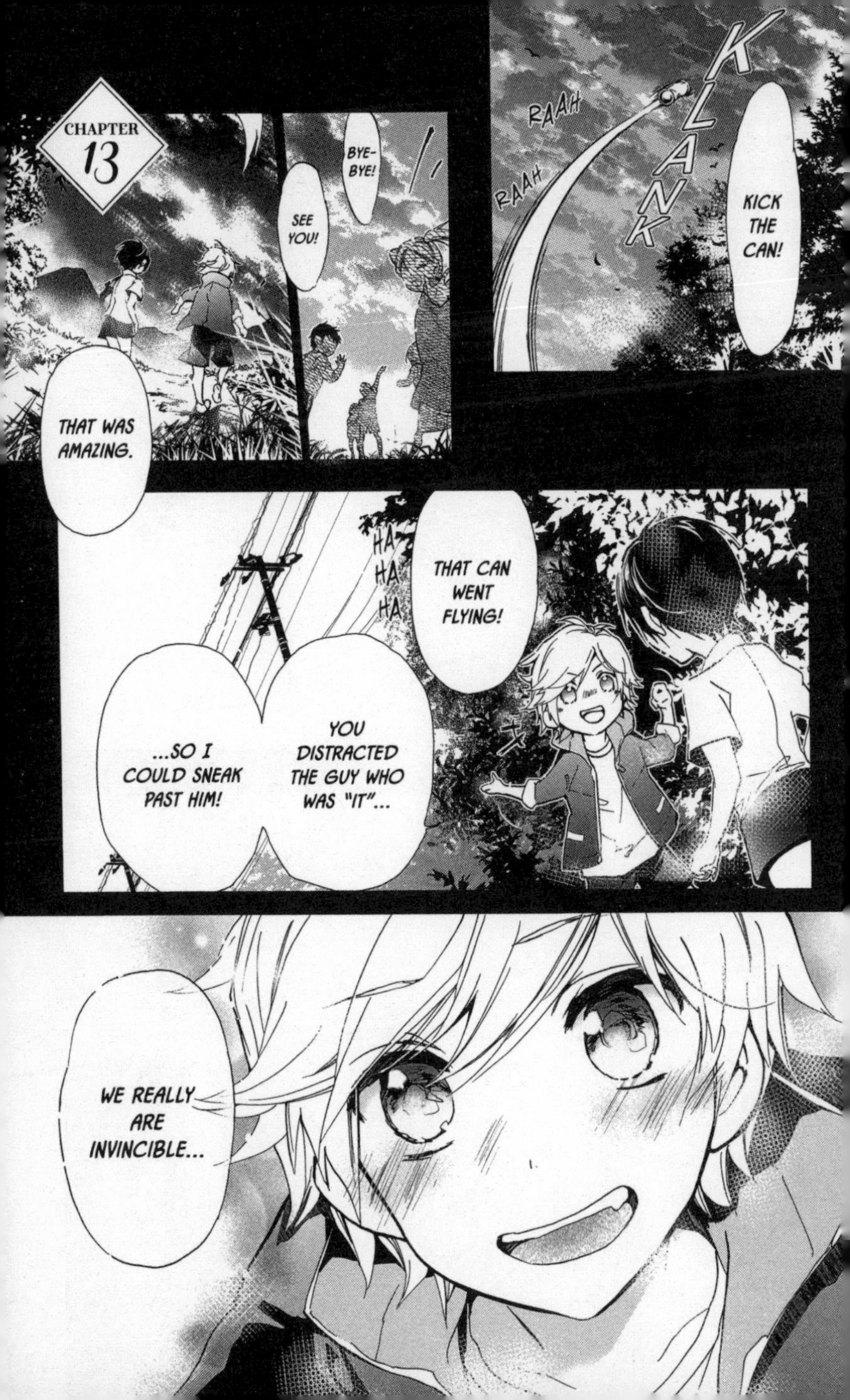
KICK THE CAN!
KLANK
RAAH
RAAH
BYE-BYE!
SEE YOU!
CHAPTER 13
THAT WAS AMAZING.
THAT CAN WENT FLYING!
HA HA HA
YOU DISTRACTED THE GUY WHO WAS "IT"...
...SO I COULD SNEAK PAST HIM!
WE REALLY ARE INVINCIBLE...

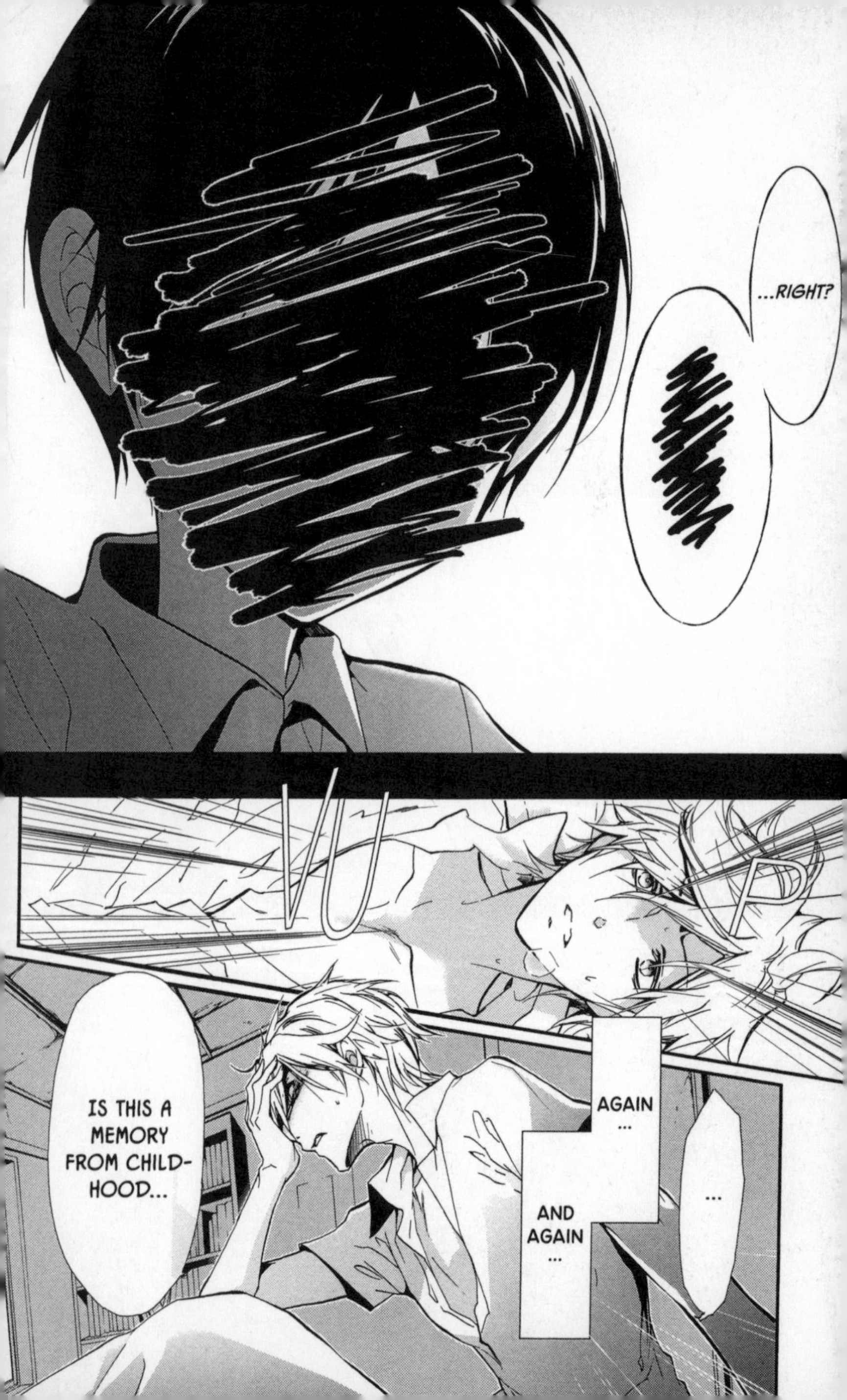
...RIGHT?
VUP
...
AGAIN ...
AND AGAIN ...
IS THIS A MEMORY FROM CHILDHOOD...

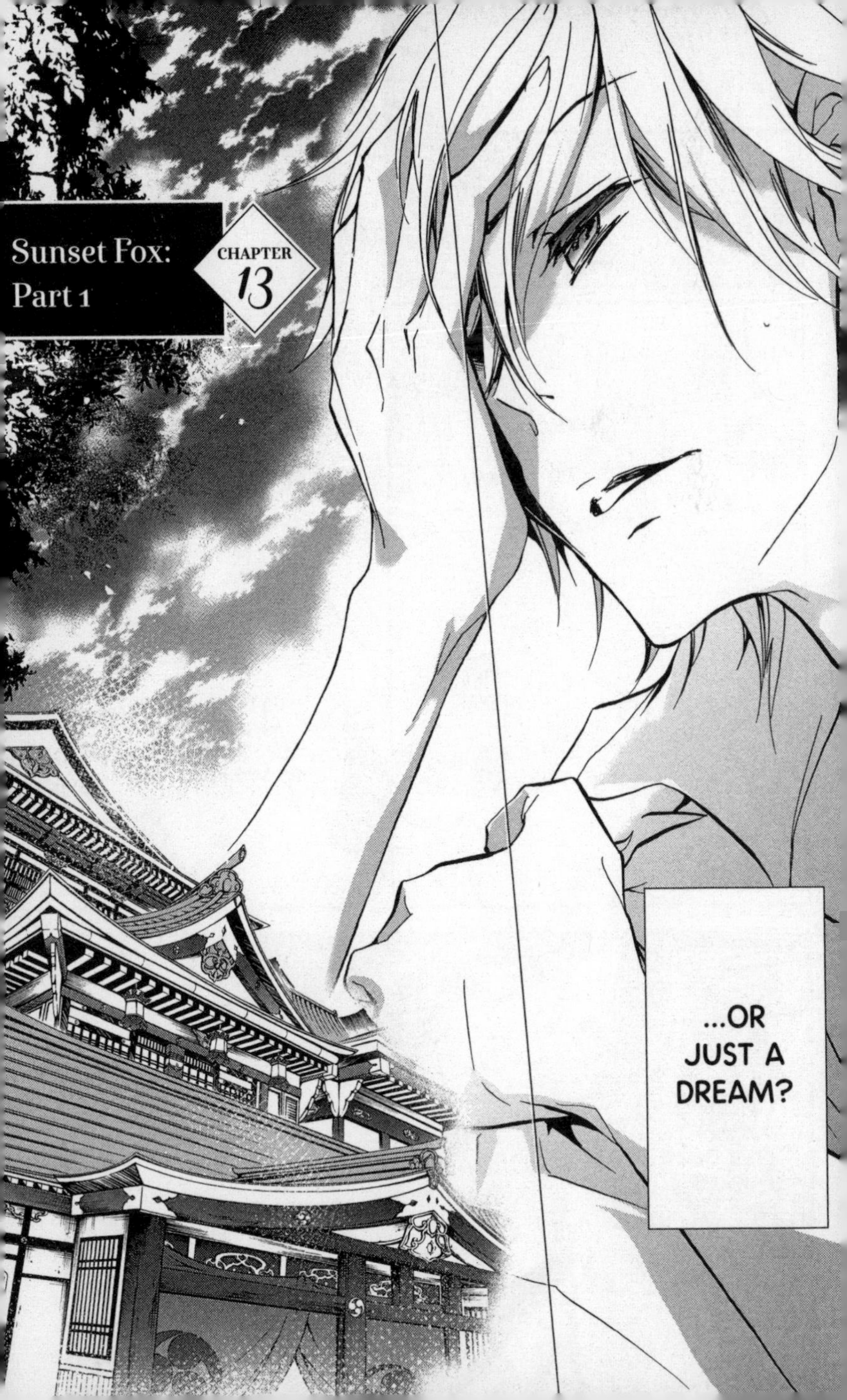
Sunset Fox: Part 1
CHAPTER 13
...OR JUST A DREAM?

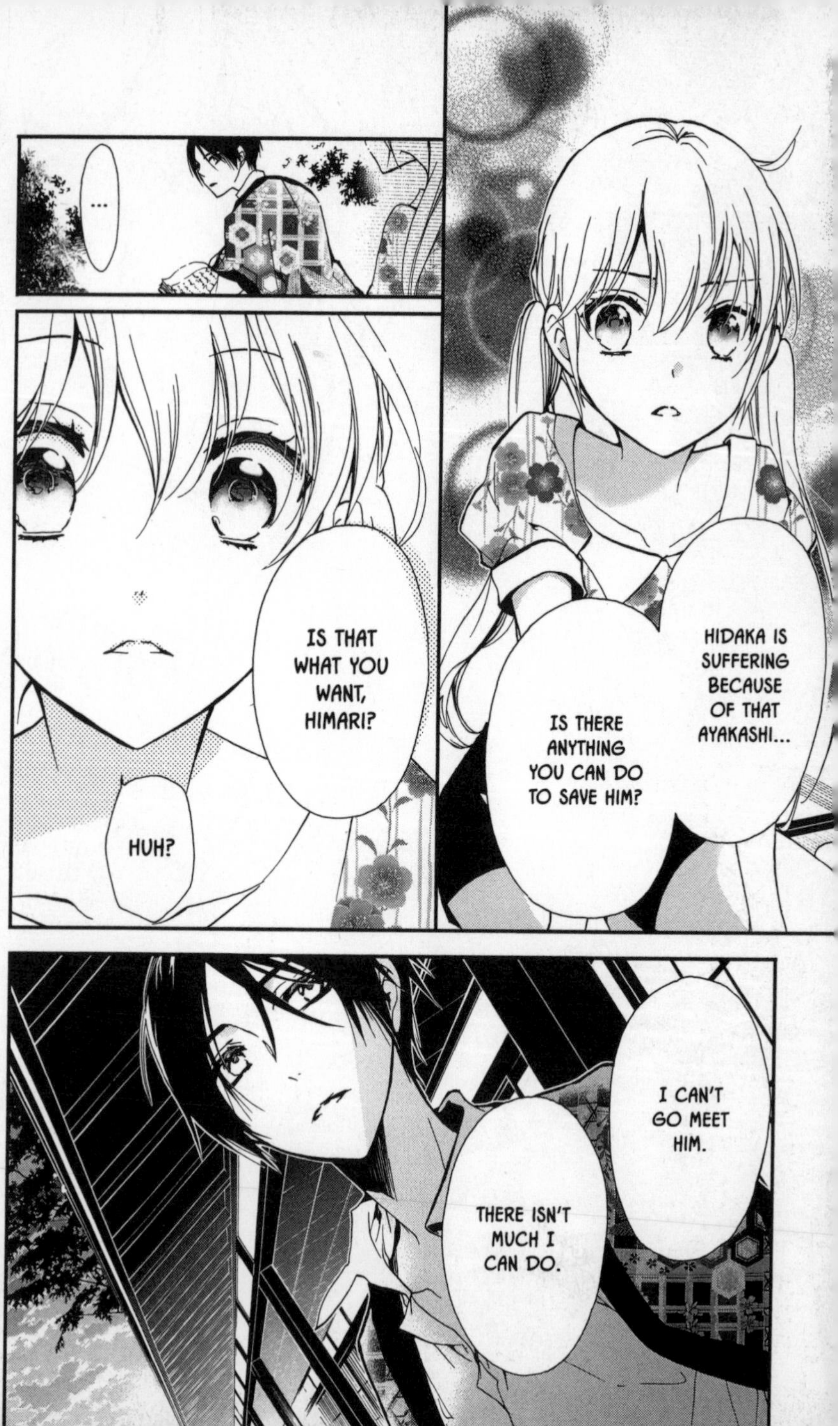
HIDAKA IS SUFFERING BECAUSE OF THAT AYAKASHI...
IS THERE ANYTHING YOU CAN DO TO SAVE HIM?
...
IS THAT WHAT YOU WANT, HIMARI?
HUH?
I CAN'T GO MEET HIM.
THERE ISN'T MUCH I CAN DO.

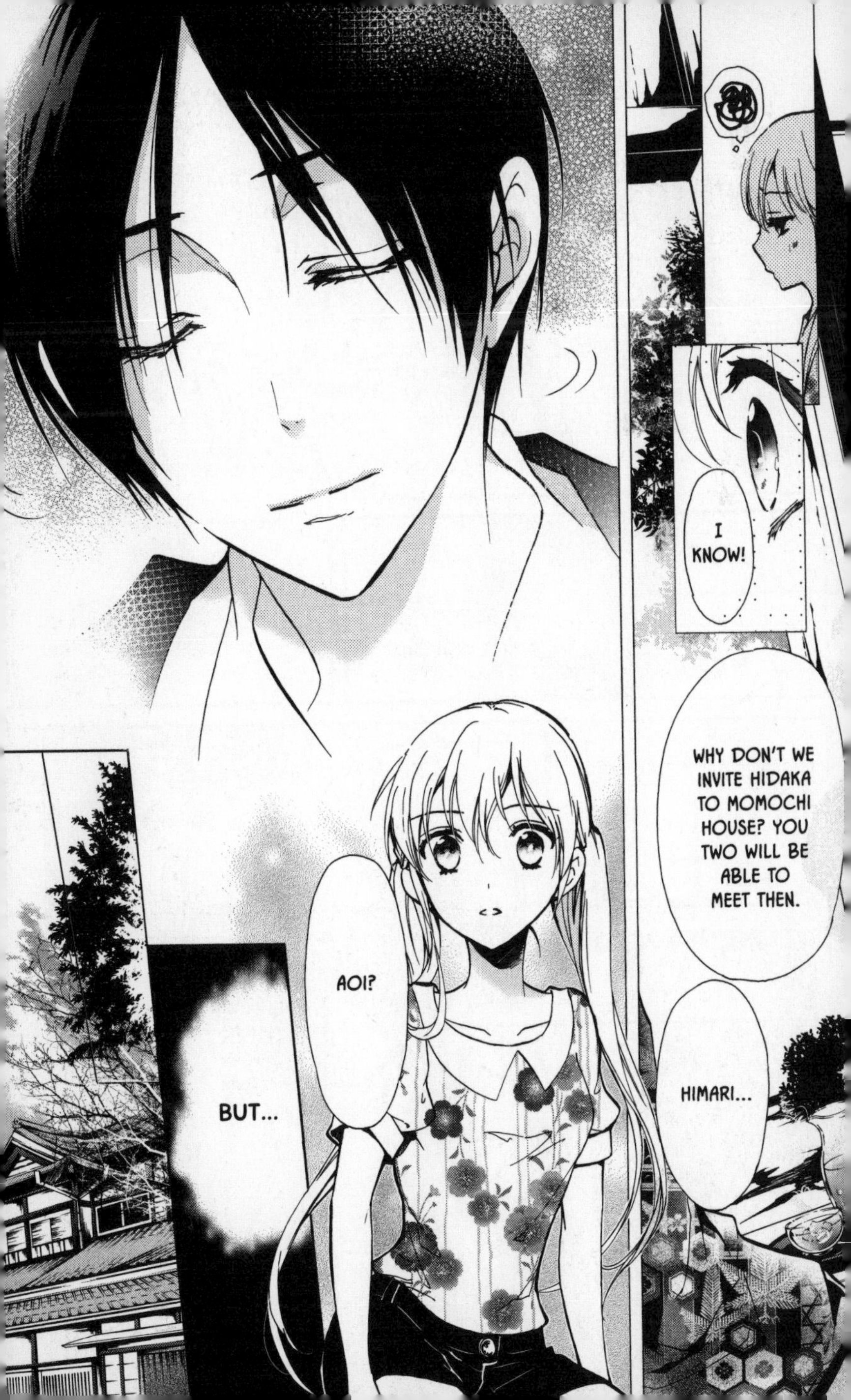
I KNOW!
WHY DON'T WE INVITE HIDAKA TO MOMOCHI HOUSE? YOU TWO WILL BE ABLE TO MEET THEN.
HIMARI...
AOI?
BUT...

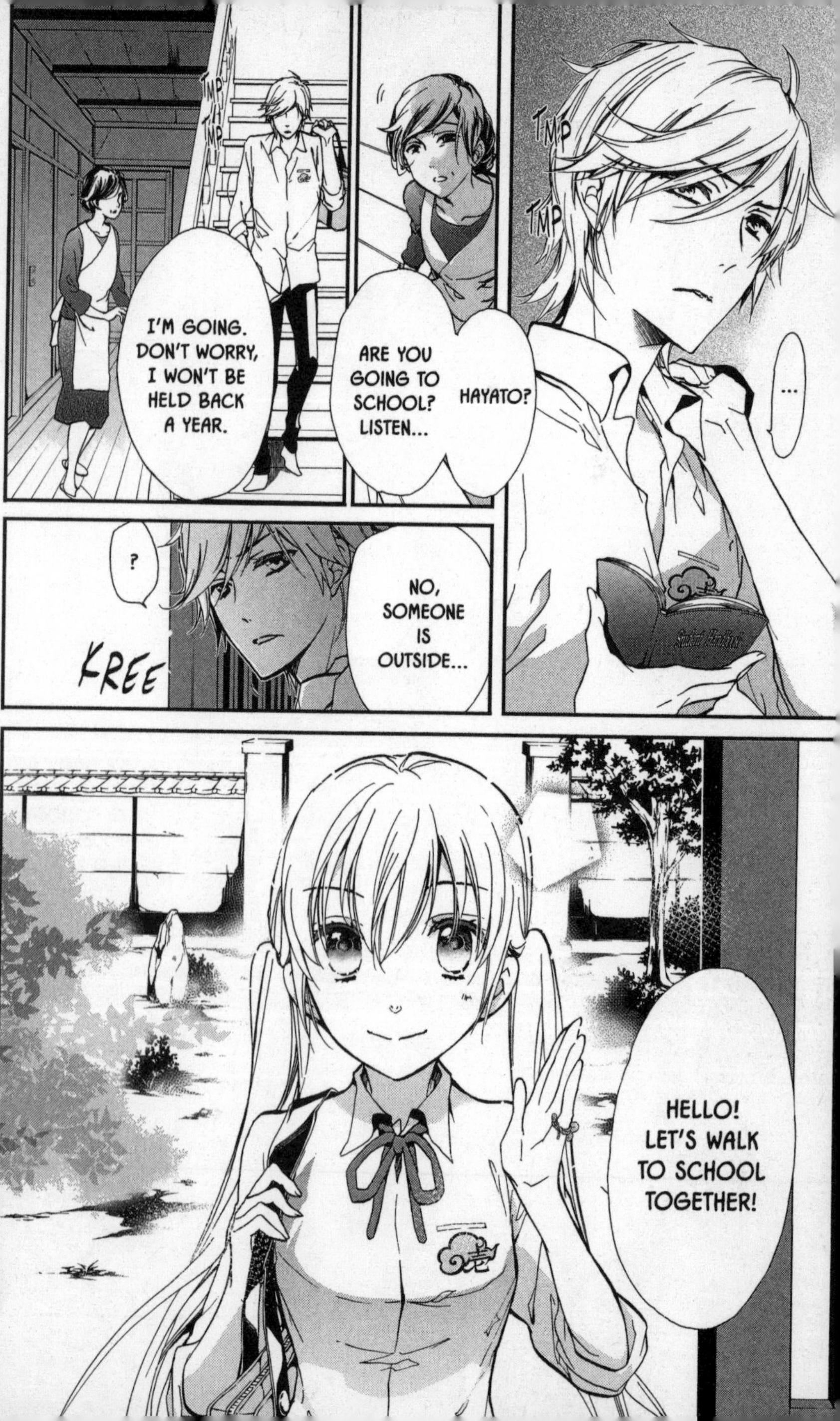
TMP
TMP
...
HAYATO?
ARE YOU GOING TO SCHOOL? LISTEN...
TMP
TMP
I'M GOING. DON'T WORRY, I WON'T BE HELD BACK A YEAR.
NO, SOMEONE IS OUTSIDE...
?
KREE
HELLO! LET'S WALK TO SCHOOL TOGETHER!

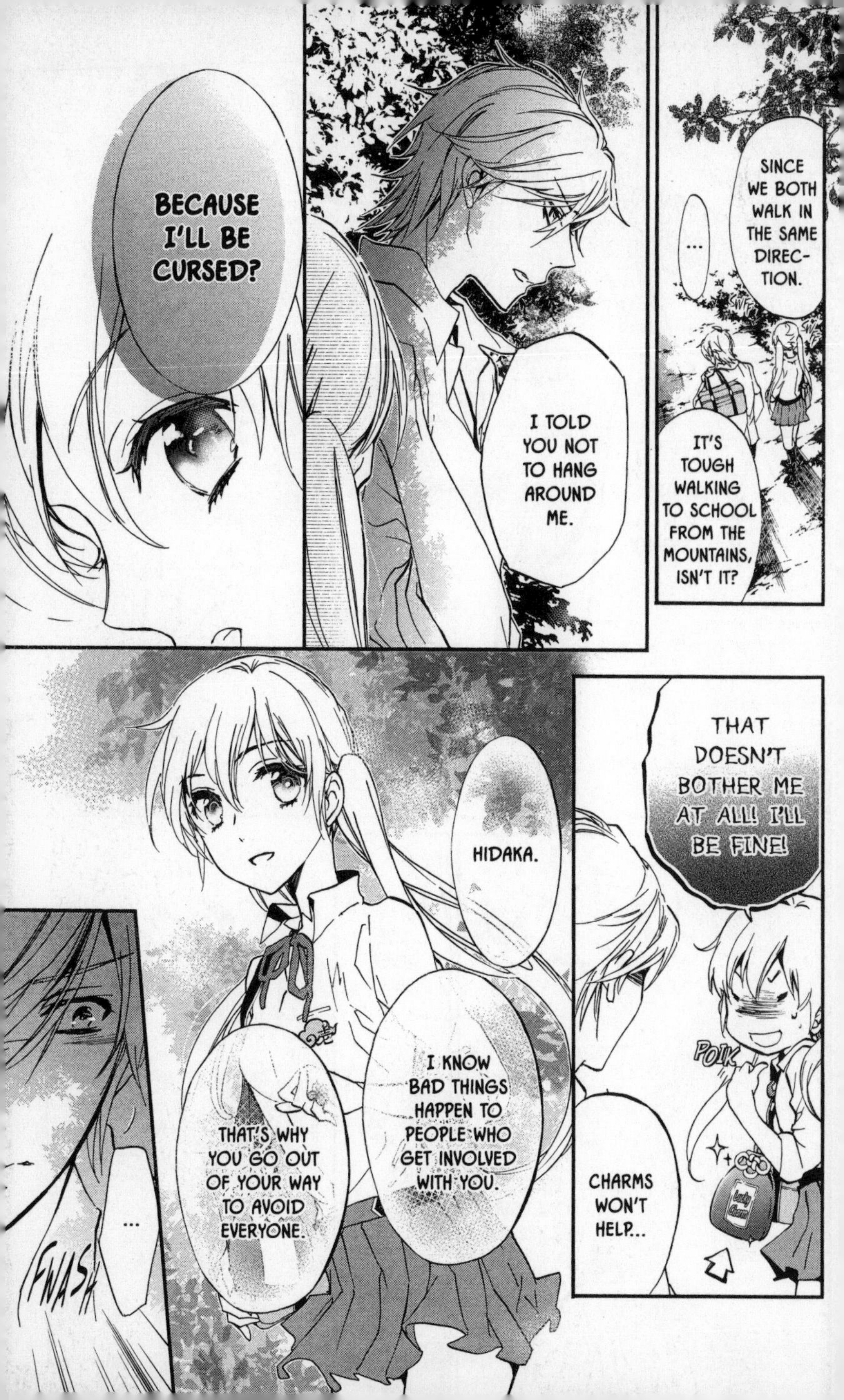
SINCE WE BOTH WALK IN THE SAME DIREC-TION.
...
SWF
IT'S TOUGH WALKING TO SCHOOL FROM THE MOUNTAINS, ISN'T IT?
I TOLD YOU NOT TO HANG AROUND ME.
BECAUSE I'LL BE CURSED?
THAT DOESN'T BOTHER ME AT ALL! I'LL BE FINE!
POIK
Lucky Charm
CHARMS WON'T HELP...
HIDAKA.
I KNOW BAD THINGS HAPPEN TO PEOPLE WHO GET INVOLVED WITH YOU.
THAT'S WHY YOU GO OUT OF YOUR WAY TO AVOID EVERYONE.
...
FWASH

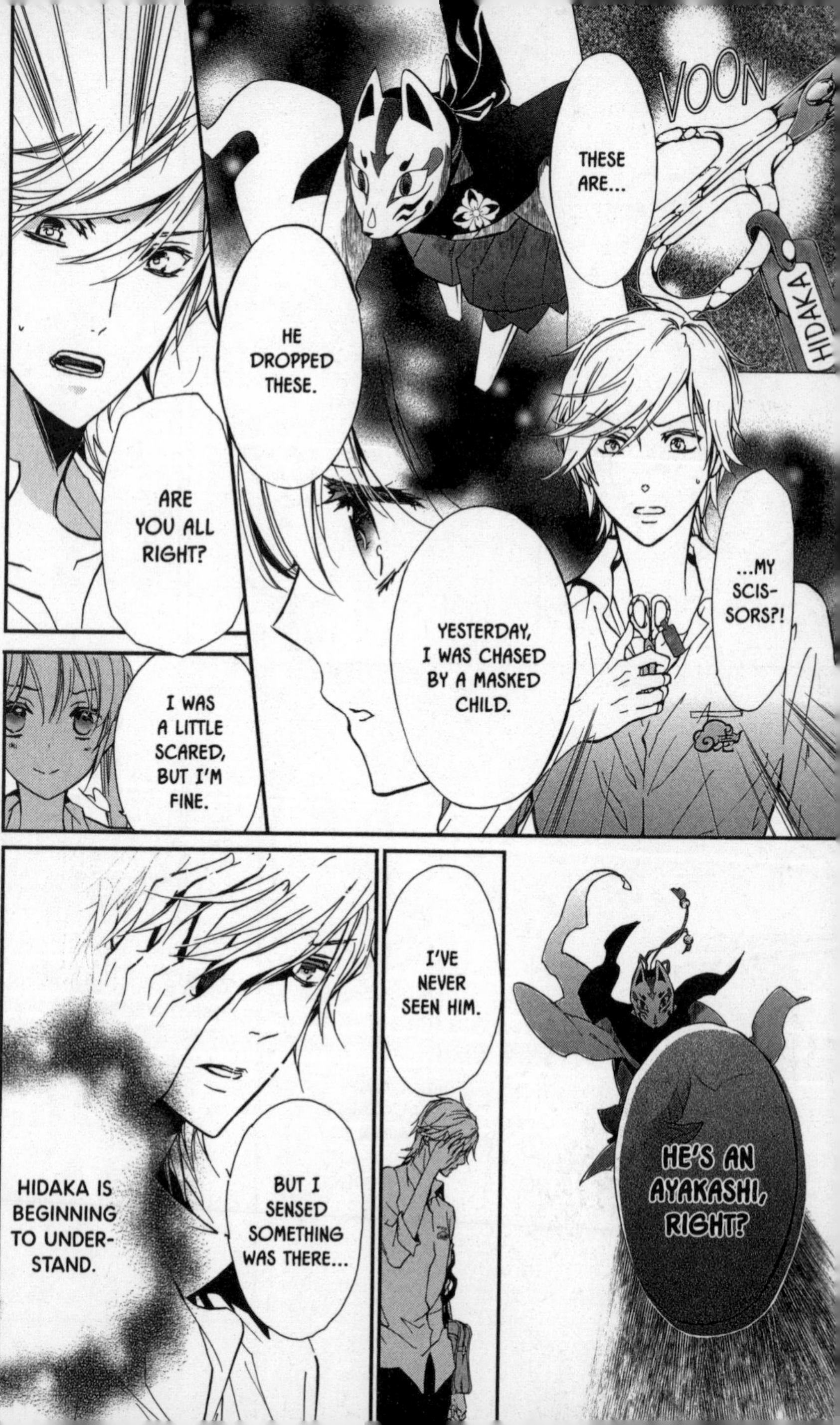
VOON
HIDAKA
THESE ARE...
...MY SCIS-SORS?!
HE DROPPED THESE.
YESTERDAY, I WAS CHASED BY A MASKED CHILD.
ARE YOU ALL RIGHT?
I WAS A LITTLE SCARED, BUT I'M FINE.
HE'S AN AYAKASHI, RIGHT?
I'VE NEVER SEEN HIM.
BUT I SENSED SOMETHING WAS THERE...
HIDAKA IS BEGINNING TO UNDER-STAND.

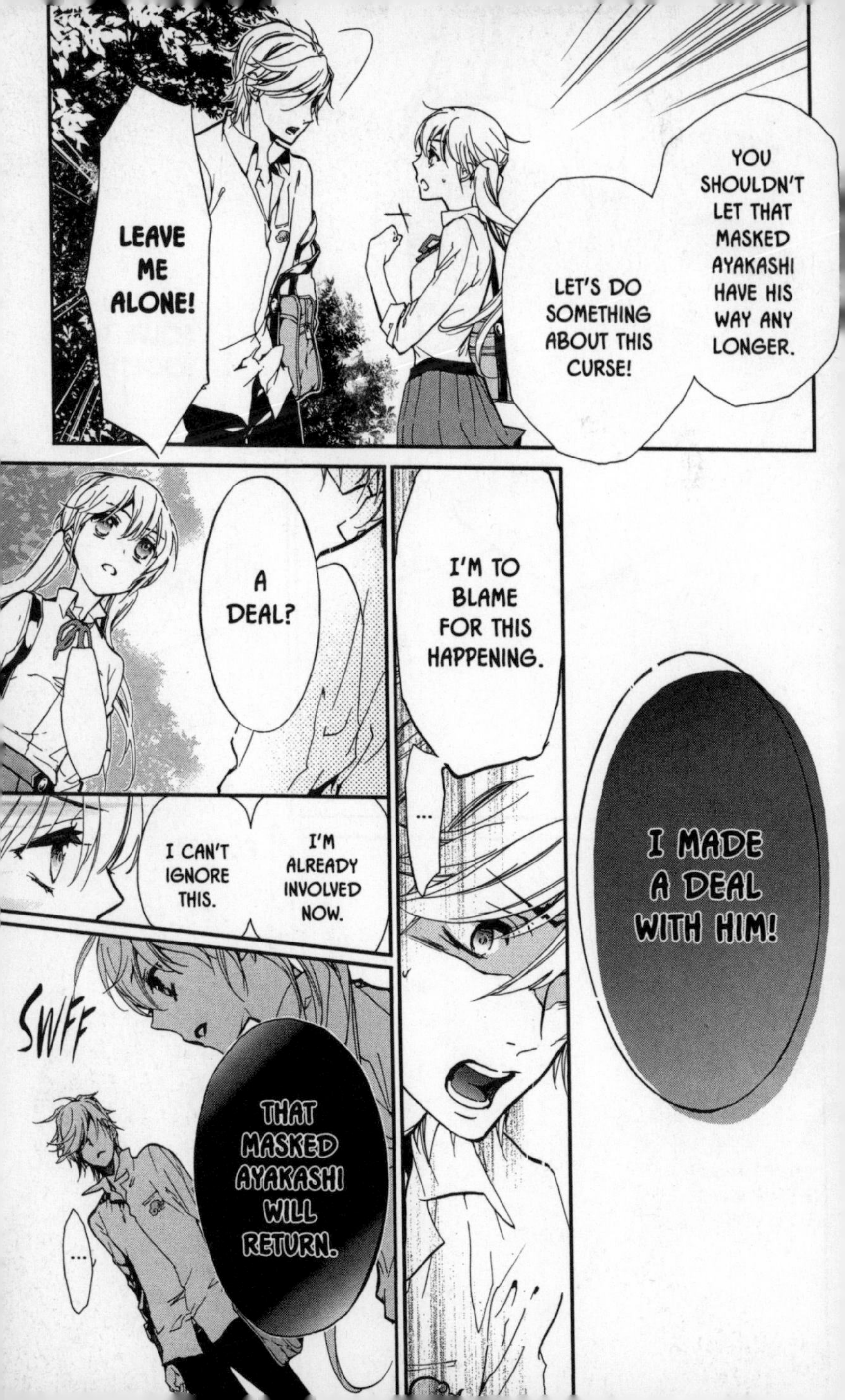
YOU SHOULDN'T LET THAT MASKED AYAKASHI HAVE HIS WAY ANY LONGER.
LET'S DO SOMETHING ABOUT THIS CURSE!
LEAVE ME ALONE!
I'M TO BLAME FOR THIS HAPPENING.
I MADE A DEAL WITH HIM!
A DEAL?
...
I'M ALREADY INVOLVED NOW.
I CAN'T IGNORE THIS.
THAT MASKED AYAKASHI WILL RETURN.
SWFF
...

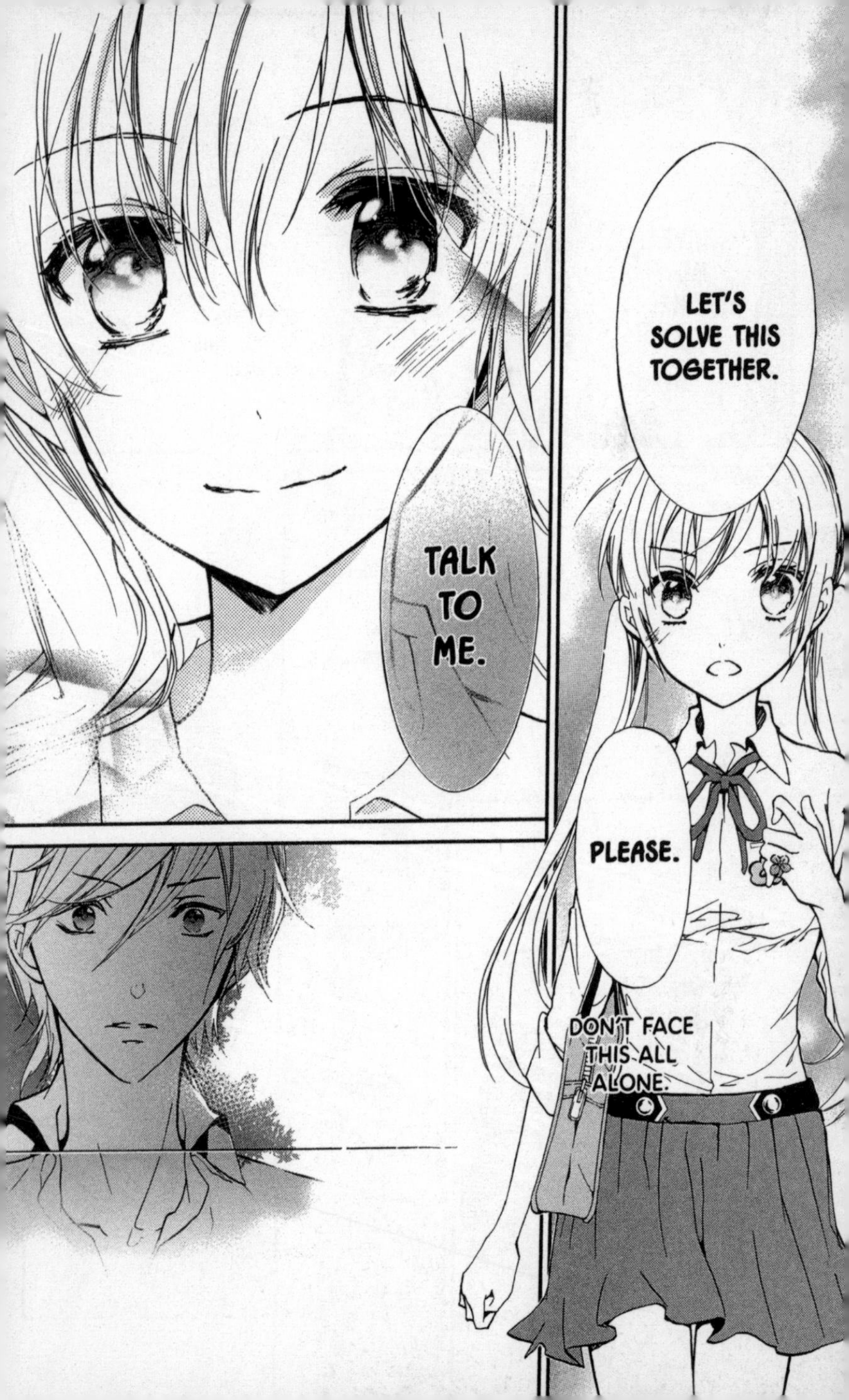
LET'S SOLVE THIS TOGETHER.
PLEASE.
DON'T FACE THIS ALL ALONE.
TALK TO ME.

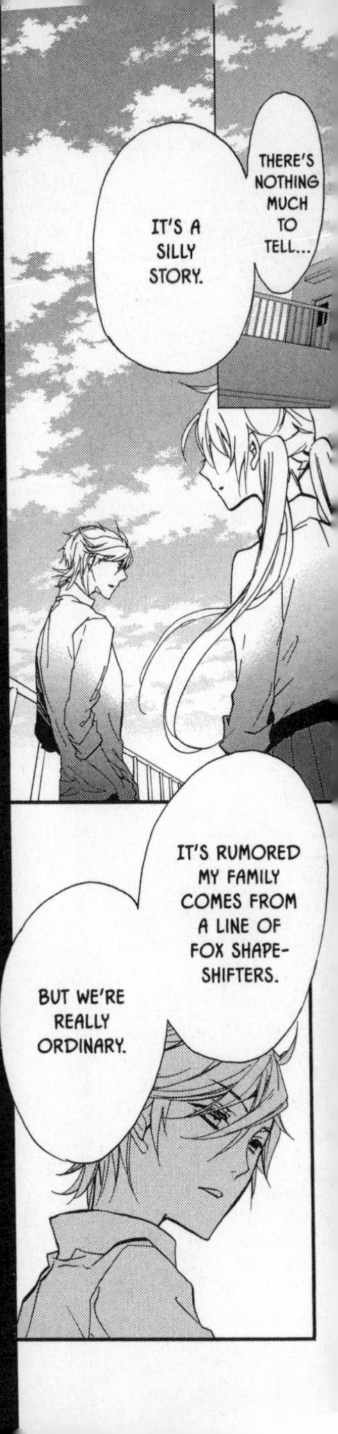
THERE'S NOTHING MUCH TO TELL...
IT'S A SILLY STORY.
IT'S RUMORED MY FAMILY COMES FROM A LINE OF FOX SHAPE-SHIFTERS.
BUT WE'RE REALLY ORDINARY.

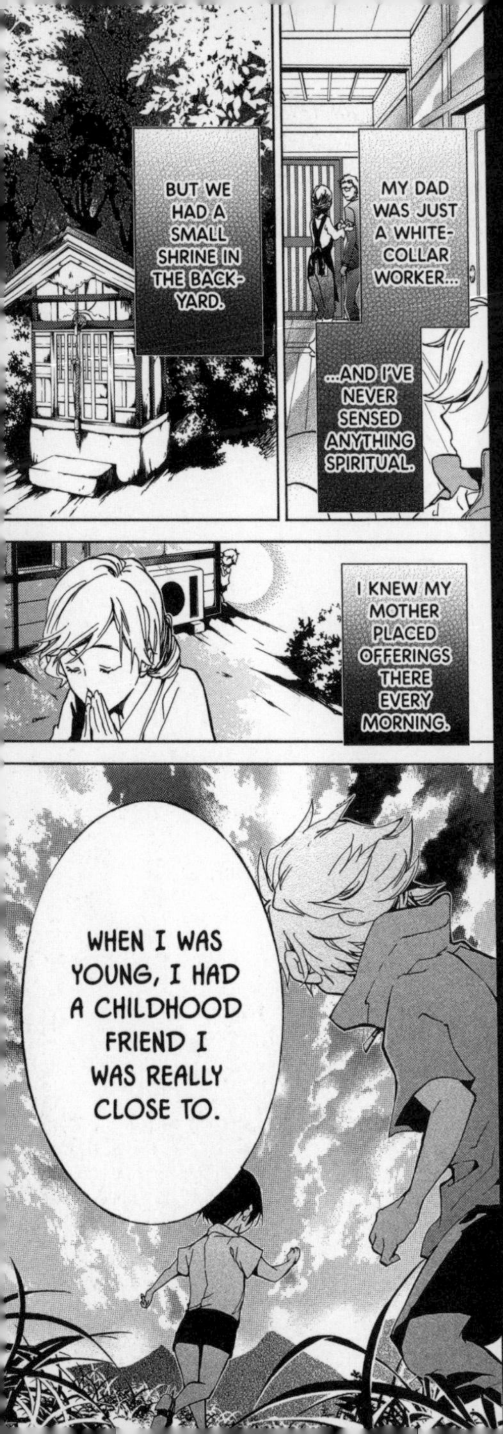
MY DAD WAS JUST A WHITE-COLLAR WORKER...
...AND I'VE NEVER SENSED ANYTHING SPIRITUAL.
BUT WE HAD A SMALL SHRINE IN THE BACK-YARD.
I KNEW MY MOTHER PLACED OFFERINGS THERE EVERY MORNING.
WHEN I WAS YOUNG, I HAD A CHILDHOOD FRIEND I WAS REALLY CLOSE TO.

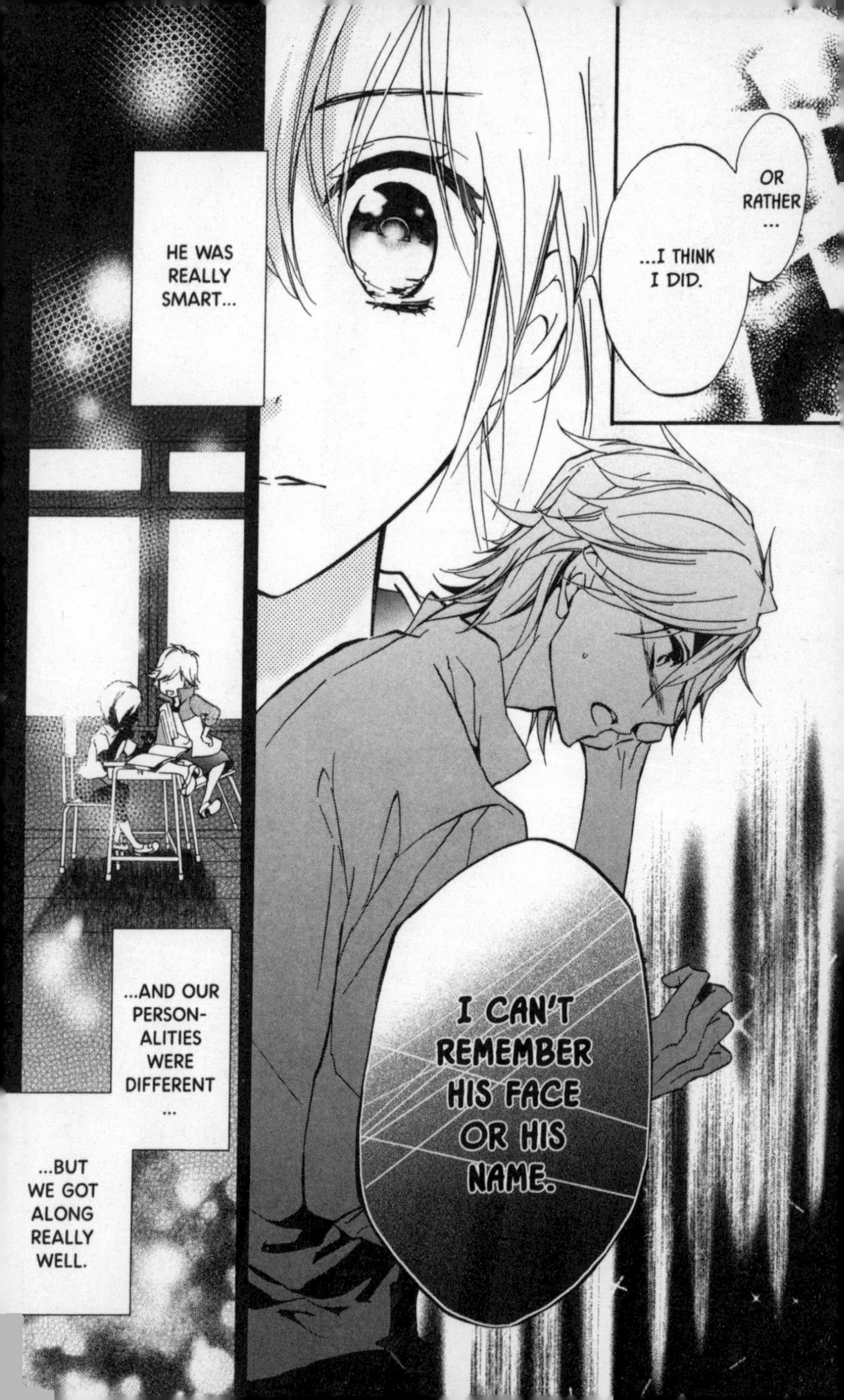
OR RATHER...
...I THINK I DID.
I CAN'T REMEMBER HIS FACE OR HIS NAME.
HE WAS REALLY SMART...
...AND OUR PERSON-ALITIES WERE DIFFERENT...
...BUT WE GOT ALONG REALLY WELL.

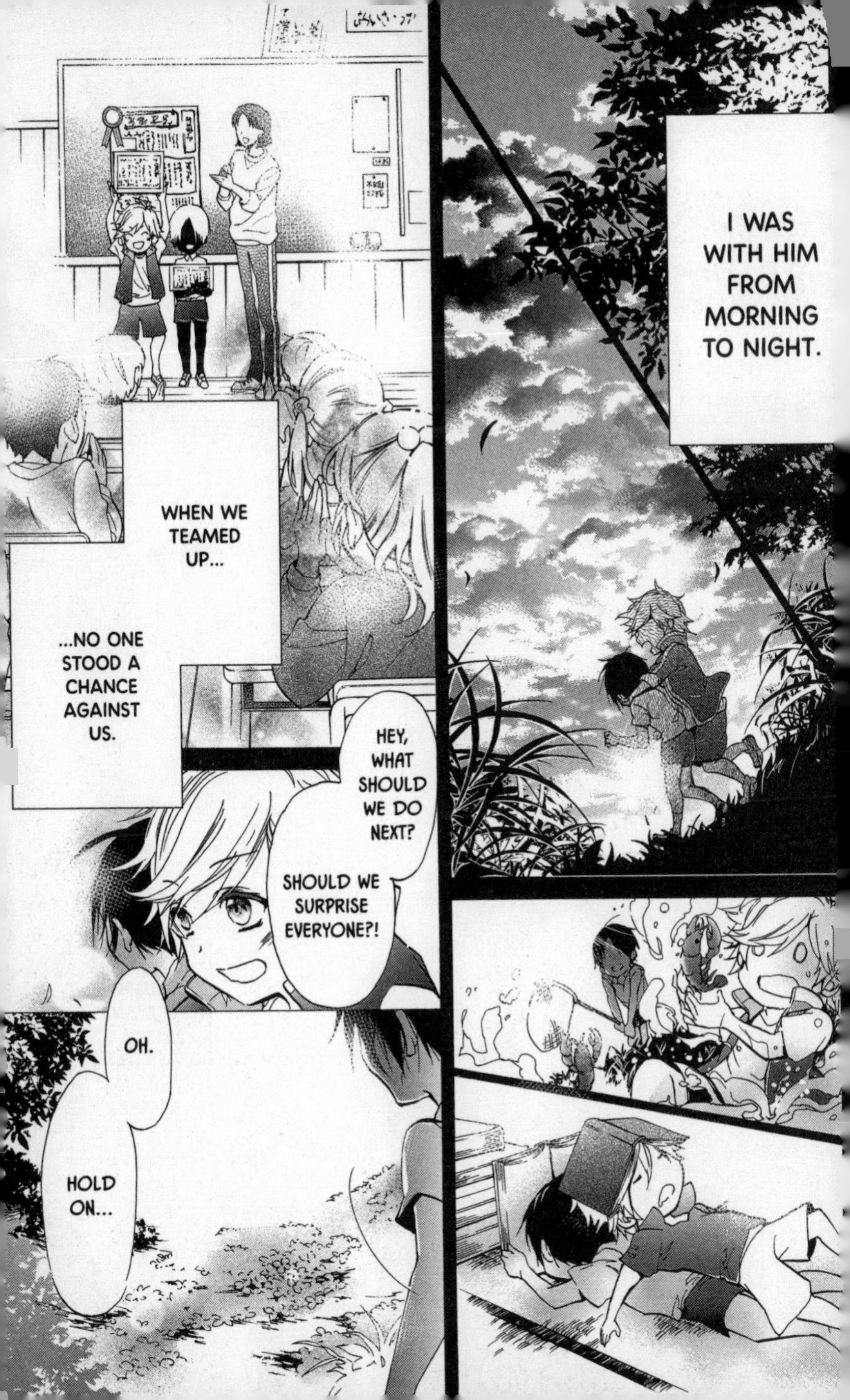
I WAS WITH HIM FROM MORNING TO NIGHT.
WHEN WE TEAMED UP...
...NO ONE STOOD A CHANCE AGAINST US.
HEY, WHAT SHOULD WE DO NEXT?
SHOULD WE SURPRISE EVERYONE?!
OH.
HOLD ON...

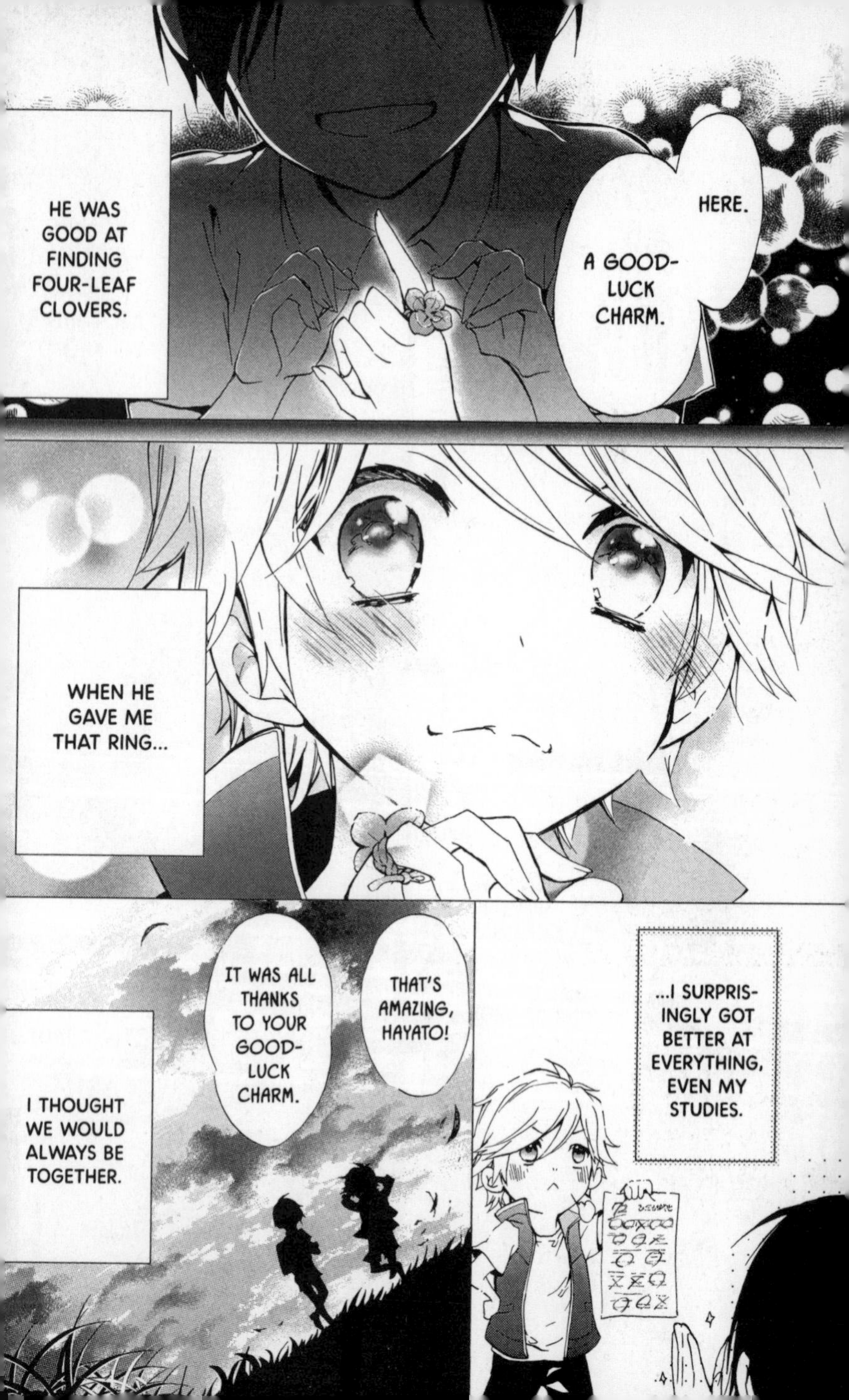
HERE.
A GOOD-LUCK CHARM.
HE WAS GOOD AT FINDING FOUR-LEAF CLOVERS.
WHEN HE GAVE ME THAT RING...
...I SURPRISINGLY GOT BETTER AT EVERYTHING, EVEN MY STUDIES.
THAT'S AMAZING, HAYATO!
IT WAS ALL THANKS TO YOUR GOOD-LUCK CHARM.
I THOUGHT WE WOULD ALWAYS BE TOGETHER.

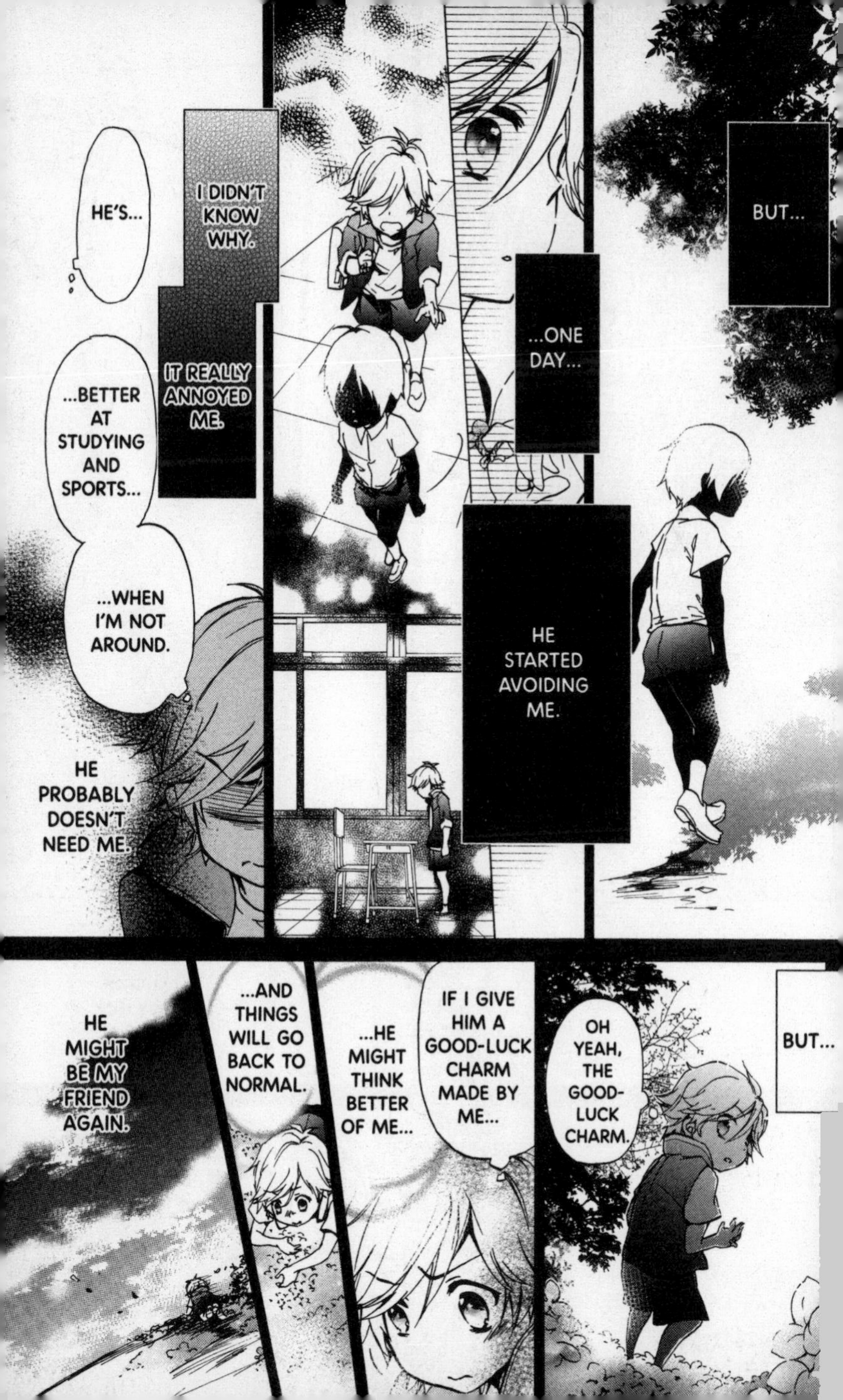
BUT...
...ONE DAY...
HE STARTED AVOIDING ME.
I DIDN'T KNOW WHY.
IT REALLY ANNOYED ME.
HE'S...
...BETTER AT STUDYING AND SPORTS...
...WHEN I'M NOT AROUND.
HE PROBABLY DOESN'T NEED ME.
BUT...
OH YEAH, THE GOOD-LUCK CHARM.
IF I GIVE HIM A GOOD-LUCK CHARM MADE BY ME...
...HE MIGHT THINK BETTER OF ME...
...AND THINGS WILL GO BACK TO NORMAL.
HE MIGHT BE MY FRIEND AGAIN.

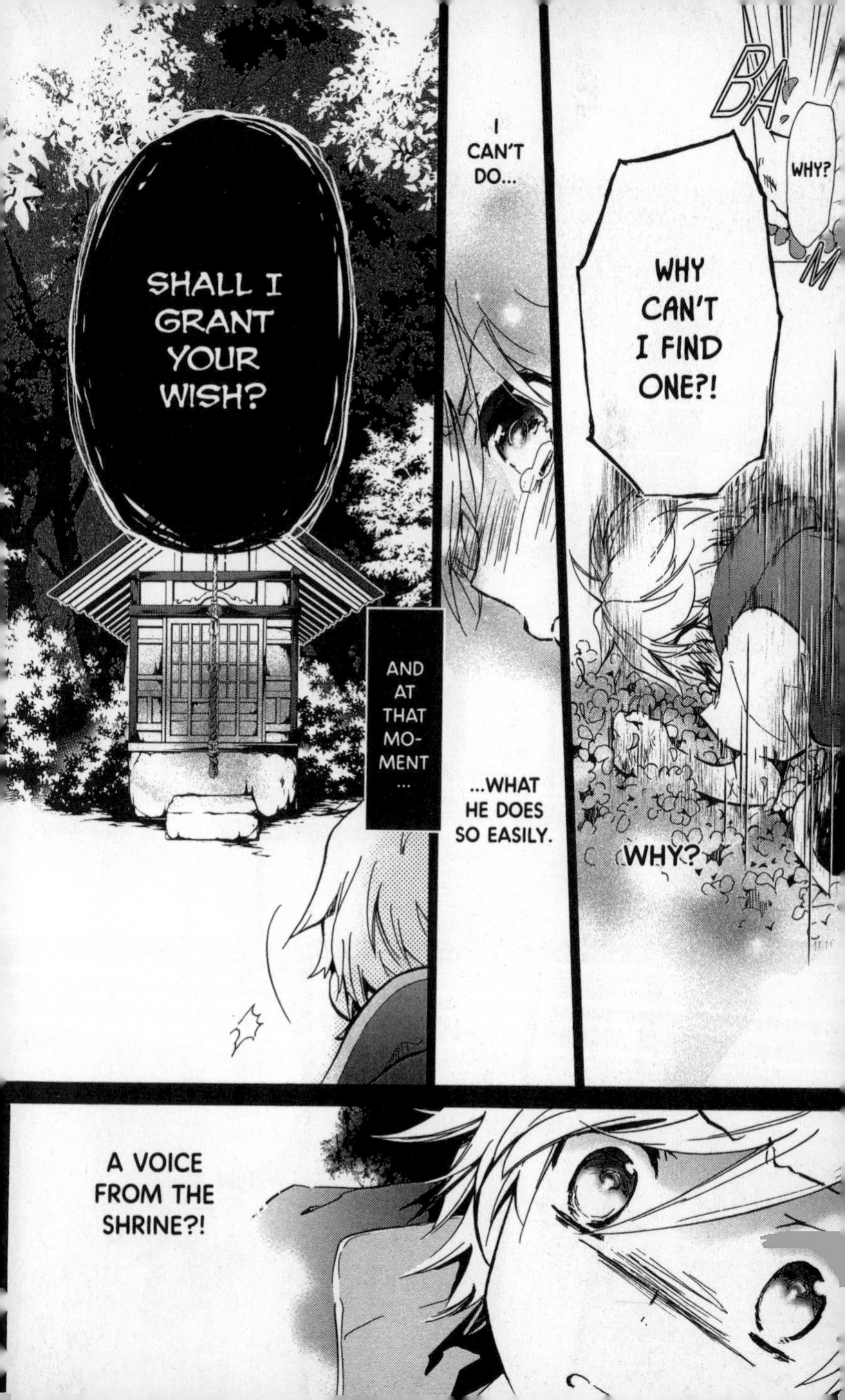
BAM
WHY?
WHY CAN'T I FIND ONE?!
WHY?
I CAN'T DO...
...WHAT HE DOES SO EASILY.
AND AT THAT MOMENT...
SHALL I GRANT YOUR WISH?
A VOICE FROM THE SHRINE?!

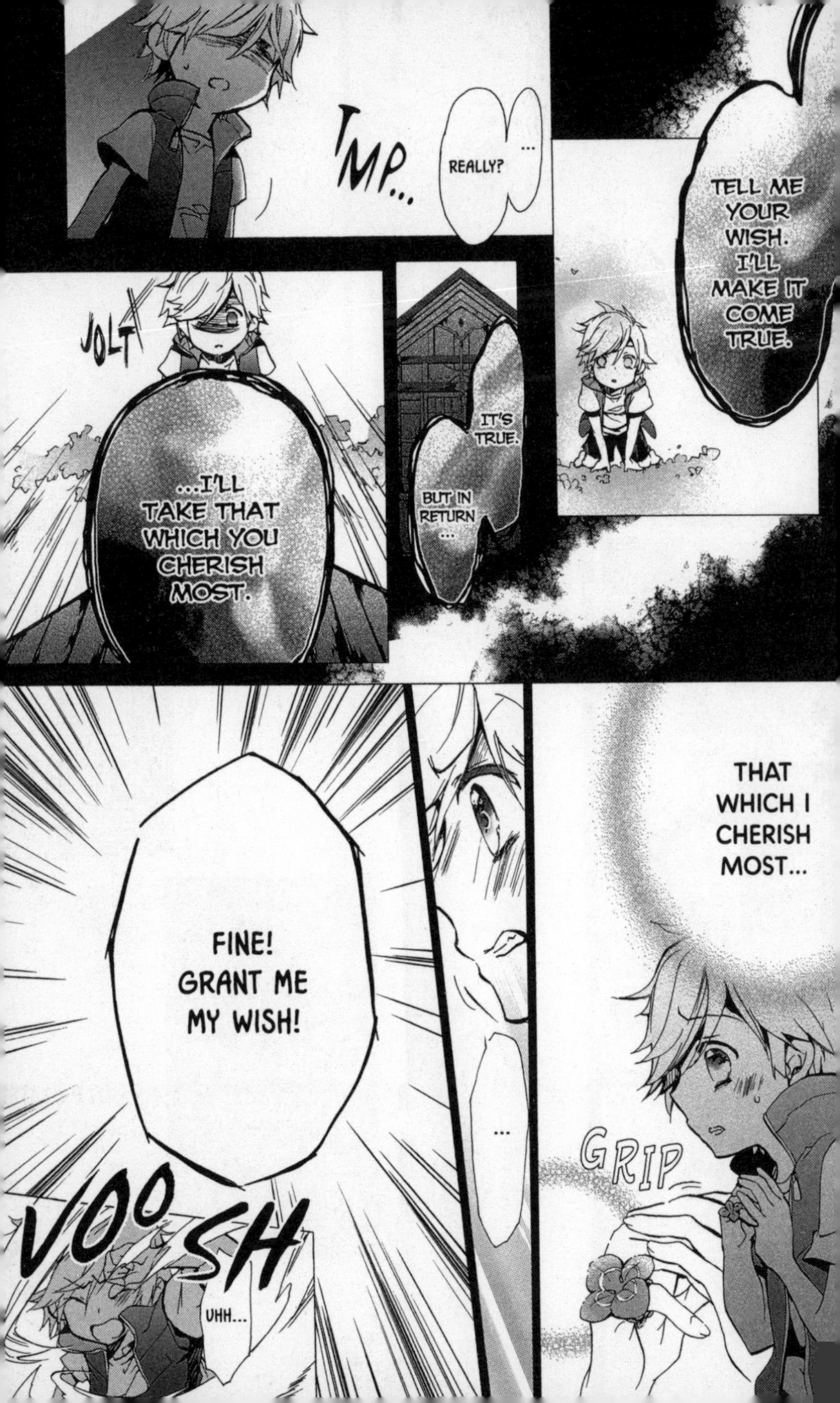
TELL ME YOUR WISH. I'LL MAKE IT COME TRUE.
...
REALLY?
TMP...
IT'S TRUE.
BUT IN RETURN ...
JOLT
...I'LL TAKE THAT WHICH YOU CHERISH MOST.
THAT WHICH I CHERISH MOST...
GRIP
...
FINE! GRANT ME MY WISH!
VOOSH
UHH...

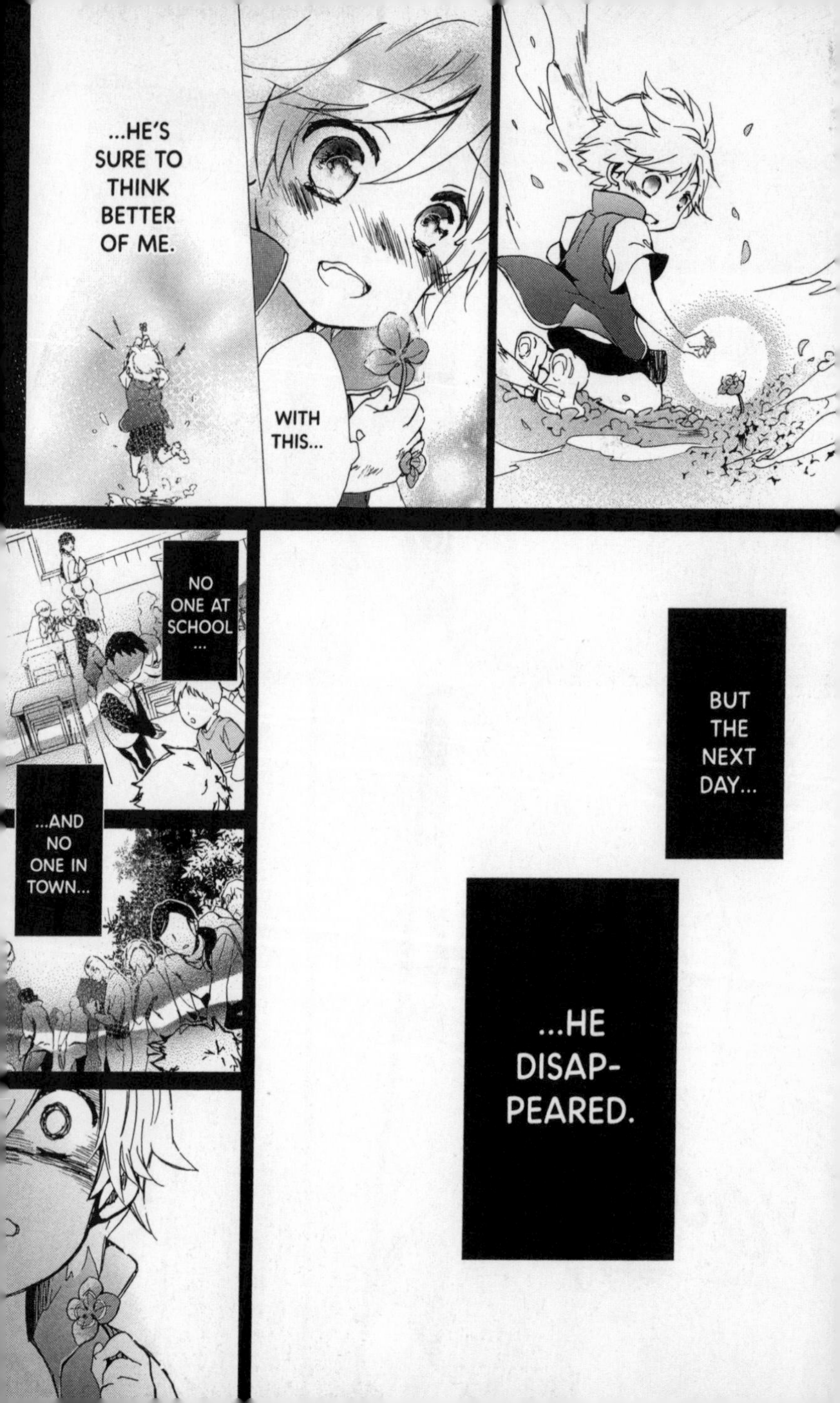
WITH THIS...
...HE'S SURE TO THINK BETTER OF ME.
BUT THE NEXT DAY...
...HE DISAPPEARED.
NO ONE AT SCHOOL ...
...AND NO ONE IN TOWN...

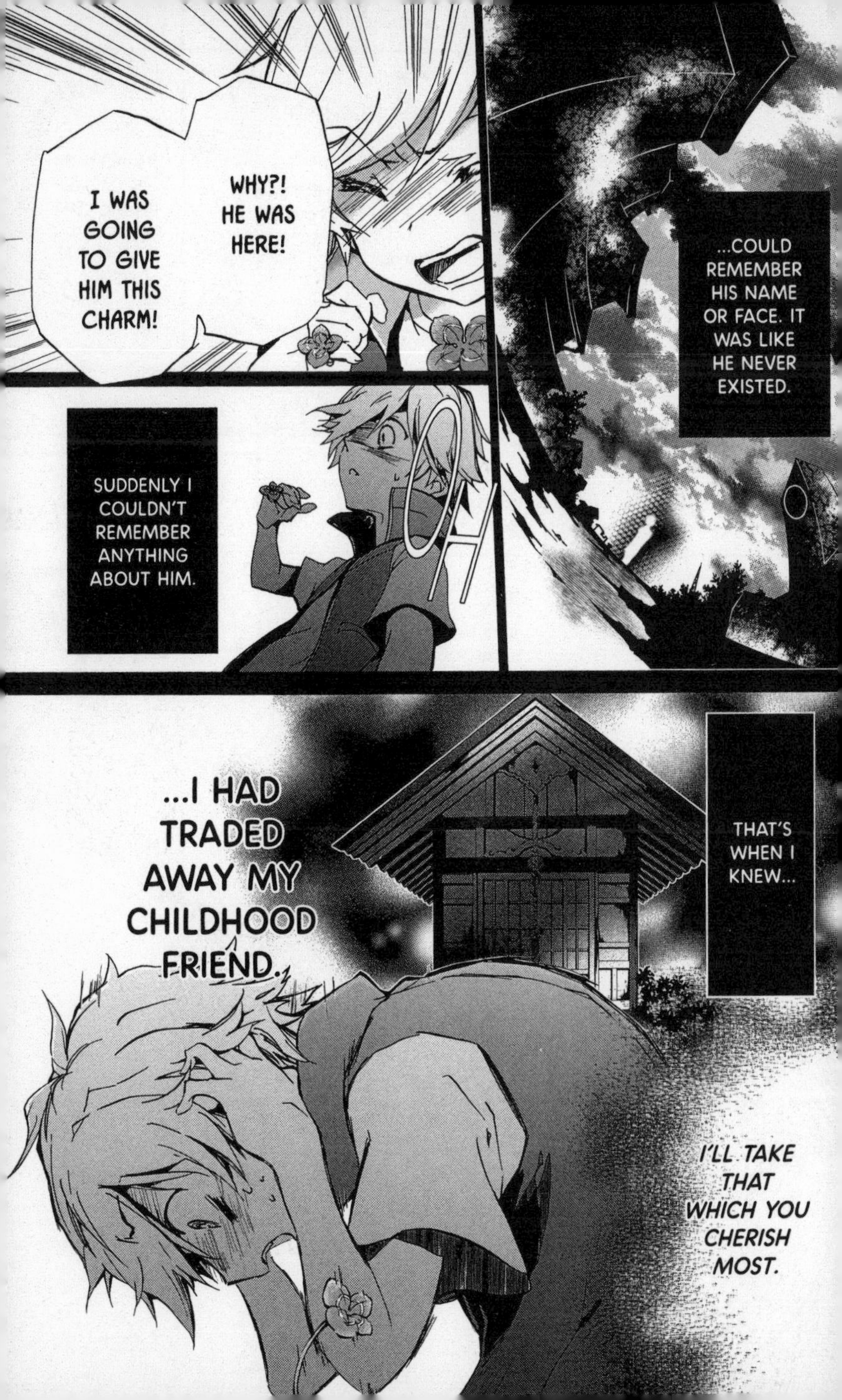
...COULD REMEMBER HIS NAME OR FACE. IT WAS LIKE HE NEVER EXISTED.
WHY?! HE WAS HERE!
I WAS GOING TO GIVE HIM THIS CHARM!
SUDDENLY I COULDN'T REMEMBER ANYTHING ABOUT HIM.
OH
THAT'S WHEN I KNEW...
...I HAD TRADED AWAY MY CHILDHOOD FRIEND.
I'LL TAKE THAT WHICH YOU CHERISH MOST.

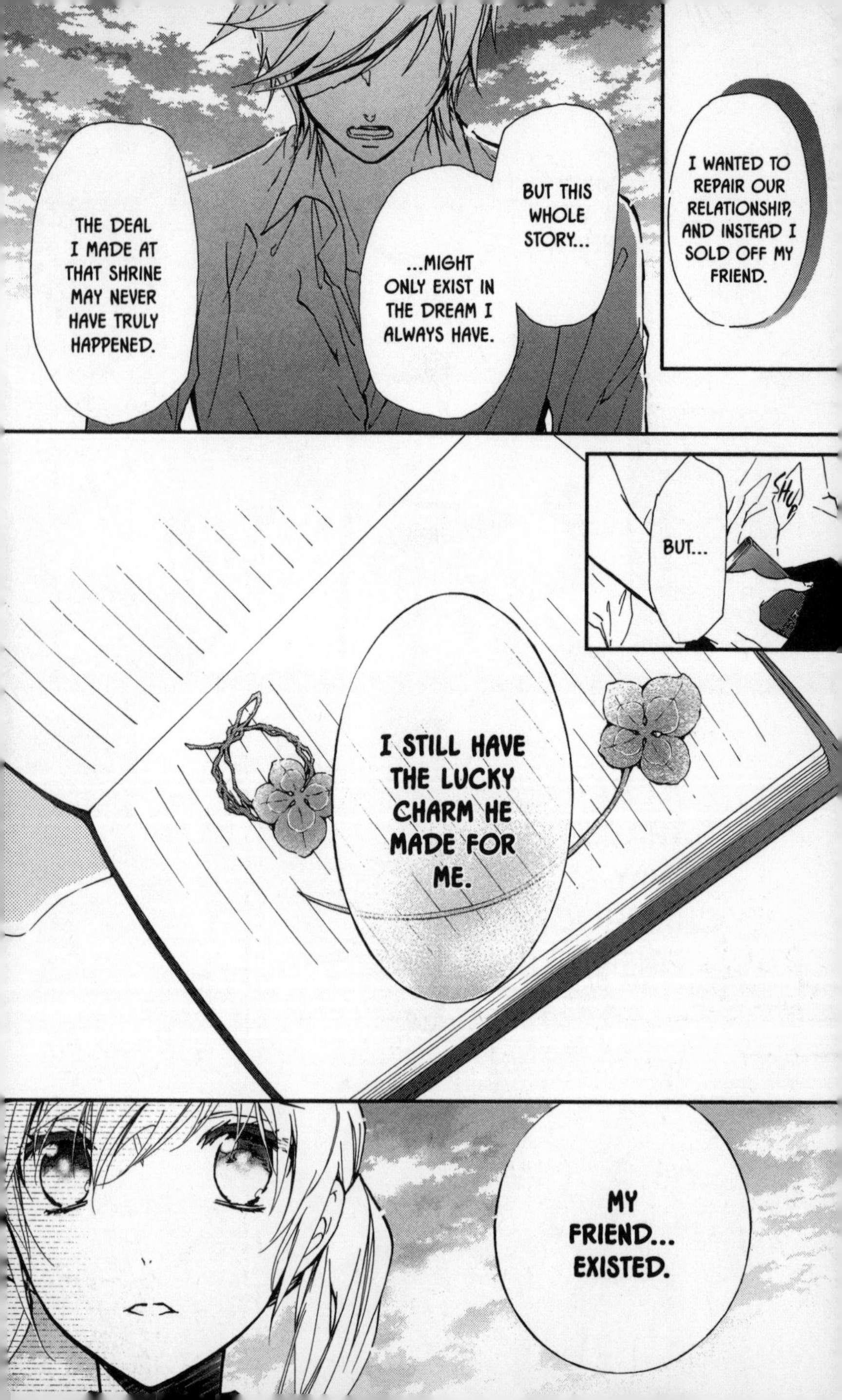
I WANTED TO REPAIR OUR RELATIONSHIP, AND INSTEAD I SOLD OFF MY FRIEND.
BUT THIS WHOLE STORY...
...MIGHT ONLY EXIST IN THE DREAM I ALWAYS HAVE.
THE DEAL I MADE AT THAT SHRINE MAY NEVER HAVE TRULY HAPPENED.
SHUP
BUT...
I STILL HAVE THE LUCKY CHARM HE MADE FOR ME.
MY FRIEND... EXISTED.

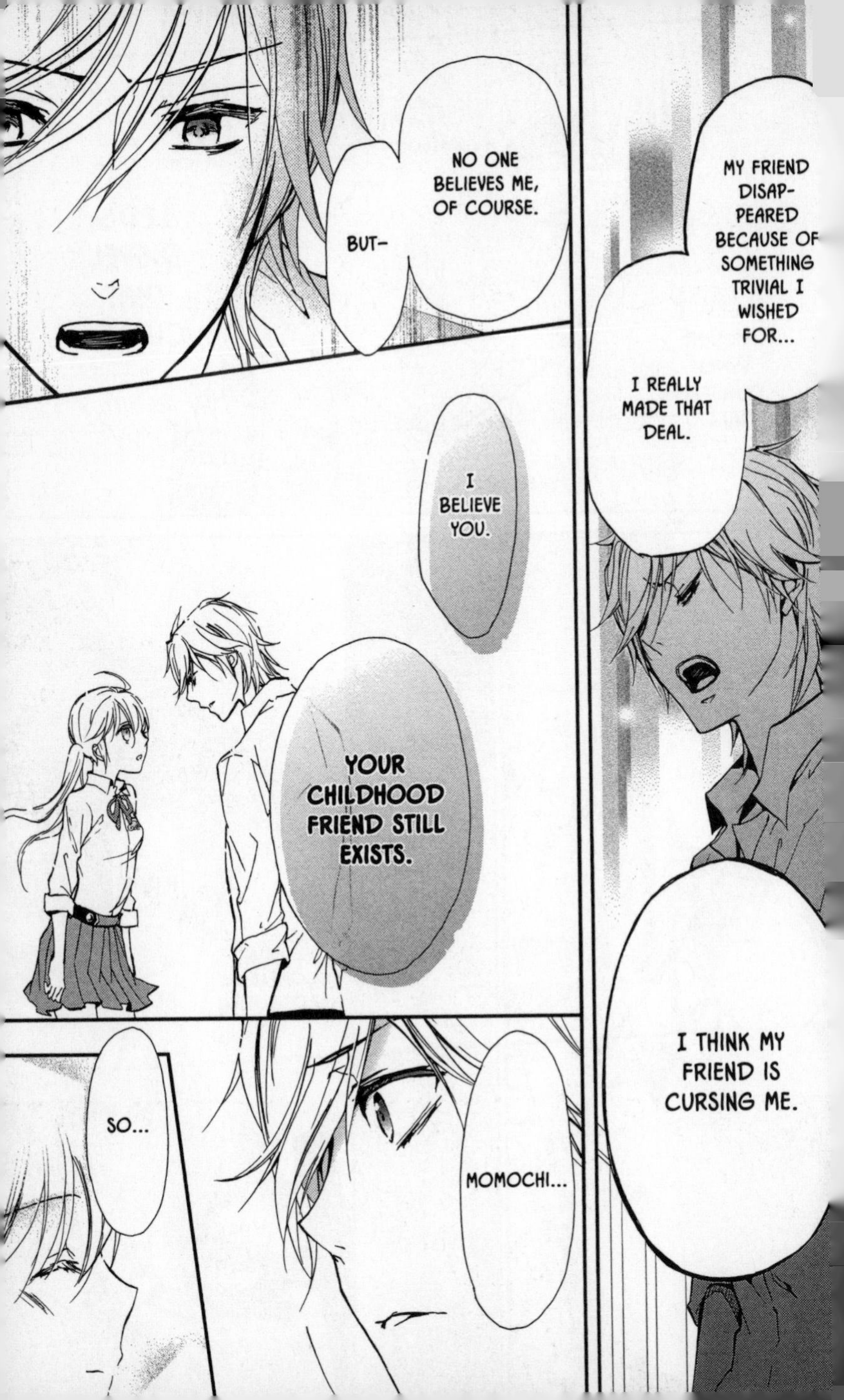
MY FRIEND DISAP- PEARED BECAUSE OF SOMETHING TRIVIAL I WISHED FOR...
I REALLY MADE THAT DEAL.
I THINK MY FRIEND IS CURSING ME.
NO ONE BELIEVES ME, OF COURSE.
BUT–
I BELIEVE YOU.
YOUR CHILDHOOD FRIEND STILL EXISTS.
MOMOCHI...
SO...

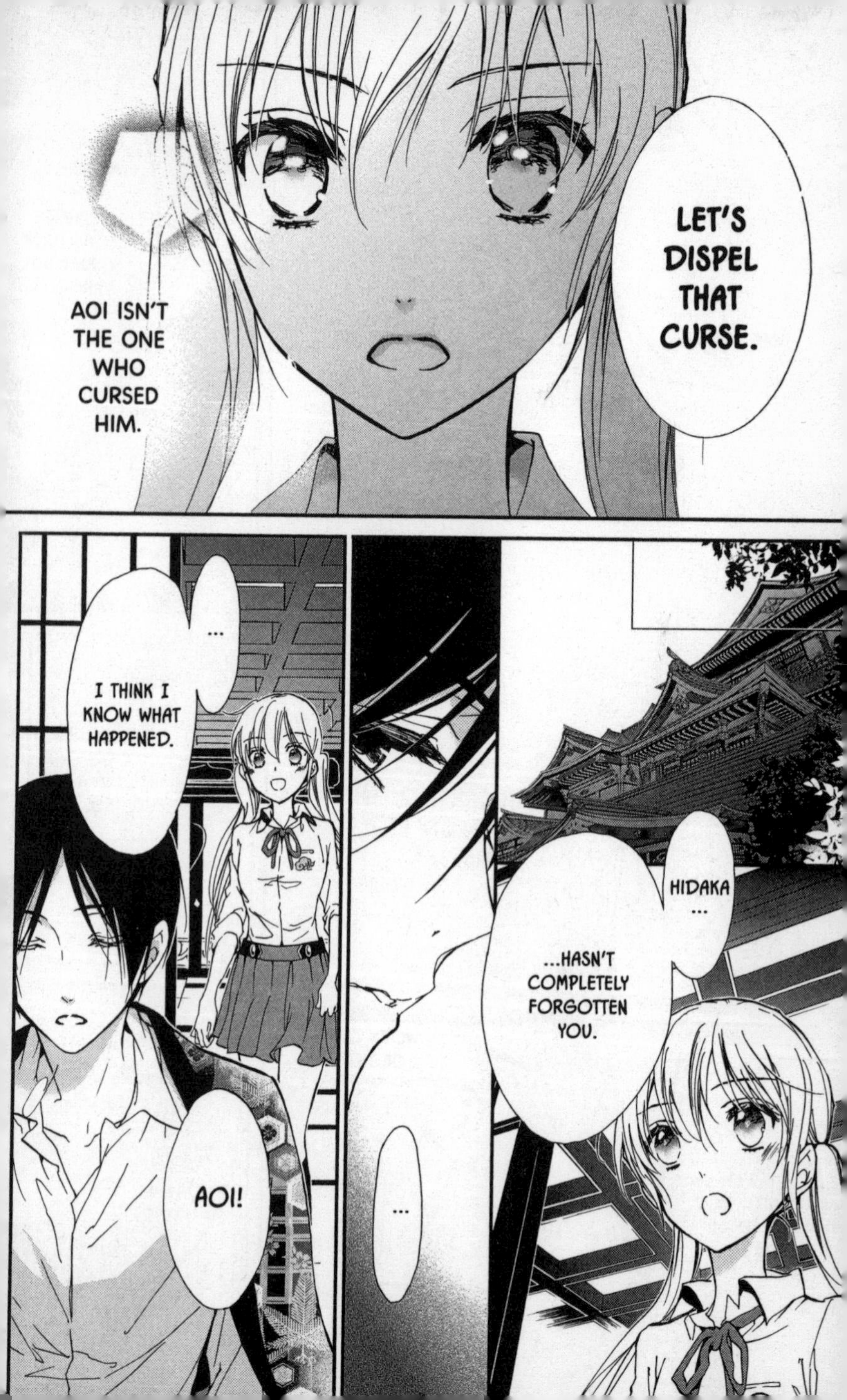
LET'S DISPEL THAT CURSE.
AOI ISN'T THE ONE WHO CURSED HIM.
HIDAKA...
...HASN'T COMPLETELY FORGOTTEN YOU.
...
...
I THINK I KNOW WHAT HAPPENED.
AOI!

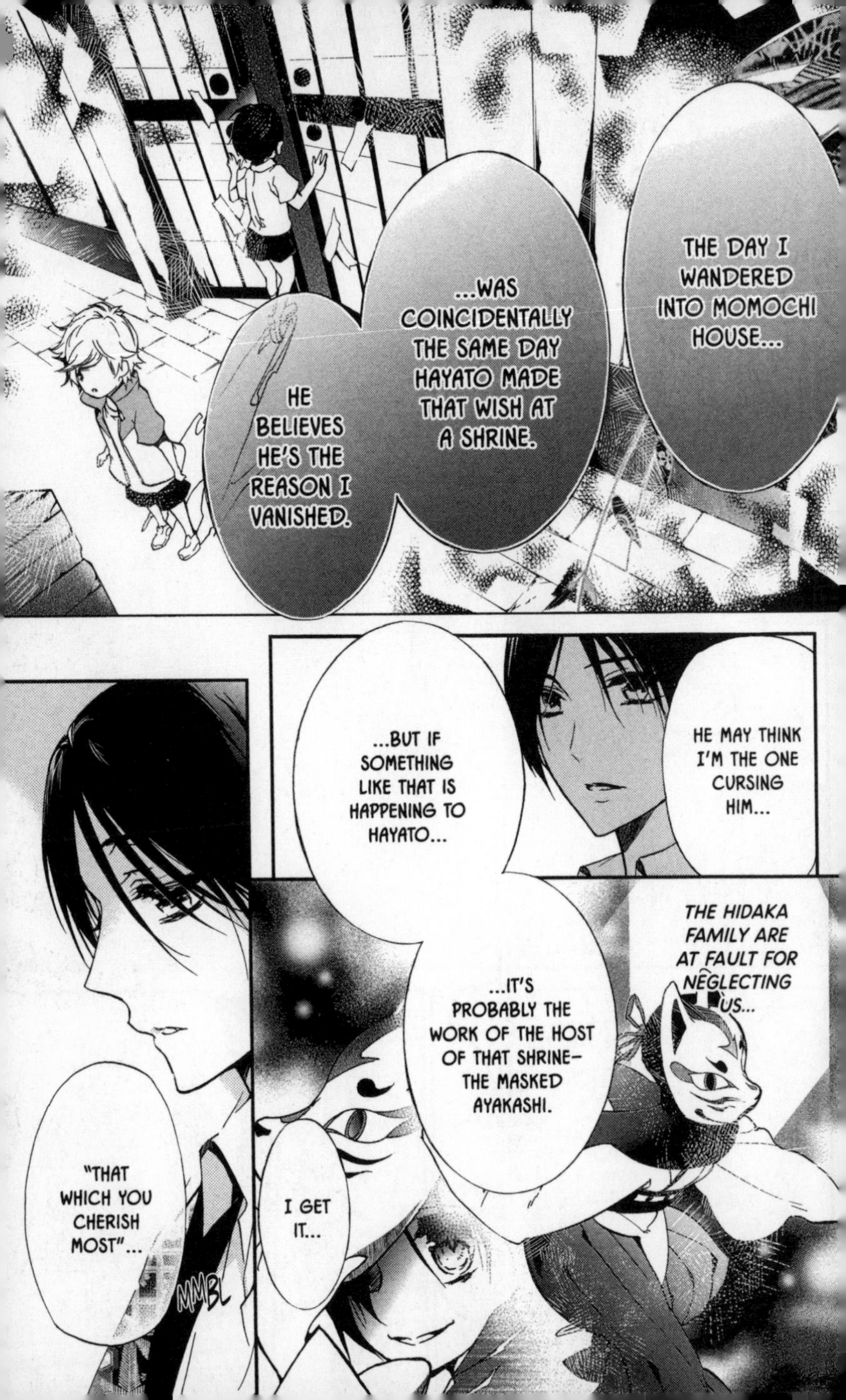
THE DAY I WANDERED INTO MOMOCHI HOUSE...
...WAS COINCIDENTALLY THE SAME DAY HAYATO MADE THAT WISH AT A SHRINE.
HE BELIEVES HE'S THE REASON I VANISHED.
HE MAY THINK I'M THE ONE CURSING HIM...
...BUT IF SOMETHING LIKE THAT IS HAPPENING TO HAYATO...
...IT'S PROBABLY THE WORK OF THE HOST OF THAT SHRINE—THE MASKED AYAKASHI.
THE HIDAKA FAMILY ARE AT FAULT FOR NEGLECTING US...
I GET IT...
"THAT WHICH YOU CHERISH MOST"...
MMBL

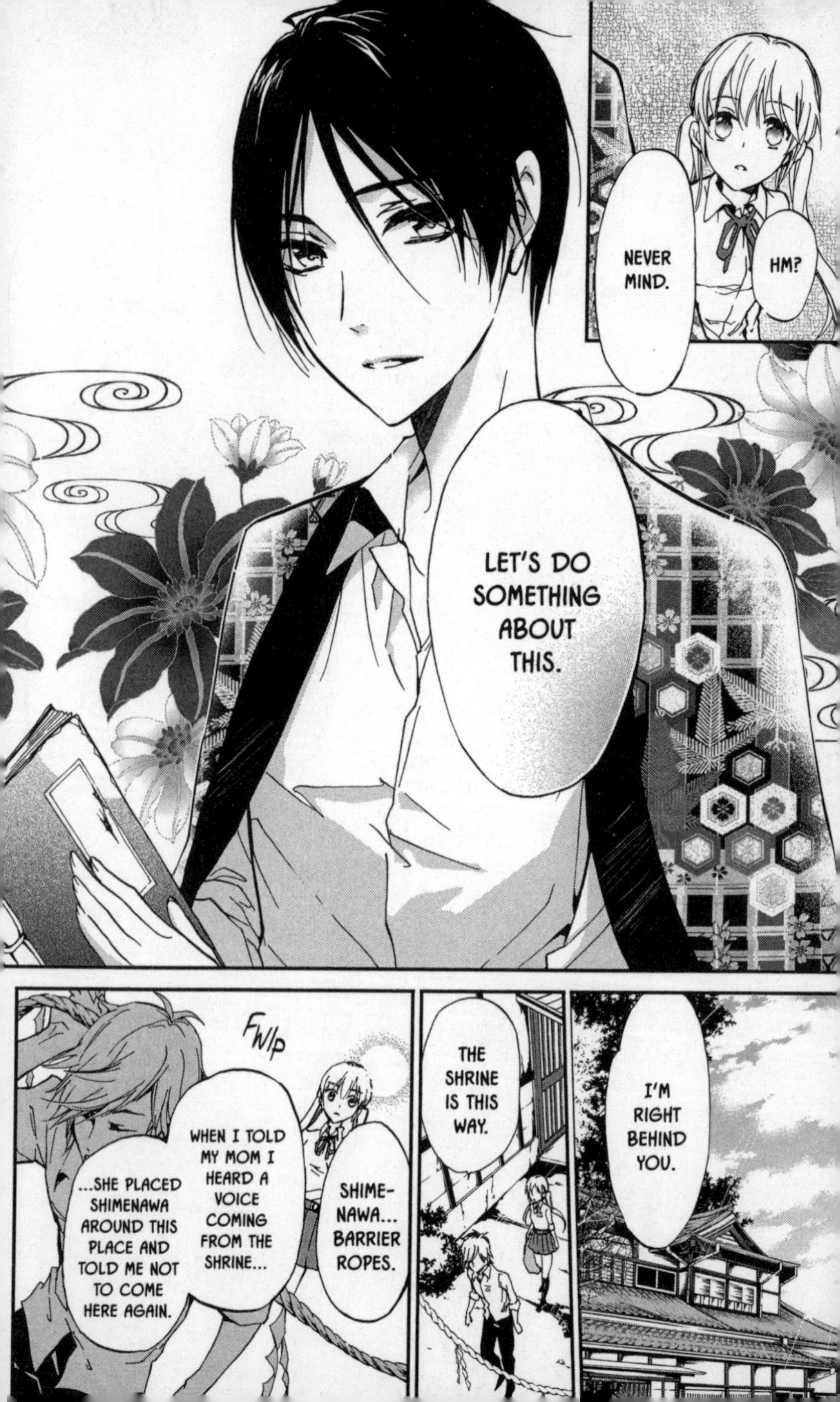
HM?
NEVER MIND.
LET'S DO SOMETHING ABOUT THIS.
I'M RIGHT BEHIND YOU.
THE SHRINE IS THIS WAY.
FWIP
SHIME-NAWA... BARRIER ROPES.
WHEN I TOLD MY MOM I HEARD A VOICE COMING FROM THE SHRINE...
...SHE PLACED SHIMENAWA AROUND THIS PLACE AND TOLD ME NOT TO COME HERE AGAIN.

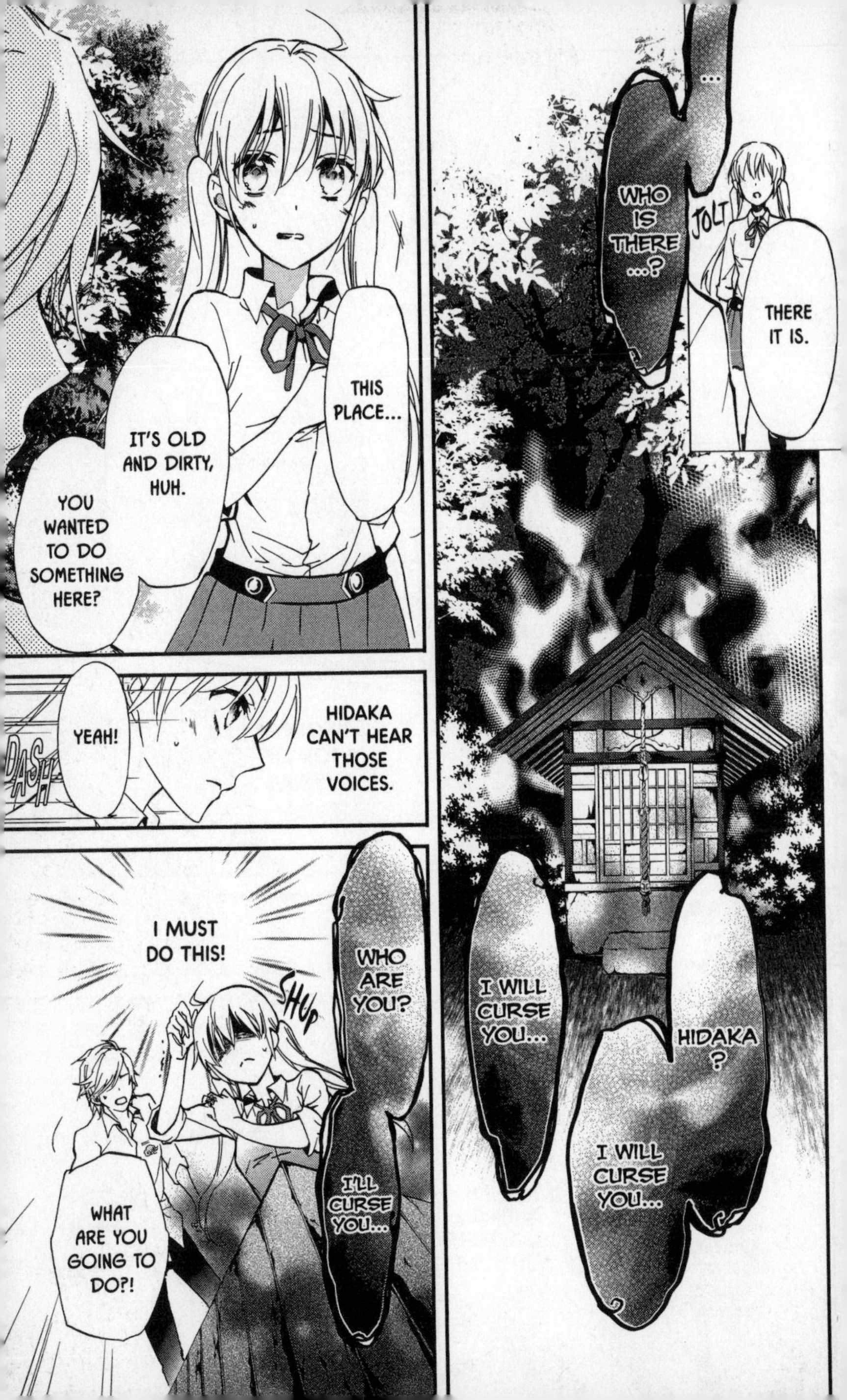
THERE IT IS.
JOLT
...
WHO IS THERE ...?
HIDAKA ?
I WILL CURSE YOU...
I WILL CURSE YOU...
THIS PLACE...
IT'S OLD AND DIRTY, HUH.
YOU WANTED TO DO SOMETHING HERE?
HIDAKA CAN'T HEAR THOSE VOICES.
YEAH!
DASH
WHO ARE YOU?
I'LL CURSE YOU...
I MUST DO THIS!
SHUP
WHAT ARE YOU GOING TO DO?!

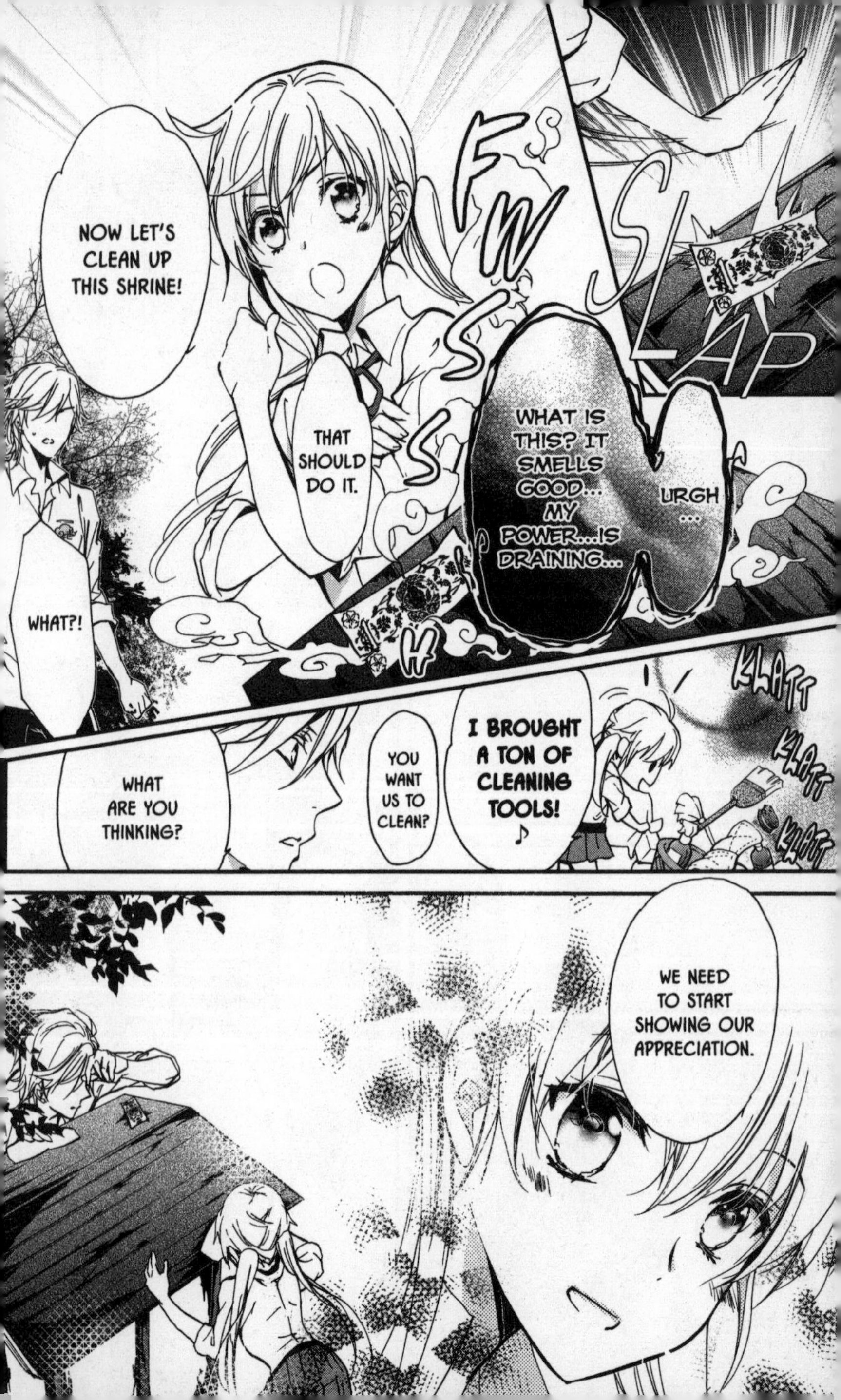
SLAP
URGH...
WHAT IS THIS? IT SMELLS GOOD... MY POWER...IS DRAINING...
FWSSH
THAT SHOULD DO IT.
NOW LET'S CLEAN UP THIS SHRINE!
WHAT?!
KLATT
KLATT
KLATT
I BROUGHT A TON OF CLEANING TOOLS! ♪
YOU WANT US TO CLEAN?
WHAT ARE YOU THINKING?
WE NEED TO START SHOWING OUR APPRECIATION.

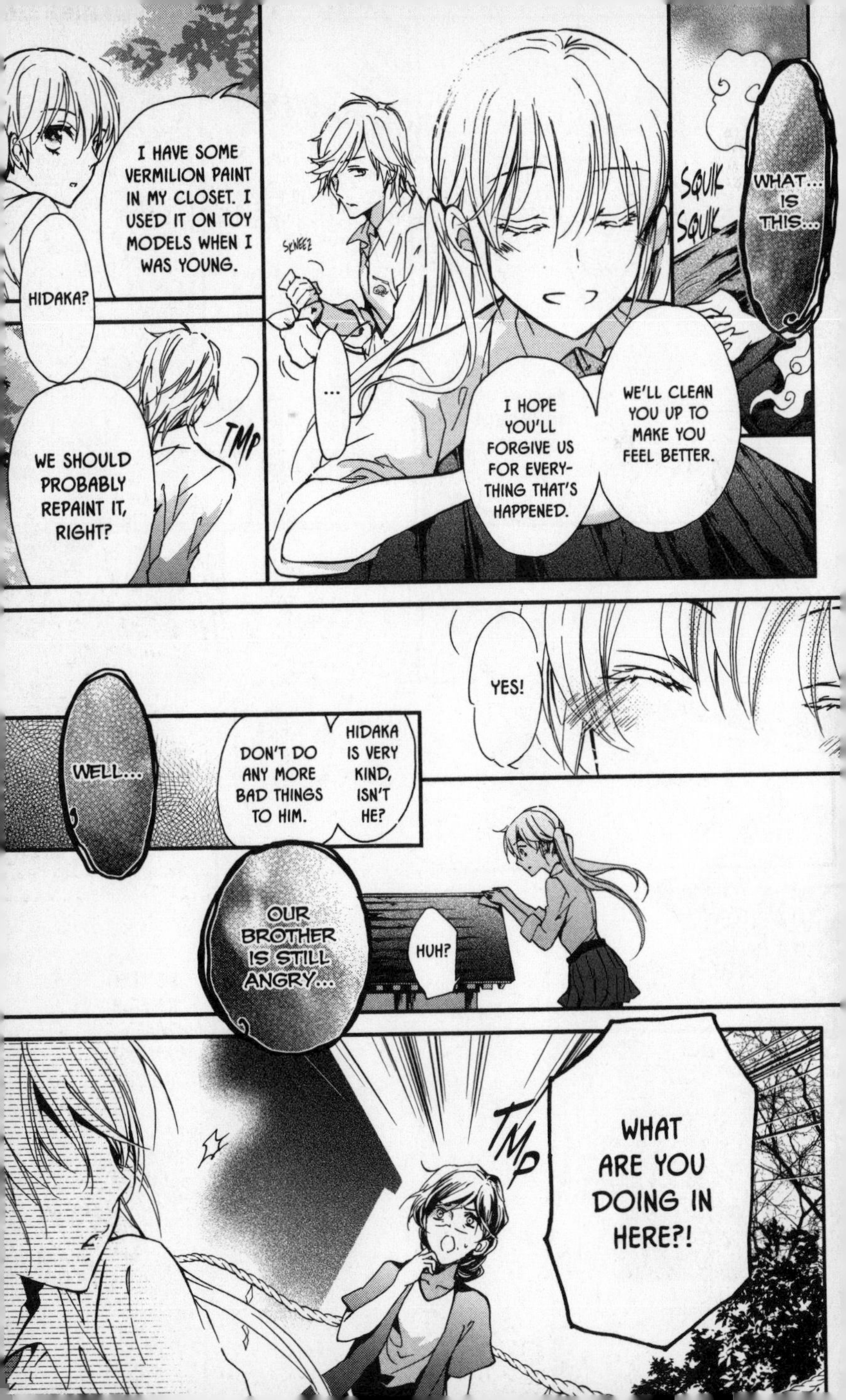
SQUIK SQUIK
WHAT... IS THIS...
WE'LL CLEAN YOU UP TO MAKE YOU FEEL BETTER.
I HOPE YOU'LL FORGIVE US FOR EVERY-THING THAT'S HAPPENED.
SKWEEZ
...
I HAVE SOME VERMILION PAINT IN MY CLOSET. I USED IT ON TOY MODELS WHEN I WAS YOUNG.
HIDAKA?
TMP
WE SHOULD PROBABLY REPAINT IT, RIGHT?
YES!
HIDAKA IS VERY KIND, ISN'T HE?
DON'T DO ANY MORE BAD THINGS TO HIM.
WELL...
OUR BROTHER IS STILL ANGRY...
HUH?
TMP
WHAT ARE YOU DOING IN HERE?!

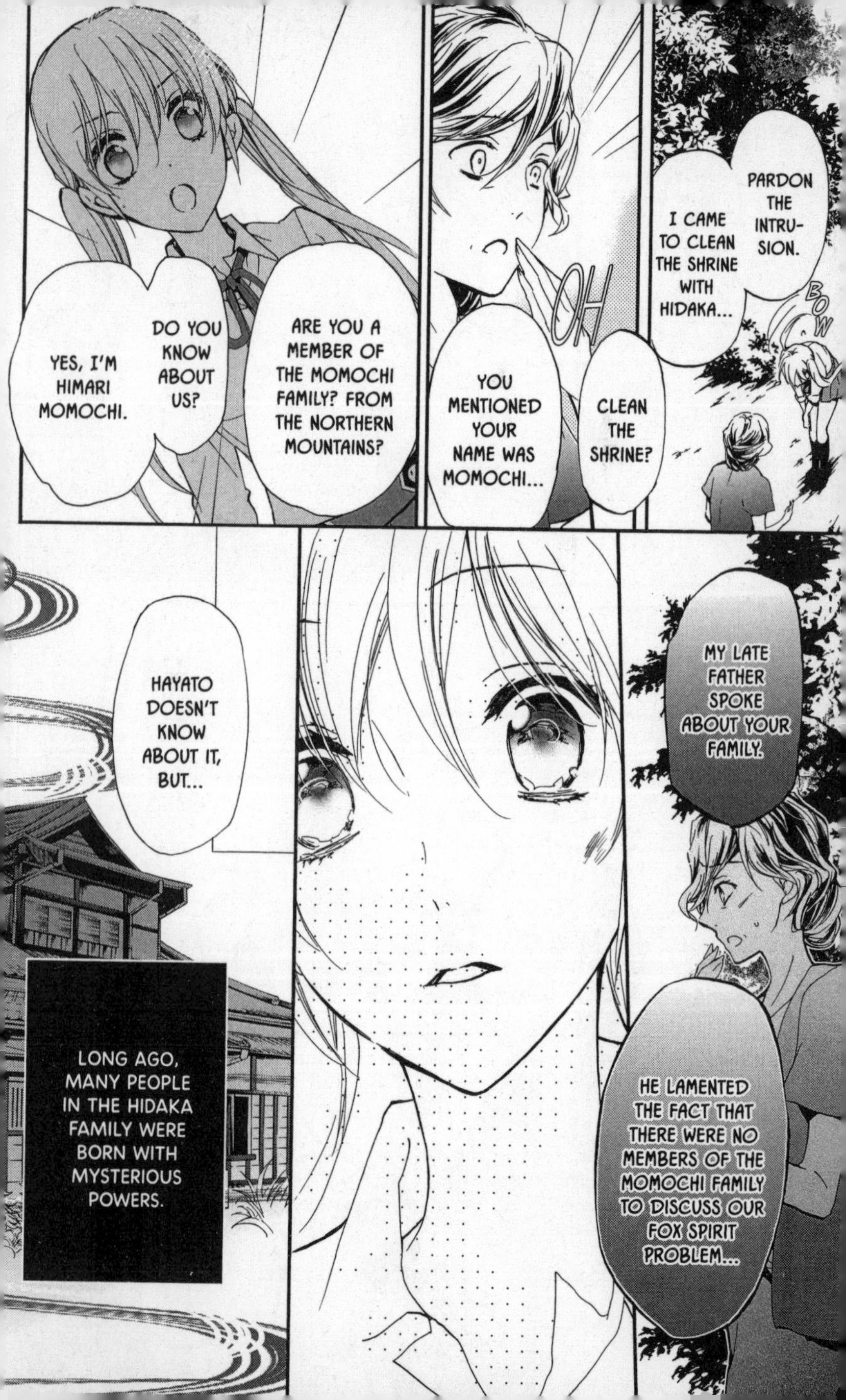
PARDON THE INTRUSION.
I CAME TO CLEAN THE SHRINE WITH HIDAKA...
BOW
OH
CLEAN THE SHRINE?
YOU MENTIONED YOUR NAME WAS MOMOCHI...
ARE YOU A MEMBER OF THE MOMOCHI FAMILY? FROM THE NORTHERN MOUNTAINS?
DO YOU KNOW ABOUT US?
YES, I'M HIMARI MOMOCHI.
MY LATE FATHER SPOKE ABOUT YOUR FAMILY.
HE LAMENTED THE FACT THAT THERE WERE NO MEMBERS OF THE MOMOCHI FAMILY TO DISCUSS OUR FOX SPIRIT PROBLEM...
HAYATO DOESN'T KNOW ABOUT IT, BUT...
LONG AGO, MANY PEOPLE IN THE HIDAKA FAMILY WERE BORN WITH MYSTERIOUS POWERS.

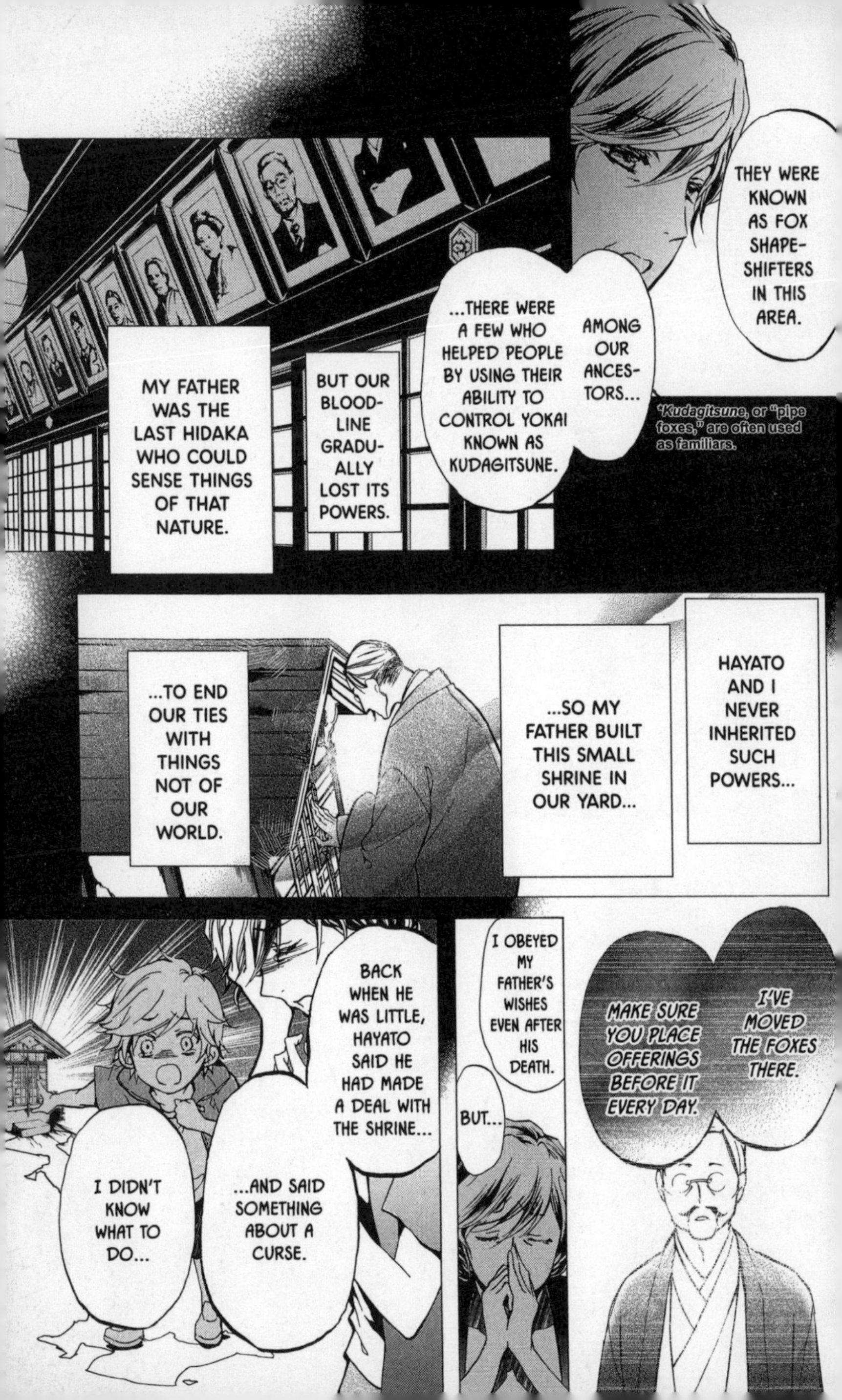
THEY WERE KNOWN AS FOX SHAPE-SHIFTERS IN THIS AREA.
AMONG OUR ANCESTORS...
...THERE WERE A FEW WHO HELPED PEOPLE BY USING THEIR ABILITY TO CONTROL YOKAI KNOWN AS KUDAGITSUNE.
*Kudagitsune, or "pipe foxes," are often used as familiars.
BUT OUR BLOODLINE GRADUALLY LOST ITS POWERS.
MY FATHER WAS THE LAST HIDAKA WHO COULD SENSE THINGS OF THAT NATURE.
HAYATO AND I NEVER INHERITED SUCH POWERS...
...SO MY FATHER BUILT THIS SMALL SHRINE IN OUR YARD...
...TO END OUR TIES WITH THINGS NOT OF OUR WORLD.
I'VE MOVED THE FOXES THERE.
MAKE SURE YOU PLACE OFFERINGS BEFORE IT EVERY DAY.
I OBEYED MY FATHER'S WISHES EVEN AFTER HIS DEATH.
BUT...
BACK WHEN HE WAS LITTLE, HAYATO SAID HE HAD MADE A DEAL WITH THE SHRINE...
...AND SAID SOMETHING ABOUT A CURSE.
I DIDN'T KNOW WHAT TO DO...

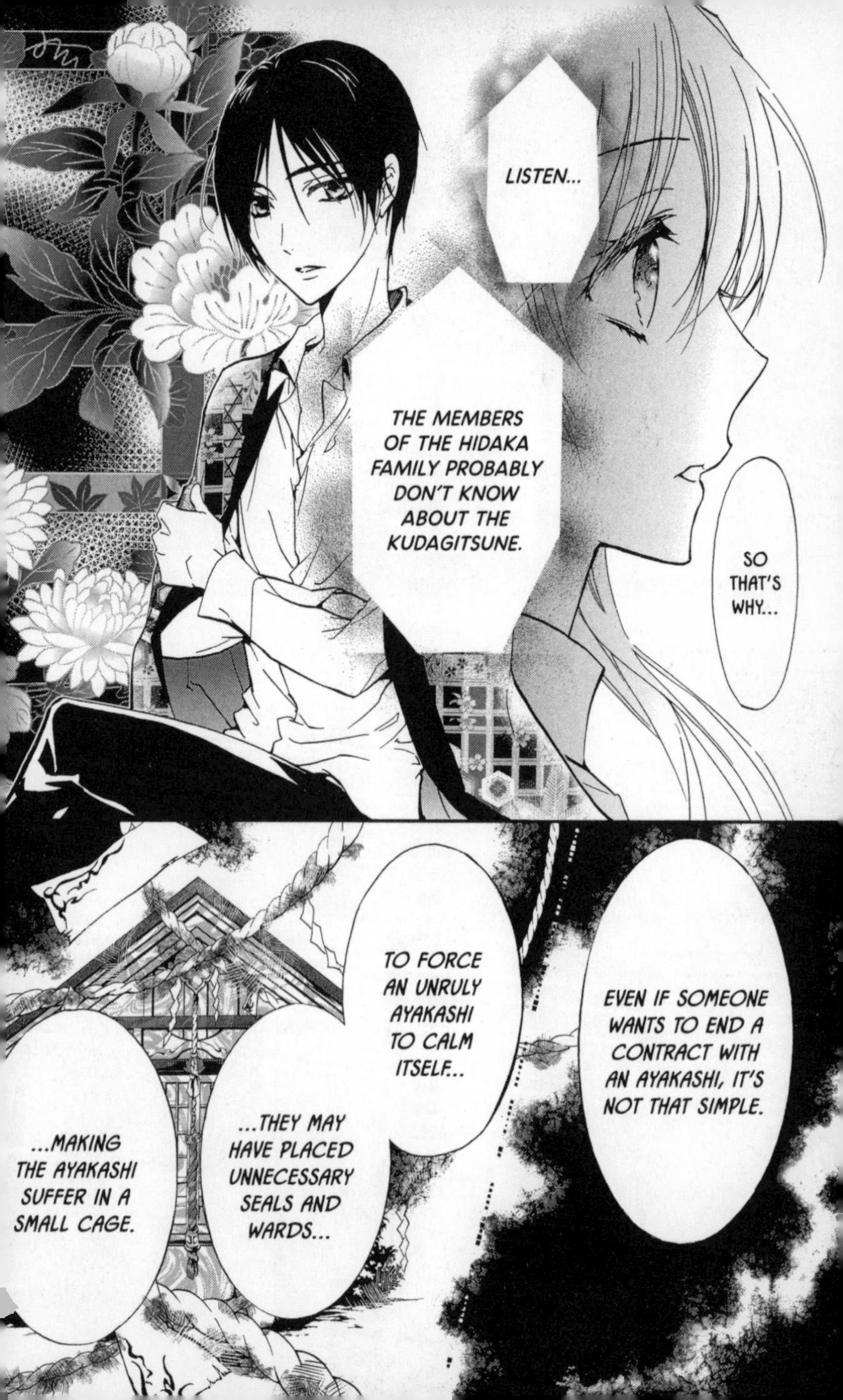
LISTEN...
THE MEMBERS OF THE HIDAKA FAMILY PROBABLY DON'T KNOW ABOUT THE KUDAGITSUNE.
SO THAT'S WHY...
EVEN IF SOMEONE WANTS TO END A CONTRACT WITH AN AYAKASHI, IT'S NOT THAT SIMPLE.
TO FORCE AN UNRULY AYAKASHI TO CALM ITSELF...
...THEY MAY HAVE PLACED UNNECESSARY SEALS AND WARDS...
...MAKING THE AYAKASHI SUFFER IN A SMALL CAGE.

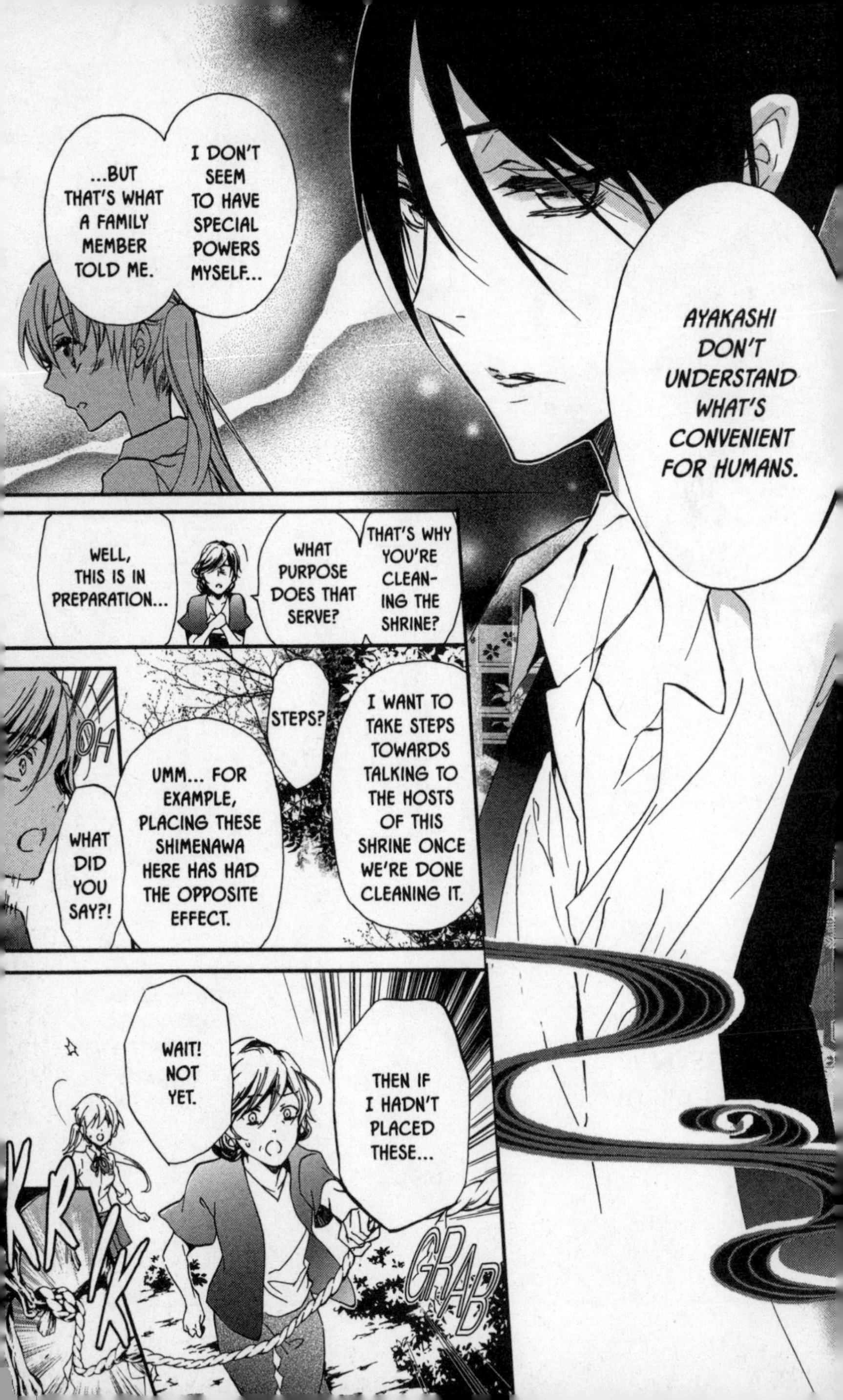
AYAKASHI DON'T UNDERSTAND WHAT'S CONVENIENT FOR HUMANS.
I DON'T SEEM TO HAVE SPECIAL POWERS MYSELF...
...BUT THAT'S WHAT A FAMILY MEMBER TOLD ME.
THAT'S WHY YOU'RE CLEAN-ING THE SHRINE?
WHAT PURPOSE DOES THAT SERVE?
WELL, THIS IS IN PREPARATION...
I WANT TO TAKE STEPS TOWARDS TALKING TO THE HOSTS OF THIS SHRINE ONCE WE'RE DONE CLEANING IT.
STEPS?
UMM... FOR EXAMPLE, PLACING THESE SHIMENAWA HERE HAS HAD THE OPPOSITE EFFECT.
OH
WHAT DID YOU SAY?!
THEN IF I HADN'T PLACED THESE...
GRAB
WAIT! NOT YET.
KRK

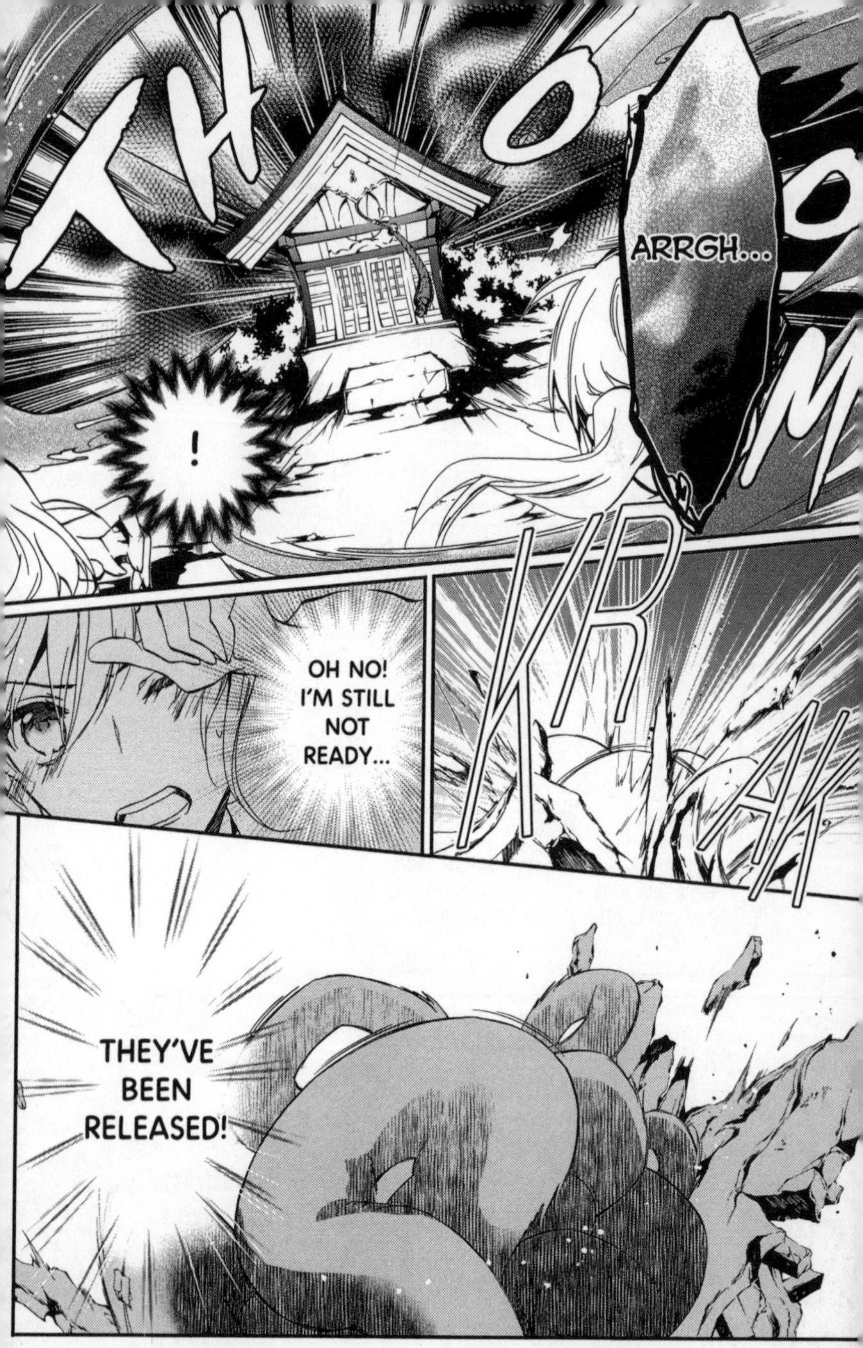
ARRGH...
!
KRAK
OH NO! I'M STILL NOT READY...
THEY'VE BEEN RELEASED!

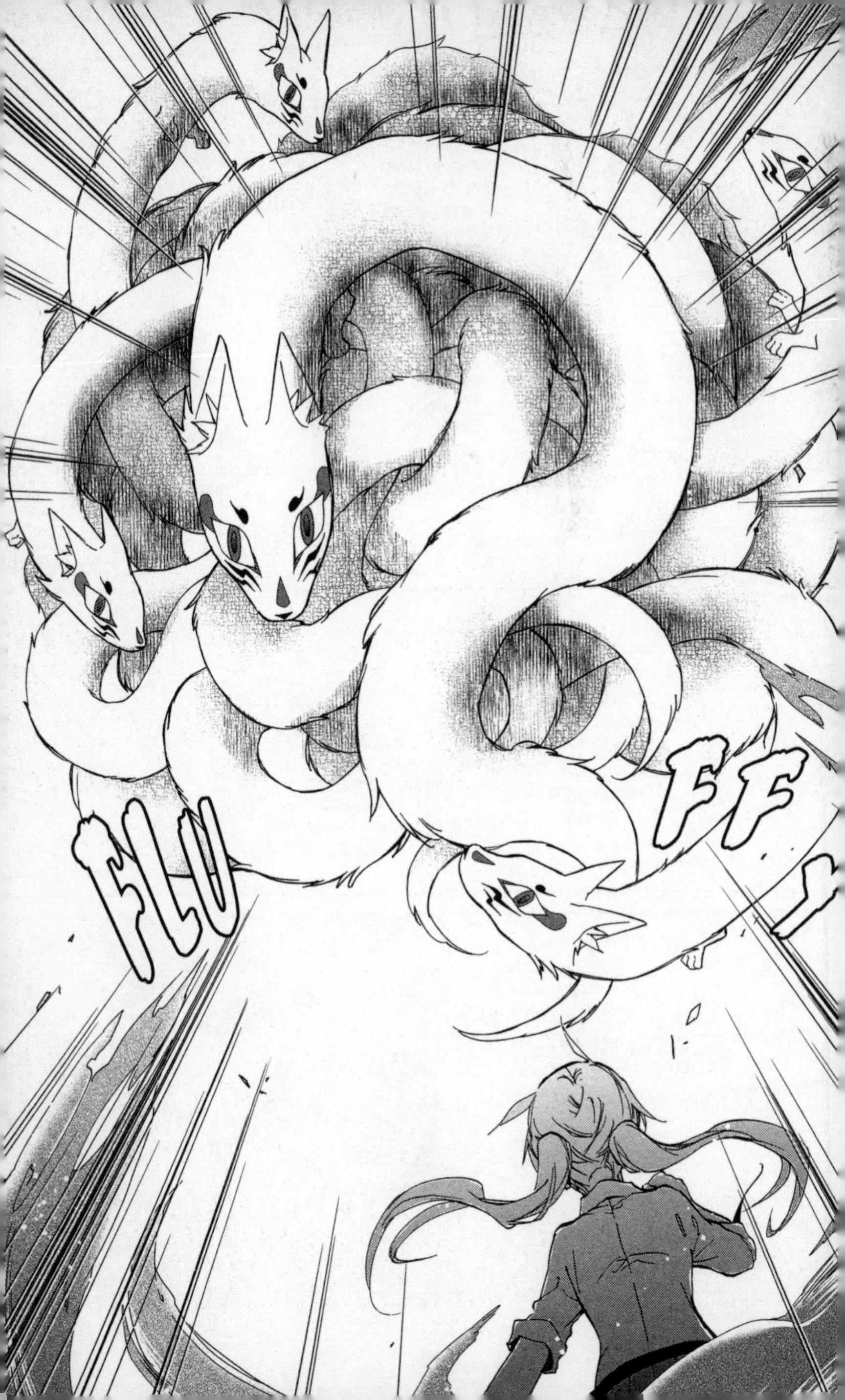
FLUFFY

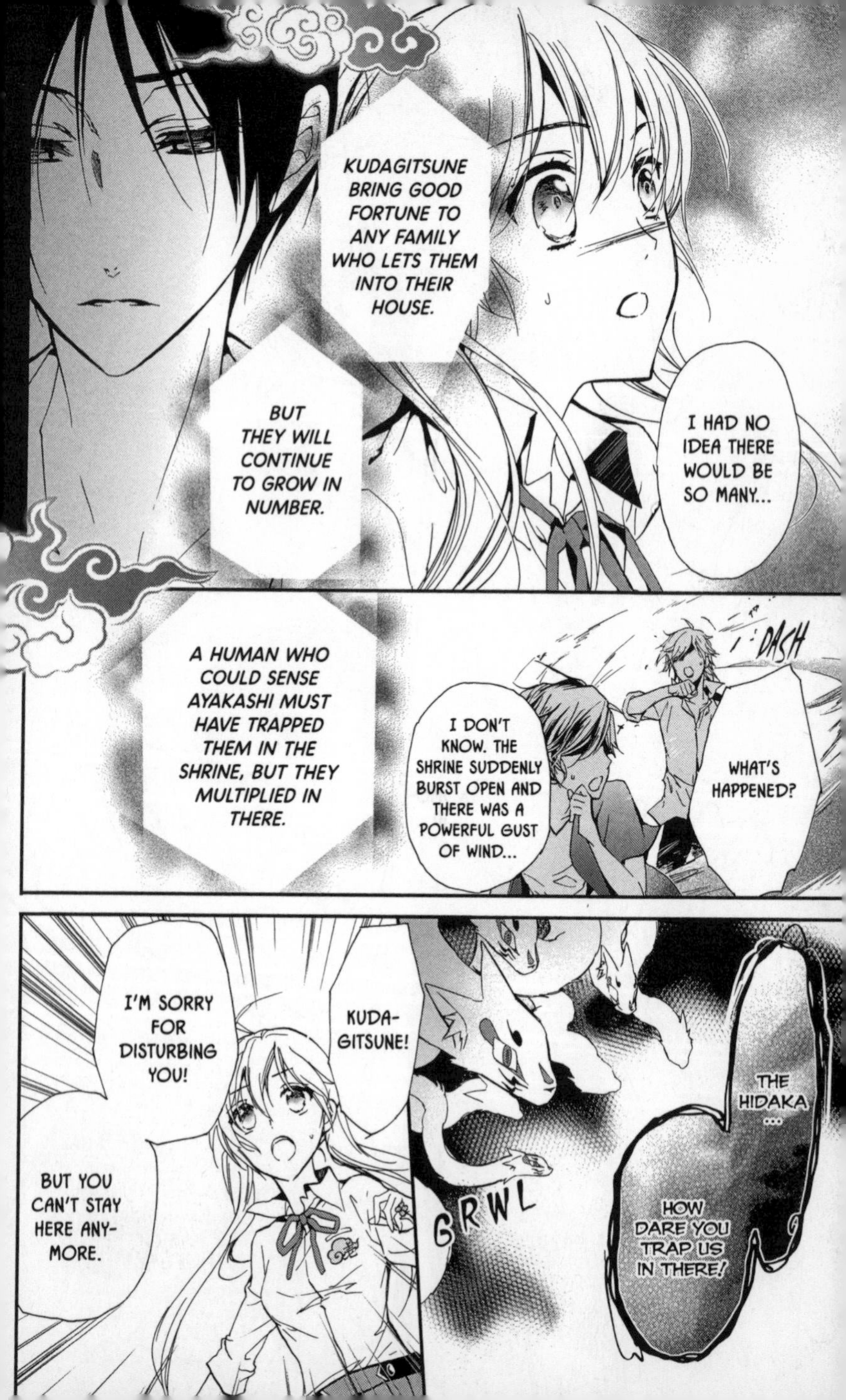
I HAD NO IDEA THERE WOULD BE SO MANY...
KUDAGITSUNE BRING GOOD FORTUNE TO ANY FAMILY WHO LETS THEM INTO THEIR HOUSE.
BUT THEY WILL CONTINUE TO GROW IN NUMBER.
DASH
WHAT'S HAPPENED?
I DON'T KNOW. THE SHRINE SUDDENLY BURST OPEN AND THERE WAS A POWERFUL GUST OF WIND...
A HUMAN WHO COULD SENSE AYAKASHI MUST HAVE TRAPPED THEM IN THE SHRINE, BUT THEY MULTIPLIED IN THERE.
THE HIDAKA...
HOW DARE YOU TRAP US IN THERE!
GRWL
KUDA-GITSUNE!
I'M SORRY FOR DISTURBING YOU!
BUT YOU CAN'T STAY HERE ANY-MORE.

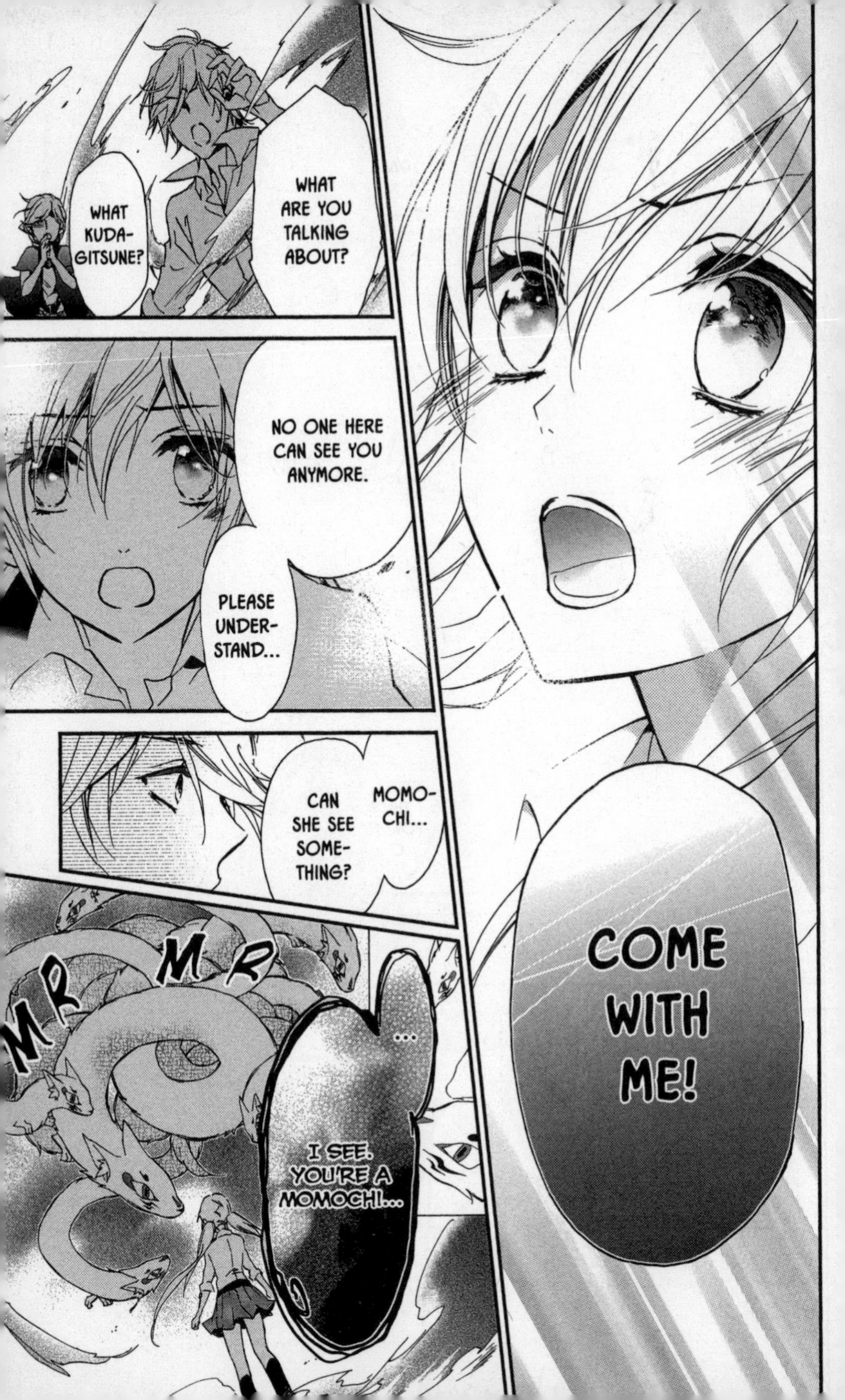
COME WITH ME!
WHAT ARE YOU TALKING ABOUT?
WHAT KUDA-GITSUNE?
NO ONE HERE CAN SEE YOU ANYMORE.
PLEASE UNDER-STAND...
MOMO-CHI...
CAN SHE SEE SOME-THING?
...
M R
M R
I SEE. YOU'RE A MOMOCHI...

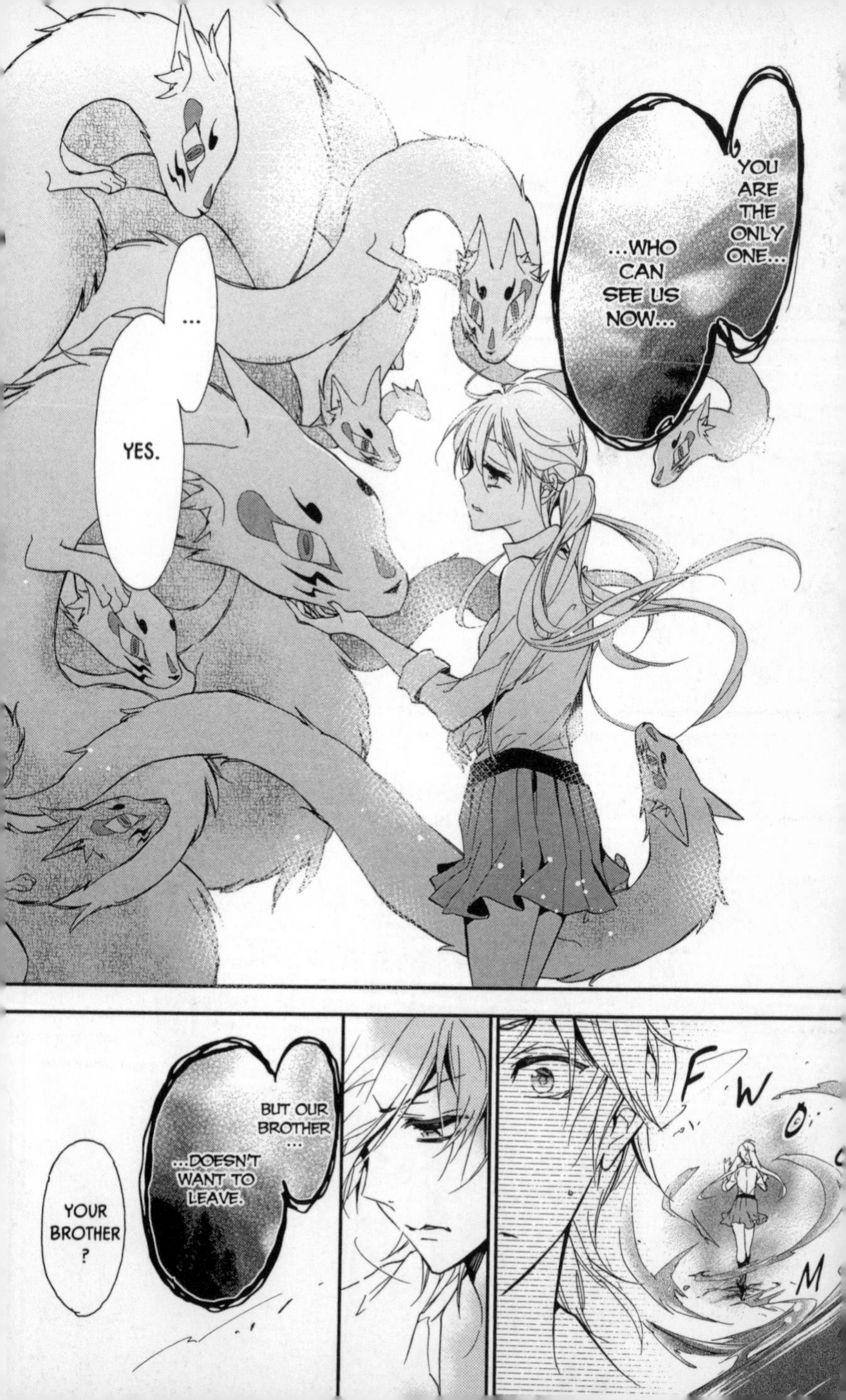
YOU ARE THE ONLY ONE...
...WHO CAN SEE US NOW...
...
YES.
FWOOM
BUT OUR BROTHER ...
...DOESN'T WANT TO LEAVE.
YOUR BROTHER ?

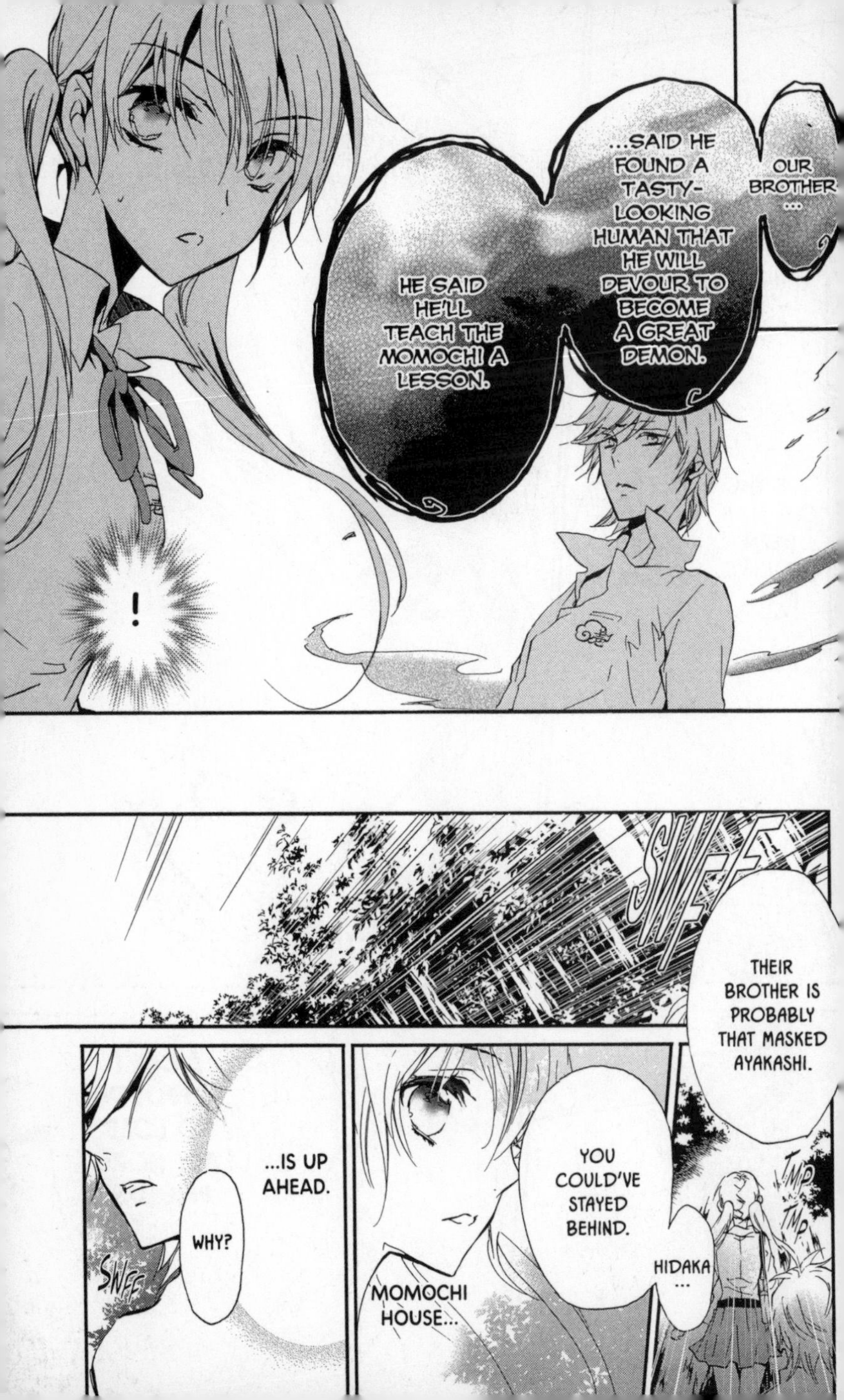
OUR BROTHER...
...SAID HE FOUND A TASTY-LOOKING HUMAN THAT HE WILL DEVOUR TO BECOME A GREAT DEMON.
HE SAID HE'LL TEACH THE MOMOCHI A LESSON.
!
SWFF
THEIR BROTHER IS PROBABLY THAT MASKED AYAKASHI.
TMP TMP
HIDAKA...
YOU COULD'VE STAYED BEHIND.
MOMOCHI HOUSE...
...IS UP AHEAD.
WHY?
SWFF

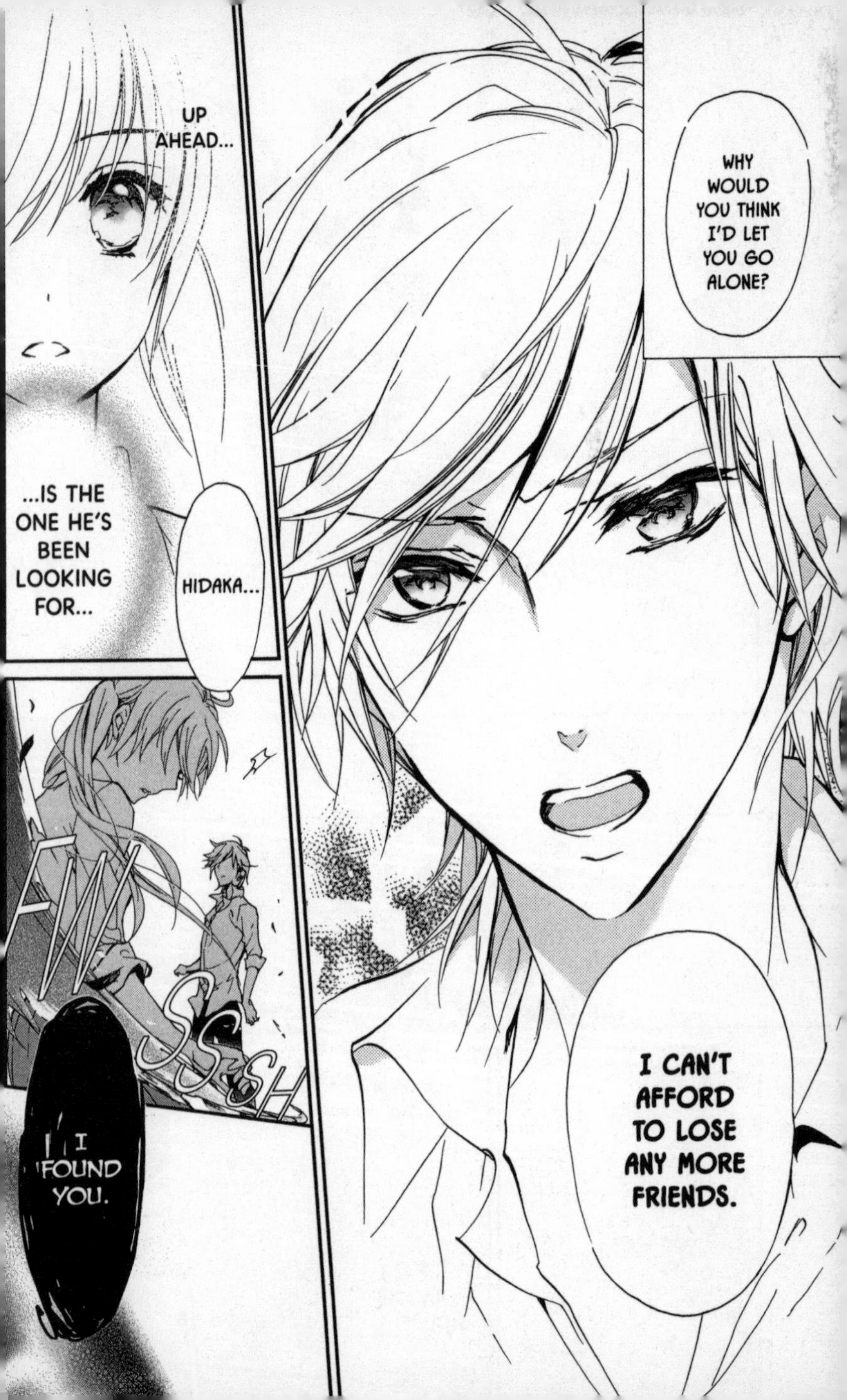
WHY WOULD YOU THINK I'D LET YOU GO ALONE?
I CAN'T AFFORD TO LOSE ANY MORE FRIENDS.
UP AHEAD...
...IS THE ONE HE'S BEEN LOOKING FOR...
HIDAKA...
FWSSSH
I FOUND YOU.

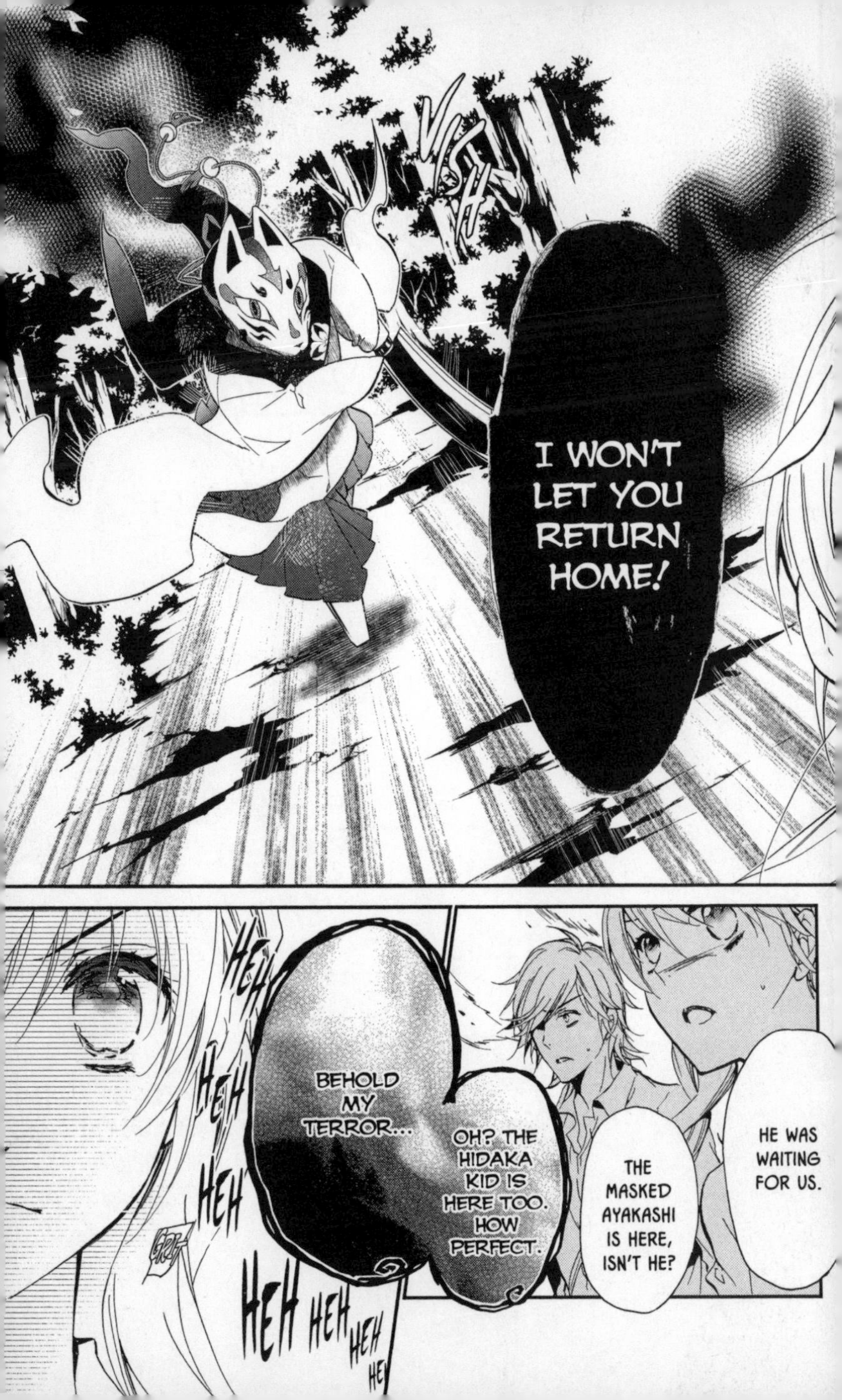
VSSH
I WON'T LET YOU RETURN HOME!
HE WAS WAITING FOR US.
THE MASKED AYAKASHI IS HERE, ISN'T HE?
OH? THE HIDAKA KID IS HERE TOO. HOW PERFECT.
BEHOLD MY TERROR...
HEH HEH HEH HEH
HEH HEH HEH HE

THIS WAY, HIDAKA!
BUT YOUR HOUSE IS IN THE OPPOSITE DIREC-TION...
IT'S OKAY.
I WON'T LET YOU ESCAPE!

I WANT TO GO HOME, BUT I CAN'T.

Chapter 13/End

The
DEMON
PRINCE
of MOMOCHI
HOUSE

The
DEMON
PRINCE
of MOMOCHI
HOUSE

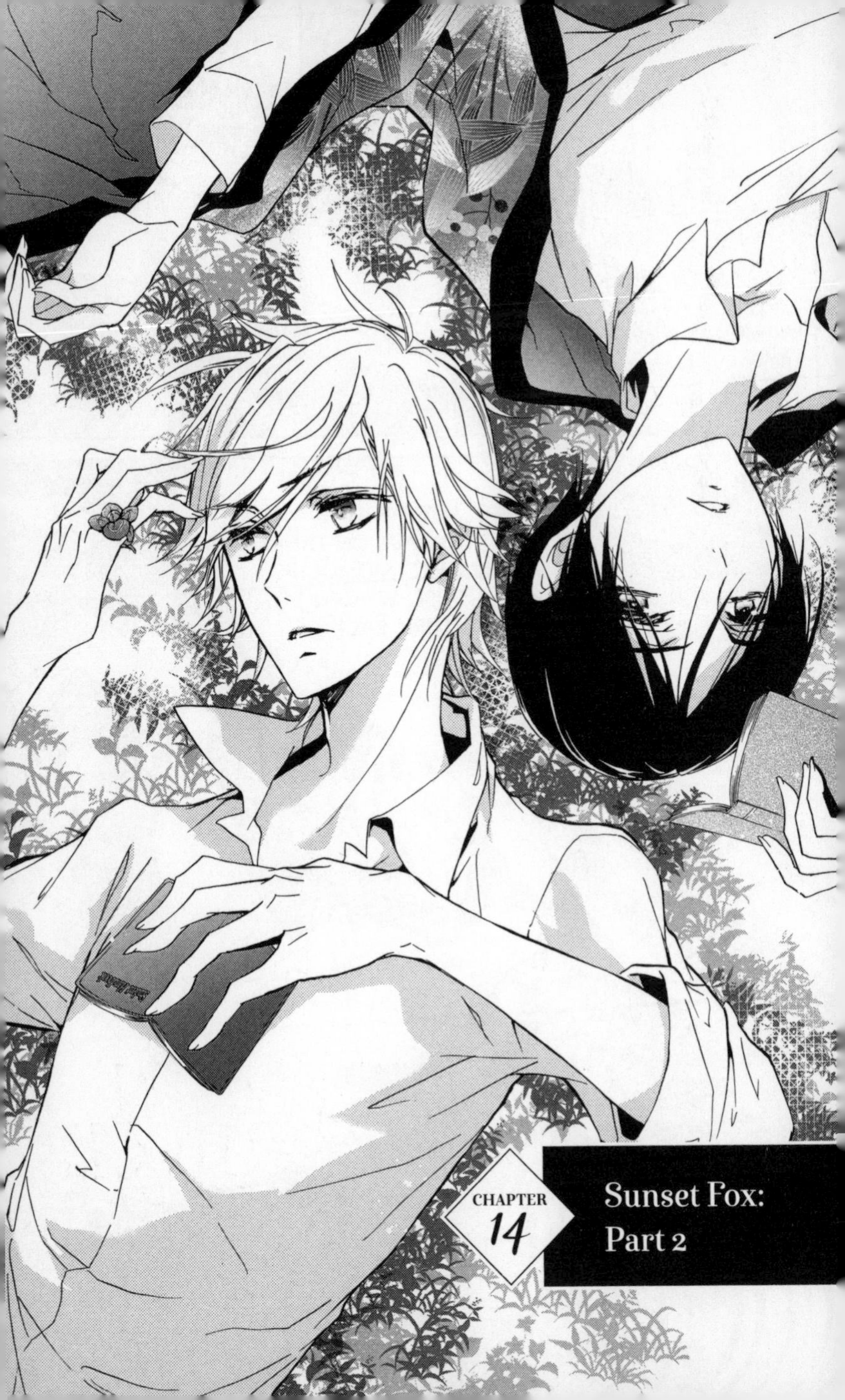
CHAPTER
14
Sunset Fox:
Part 2

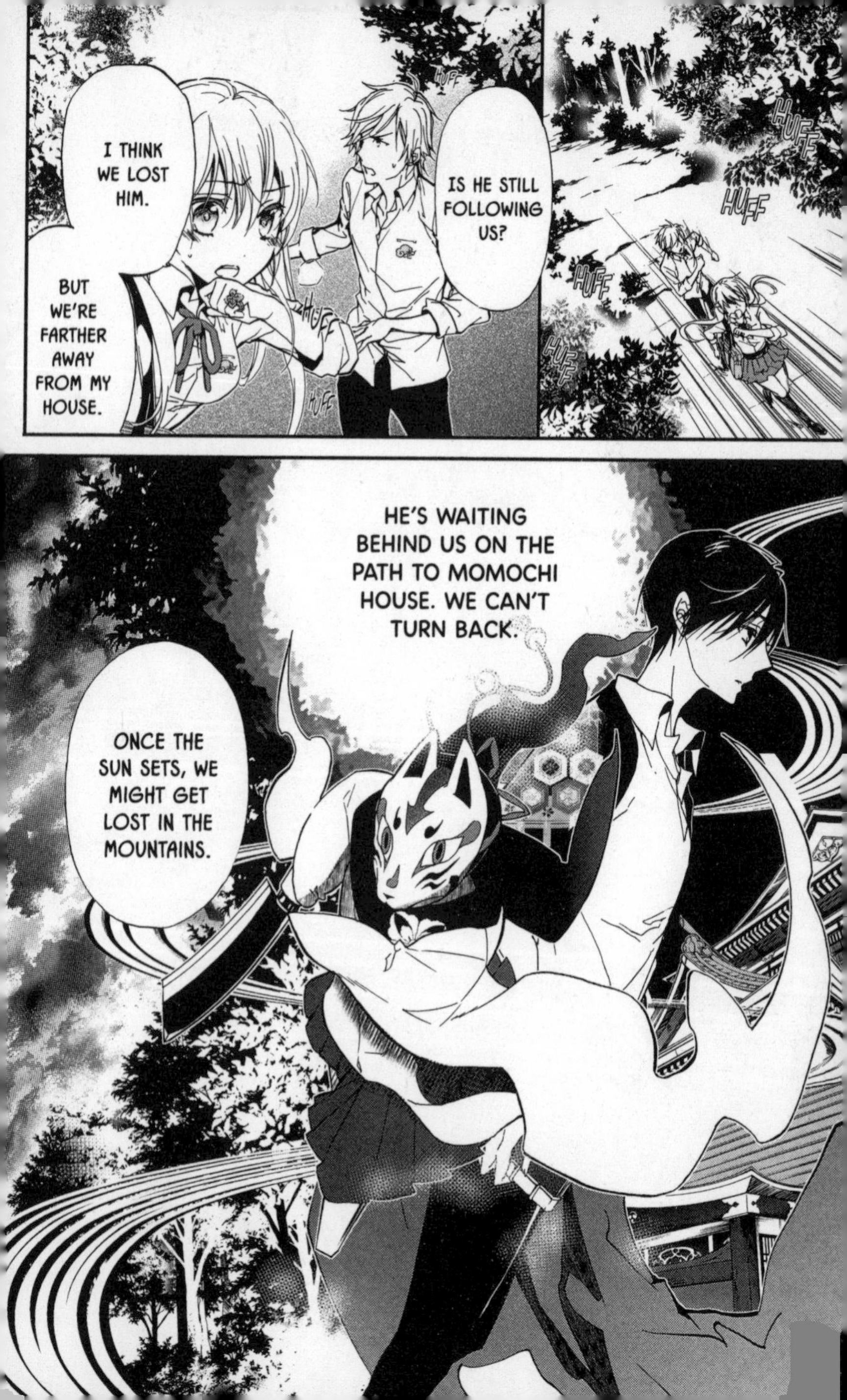
HUFF
HUFF
HUFF
HUFF
HUFF
IS HE STILL FOLLOWING US?
I THINK WE LOST HIM.
BUT WE'RE FARTHER AWAY FROM MY HOUSE.
HUFF
HUFF
HE'S WAITING BEHIND US ON THE PATH TO MOMOCHI HOUSE. WE CAN'T TURN BACK.
ONCE THE SUN SETS, WE MIGHT GET LOST IN THE MOUNTAINS.

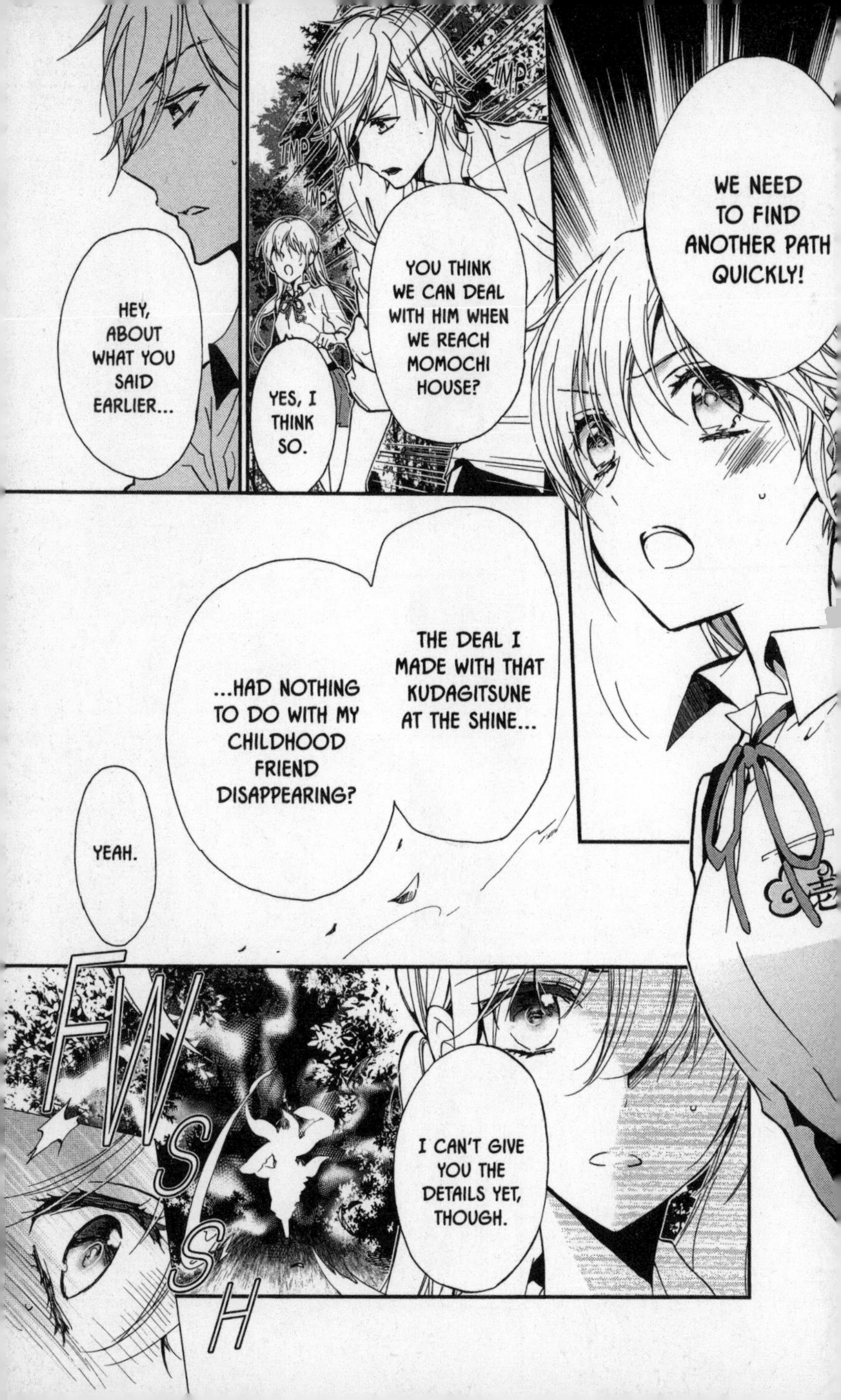
WE NEED TO FIND ANOTHER PATH QUICKLY!
TMP
TMP
TMP
YOU THINK WE CAN DEAL WITH HIM WHEN WE REACH MOMOCHI HOUSE?
YES, I THINK SO.
HEY, ABOUT WHAT YOU SAID EARLIER...
THE DEAL I MADE WITH THAT KUDAGITSUNE AT THE SHINE...
...HAD NOTHING TO DO WITH MY CHILDHOOD FRIEND DISAPPEARING?
YEAH.
I CAN'T GIVE YOU THE DETAILS YET, THOUGH.
FWSSH

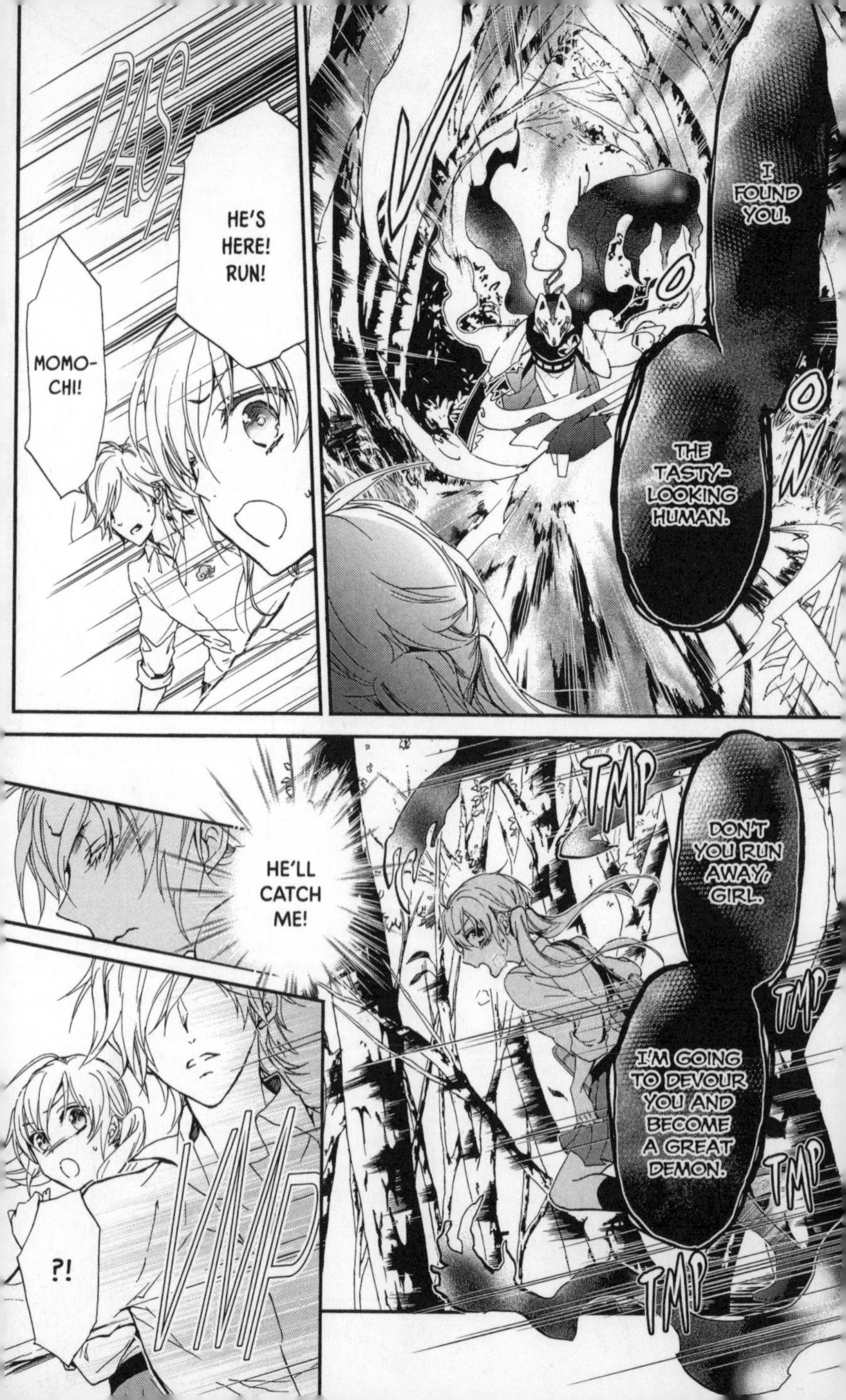
I FOUND YOU.
THE TASTY-LOOKING HUMAN.
DASH
HE'S HERE! RUN!
MOMO-CHI!
TMP
DON'T YOU RUN AWAY, GIRL.
TMP
I'M GOING TO DEVOUR YOU AND BECOME A GREAT DEMON.
TMP
TMP
HE'LL CATCH ME!
?!

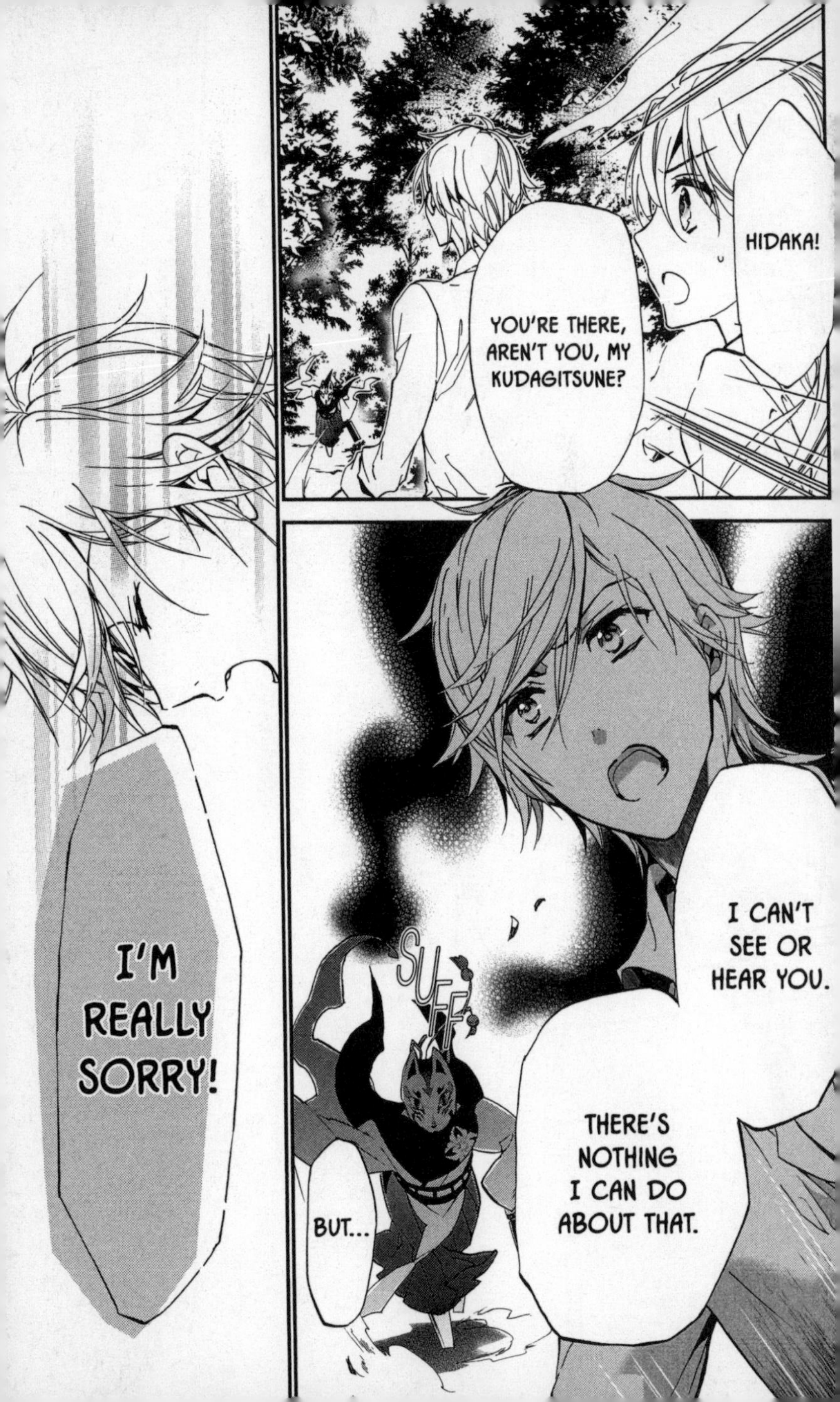
HIDAKA!
YOU'RE THERE, AREN'T YOU, MY KUDAGITSUNE?
I CAN'T SEE OR HEAR YOU.
THERE'S NOTHING I CAN DO ABOUT THAT.
SUFF
BUT...
I'M REALLY SORRY!

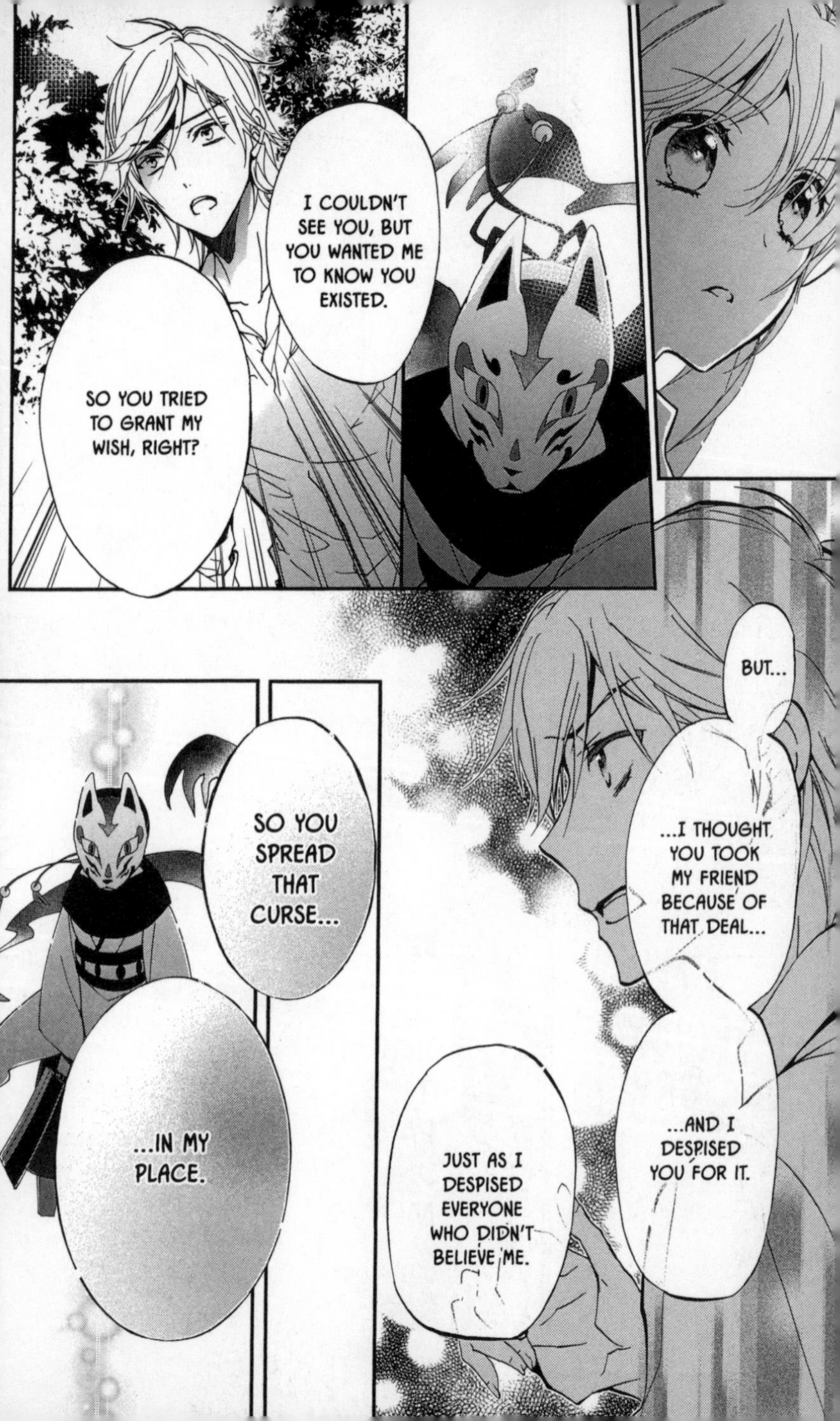
I COULDN'T SEE YOU, BUT YOU WANTED ME TO KNOW YOU EXISTED.
SO YOU TRIED TO GRANT MY WISH, RIGHT?
BUT...
...I THOUGHT YOU TOOK MY FRIEND BECAUSE OF THAT DEAL...
...AND I DESPISED YOU FOR IT.
JUST AS I DESPISED EVERYONE WHO DIDN'T BELIEVE ME.
SO YOU SPREAD THAT CURSE...
...IN MY PLACE.

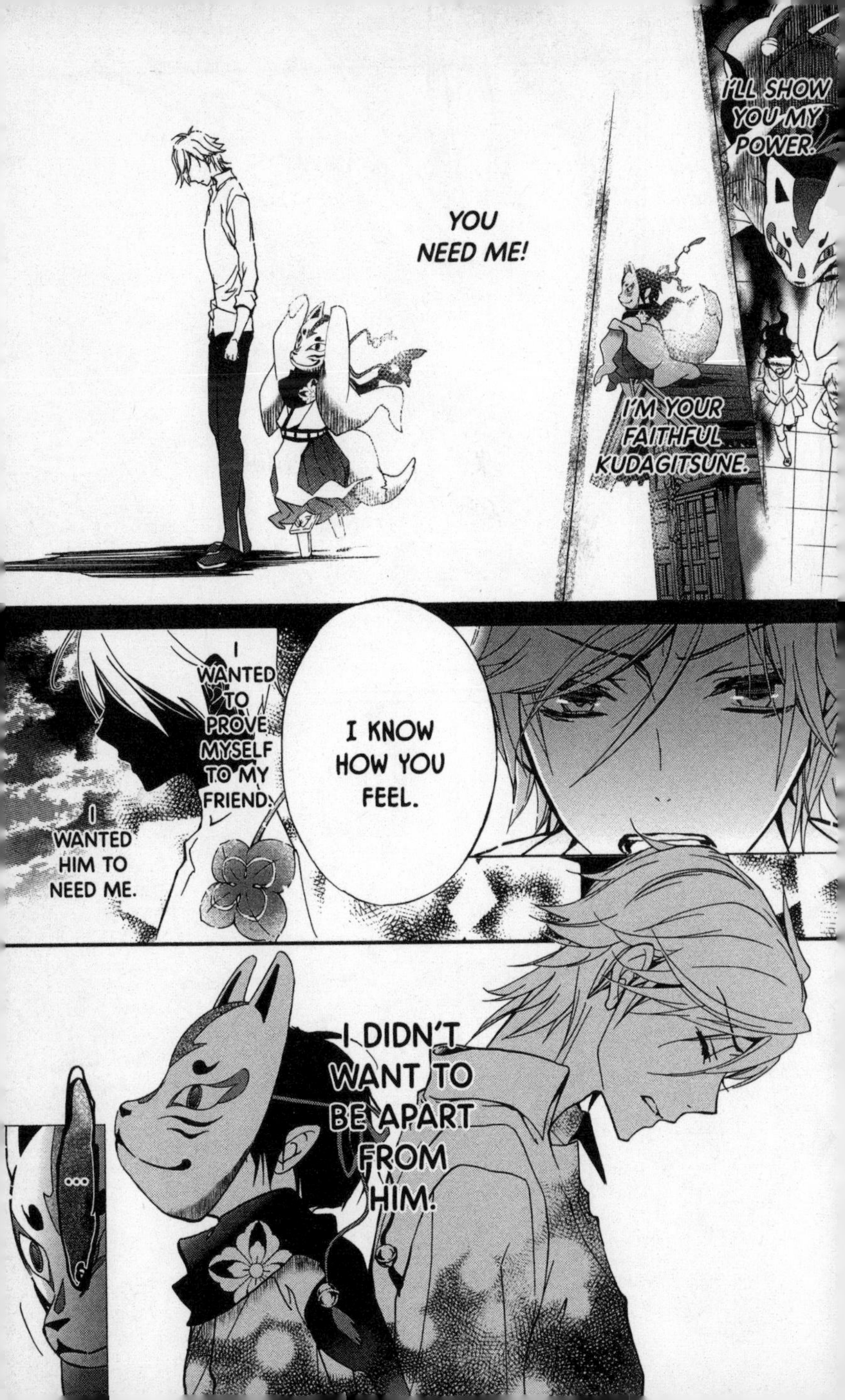
I'LL SHOW YOU MY POWER.
I'M YOUR FAITHFUL KUDAGITSUNE.
YOU NEED ME!
I KNOW HOW YOU FEEL.
I WANTED TO PROVE MYSELF TO MY FRIEND.
I WANTED HIM TO NEED ME.
I DIDN'T WANT TO BE APART FROM HIM.
...

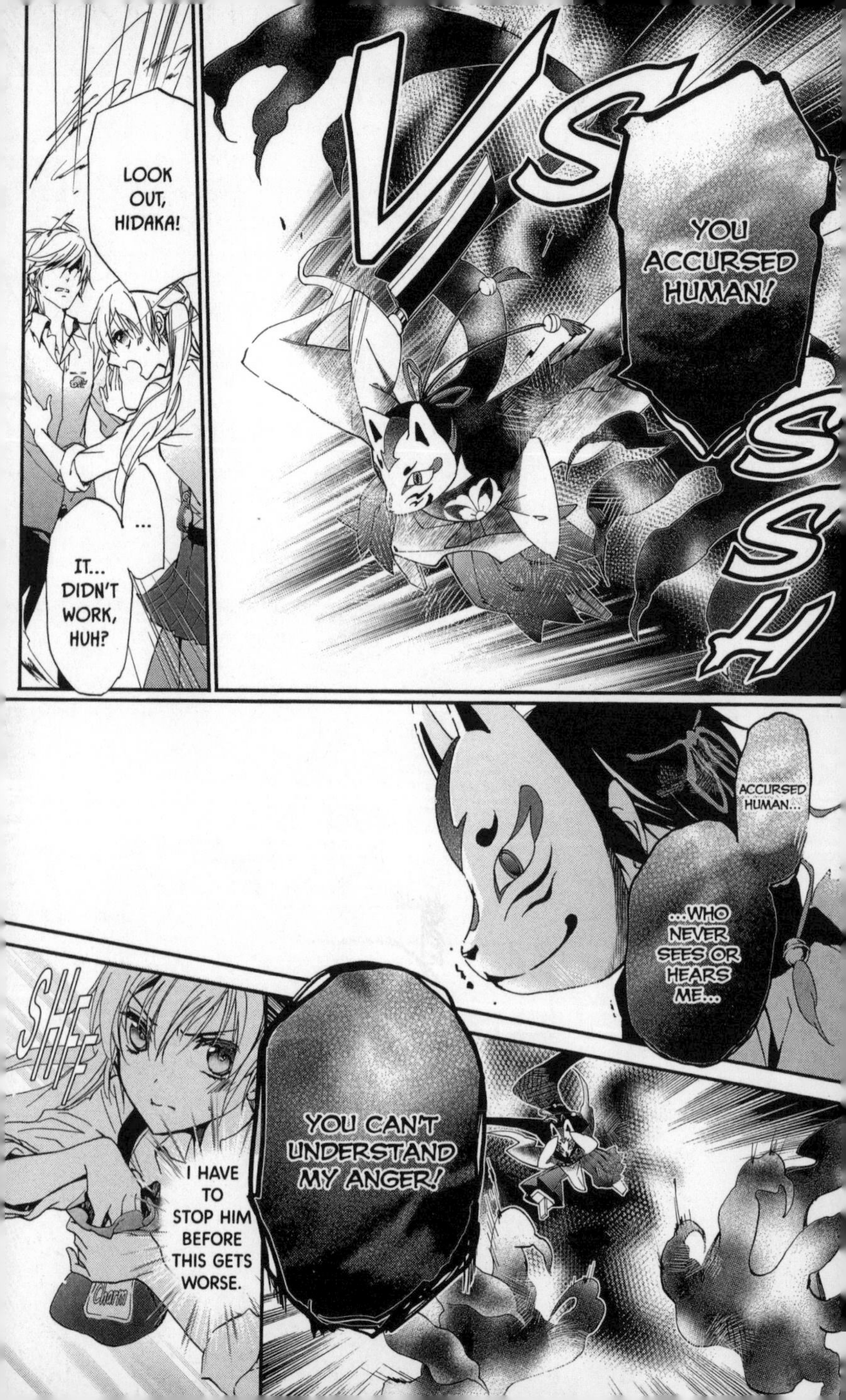
VS
YOU ACCURSED HUMAN!
SSSH
LOOK OUT, HIDAKA!
...
IT... DIDN'T WORK, HUH?
ACCURSED HUMAN...
...WHO NEVER SEES OR HEARS ME...
YOU CAN'T UNDERSTAND MY ANGER!
SHFF
I HAVE TO STOP HIM BEFORE THIS GETS WORSE.
Charm

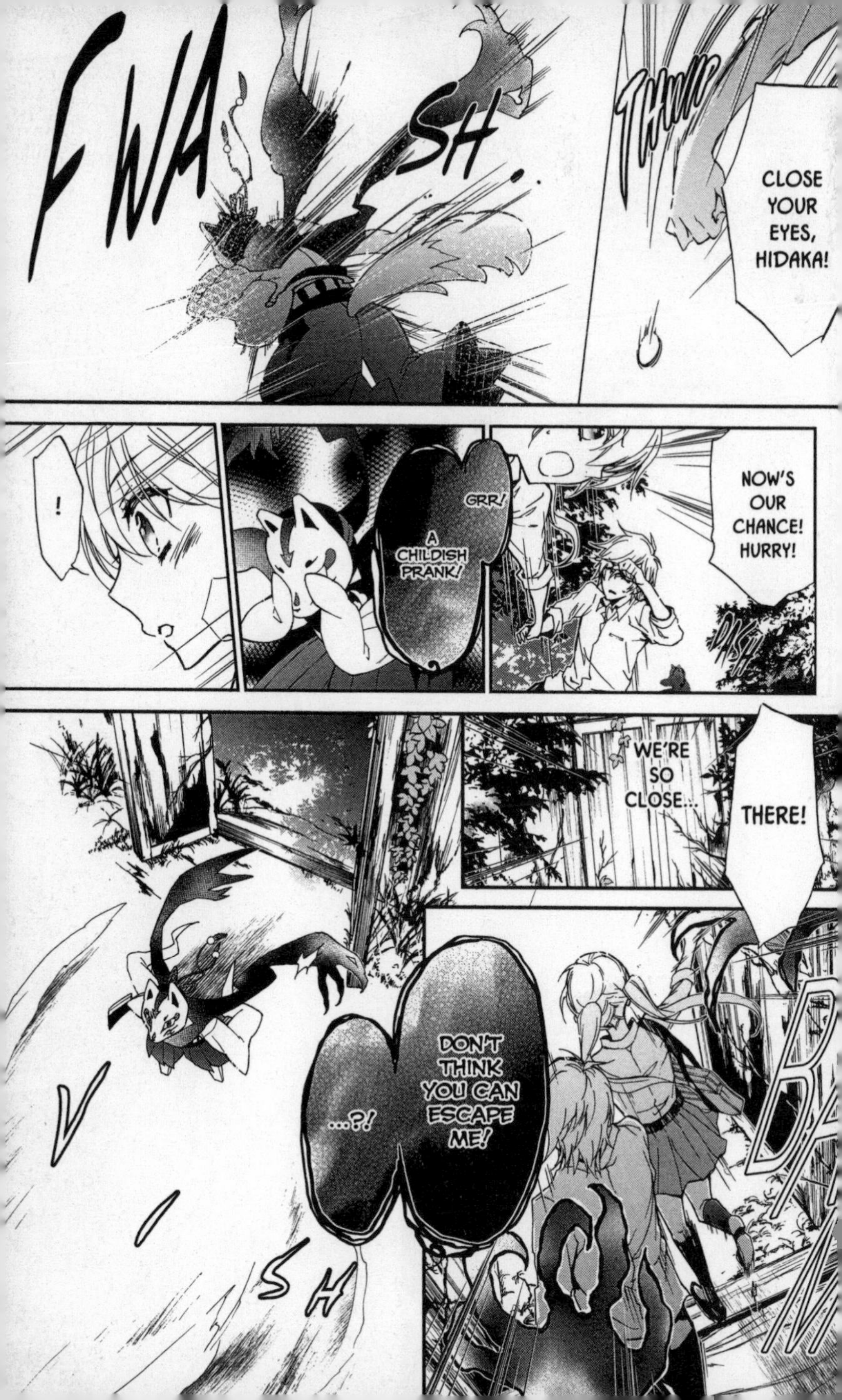
CLOSE YOUR EYES, HIDAKA!
FWASH
NOW'S OUR CHANCE! HURRY!
DASH
GRR!
A CHILDISH PRANK!
!
THERE!
WE'RE SO CLOSE...
DON'T THINK YOU CAN ESCAPE ME!
...?!
VISH

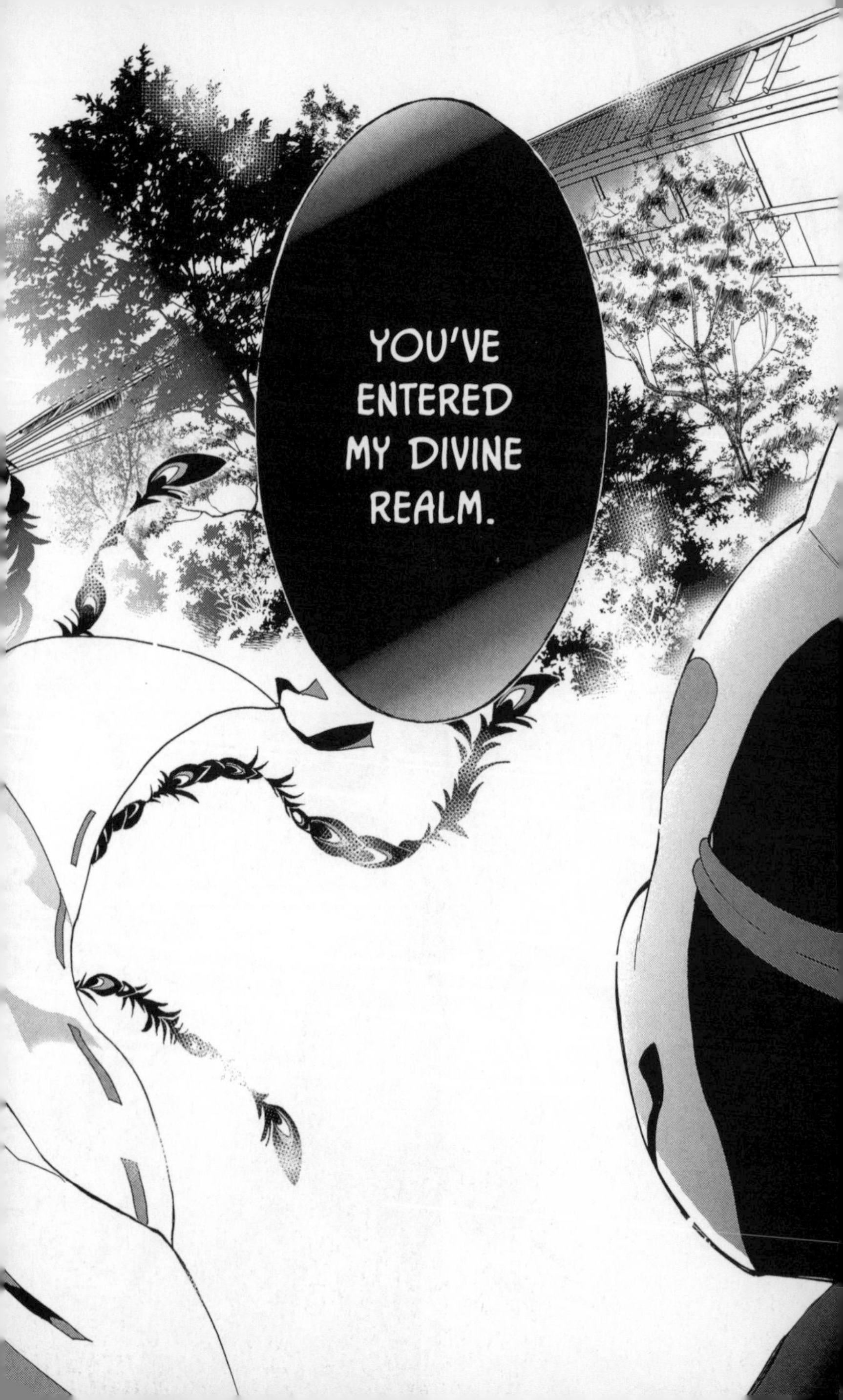
YOU'VE ENTERED MY DIVINE REALM.

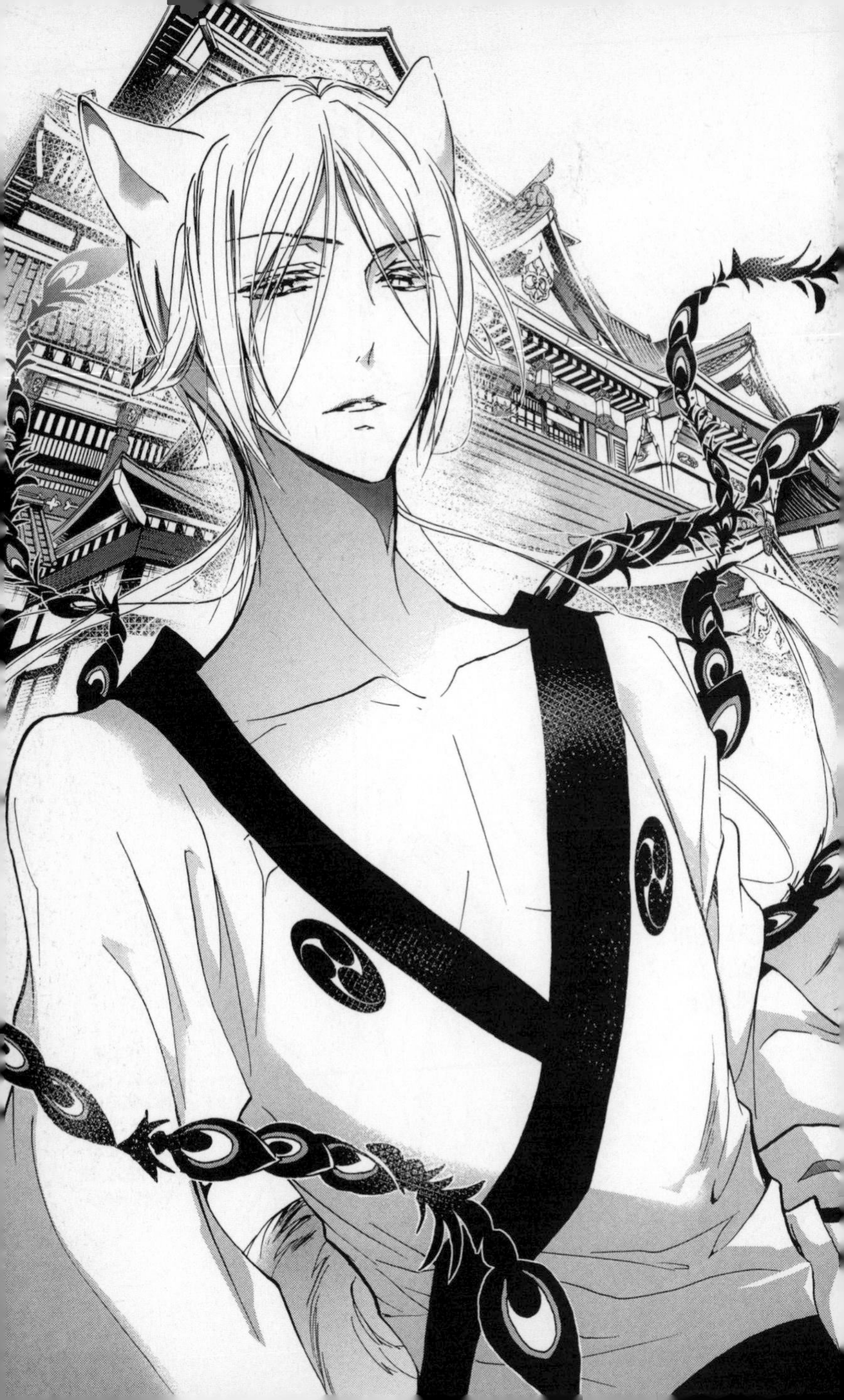

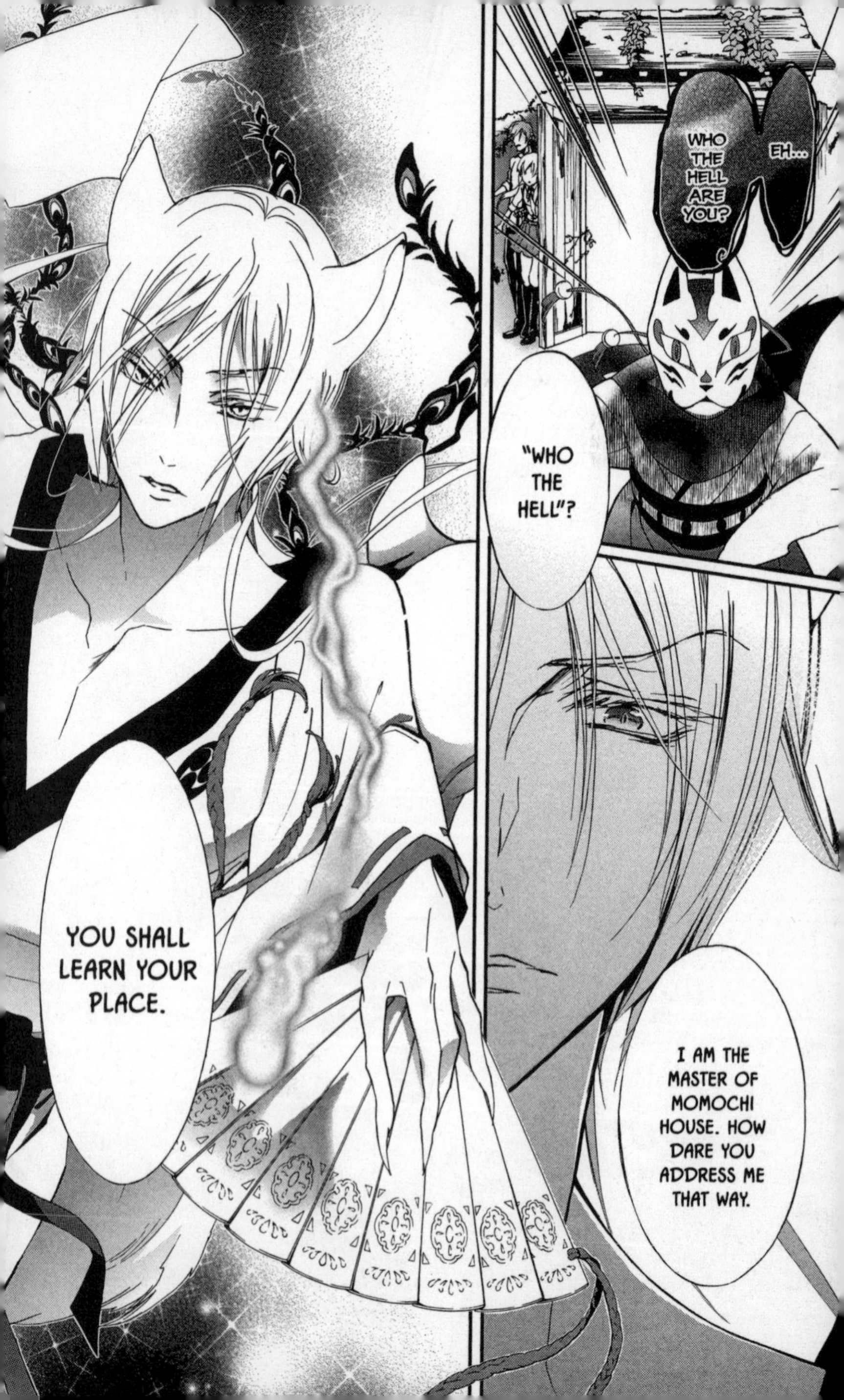
EH...
WHO THE HELL ARE YOU?
"WHO THE HELL"?
I AM THE MASTER OF MOMOCHI HOUSE. HOW DARE YOU ADDRESS ME THAT WAY.
YOU SHALL LEARN YOUR PLACE.

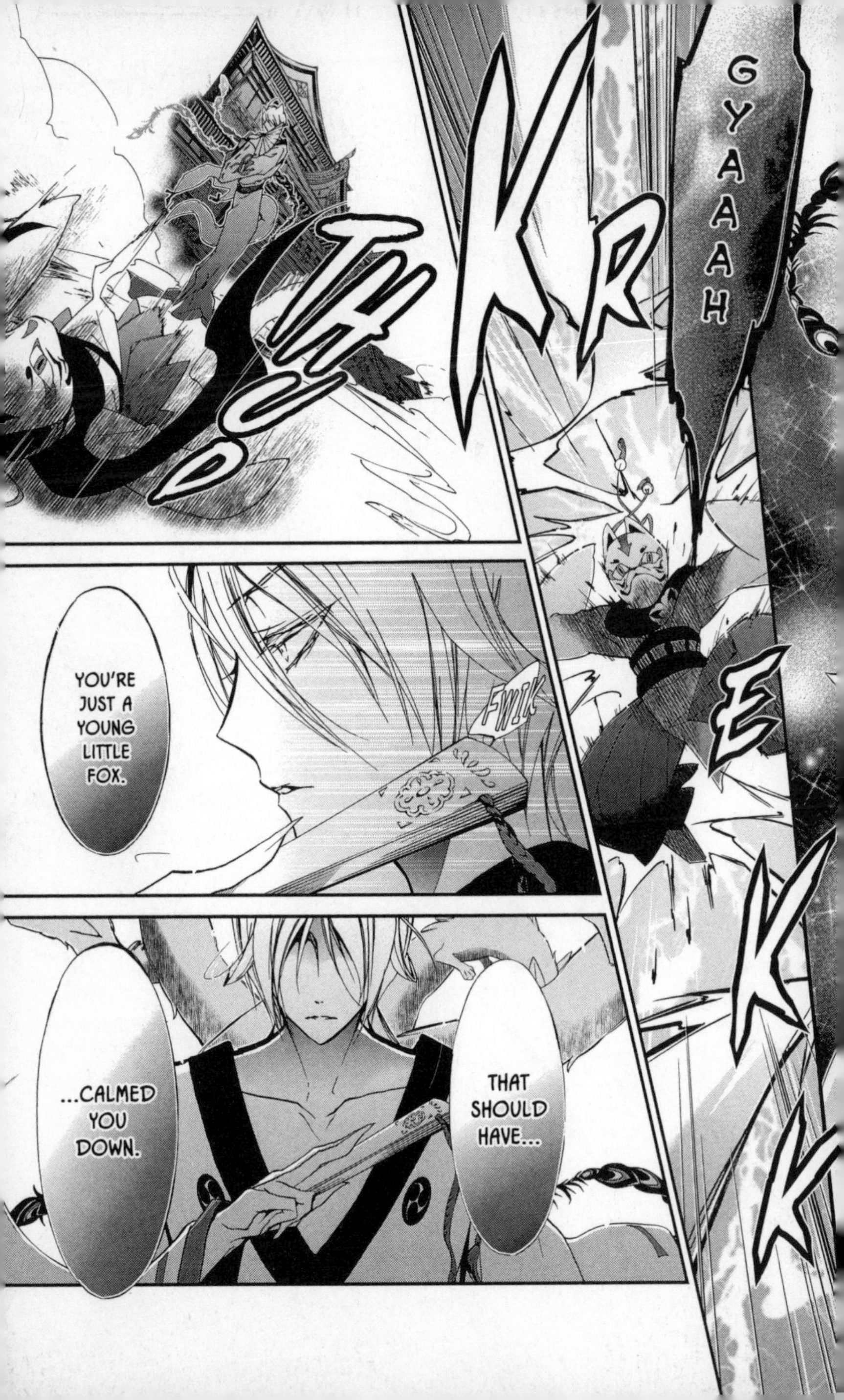
GYAAAH
EKK
KR
THUD
FWIK
YOU'RE JUST A YOUNG LITTLE FOX.
THAT SHOULD HAVE...
...CALMED YOU DOWN.

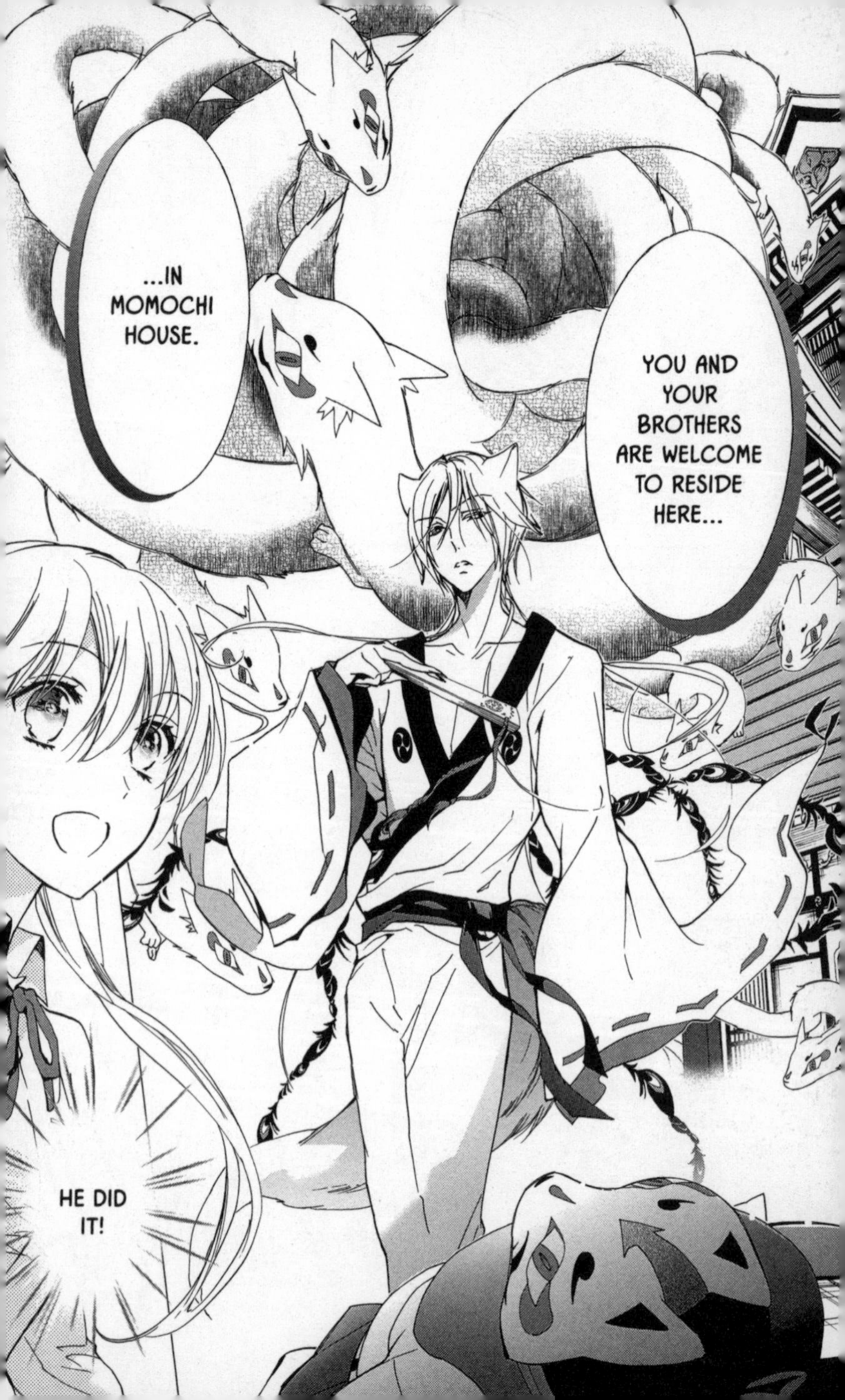
YOU AND YOUR BROTHERS ARE WELCOME TO RESIDE HERE...
...IN MOMOCHI HOUSE.
HE DID IT!

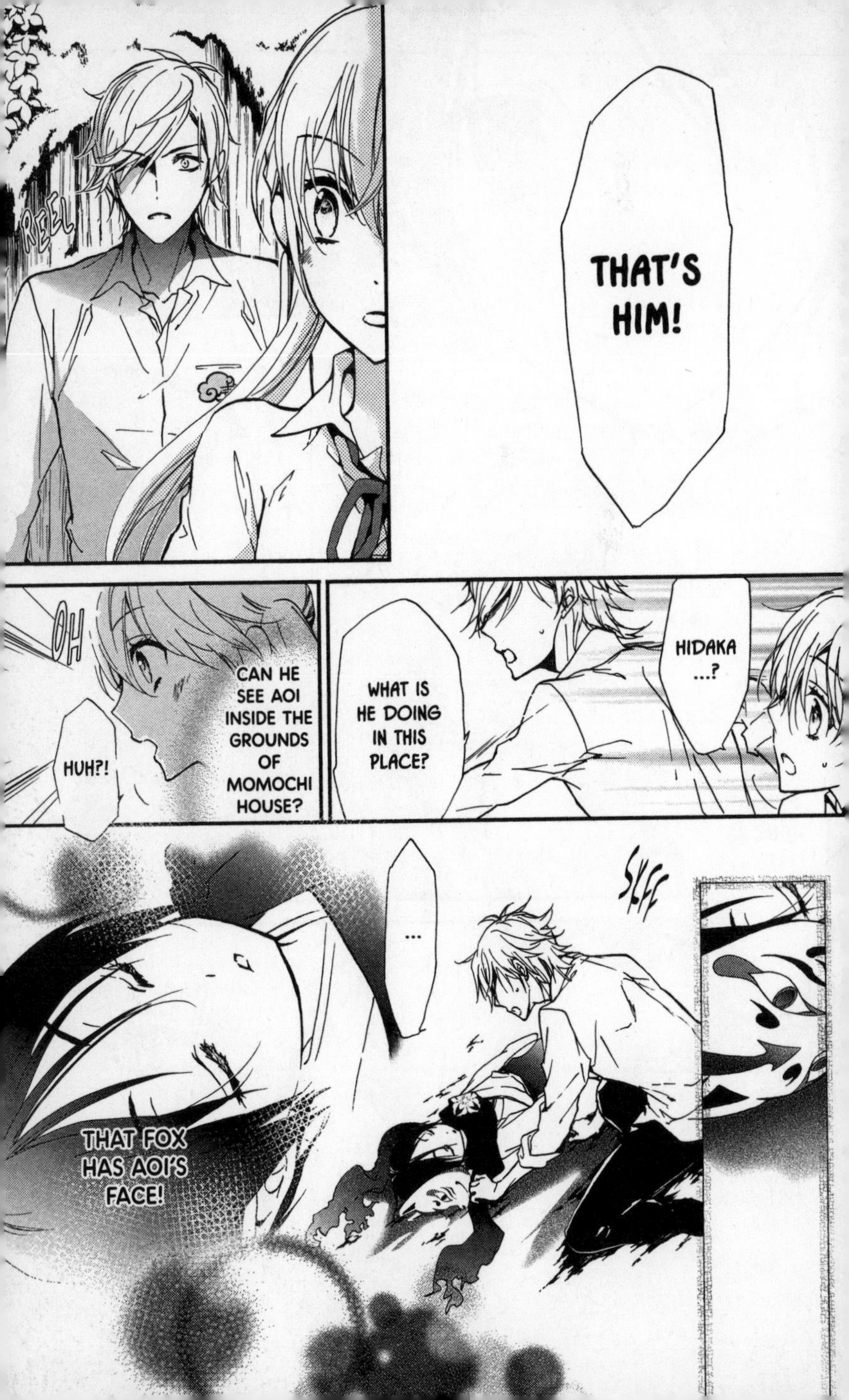
THAT'S HIM!
REEL
HIDAKA ...?
WHAT IS HE DOING IN THIS PLACE?
CAN HE SEE AOI INSIDE THE GROUNDS OF MOMOCHI HOUSE?
OH
HUH?!
SLFF
...
THAT FOX HAS AOI'S FACE!

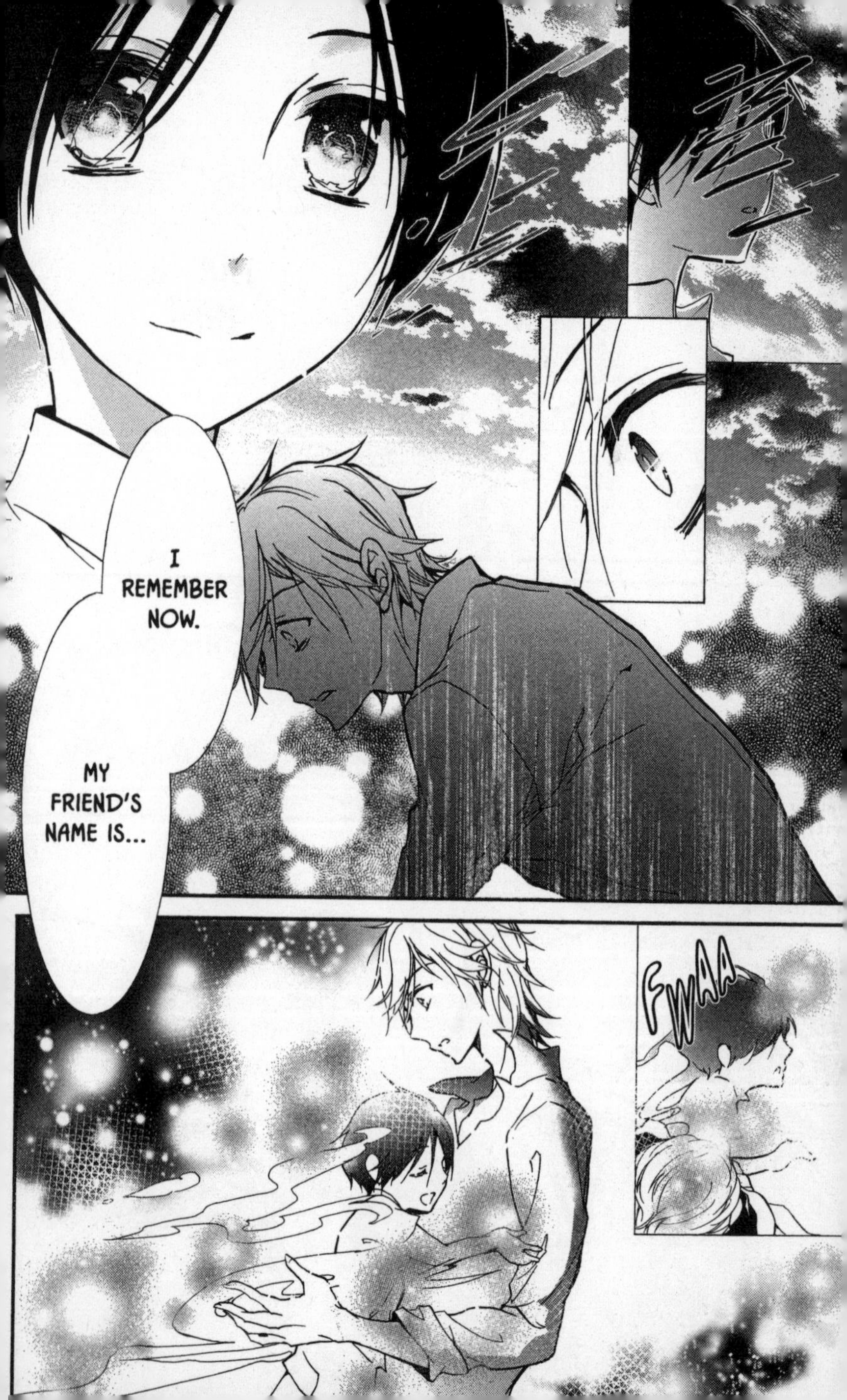
I REMEMBER NOW.
MY FRIEND'S NAME IS...
FWAA

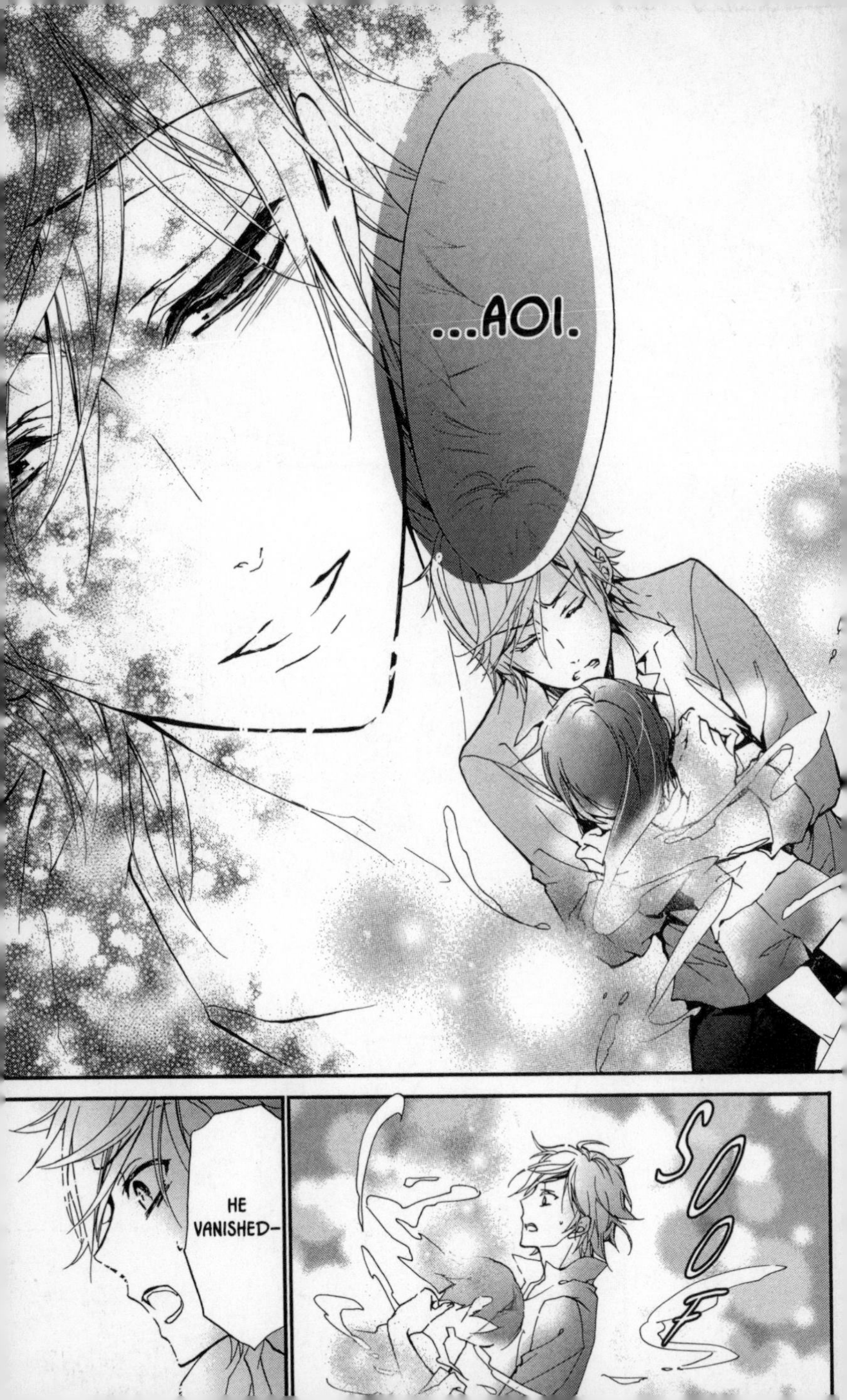
...AOI.
SOOF
HE VANISHED—

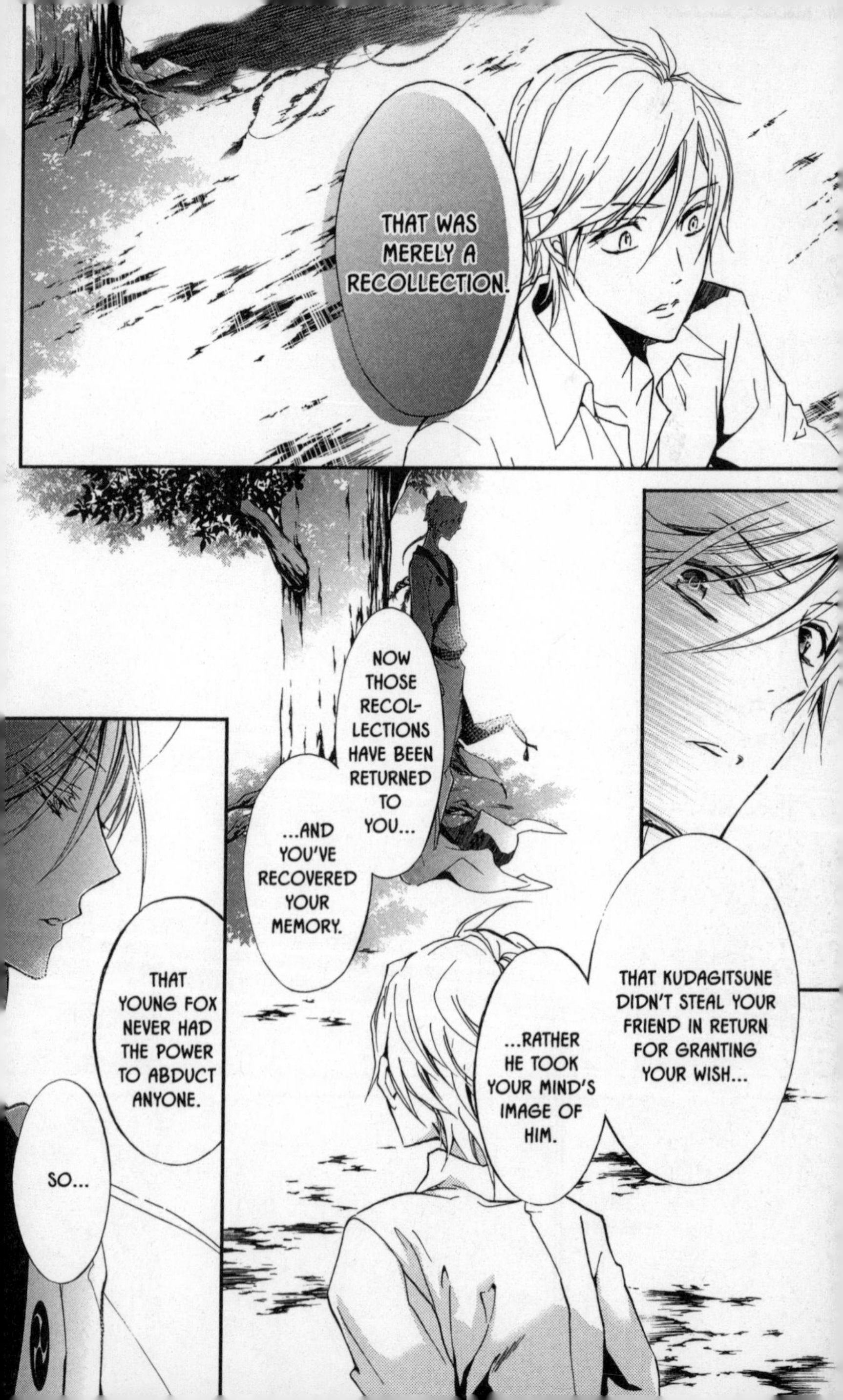

THAT WAS MERELY A RECOLLECTION.
NOW THOSE RECOL-LECTIONS HAVE BEEN RETURNED TO YOU...
...AND YOU'VE RECOVERED YOUR MEMORY.
THAT KUDAGITSUNE DIDN'T STEAL YOUR FRIEND IN RETURN FOR GRANTING YOUR WISH...
...RATHER HE TOOK YOUR MIND'S IMAGE OF HIM.
THAT YOUNG FOX NEVER HAD THE POWER TO ABDUCT ANYONE.
SO...

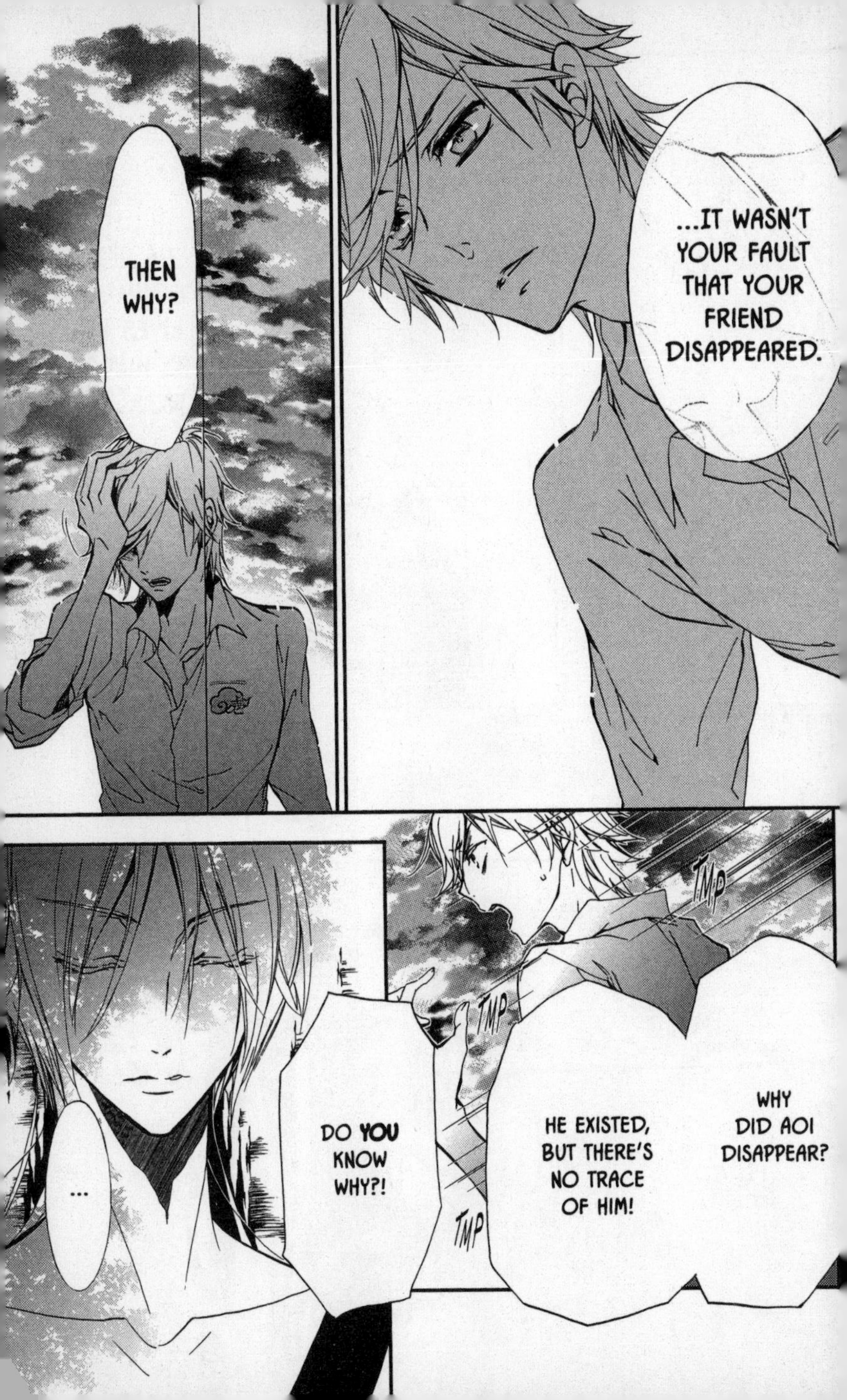
...IT WASN'T YOUR FAULT THAT YOUR FRIEND DISAPPEARED.
THEN WHY?
TMP
WHY DID AOI DISAPPEAR?
HE EXISTED, BUT THERE'S NO TRACE OF HIM!
TMP
DO **YOU** KNOW WHY?!
TMP
...

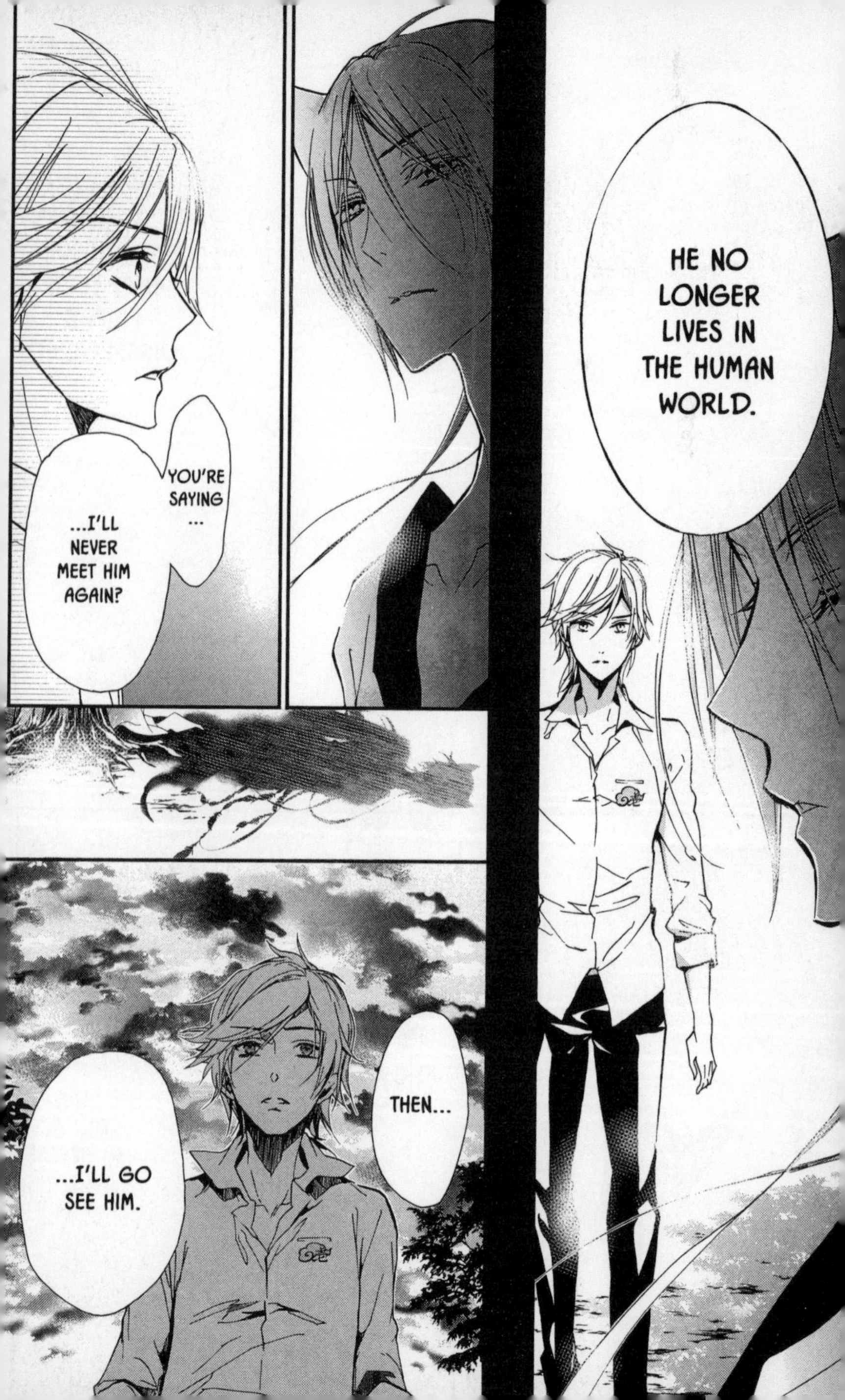
HE NO LONGER LIVES IN THE HUMAN WORLD.
YOU'RE SAYING...
...I'LL NEVER MEET HIM AGAIN?
THEN...
...I'LL GO SEE HIM.

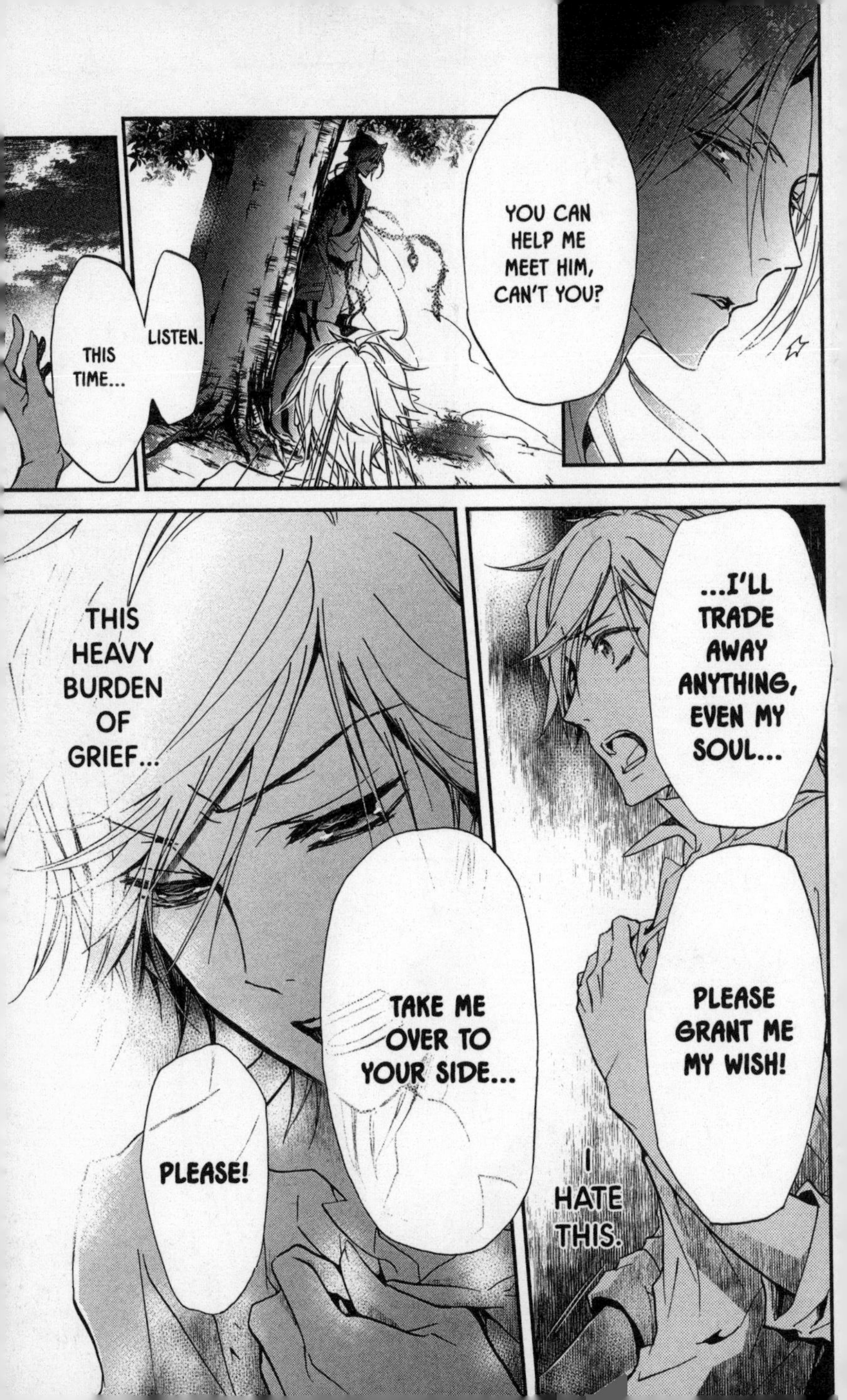
YOU CAN HELP ME MEET HIM, CAN'T YOU?
LISTEN.
THIS TIME...
...I'LL TRADE AWAY ANYTHING, EVEN MY SOUL...
PLEASE GRANT ME MY WISH!
I HATE THIS.
THIS HEAVY BURDEN OF GRIEF...
TAKE ME OVER TO YOUR SIDE...
PLEASE!

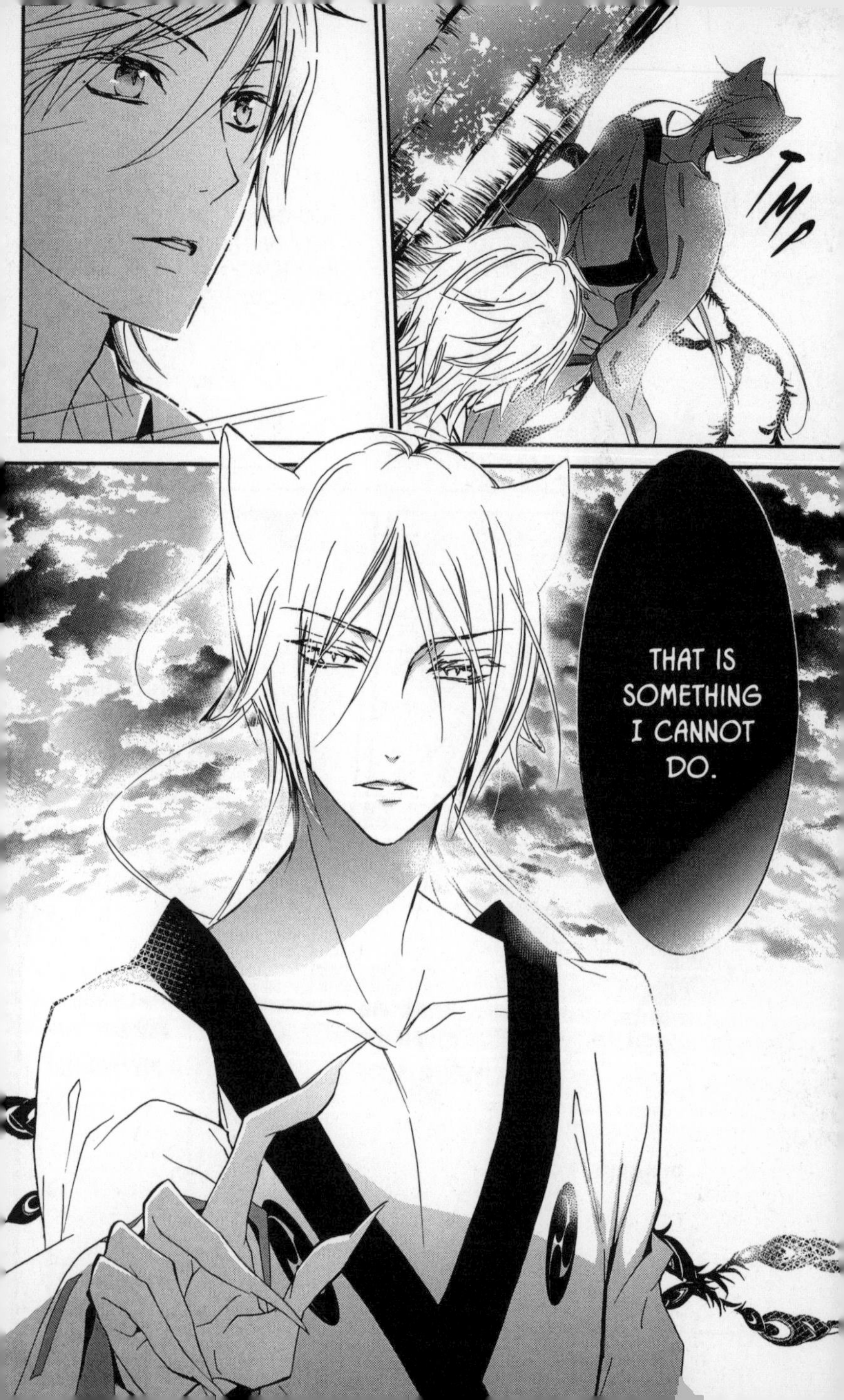
TMP
THAT IS SOMETHING I CANNOT DO.

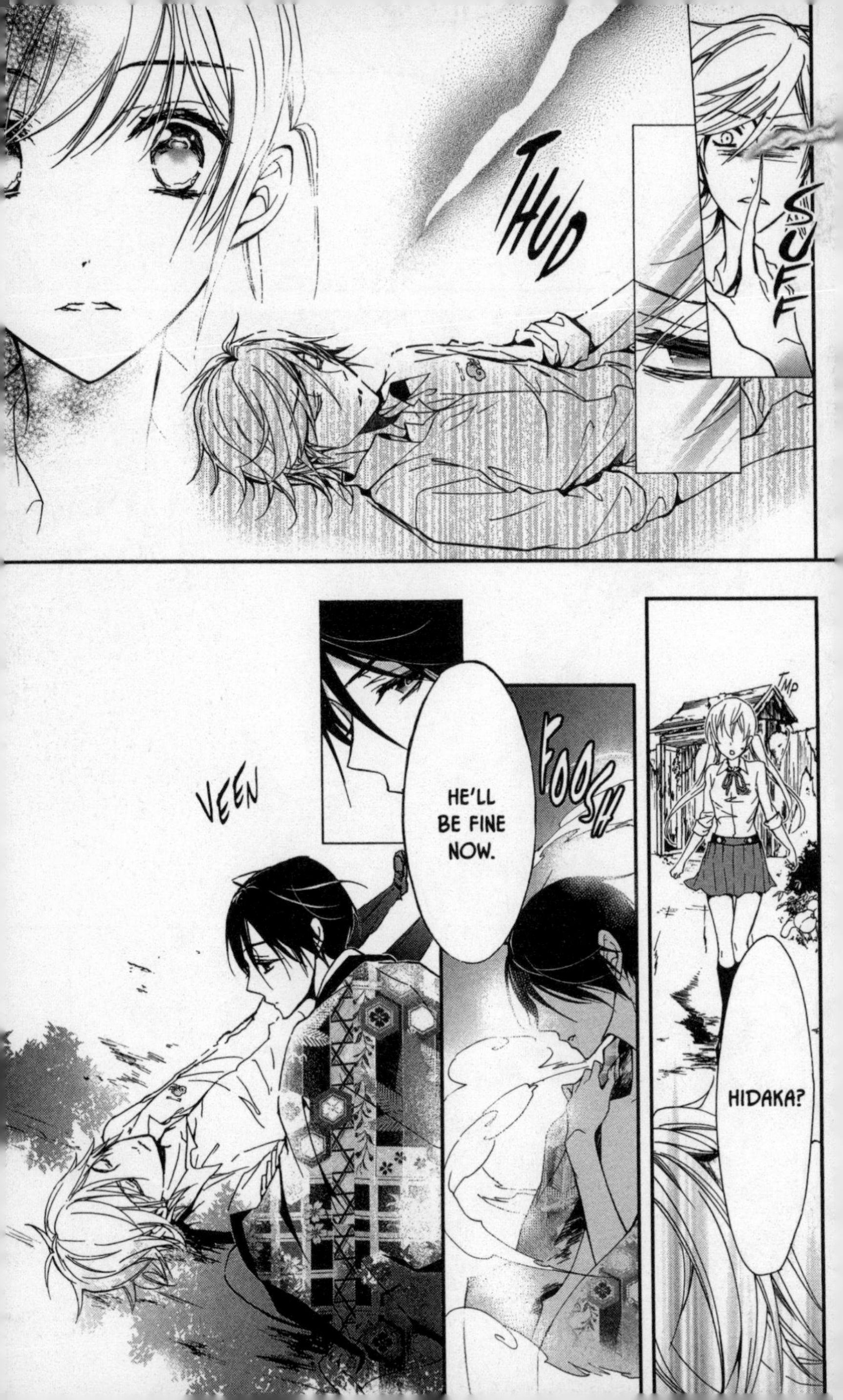
SNIFF
THUD
TMP
HIDAKA?
FOOSH
HE'LL BE FINE NOW.
VEEN

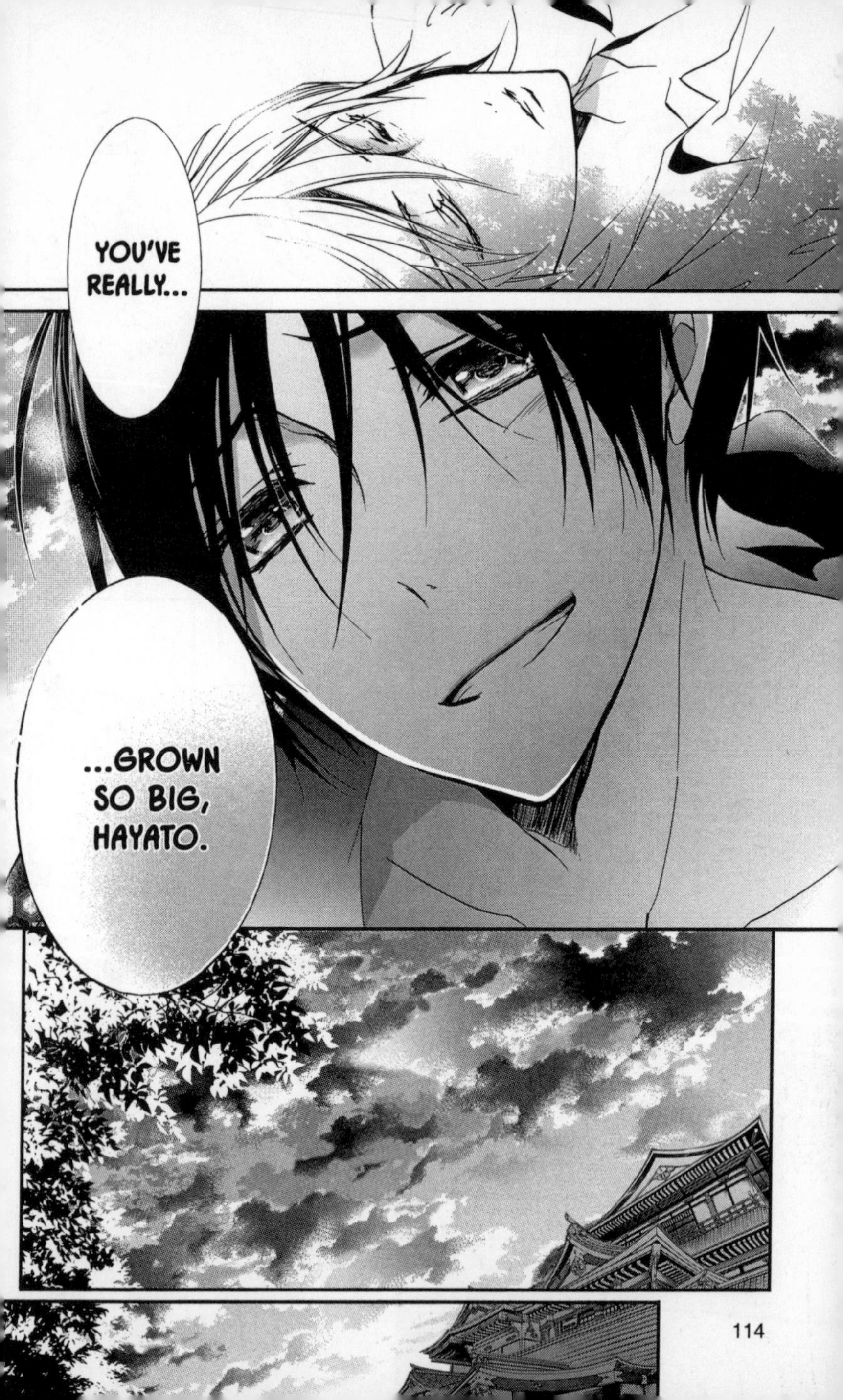
YOU'VE REALLY...
...GROWN SO BIG, HAYATO.

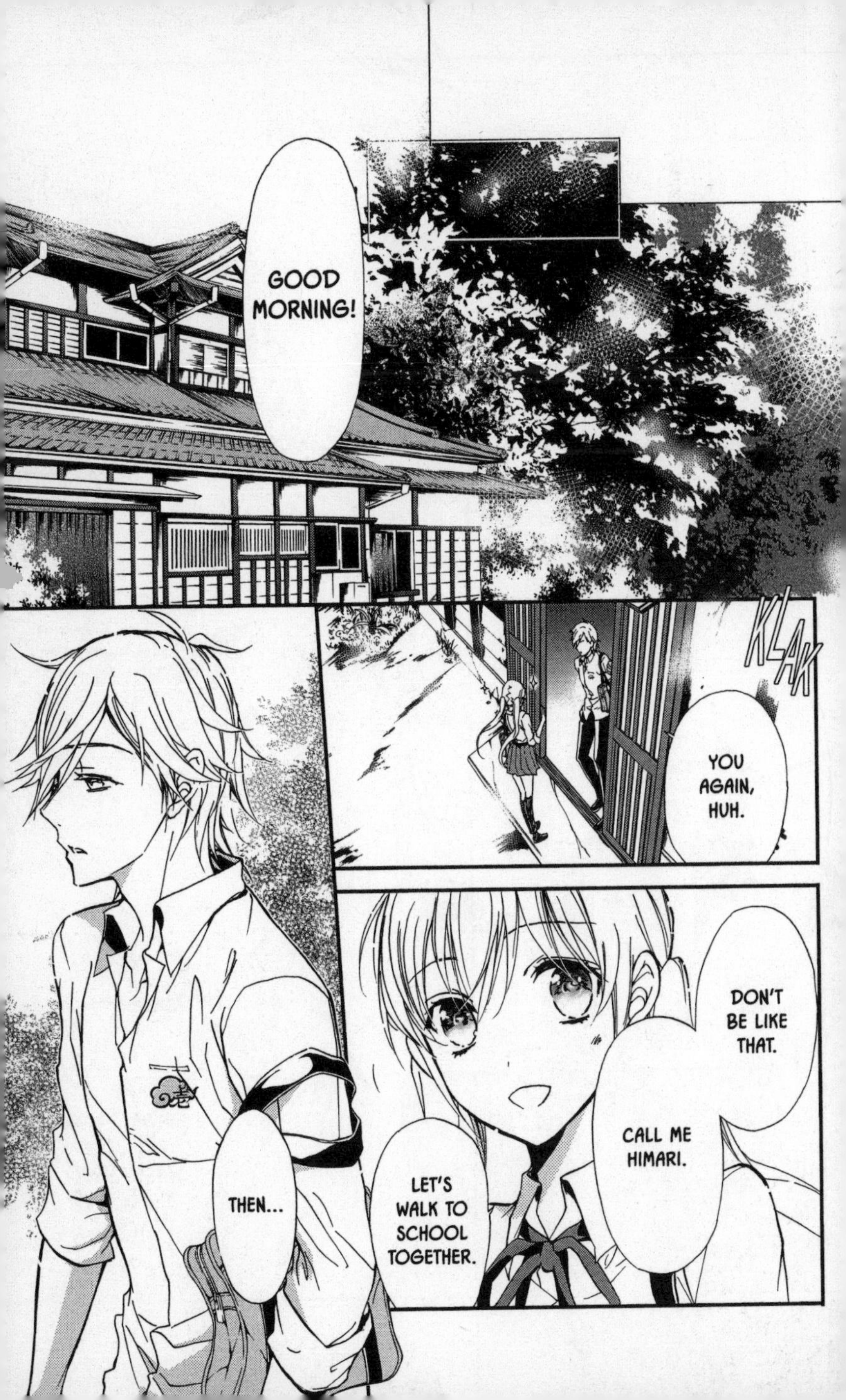
GOOD MORNING!
KLAK
YOU AGAIN, HUH.
DON'T BE LIKE THAT.
CALL ME HIMARI.
LET'S WALK TO SCHOOL TOGETHER.
THEN...

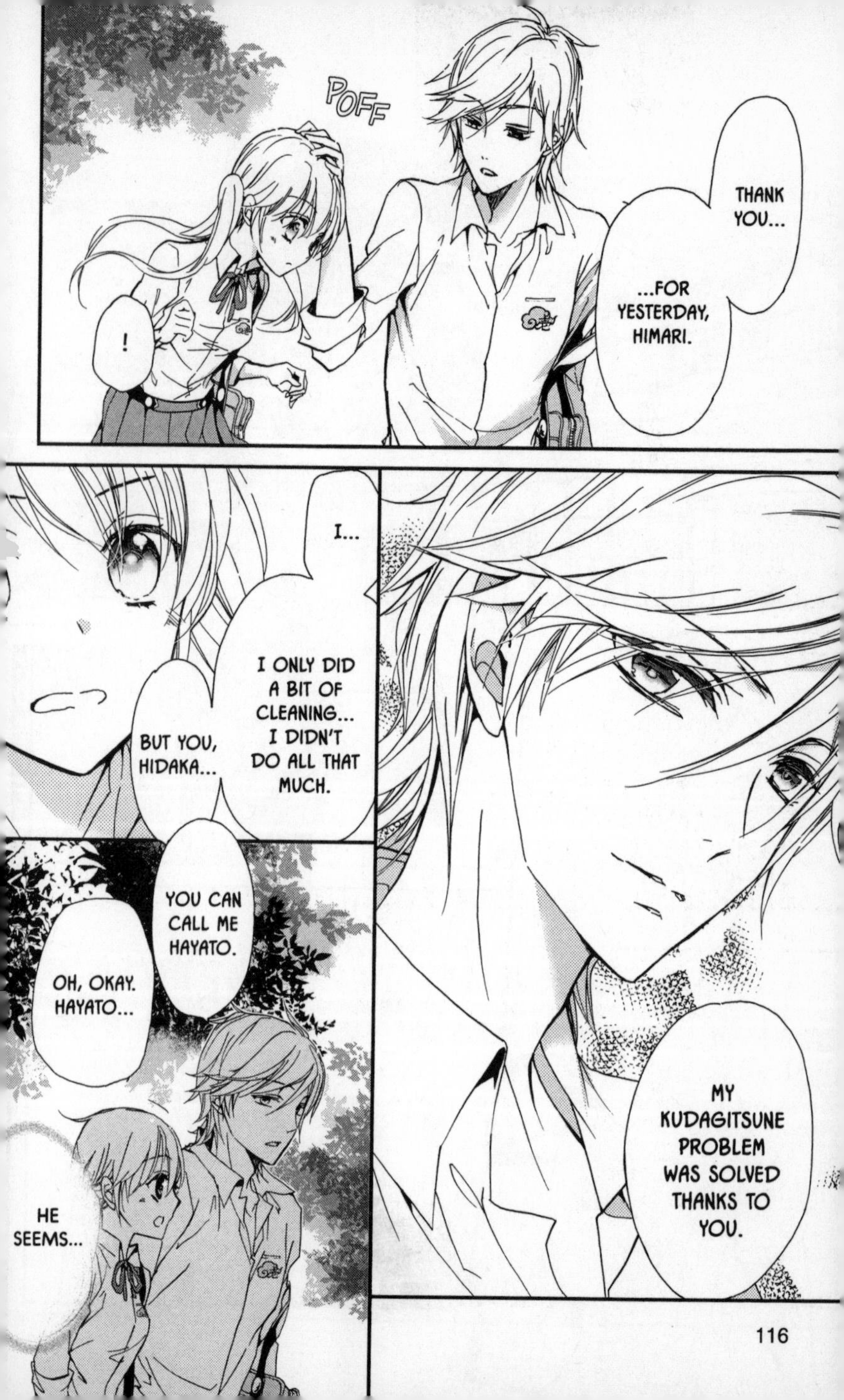
POFF
THANK YOU...
...FOR YESTERDAY, HIMARI.
!
MY KUDAGITSUNE PROBLEM WAS SOLVED THANKS TO YOU.
I...
I ONLY DID A BIT OF CLEANING... I DIDN'T DO ALL THAT MUCH.
BUT YOU, HIDAKA...
YOU CAN CALL ME HAYATO.
OH, OKAY. HAYATO...
HE SEEMS...

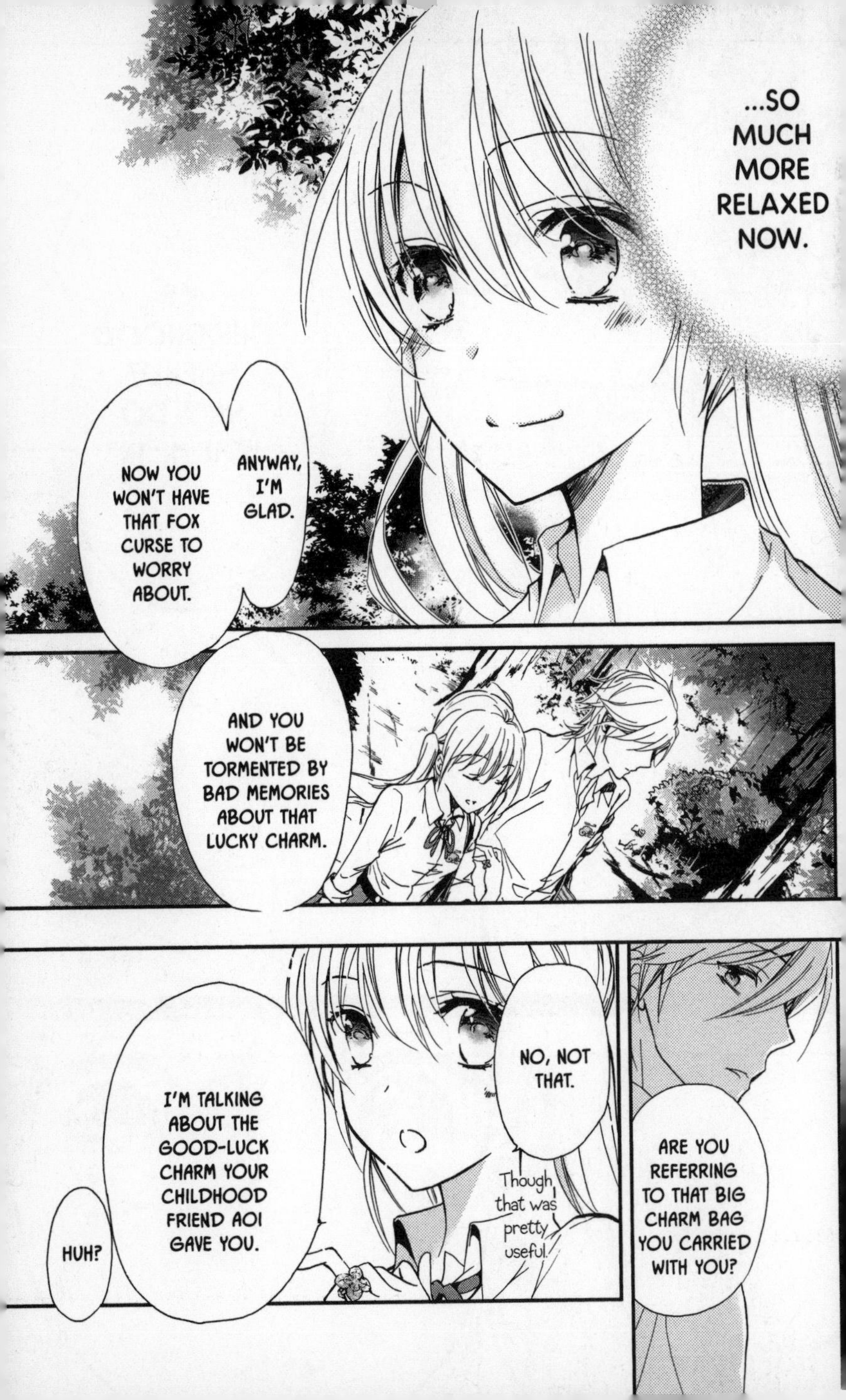
...SO MUCH MORE RELAXED NOW.
ANYWAY, I'M GLAD.
NOW YOU WON'T HAVE THAT FOX CURSE TO WORRY ABOUT.
AND YOU WON'T BE TORMENTED BY BAD MEMORIES ABOUT THAT LUCKY CHARM.
ARE YOU REFERRING TO THAT BIG CHARM BAG YOU CARRIED WITH YOU?
NO, NOT THAT.
Though that was pretty useful.
I'M TALKING ABOUT THE GOOD-LUCK CHARM YOUR CHILDHOOD FRIEND AOI GAVE YOU.
HUH?

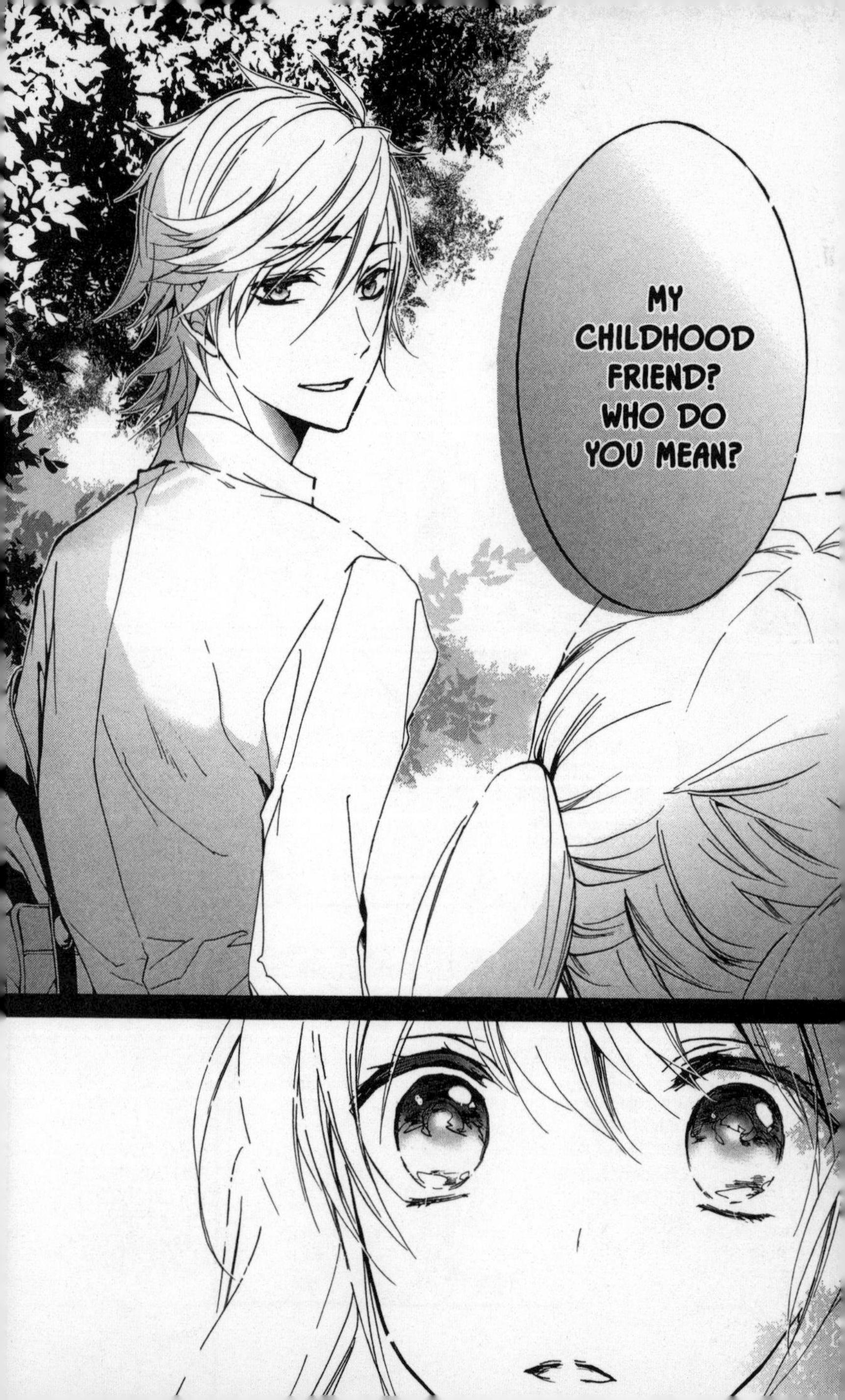
MY CHILDHOOD FRIEND? WHO DO YOU MEAN?

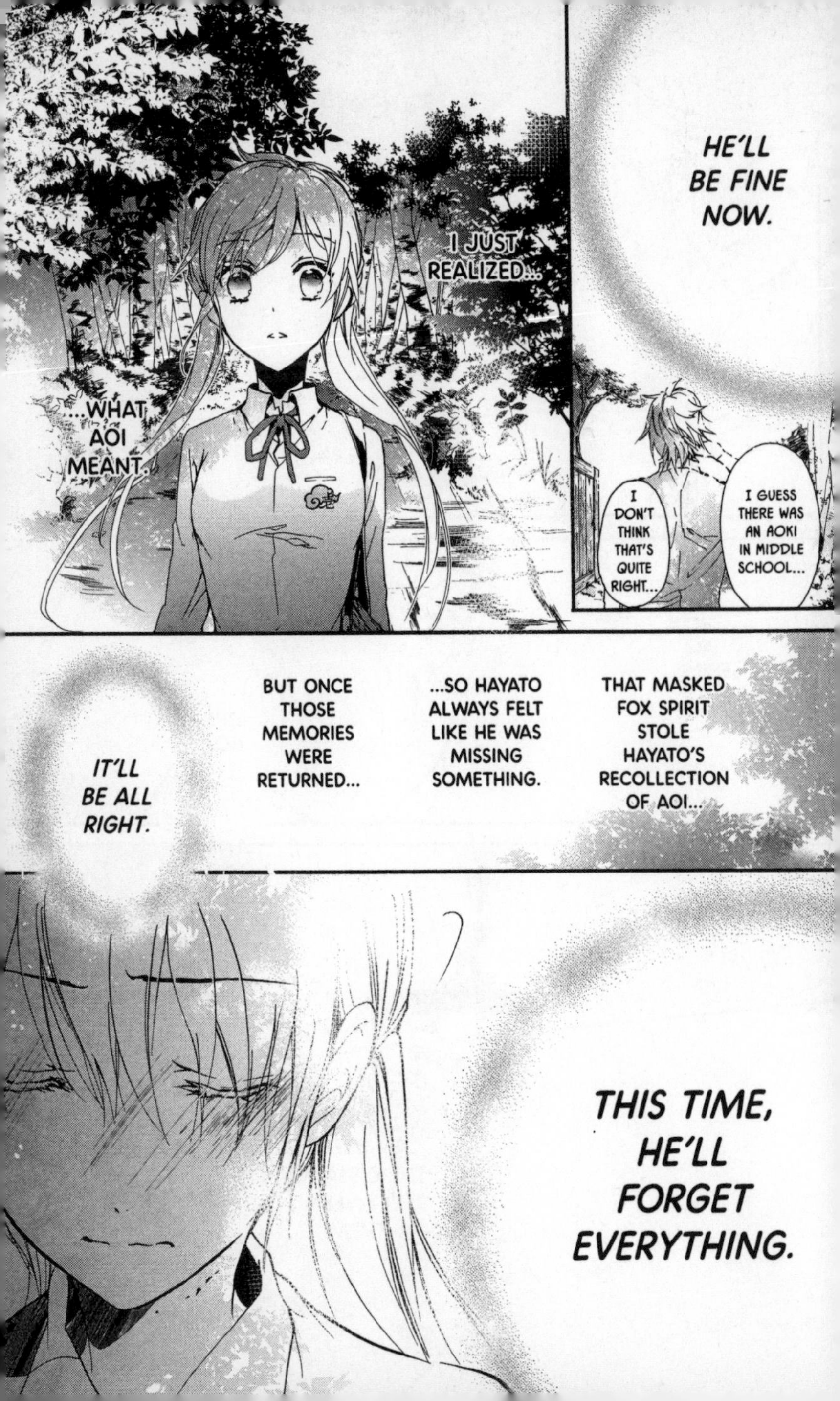
HE'LL BE FINE NOW.
I GUESS THERE WAS AN AOKI IN MIDDLE SCHOOL...
I DON'T THINK THAT'S QUITE RIGHT...
I JUST REALIZED...
...WHAT AOI MEANT.
THAT MASKED FOX SPIRIT STOLE HAYATO'S RECOLLECTION OF AOI...
...SO HAYATO ALWAYS FELT LIKE HE WAS MISSING SOMETHING.
BUT ONCE THOSE MEMORIES WERE RETURNED...
IT'LL BE ALL RIGHT.
THIS TIME, HE'LL FORGET EVERYTHING.

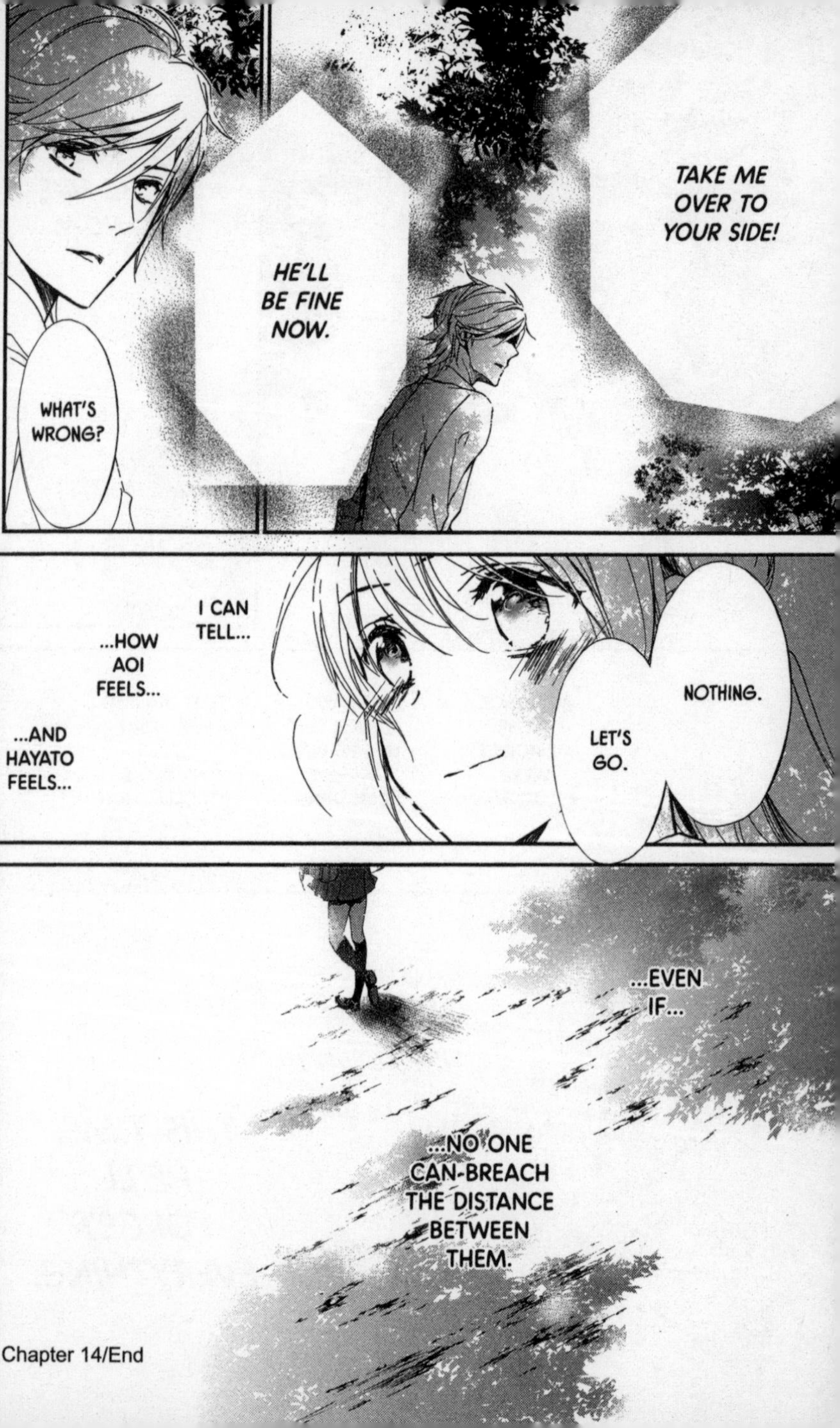
TAKE ME OVER TO YOUR SIDE!
HE'LL BE FINE NOW.
WHAT'S WRONG?
NOTHING.
LET'S GO.
I CAN TELL...
...HOW AOI FEELS...
...AND HAYATO FEELS...
...EVEN IF...
...NO ONE CAN BREACH THE DISTANCE BETWEEN THEM.
Chapter 14/End

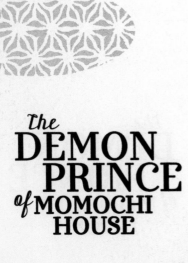

The
DEMON
PRINCE
of MOMOCHI
HOUSE

The
DEMON
PRINCE
of MOMOCHI
HOUSE

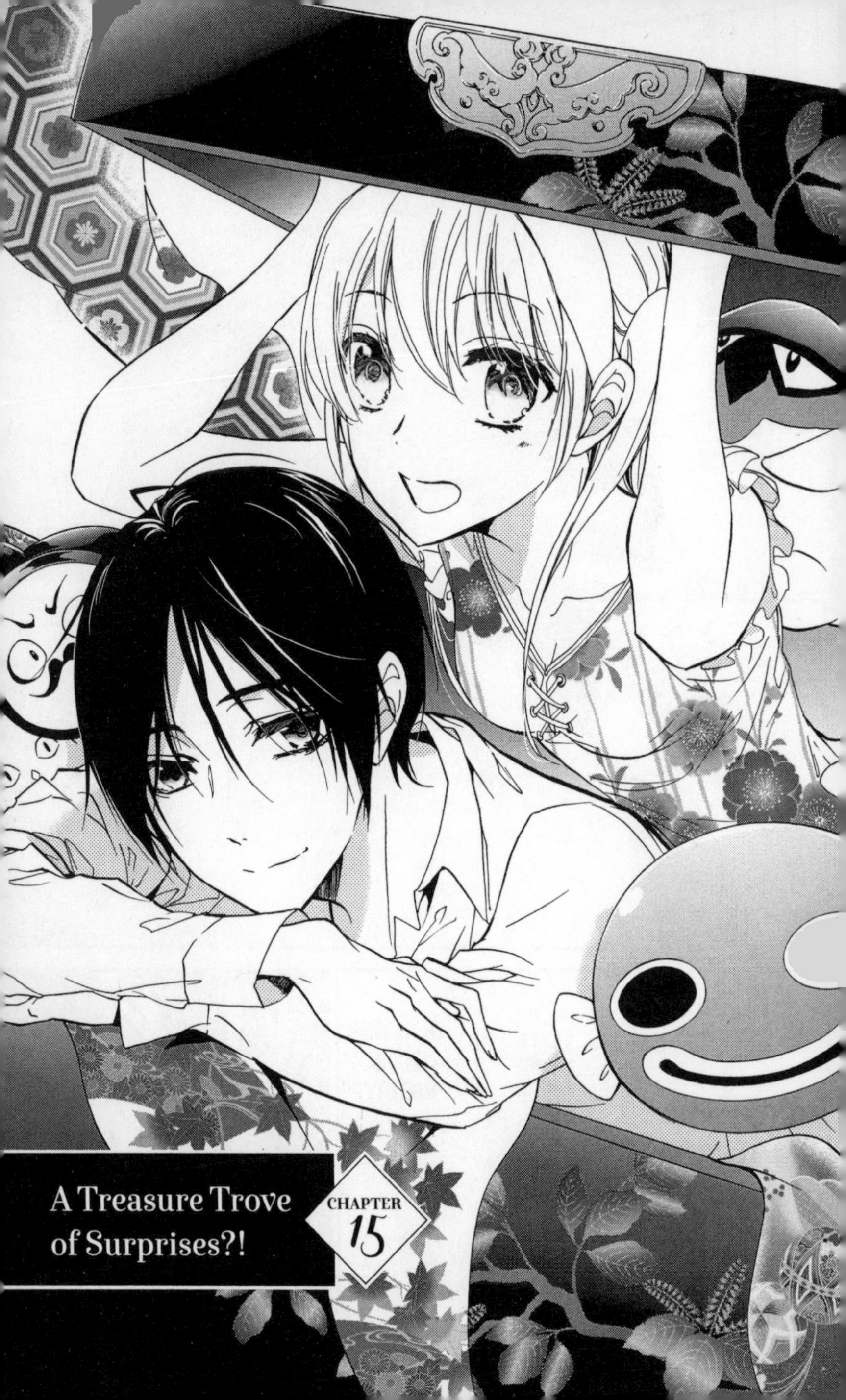
A Treasure Trove of Surprises?!
CHAPTER 15

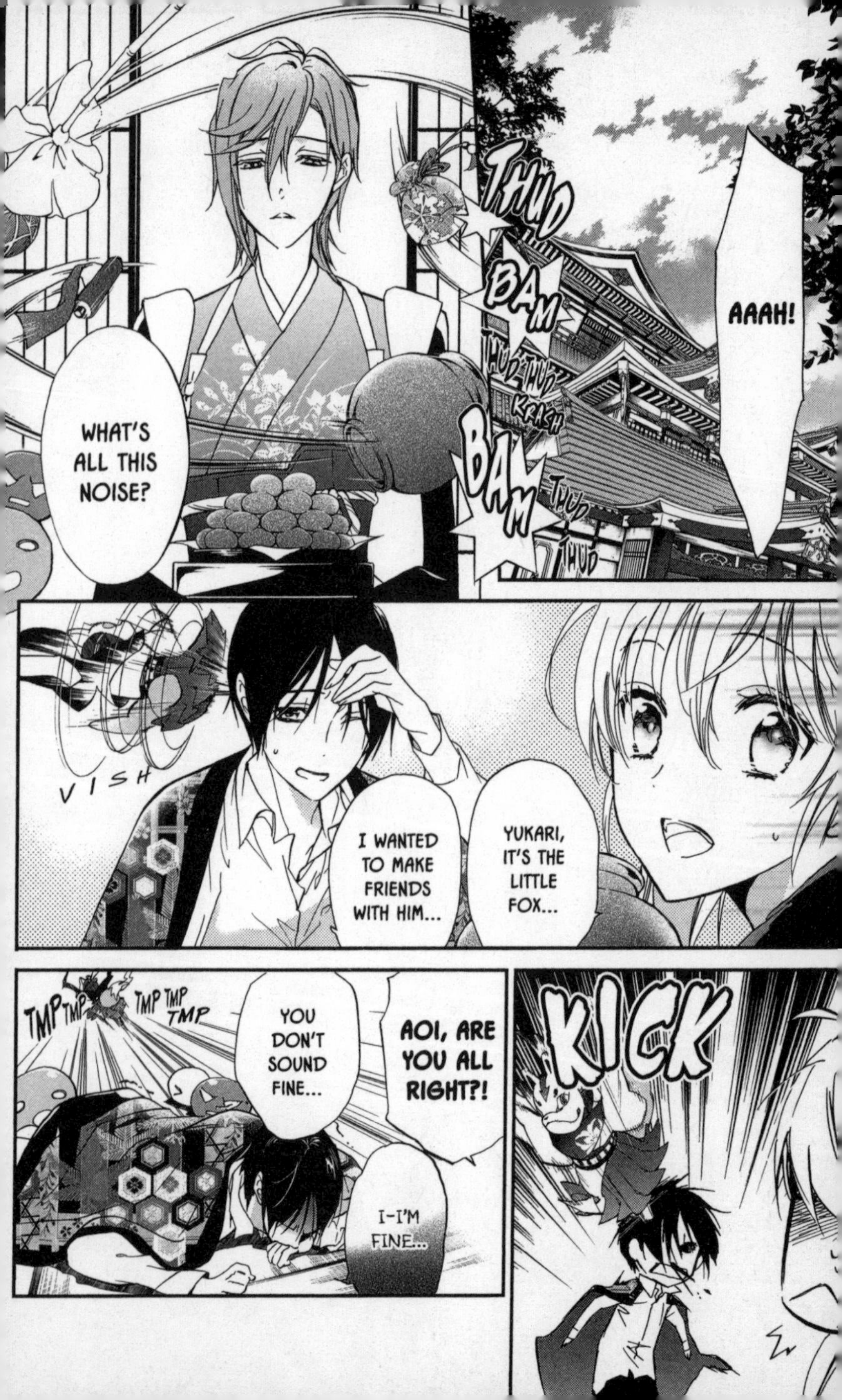
AAAH!
THUD
BAM
THUD THUD
KRASH
BAM
THUD
THUD
WHAT'S ALL THIS NOISE?
YUKARI, IT'S THE LITTLE FOX...
I WANTED TO MAKE FRIENDS WITH HIM...
VISH
KICK
AOI, ARE YOU ALL RIGHT?!
I-I'M FINE...
YOU DON'T SOUND FINE...
TMP TMP TMP TMP TMP

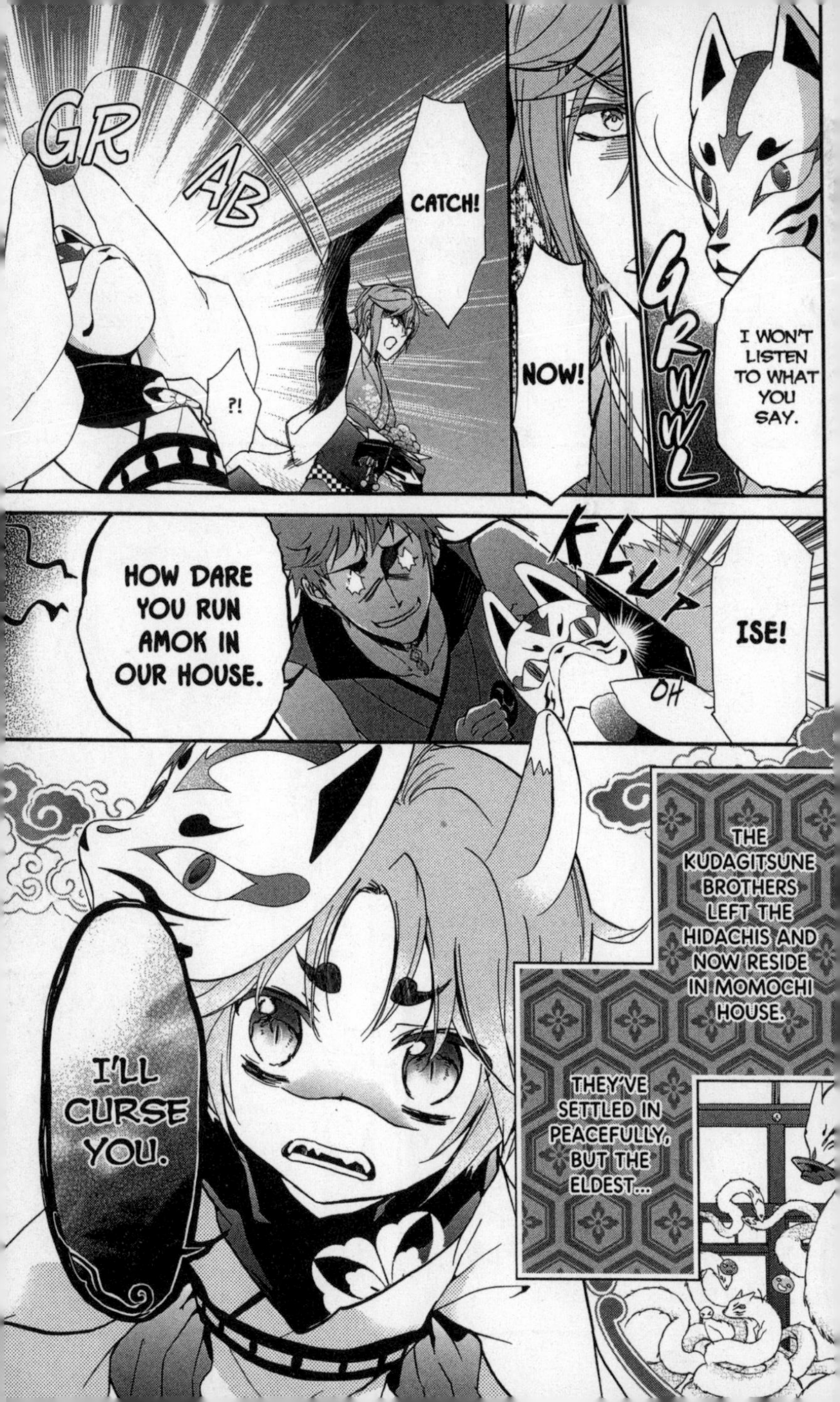
I WON'T LISTEN TO WHAT YOU SAY.
GRWWL
NOW!
CATCH!
GRAB
?!
ISE!
KLUP
OH
HOW DARE YOU RUN AMOK IN OUR HOUSE.
THE KUDAGITSUNE BROTHERS LEFT THE HIDACHIS AND NOW RESIDE IN MOMOCHI HOUSE.
THEY'VE SETTLED IN PEACEFULLY, BUT THE ELDEST...
I'LL CURSE YOU.

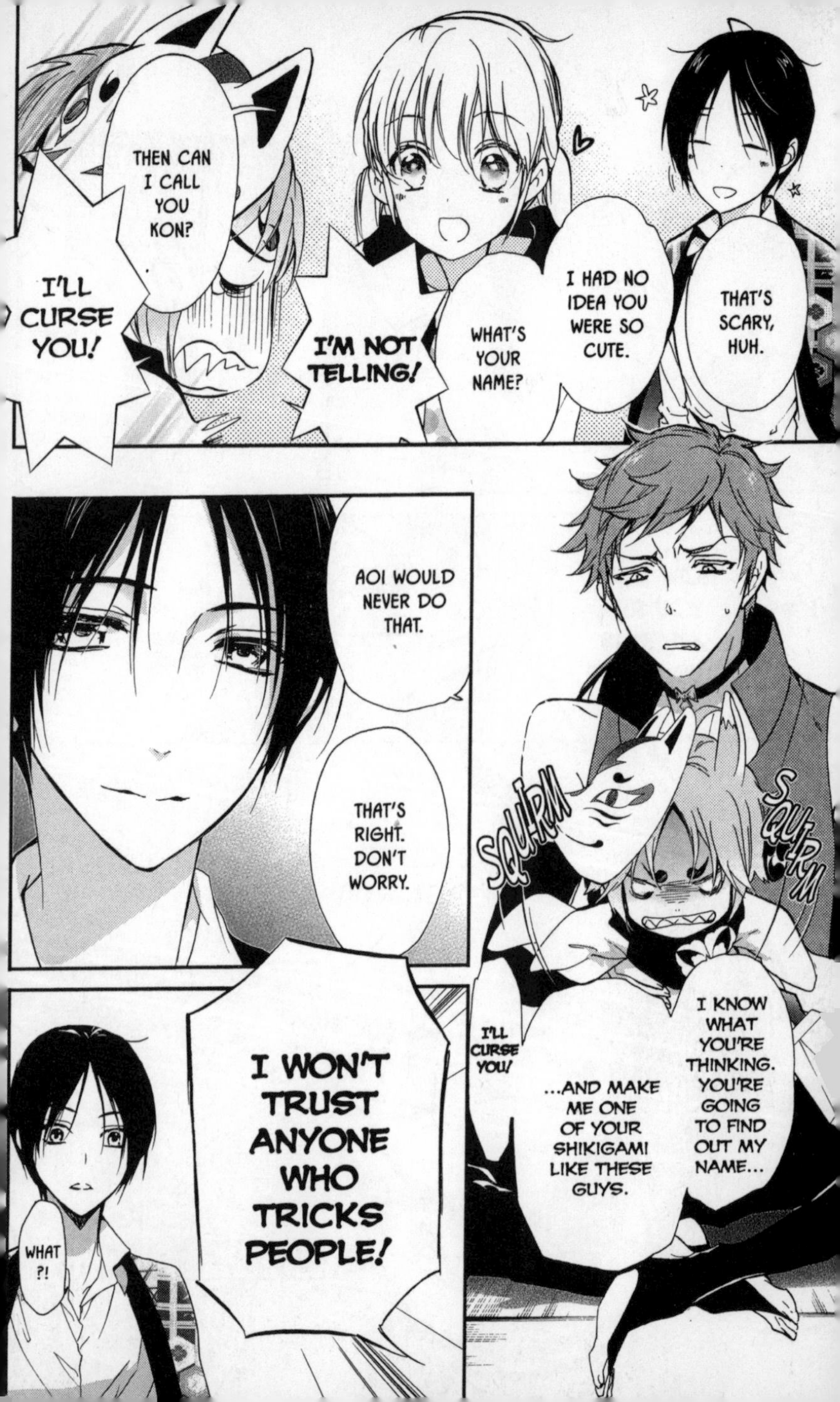

THAT'S SCARY, HUH.
I HAD NO IDEA YOU WERE SO CUTE.
WHAT'S YOUR NAME?
I'M NOT TELLING!
THEN CAN I CALL YOU KON?
I'LL CURSE YOU!
SQUIRM
SQUIRM
I KNOW WHAT YOU'RE THINKING. YOU'RE GOING TO FIND OUT MY NAME...
...AND MAKE ME ONE OF YOUR SHIKIGAMI LIKE THESE GUYS.
I'LL CURSE YOU!
AOI WOULD NEVER DO THAT.
THAT'S RIGHT. DON'T WORRY.
I WON'T TRUST ANYONE WHO TRICKS PEOPLE!
WHAT?!

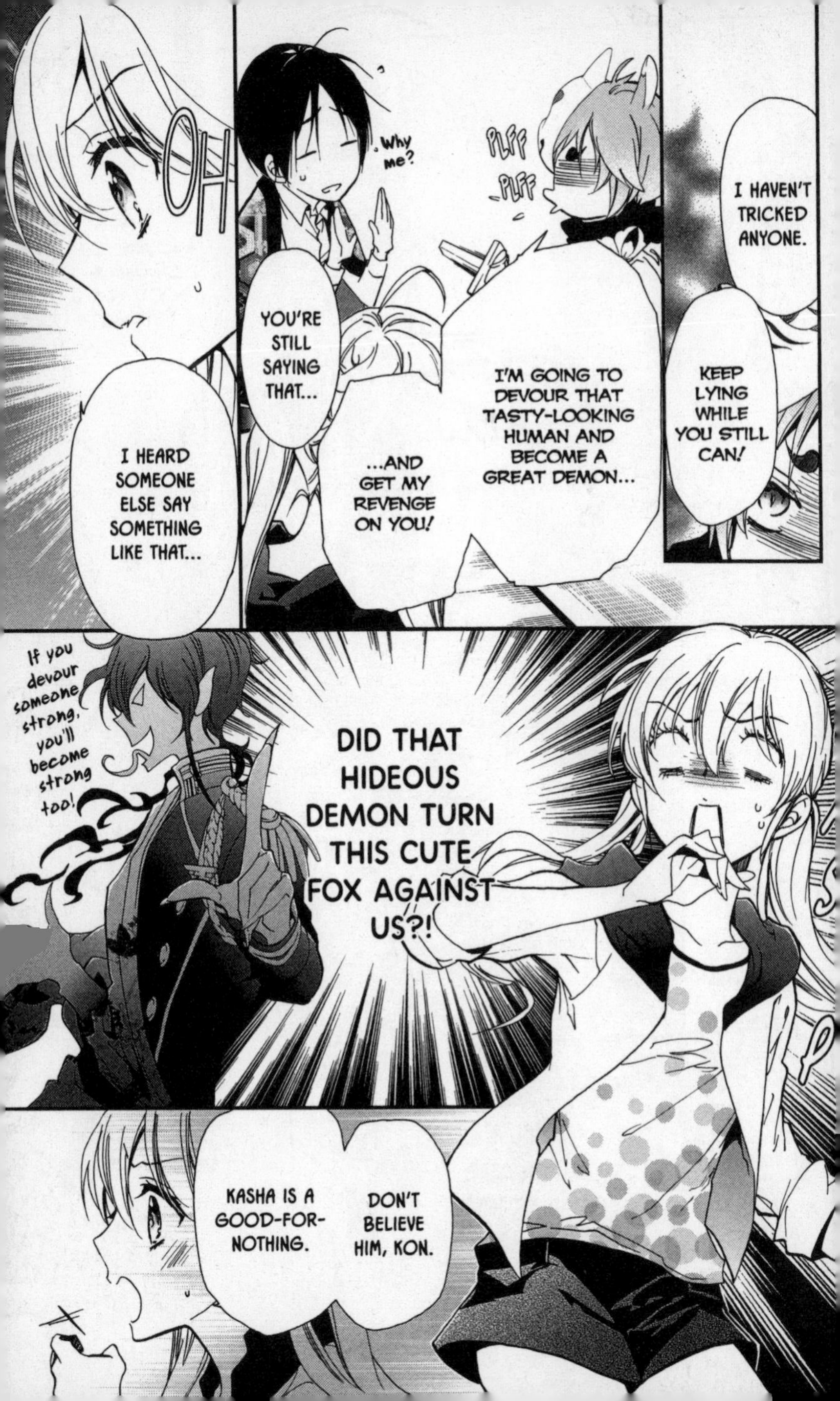
I HAVEN'T TRICKED ANYONE.
KEEP LYING WHILE YOU STILL CAN!
PLFF
PLFF
Why me?
I'M GOING TO DEVOUR THAT TASTY-LOOKING HUMAN AND BECOME A GREAT DEMON...
...AND GET MY REVENGE ON YOU!
YOU'RE STILL SAYING THAT...
OH
I HEARD SOMEONE ELSE SAY SOMETHING LIKE THAT...
DID THAT HIDEOUS DEMON TURN THIS CUTE FOX AGAINST US?!
If you devour someone strong, you'll become strong too!
DON'T BELIEVE HIM, KON.
KASHA IS A GOOD-FOR-NOTHING.

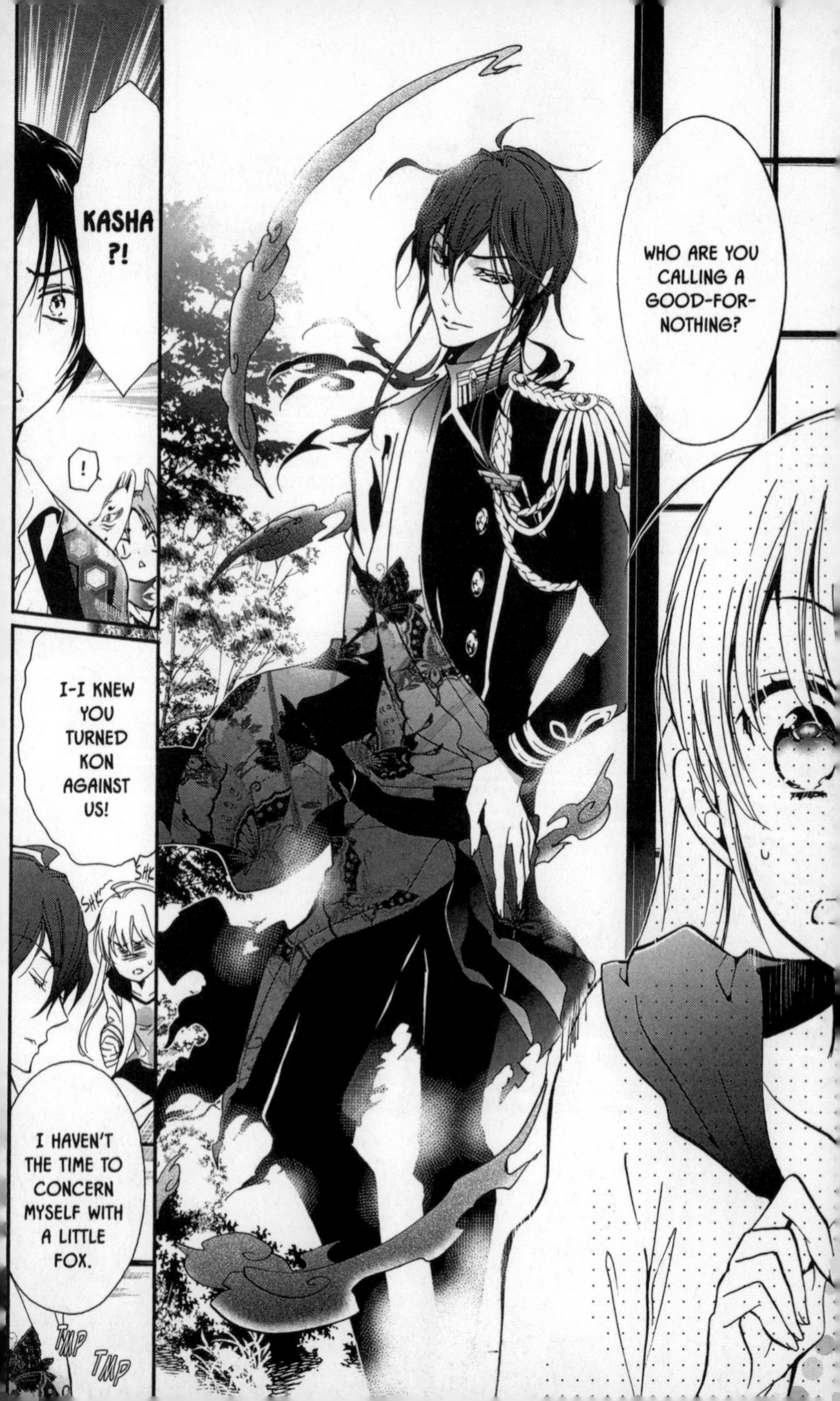
WHO ARE YOU CALLING A GOOD-FOR-NOTHING?
KASHA ?!
!
I-I KNEW YOU TURNED KON AGAINST US!
SHK
SHK
I HAVEN'T THE TIME TO CONCERN MYSELF WITH A LITTLE FOX.
TMP
TMP

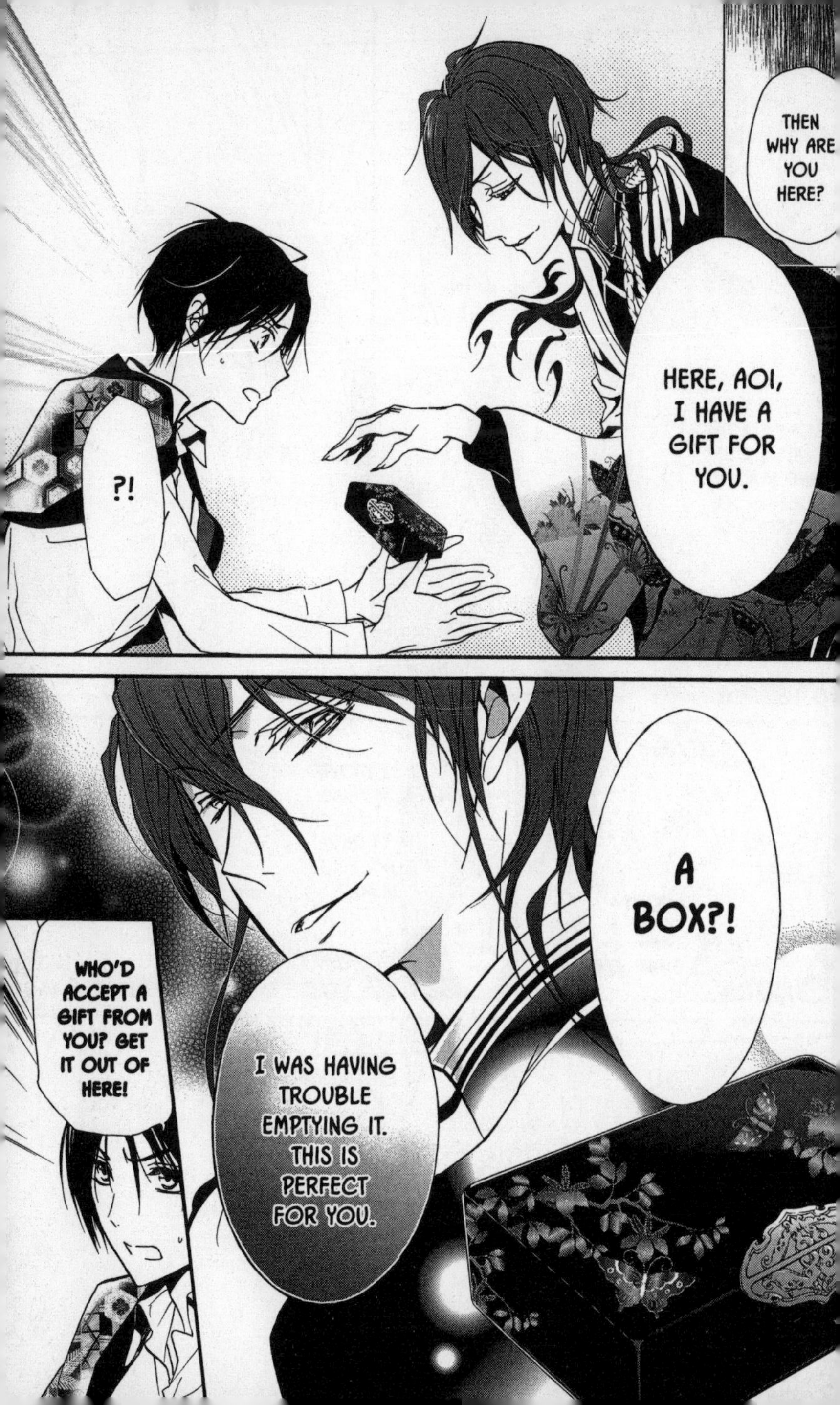
THEN WHY ARE YOU HERE?
HERE, AOI, I HAVE A GIFT FOR YOU.
?!
A BOX?!
I WAS HAVING TROUBLE EMPTYING IT. THIS IS PERFECT FOR YOU.
WHO'D ACCEPT A GIFT FROM YOU? GET IT OUT OF HERE!

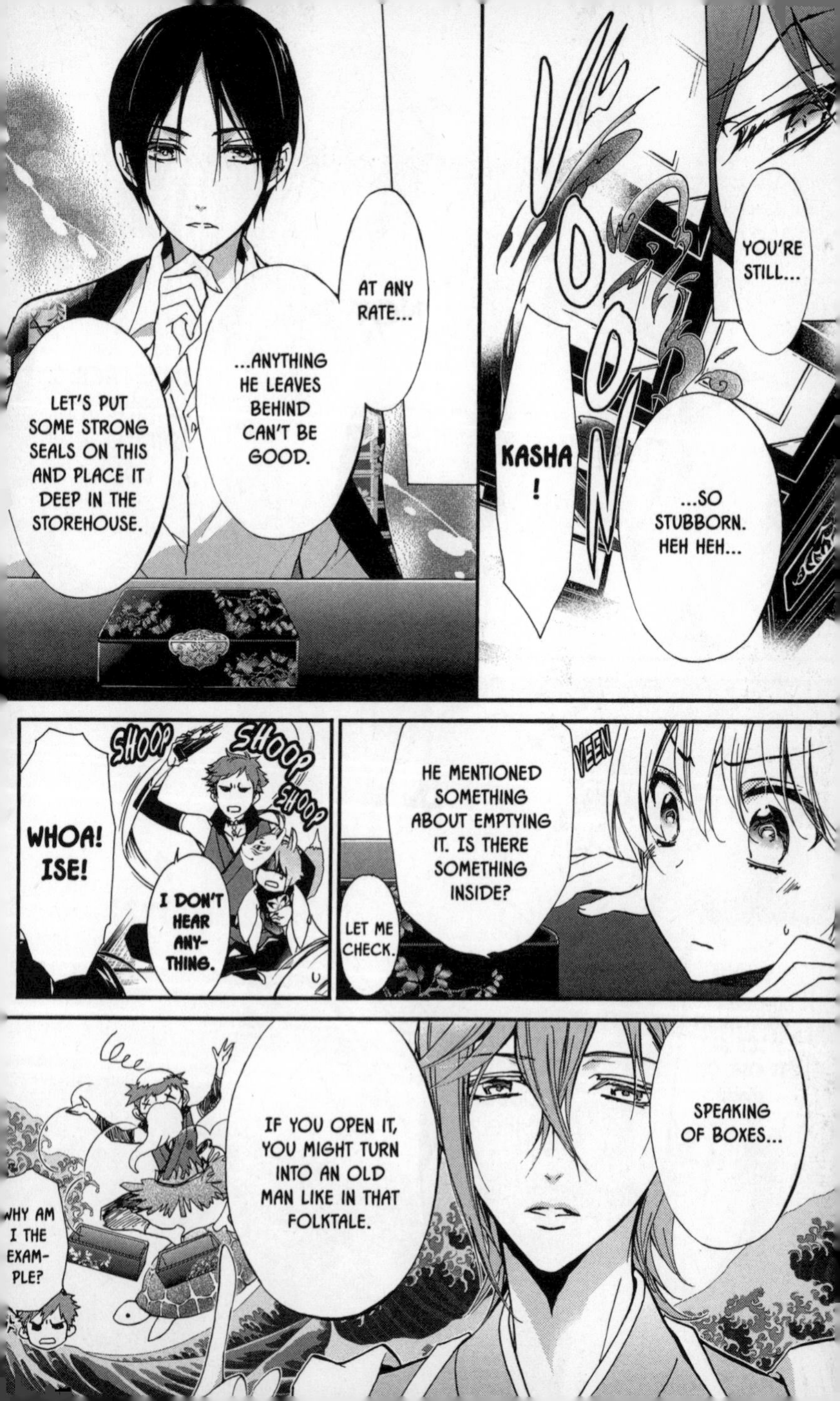
YOU'RE STILL...
...SO STUBBORN. HEH HEH...
KASHA!
AT ANY RATE...
...ANYTHING HE LEAVES BEHIND CAN'T BE GOOD.
LET'S PUT SOME STRONG SEALS ON THIS AND PLACE IT DEEP IN THE STOREHOUSE.
VEEN
HE MENTIONED SOMETHING ABOUT EMPTYING IT. IS THERE SOMETHING INSIDE?
LET ME CHECK.
SHOOP
SHOOP
SHOOP
I DON'T HEAR ANY-THING.
WHOA! ISE!
SPEAKING OF BOXES...
IF YOU OPEN IT, YOU MIGHT TURN INTO AN OLD MAN LIKE IN THAT FOLKTALE.
WHY AM I THE EXAM-PLE?

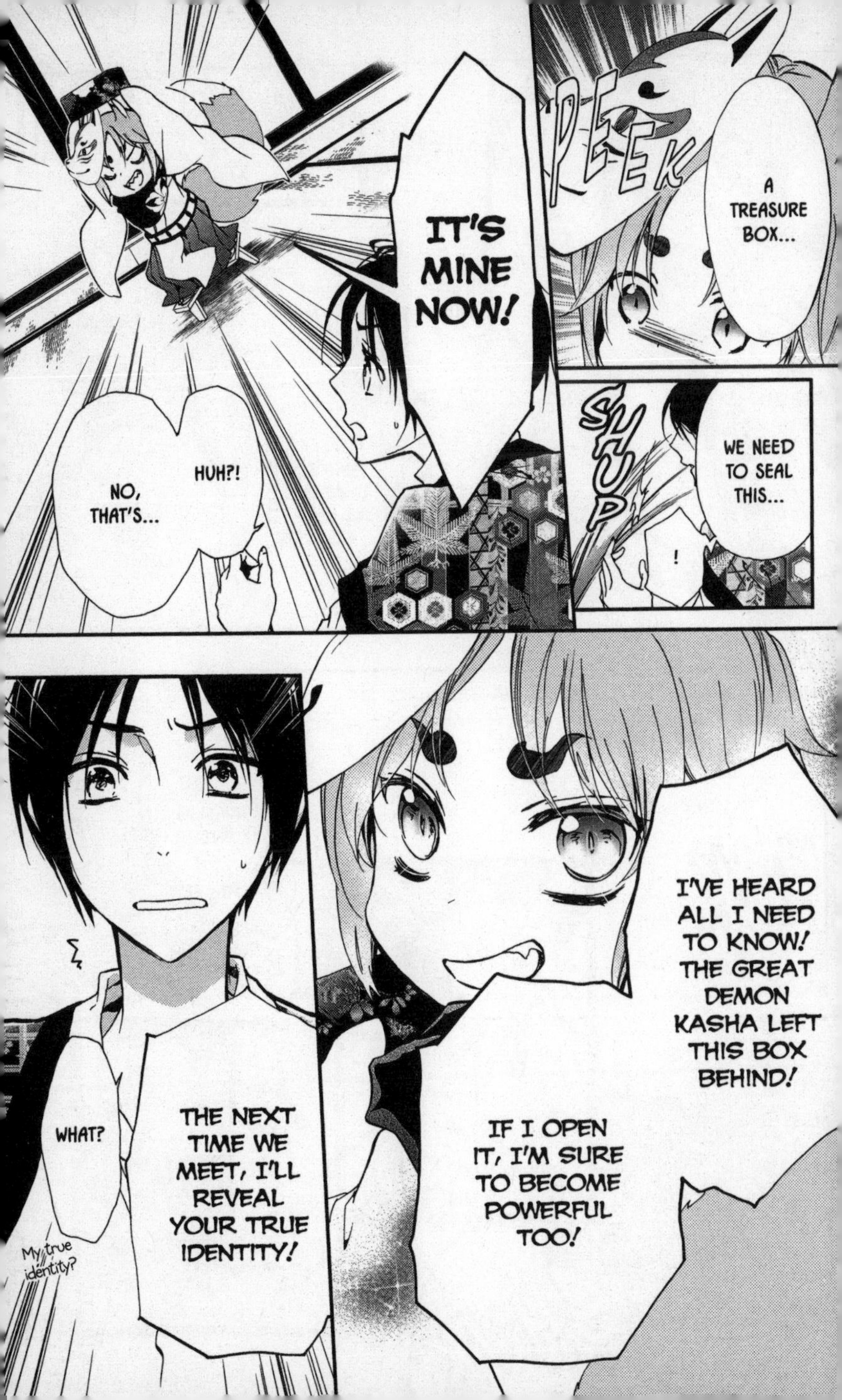
PEEK
A TREASURE BOX...
SHUP
WE NEED TO SEAL THIS...
!
IT'S MINE NOW!
HUH?!
NO, THAT'S...
I'VE HEARD ALL I NEED TO KNOW! THE GREAT DEMON KASHA LEFT THIS BOX BEHIND!
IF I OPEN IT, I'M SURE TO BECOME POWERFUL TOO!
THE NEXT TIME WE MEET, I'LL REVEAL YOUR TRUE IDENTITY!
WHAT?
My true identity?

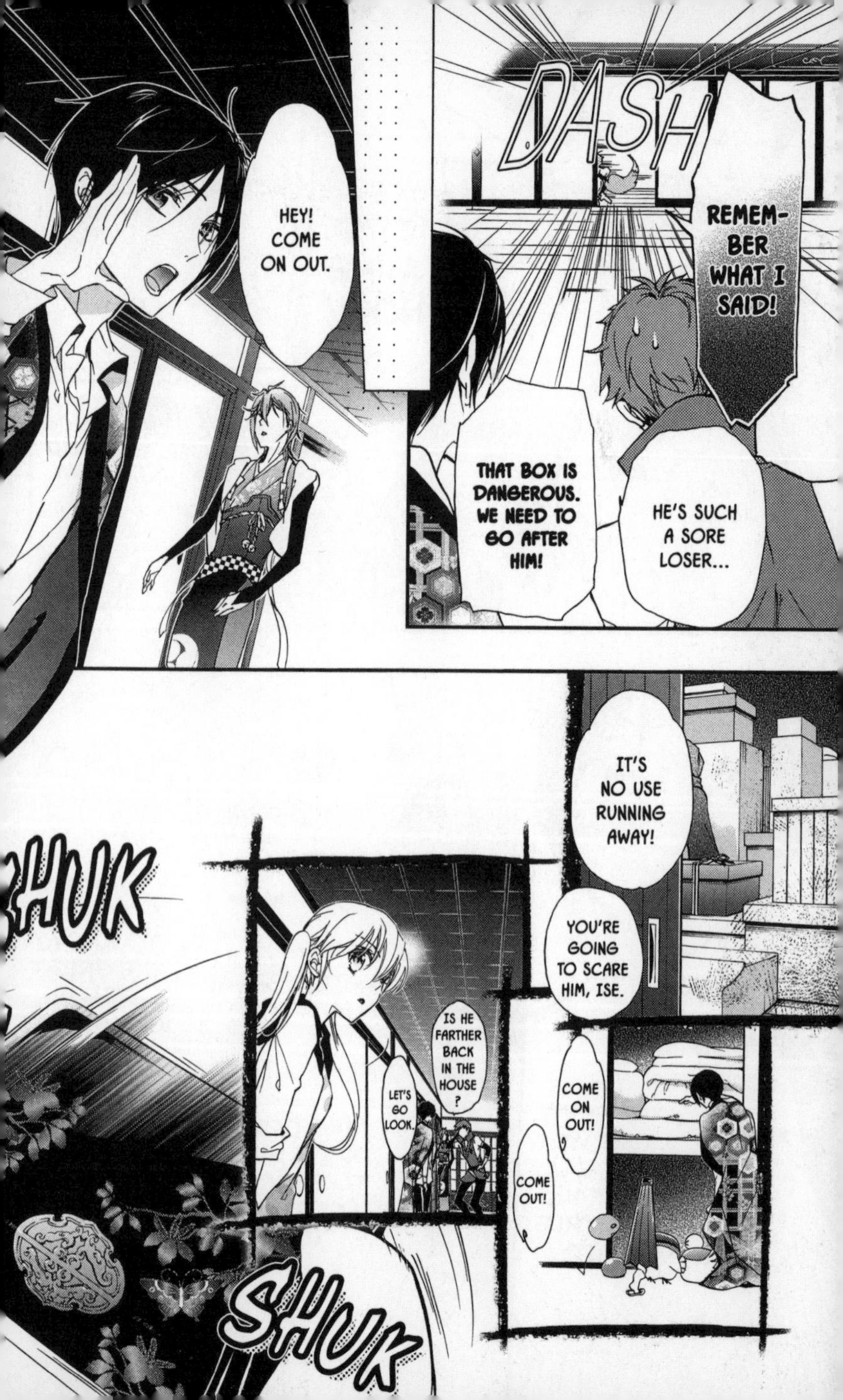
DASH
REMEMBER WHAT I SAID!
HE'S SUCH A SORE LOSER...
THAT BOX IS DANGEROUS. WE NEED TO GO AFTER HIM!
HEY! COME ON OUT.
IT'S NO USE RUNNING AWAY!
YOU'RE GOING TO SCARE HIM, ISE.
COME ON OUT!
COME OUT!
IS HE FARTHER BACK IN THE HOUSE?
LET'S GO LOOK.
SHUK
SHUK

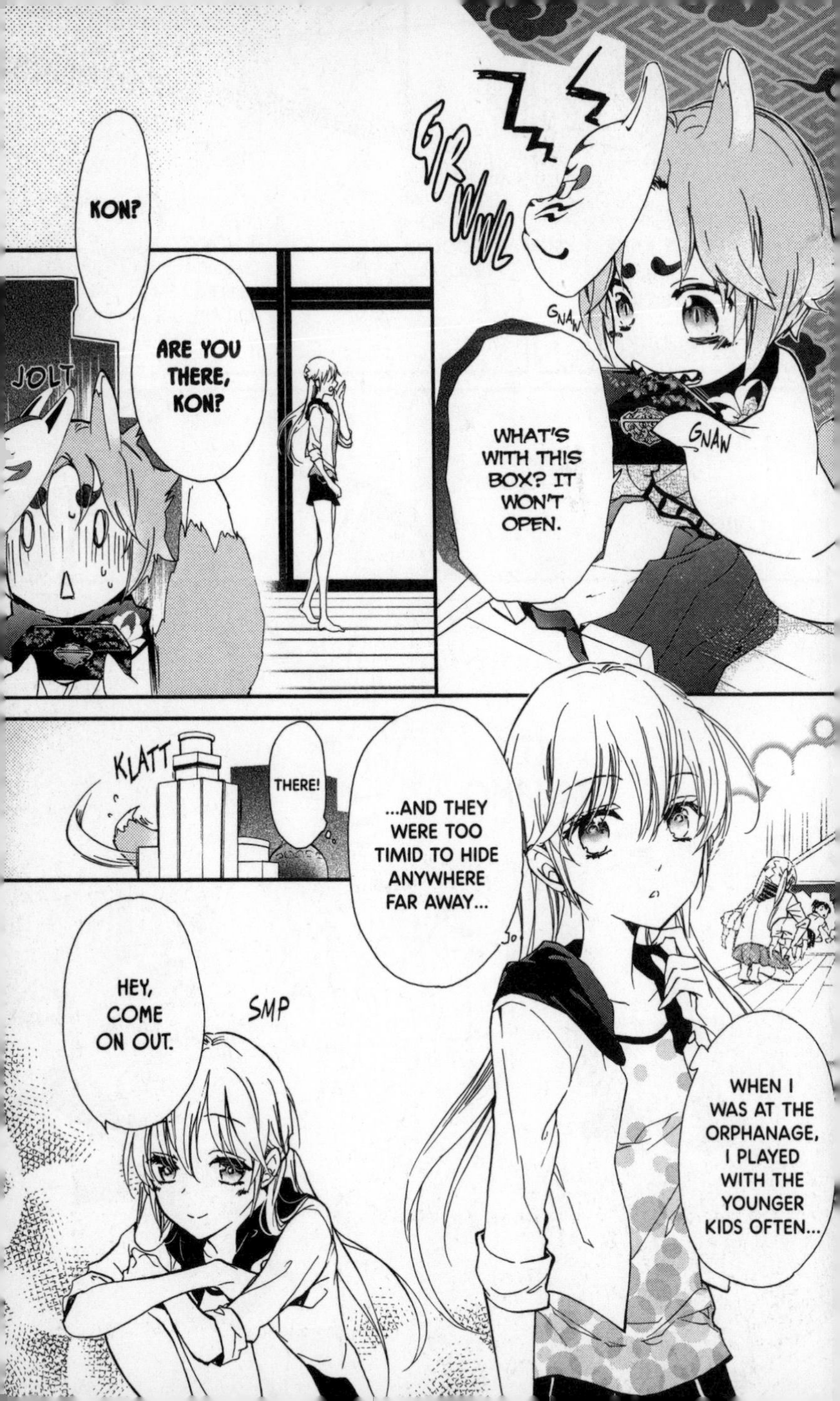
GRWWL
GNAW
GNAW
WHAT'S WITH THIS BOX? IT WON'T OPEN.
KON?
ARE YOU THERE, KON?
JOLT
WHEN I WAS AT THE ORPHANAGE, I PLAYED WITH THE YOUNGER KIDS OFTEN...
...AND THEY WERE TOO TIMID TO HIDE ANYWHERE FAR AWAY...
THERE!
KLATT
HEY, COME ON OUT.
SMP

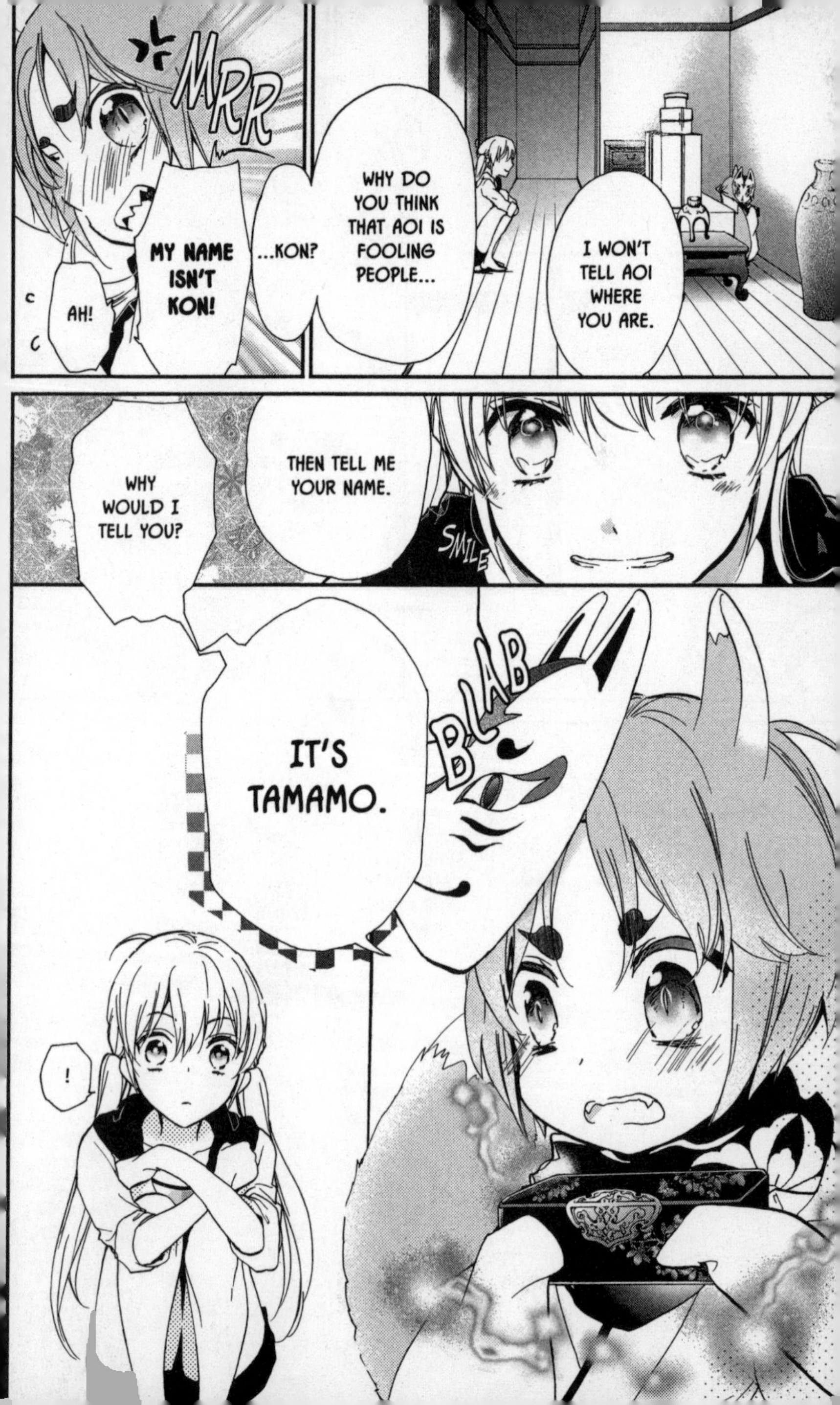

I WON'T TELL AOI WHERE YOU ARE.
WHY DO YOU THINK THAT AOI IS FOOLING PEOPLE...
...KON?
MRR
MY NAME ISN'T KON!
AH!
THEN TELL ME YOUR NAME.
SMILE
WHY WOULD I TELL YOU?
BLAB
IT'S TAMAMO.
!

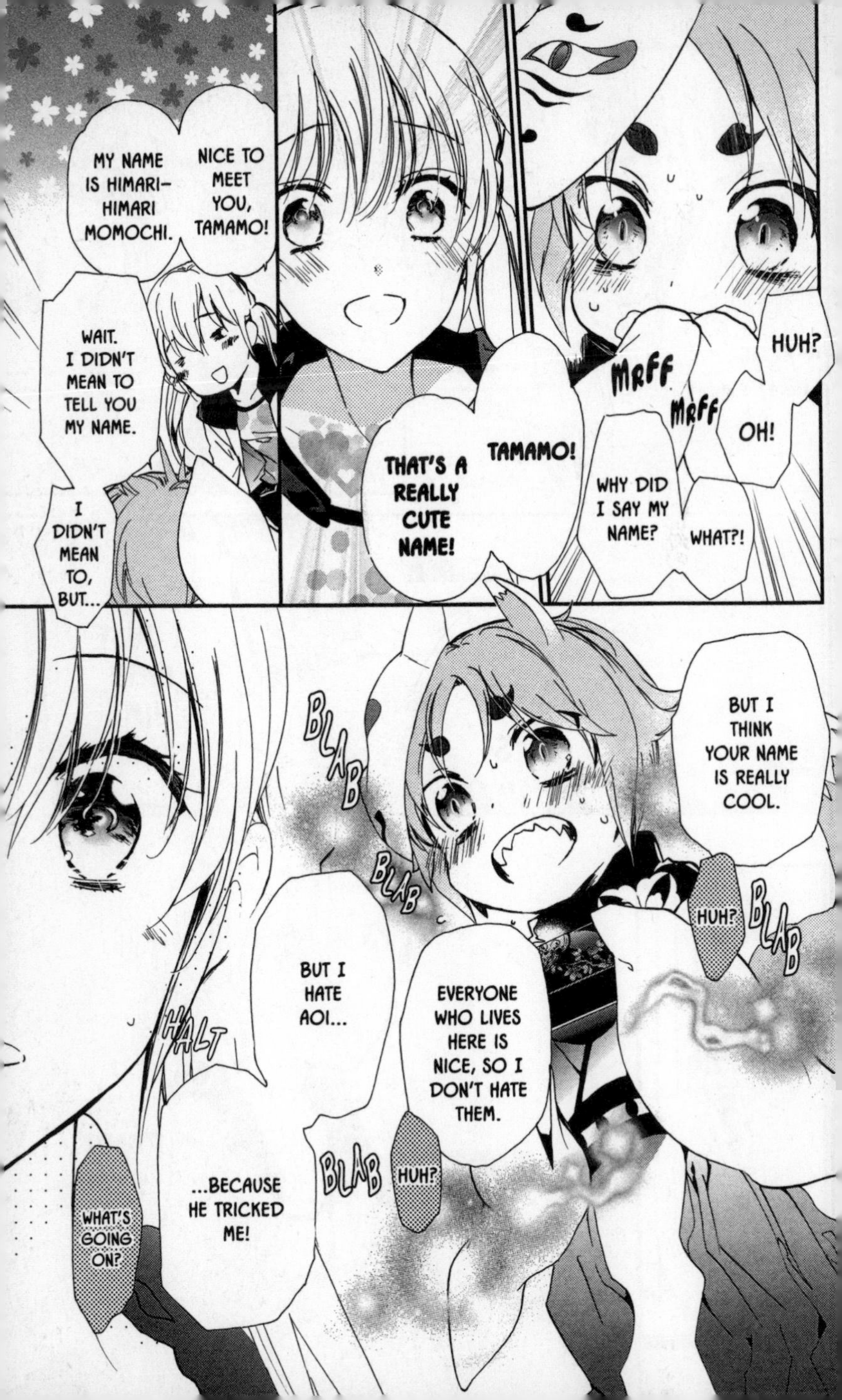
HUH?
OH!
MRFF
MRFF
WHAT?!
WHY DID I SAY MY NAME?
TAMAMO!
THAT'S A REALLY CUTE NAME!
NICE TO MEET YOU, TAMAMO!
MY NAME IS HIMARI— HIMARI MOMOCHI.
WAIT. I DIDN'T MEAN TO TELL YOU MY NAME.
I DIDN'T MEAN TO, BUT...
BUT I THINK YOUR NAME IS REALLY COOL.
BLAB
HUH?
BLAB
BLAB
EVERYONE WHO LIVES HERE IS NICE, SO I DON'T HATE THEM.
BUT I HATE AOI...
HUH?
BLAB
...BECAUSE HE TRICKED ME!
HALT
WHAT'S GOING ON?

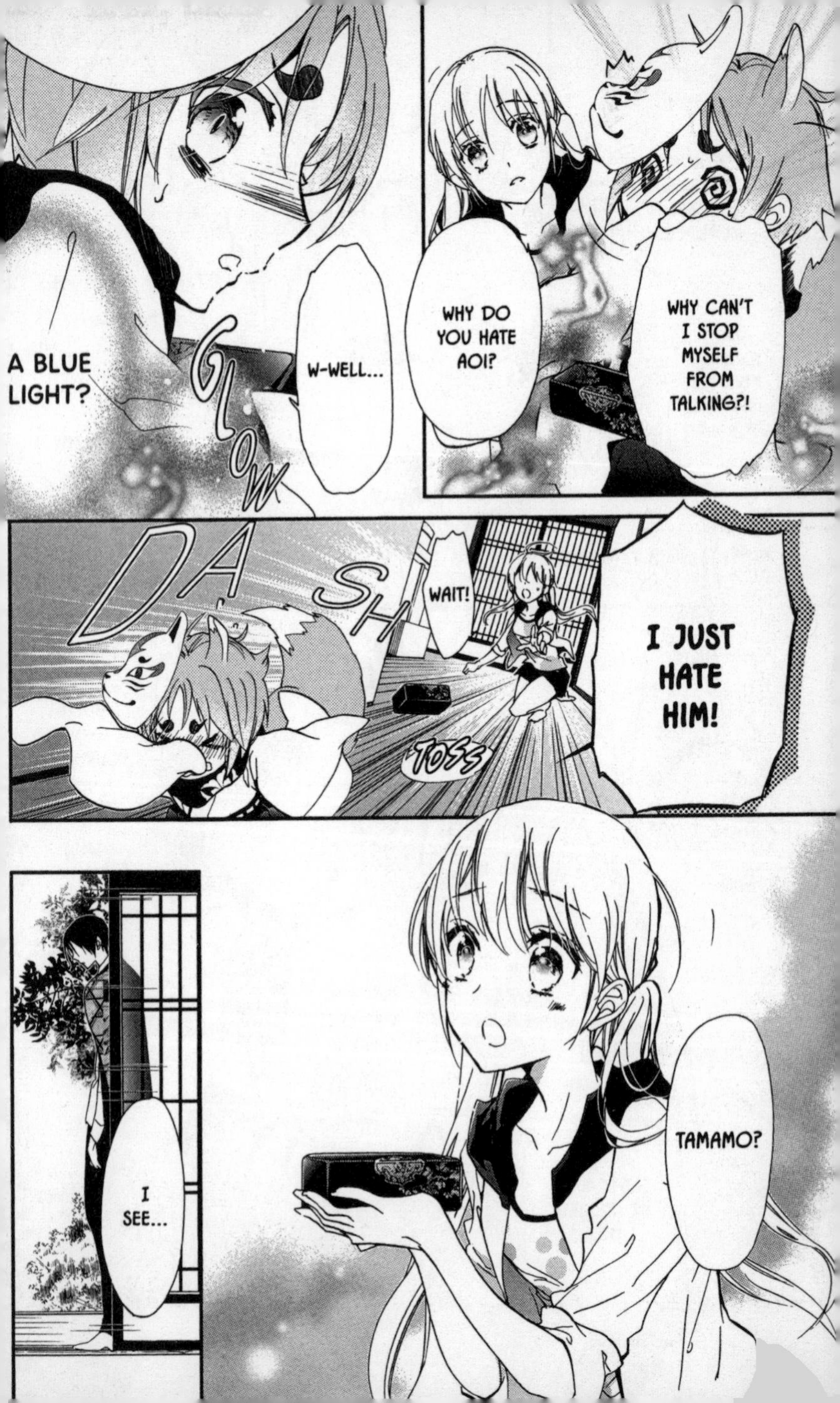
WHY CAN'T I STOP MYSELF FROM TALKING?!
WHY DO YOU HATE AOI?
W-WELL...
GLOW
A BLUE LIGHT?
I JUST HATE HIM!
WAIT!
DASH
TOSS
TAMAMO?
I SEE...

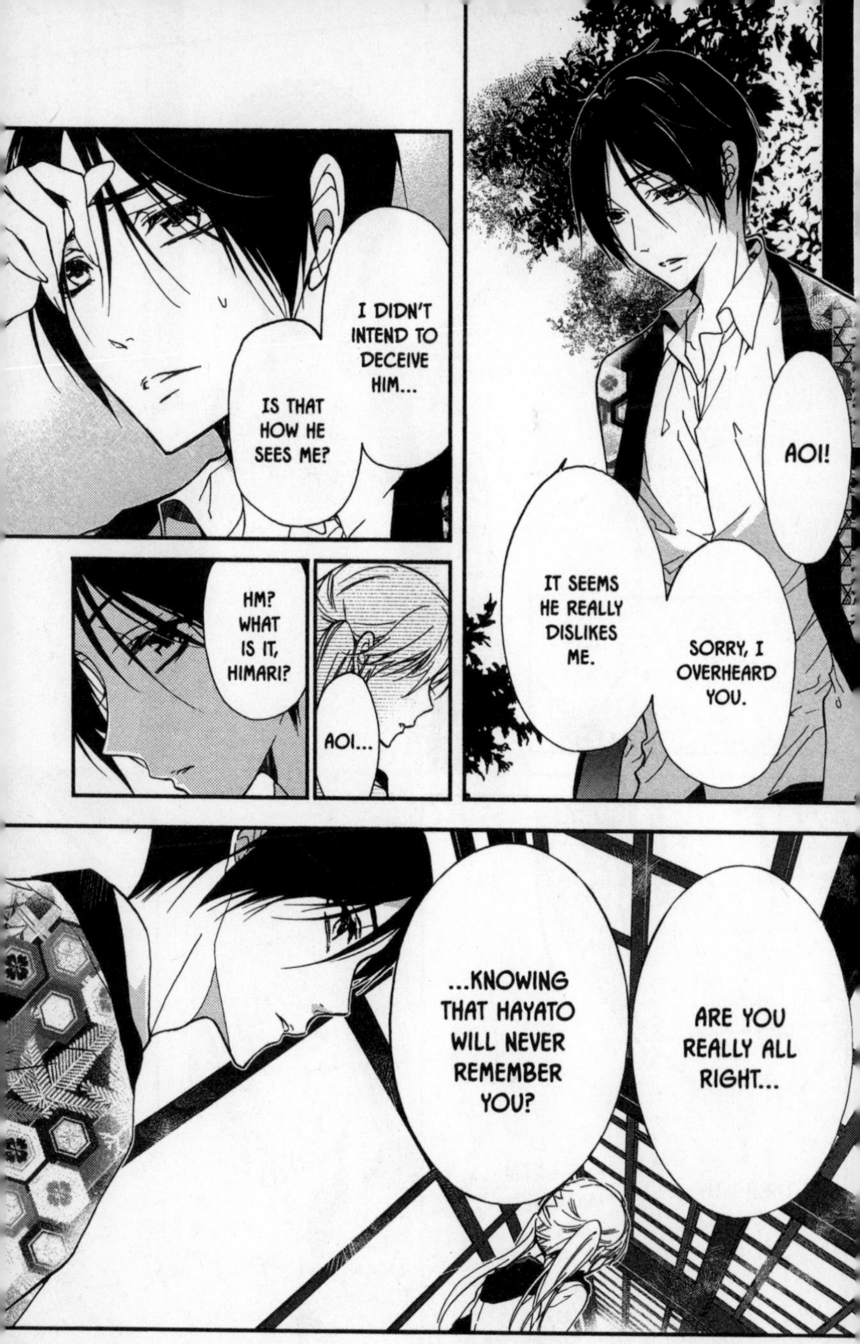
AOI!
SORRY, I OVERHEARD YOU.
IT SEEMS HE REALLY DISLIKES ME.
I DIDN'T INTEND TO DECEIVE HIM...
IS THAT HOW HE SEES ME?
AOI...
HM? WHAT IS IT, HIMARI?
ARE YOU REALLY ALL RIGHT...
...KNOWING THAT HAYATO WILL NEVER REMEMBER YOU?

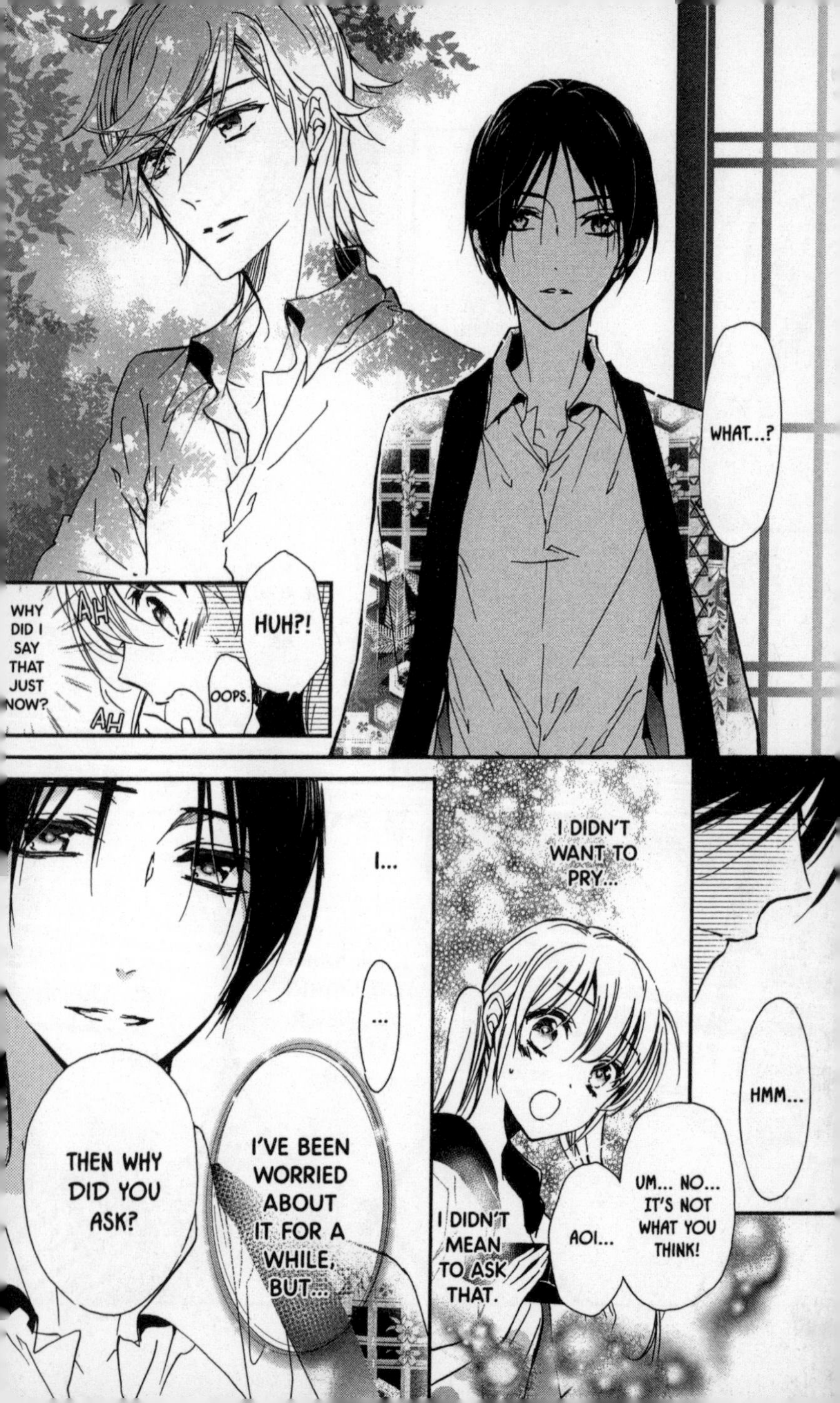
WHAT...?
HUH?!
AH
AH
OOPS.
WHY DID I SAY THAT JUST NOW?
HMM...
I DIDN'T WANT TO PRY...
UM... NO... IT'S NOT WHAT YOU THINK!
AOI...
I DIDN'T MEAN TO ASK THAT.
I...
...
I'VE BEEN WORRIED ABOUT IT FOR A WHILE, BUT...
THEN WHY DID YOU ASK?

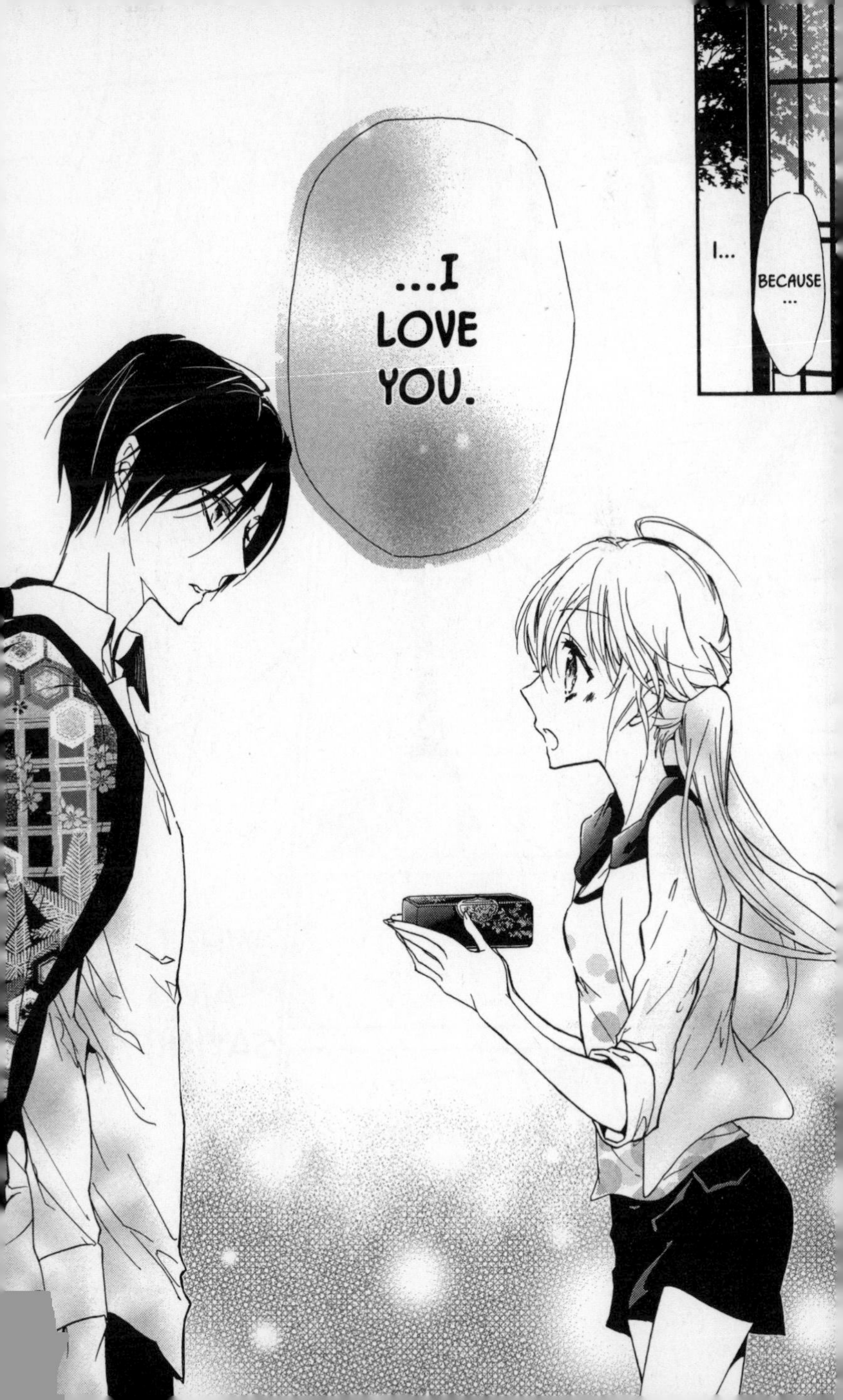
BECAUSE ...
I...
...I LOVE YOU.

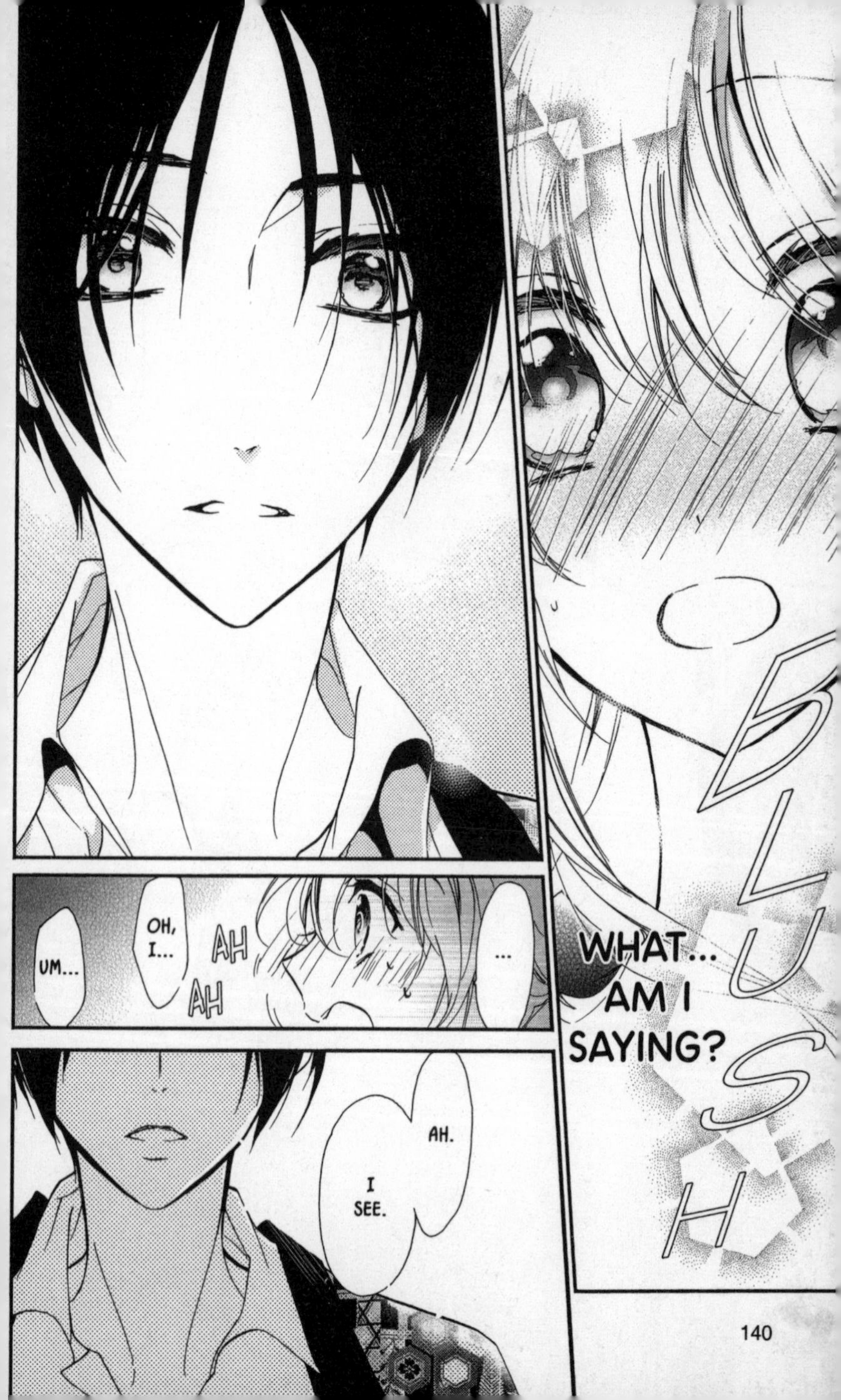
BLUSH
WHAT... AM I SAYING?
...
AH AH
OH, I...
UM...
AH.
I SEE.

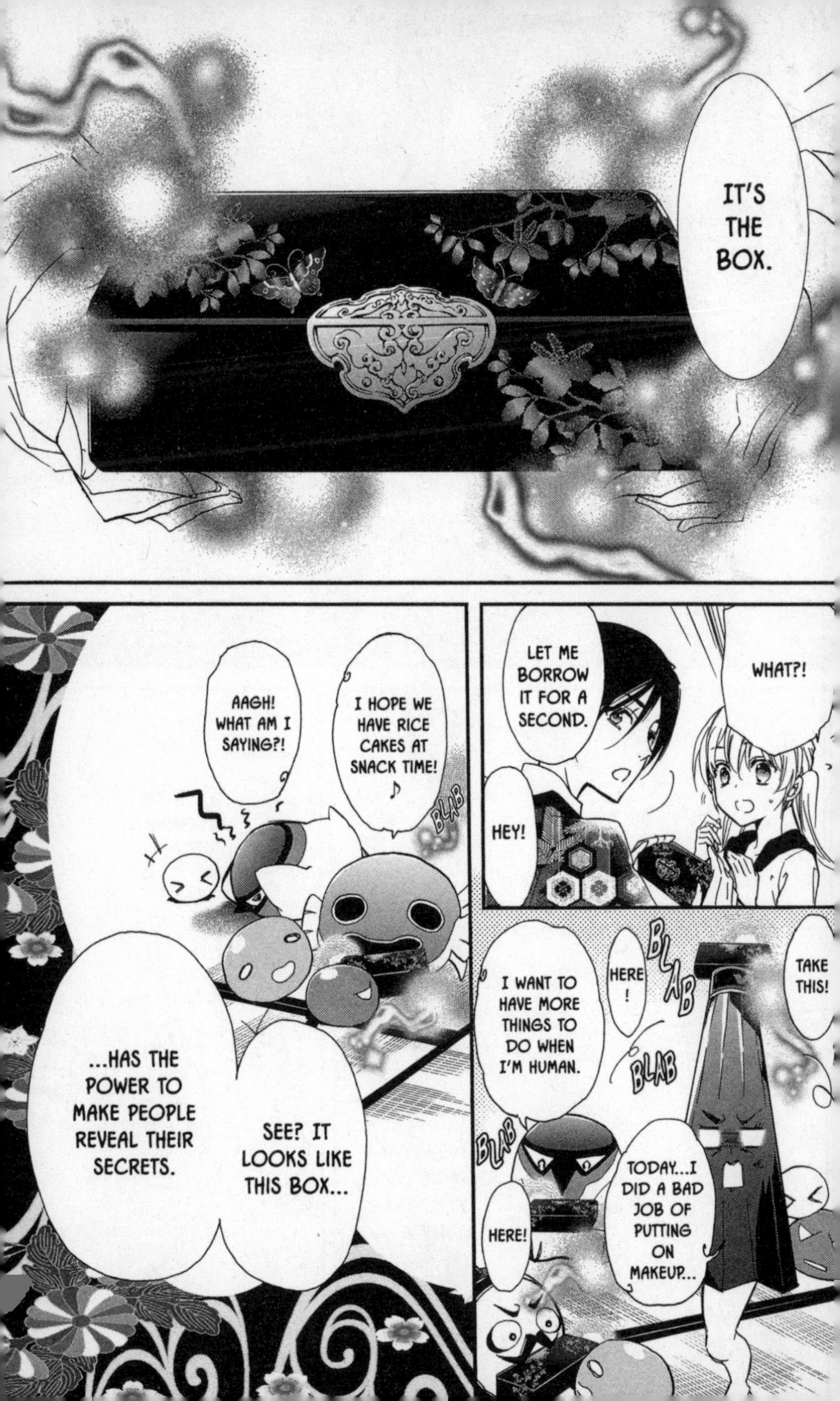
IT'S THE BOX.
WHAT?!
LET ME BORROW IT FOR A SECOND.
HEY!
TAKE THIS!
HERE!
BLAB
I WANT TO HAVE MORE THINGS TO DO WHEN I'M HUMAN.
BLAB
BLAB
TODAY...I DID A BAD JOB OF PUTTING ON MAKEUP...
HERE!
I HOPE WE HAVE RICE CAKES AT SNACK TIME! ♪
BLAB
AAGH! WHAT AM I SAYING?!
SEE? IT LOOKS LIKE THIS BOX...
...HAS THE POWER TO MAKE PEOPLE REVEAL THEIR SECRETS.

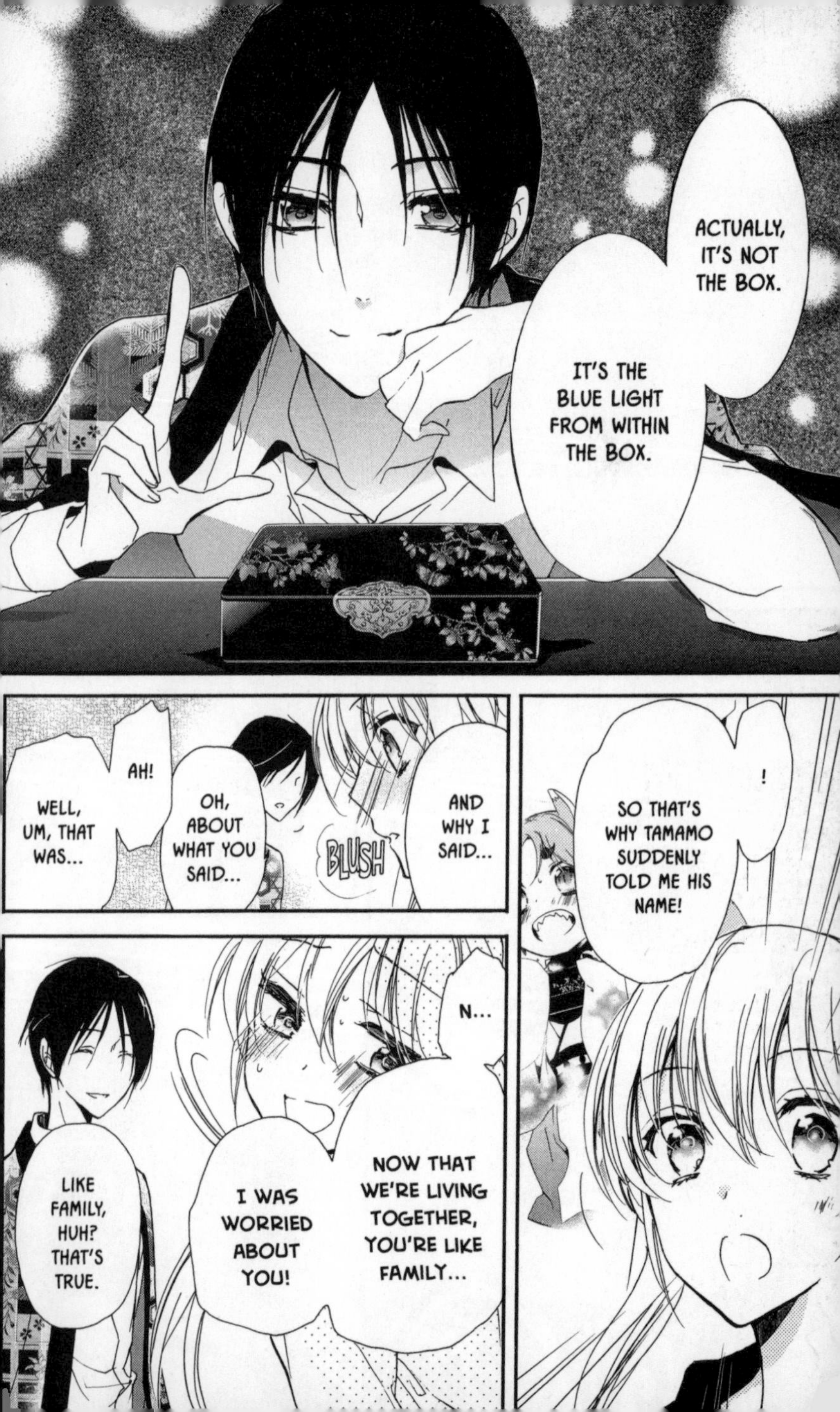
ACTUALLY, IT'S NOT THE BOX.
IT'S THE BLUE LIGHT FROM WITHIN THE BOX.
!
SO THAT'S WHY TAMAMO SUDDENLY TOLD ME HIS NAME!
AND WHY I SAID...
BLUSH
OH, ABOUT WHAT YOU SAID...
AH!
WELL, UM, THAT WAS...
N...
NOW THAT WE'RE LIVING TOGETHER, YOU'RE LIKE FAMILY...
I WAS WORRIED ABOUT YOU!
LIKE FAMILY, HUH? THAT'S TRUE.

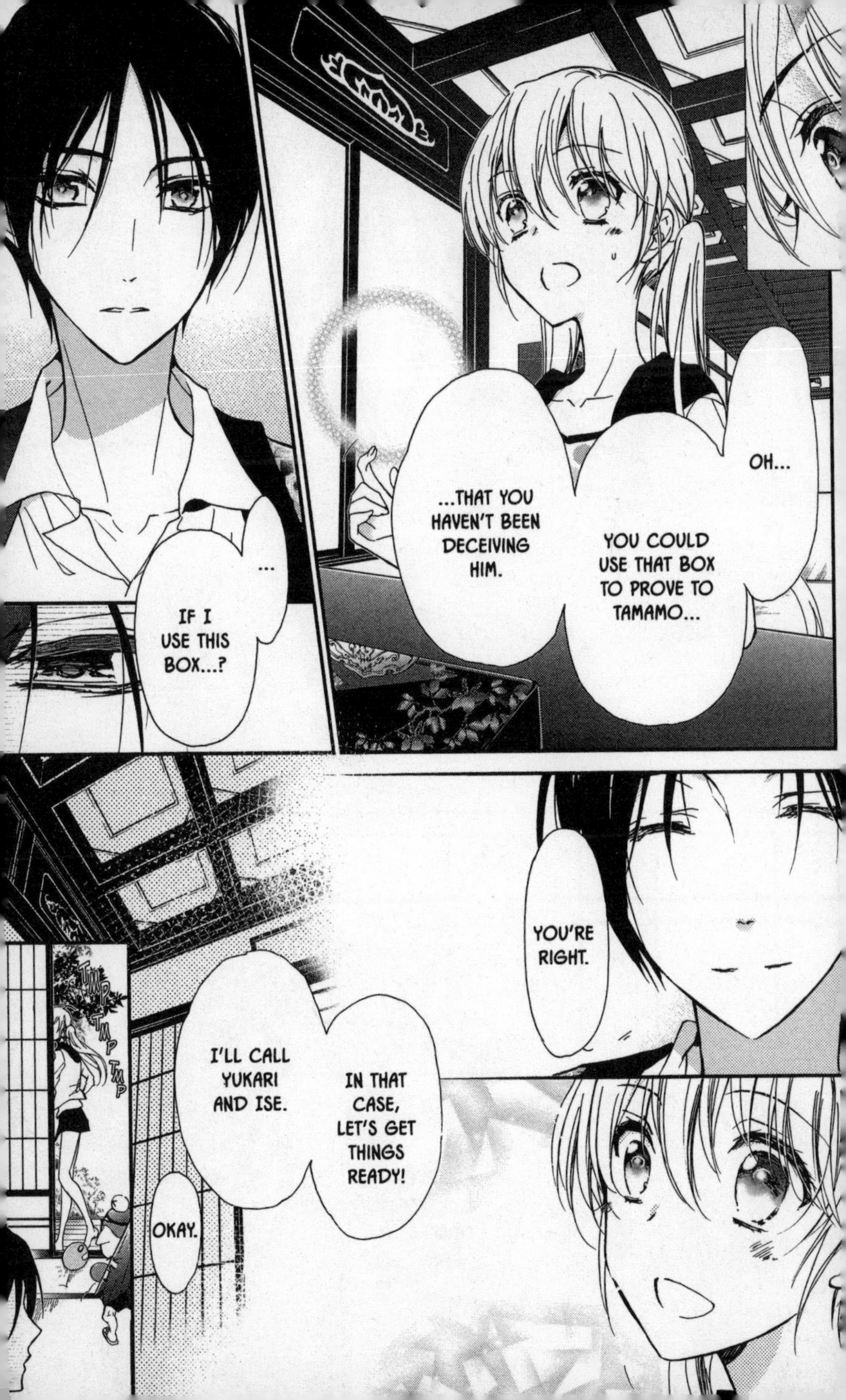
OH...
YOU COULD USE THAT BOX TO PROVE TO TAMAMO...
...THAT YOU HAVEN'T BEEN DECEIVING HIM.
...
IF I USE THIS BOX...?
YOU'RE RIGHT.
IN THAT CASE, LET'S GET THINGS READY!
I'LL CALL YUKARI AND ISE.
OKAY.
TMP TMP TMP

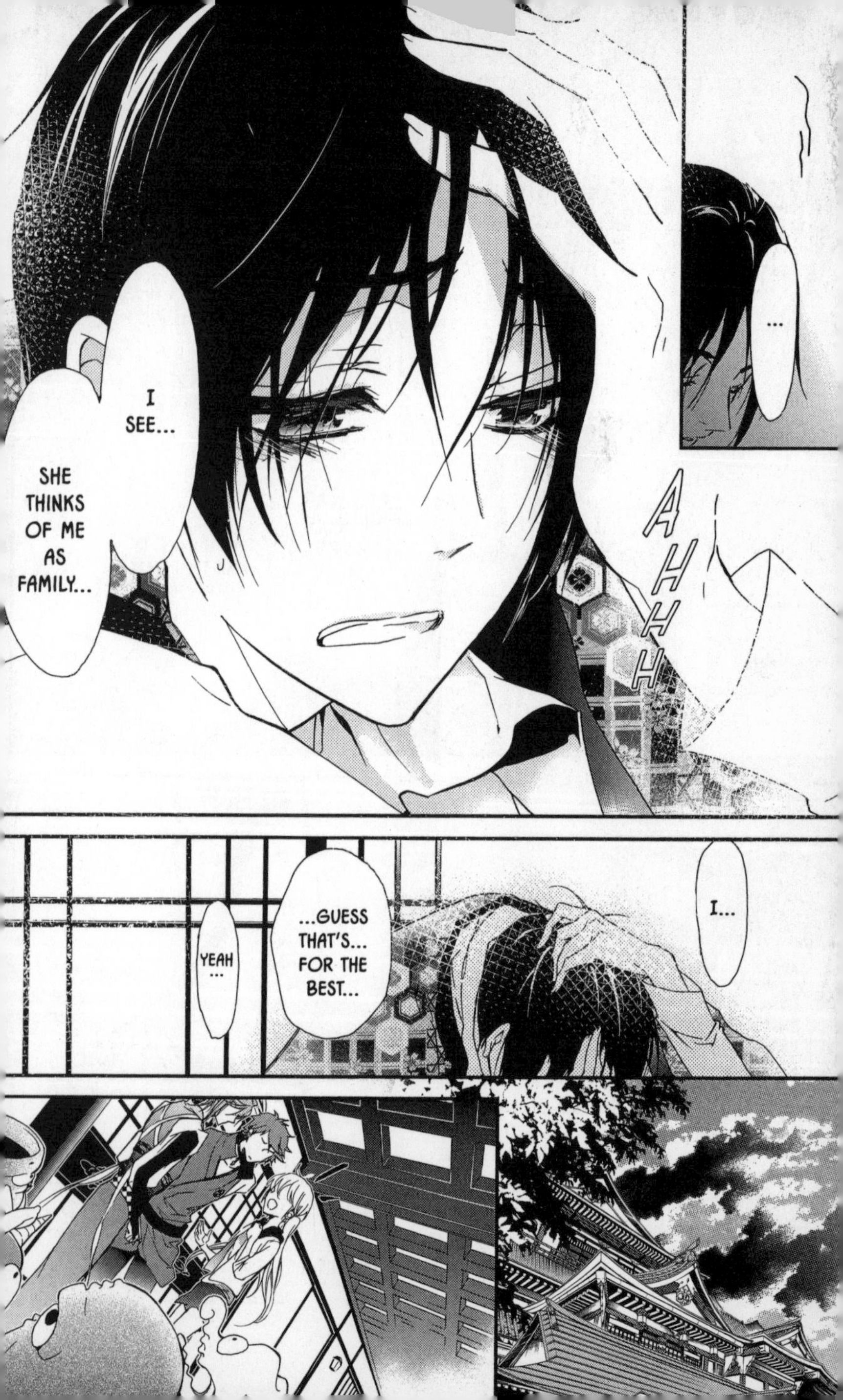
...
I SEE...
SHE THINKS OF ME AS FAMILY...
AHHHH
I...
...GUESS THAT'S... FOR THE BEST...
YEAH...

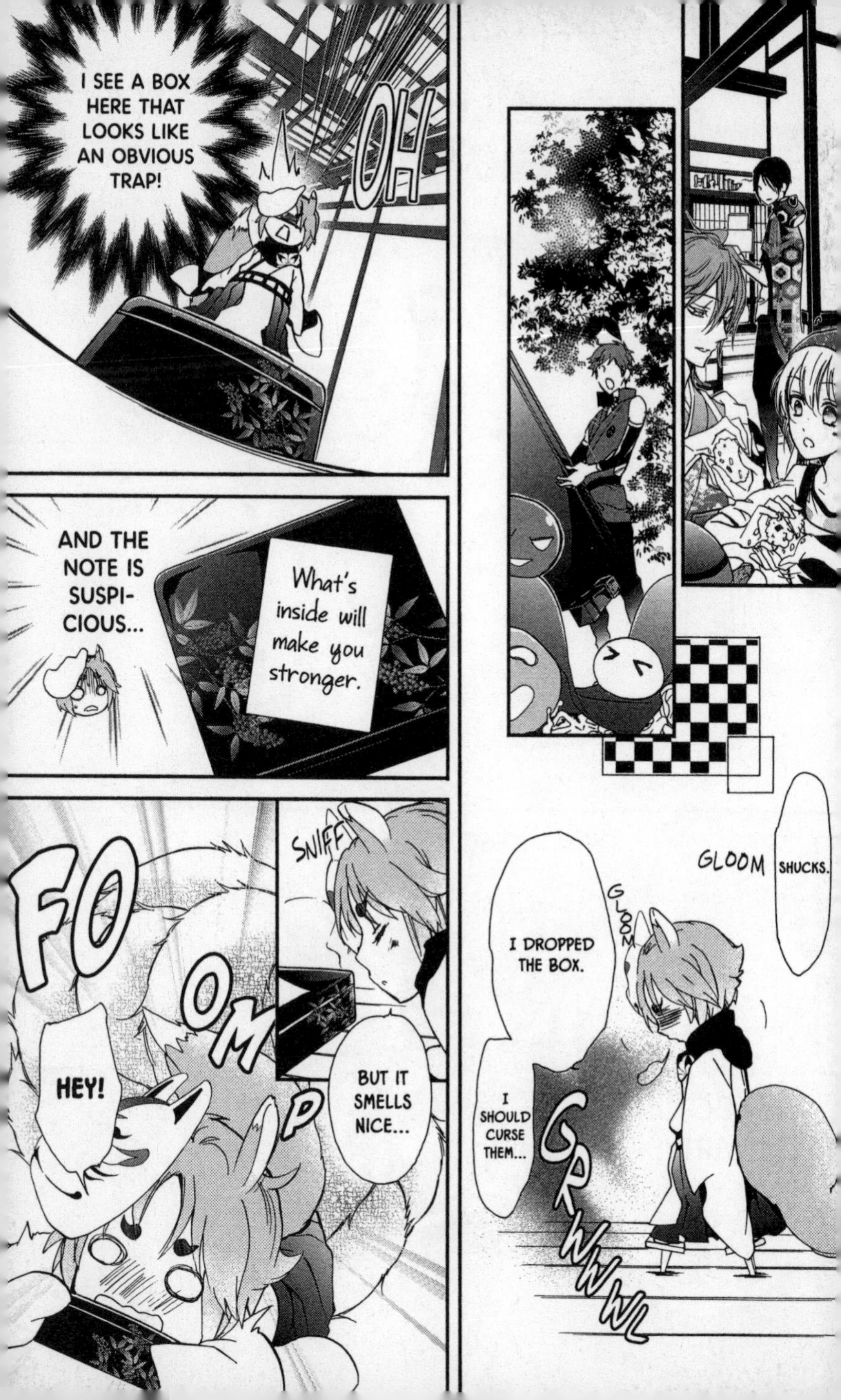
SHUCKS.
GLOOM
GLOOM
I DROPPED THE BOX.
I SHOULD CURSE THEM...
GRWWWL
OH
I SEE A BOX HERE THAT LOOKS LIKE AN OBVIOUS TRAP!
What's inside will make you stronger.
AND THE NOTE IS SUSPICIOUS...
SNIFF
BUT IT SMELLS NICE...
FOOMP
HEY!

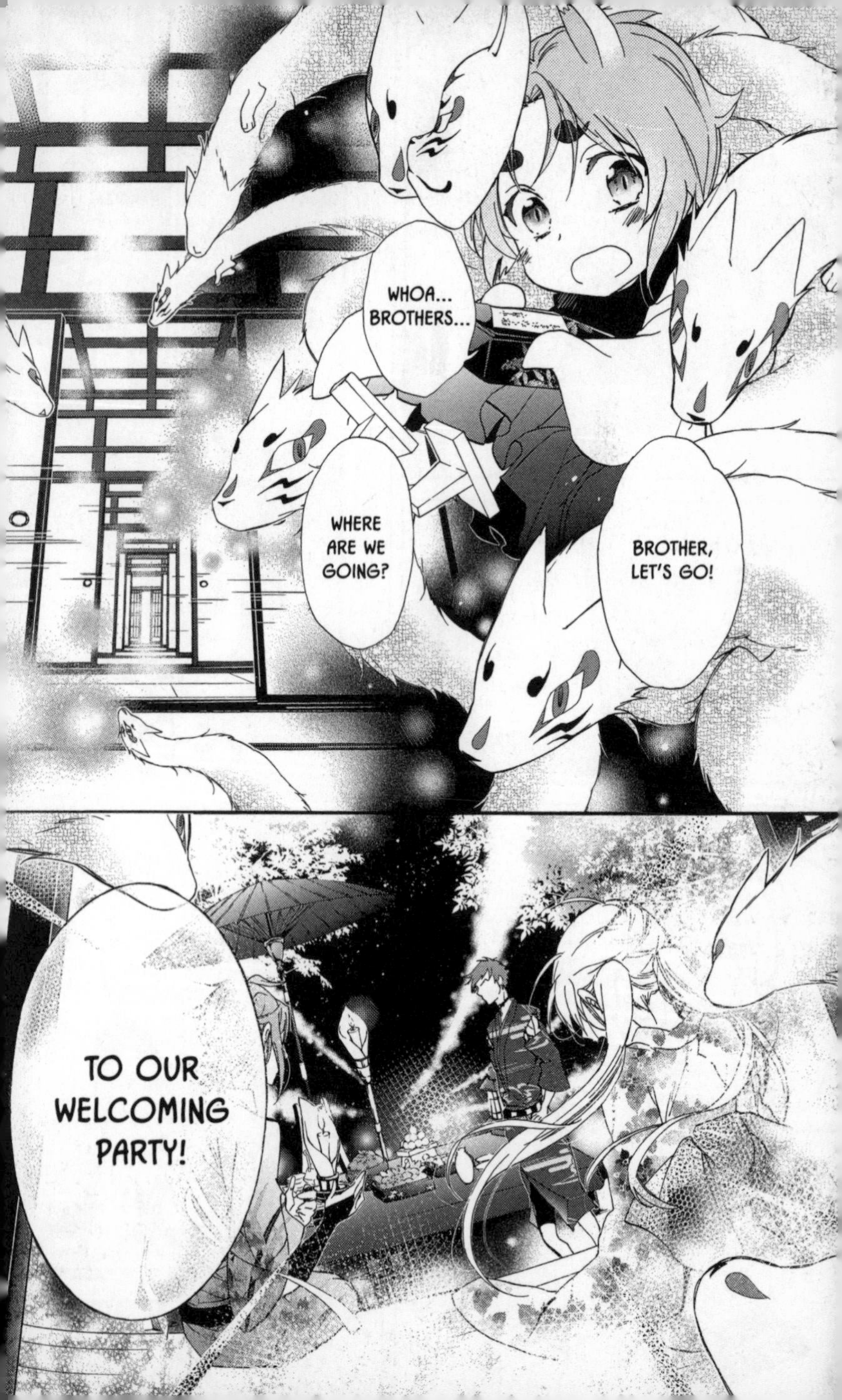
WHOA... BROTHERS...
BROTHER, LET'S GO!
WHERE ARE WE GOING?
TO OUR WELCOMING PARTY!

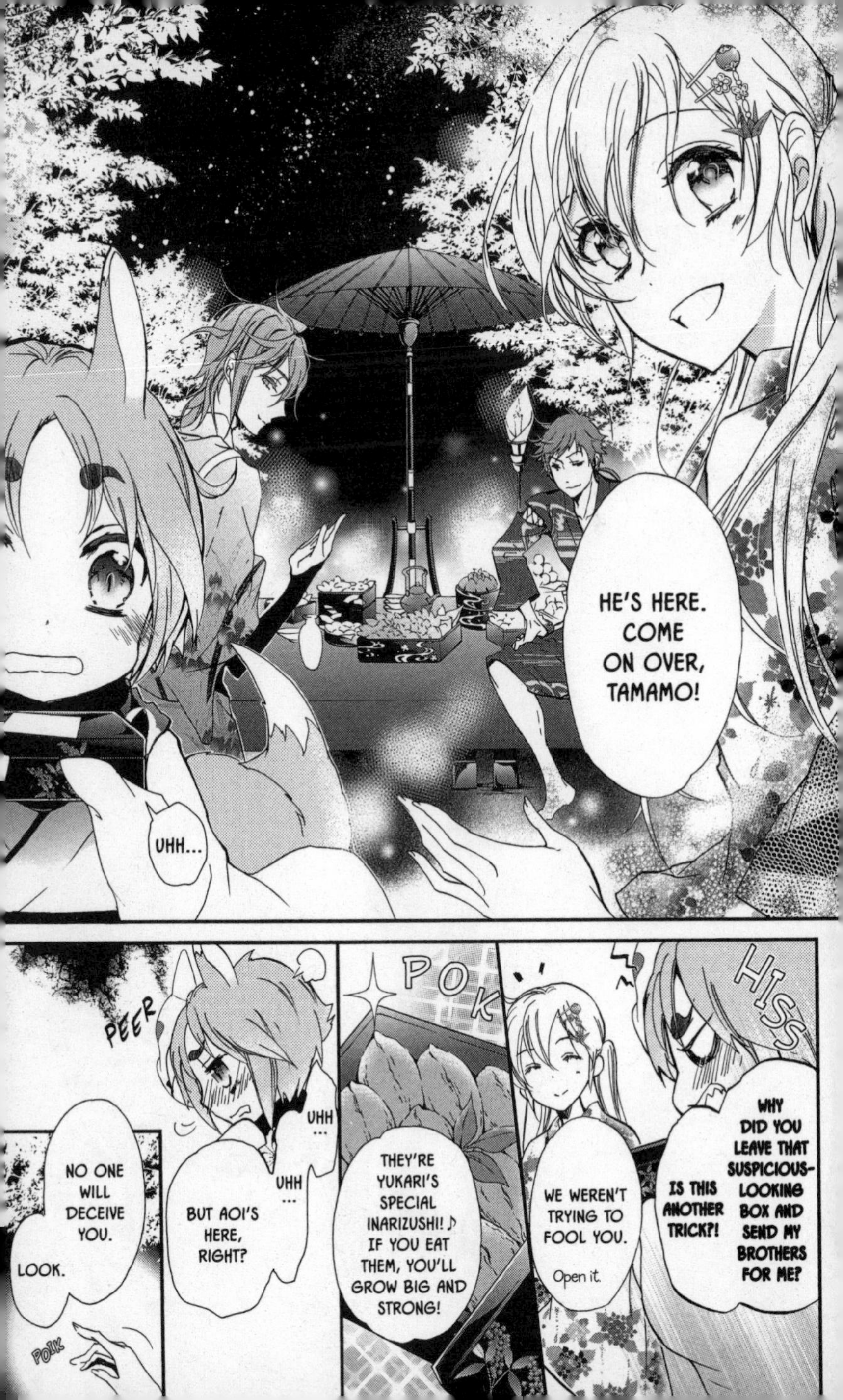
HE'S HERE. COME ON OVER, TAMAMO!
UHH...
HISS
WHY DID YOU LEAVE THAT SUSPICIOUS-LOOKING BOX AND SEND MY BROTHERS FOR ME?
IS THIS ANOTHER TRICK?!
WE WEREN'T TRYING TO FOOL YOU.
Open it.
POK
THEY'RE YUKARI'S SPECIAL INARIZUSHI!♪ IF YOU EAT THEM, YOU'LL GROW BIG AND STRONG!
PEER
UHH...
UHH...
BUT AOI'S HERE, RIGHT?
NO ONE WILL DECEIVE YOU.
LOOK.
POIK

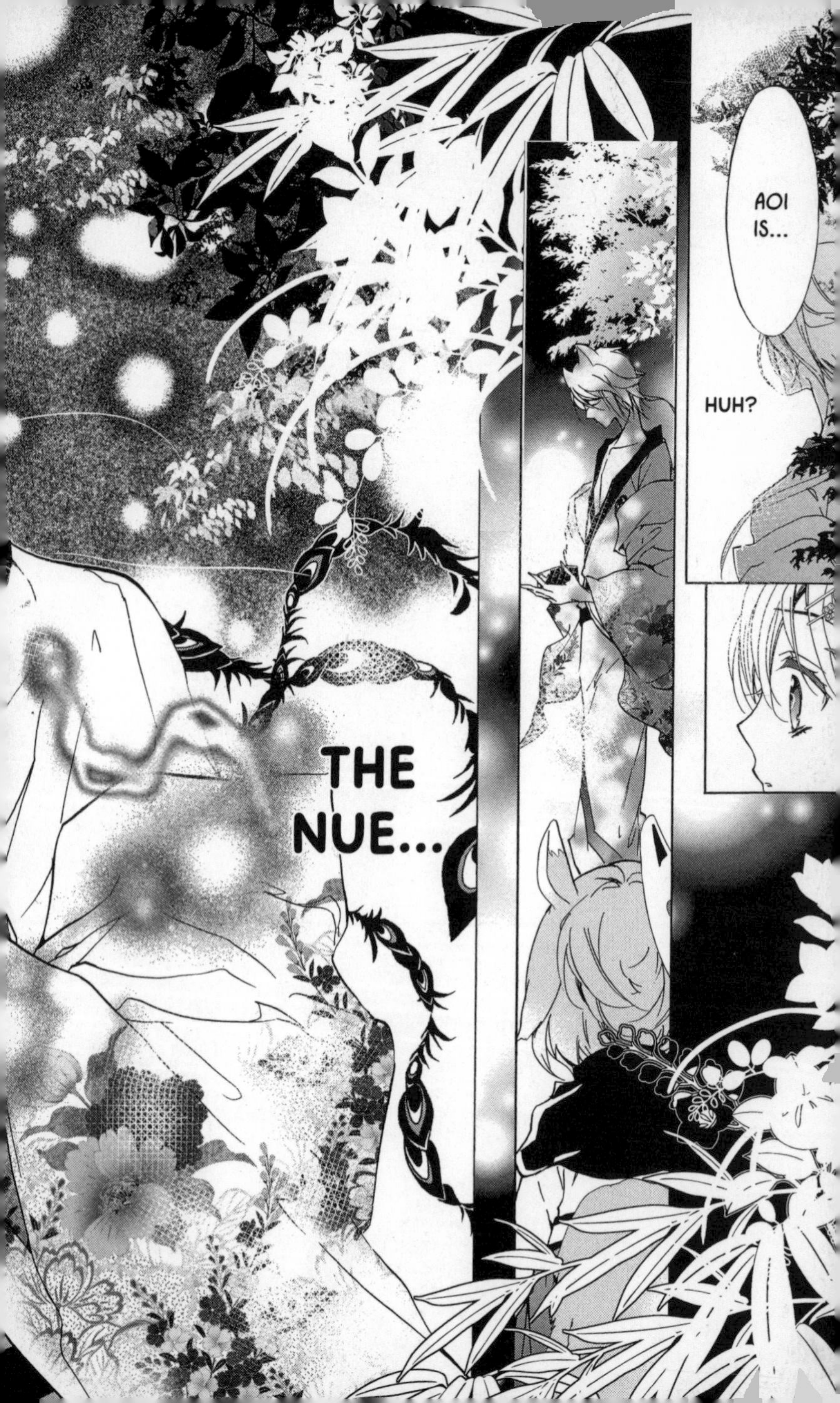
AOI IS...
HUH?
THE NUE...

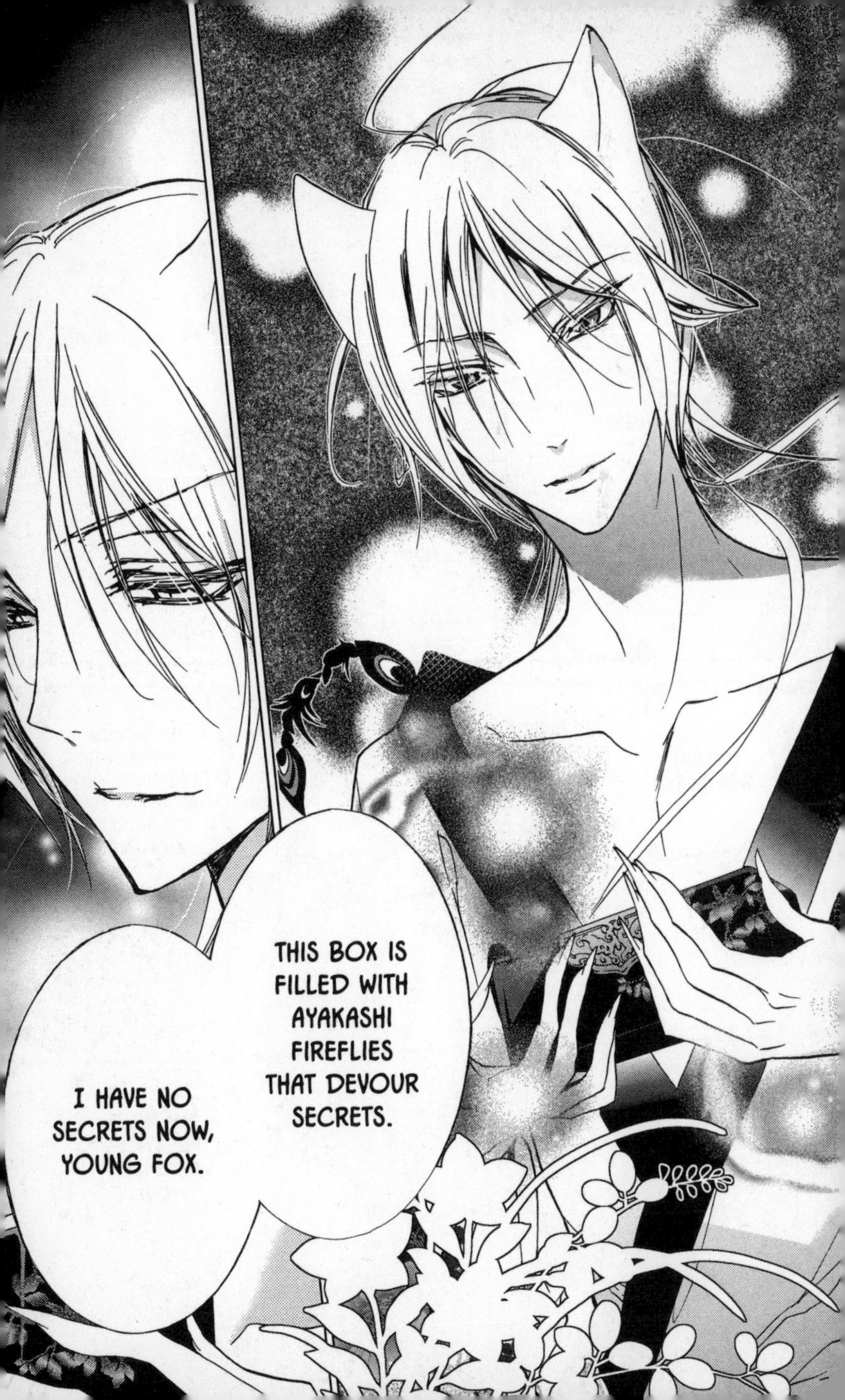
THIS BOX IS FILLED WITH AYAKASHI FIREFLIES THAT DEVOUR SECRETS.
I HAVE NO SECRETS NOW, YOUNG FOX.

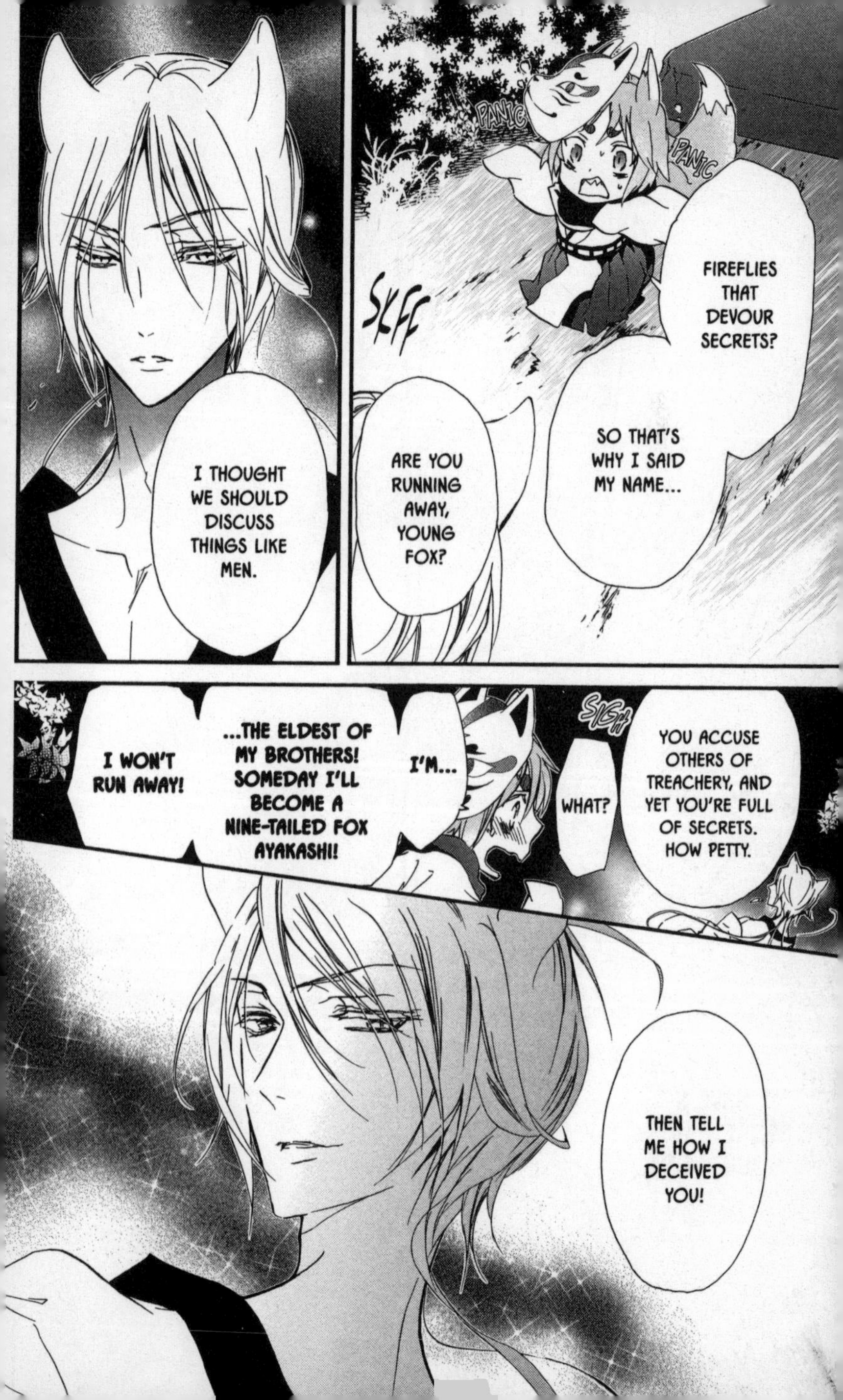
PANIC
PANIC
FIREFLIES THAT DEVOUR SECRETS?
SO THAT'S WHY I SAID MY NAME...
SKFF
ARE YOU RUNNING AWAY, YOUNG FOX?
I THOUGHT WE SHOULD DISCUSS THINGS LIKE MEN.
SIGH
YOU ACCUSE OTHERS OF TREACHERY, AND YET YOU'RE FULL OF SECRETS. HOW PETTY.
WHAT?
I'M...
...THE ELDEST OF MY BROTHERS! SOMEDAY I'LL BECOME A NINE-TAILED FOX AYAKASHI!
I WON'T RUN AWAY!
THEN TELL ME HOW I DECEIVED YOU!

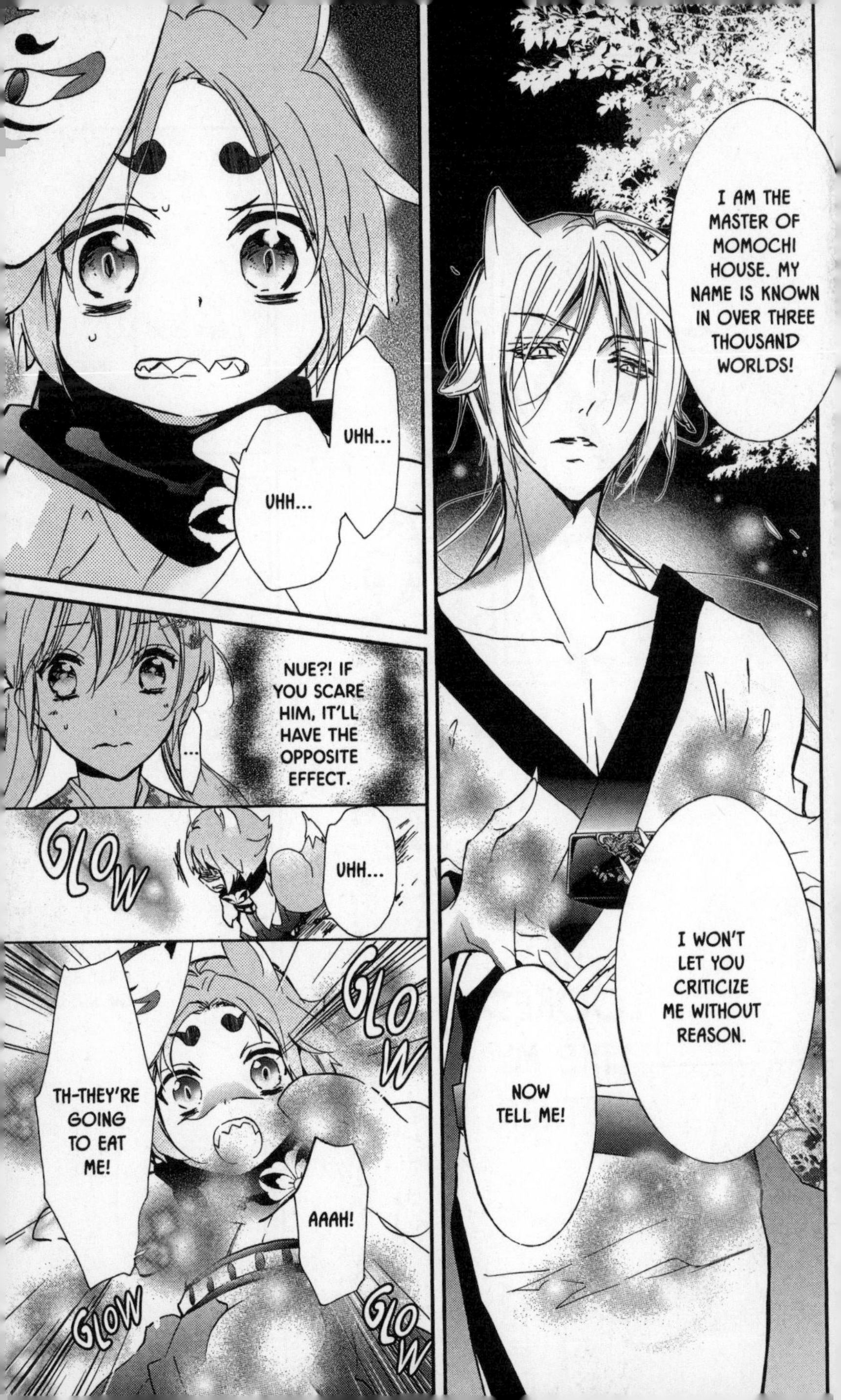
I AM THE MASTER OF MOMOCHI HOUSE. MY NAME IS KNOWN IN OVER THREE THOUSAND WORLDS!
I WON'T LET YOU CRITICIZE ME WITHOUT REASON.
NOW TELL ME!
UHH...
UHH...
NUE?! IF YOU SCARE HIM, IT'LL HAVE THE OPPOSITE EFFECT.
...
UHH...
GLOW
GLOW
GLOW
TH-THEY'RE GOING TO EAT ME!
AAAH!
GLOW
GLOW

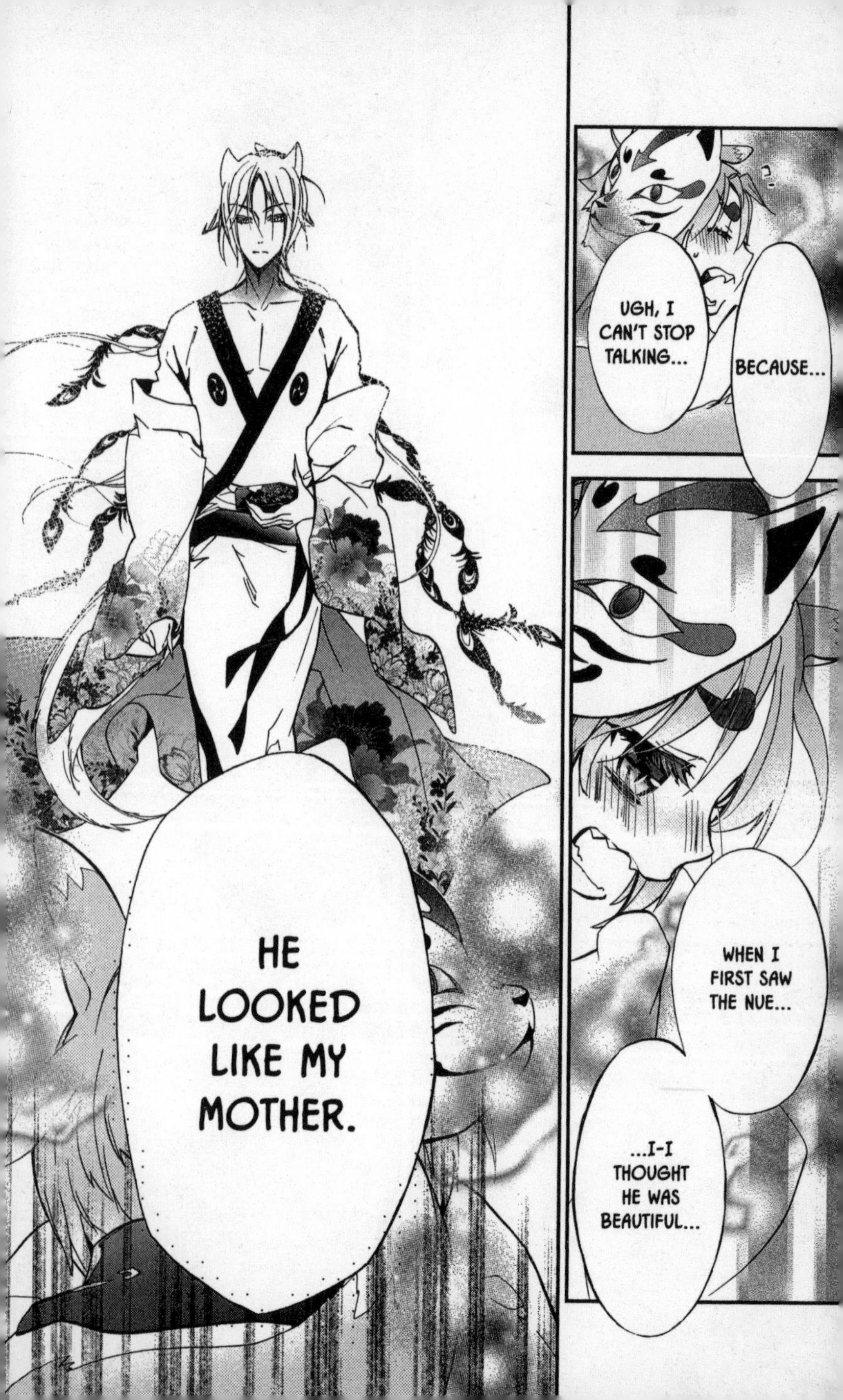
UGH, I CAN'T STOP TALKING...
BECAUSE...
WHEN I FIRST SAW THE NUE...
...I-I THOUGHT HE WAS BEAUTIFUL...
HE LOOKED LIKE MY MOTHER.

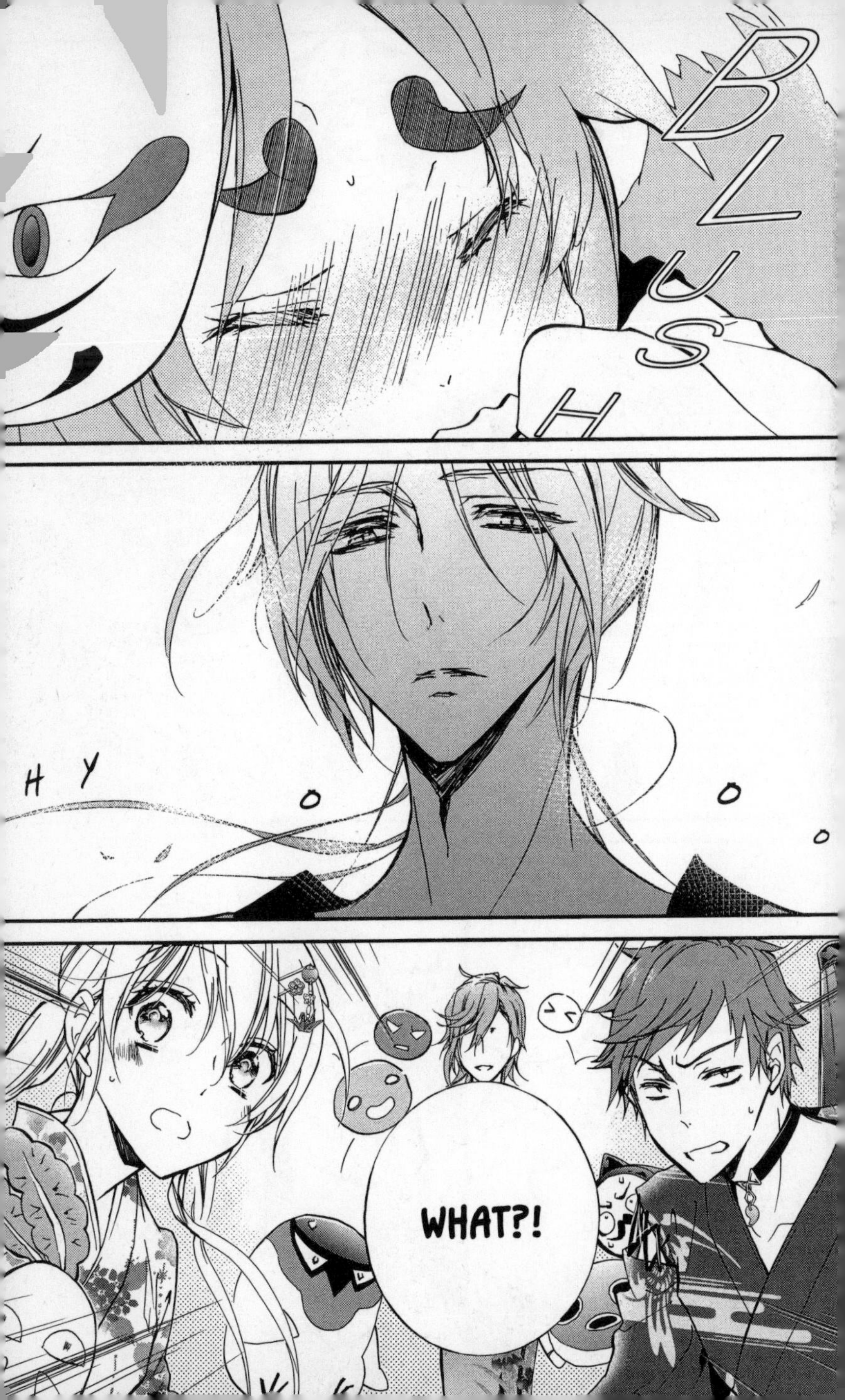
BLUSH
HYOOO
WHAT?!

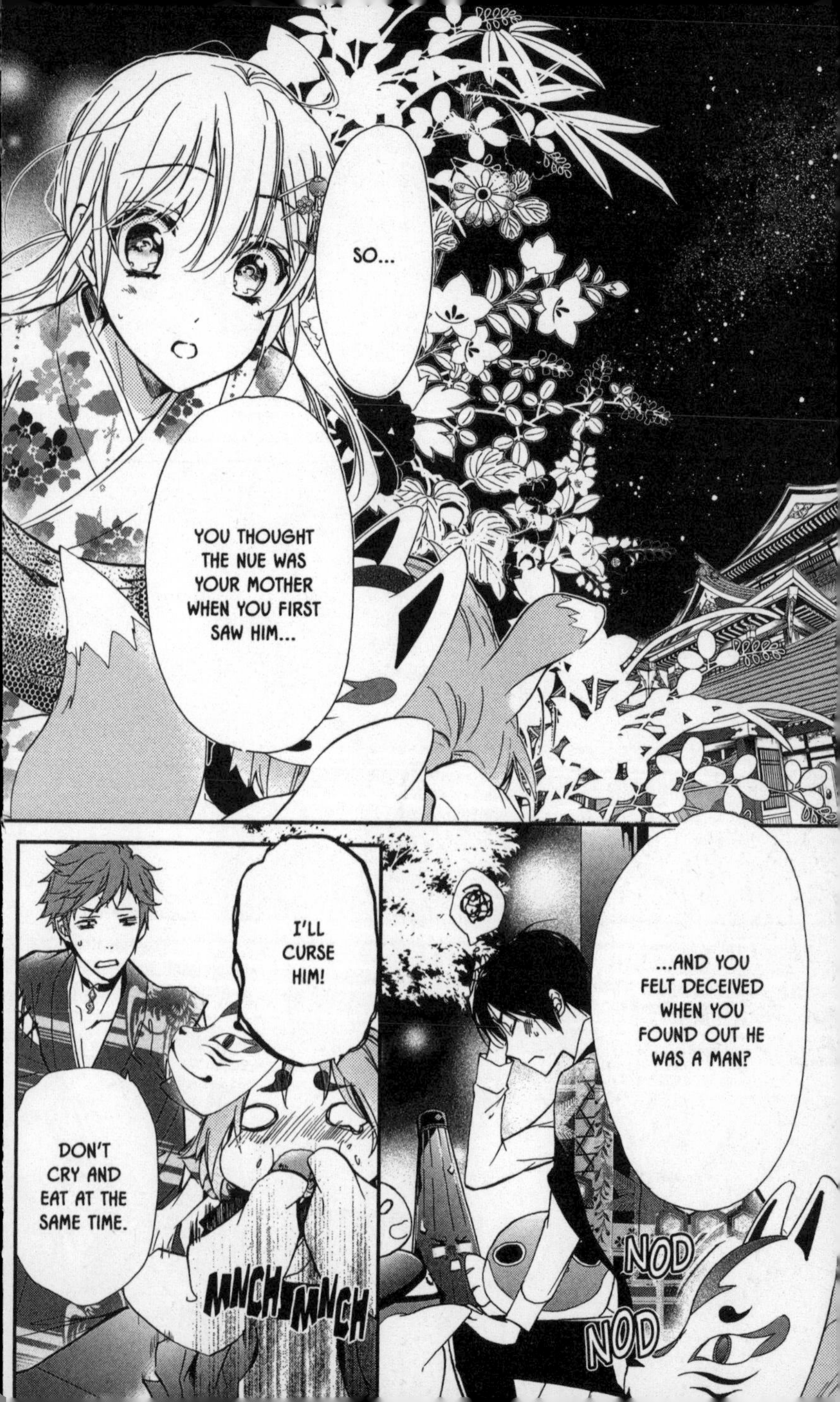
SO...
YOU THOUGHT THE NUE WAS YOUR MOTHER WHEN YOU FIRST SAW HIM...
...AND YOU FELT DECEIVED WHEN YOU FOUND OUT HE WAS A MAN?
NOD
NOD
I'LL CURSE HIM!
DON'T CRY AND EAT AT THE SAME TIME.
MNCH MNCH

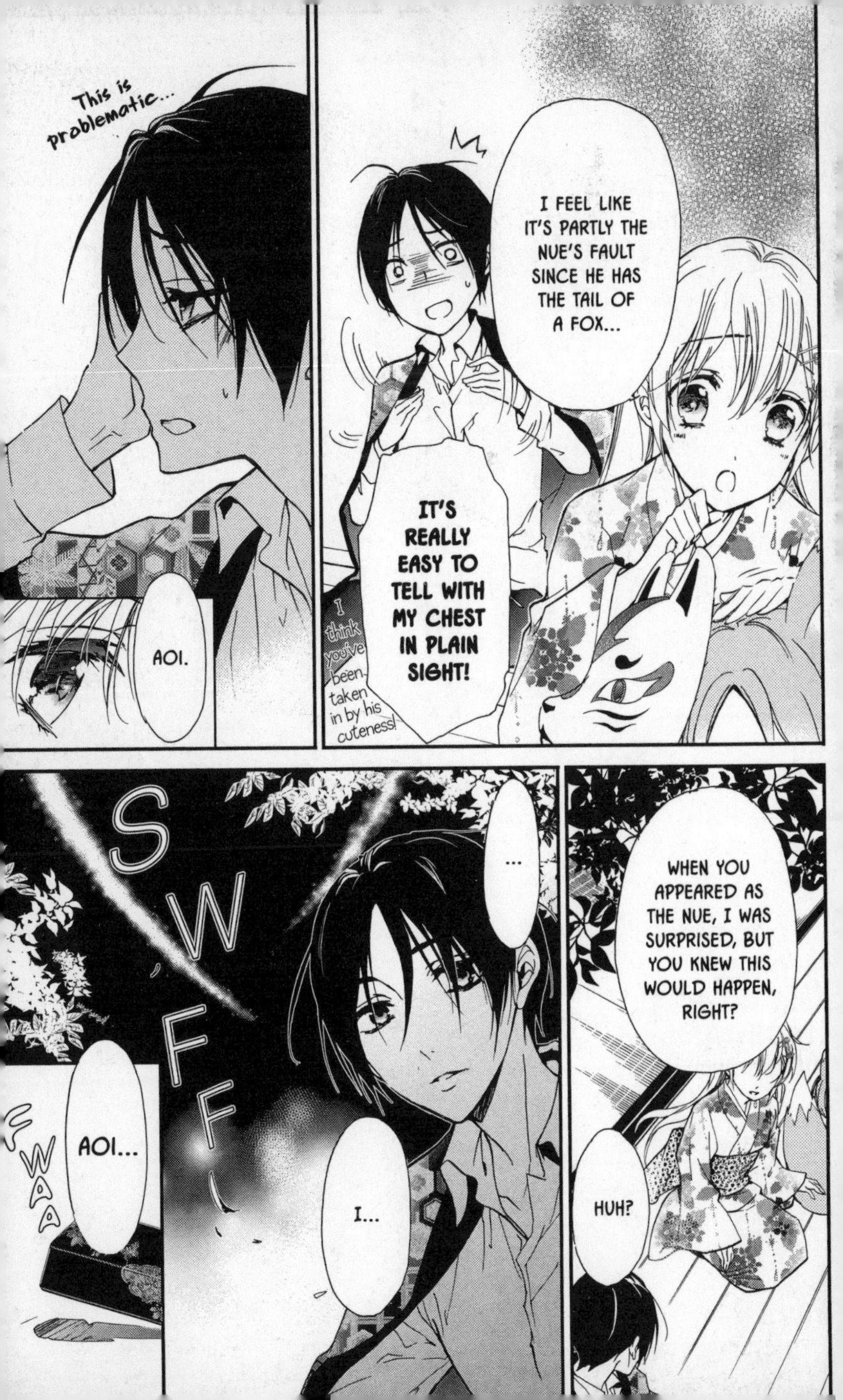
I FEEL LIKE IT'S PARTLY THE NUE'S FAULT SINCE HE HAS THE TAIL OF A FOX...
IT'S REALLY EASY TO TELL WITH MY CHEST IN PLAIN SIGHT!
I think you've been taken in by his cuteness!
This is problematic...
AOI.
WHEN YOU APPEARED AS THE NUE, I WAS SURPRISED, BUT YOU KNEW THIS WOULD HAPPEN, RIGHT?
HUH?
...
SWFF
I...
AOI...
FWAA

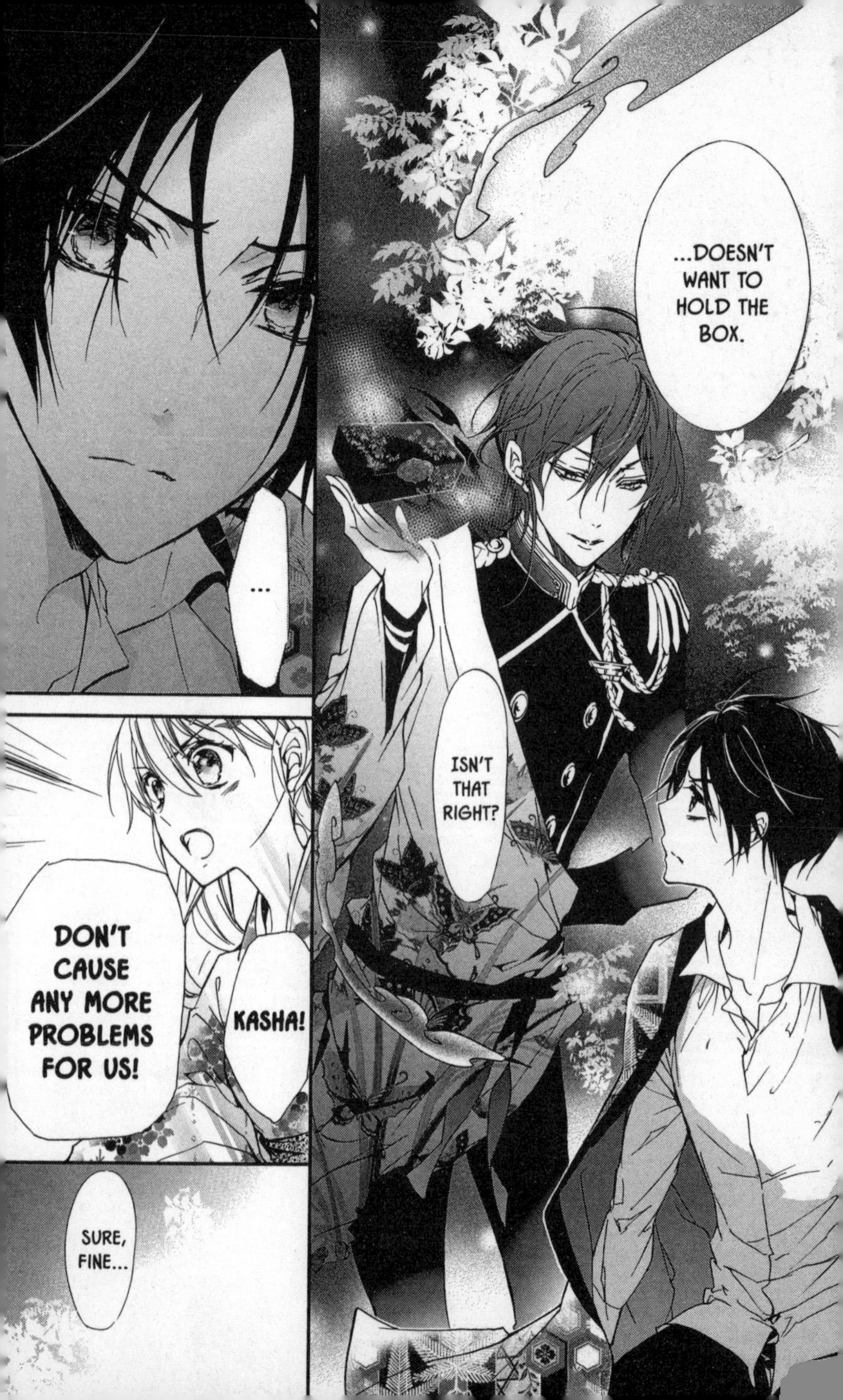
...DOESN'T WANT TO HOLD THE BOX.
ISN'T THAT RIGHT?
...
KASHA!
DON'T CAUSE ANY MORE PROBLEMS FOR US!
SURE, FINE...

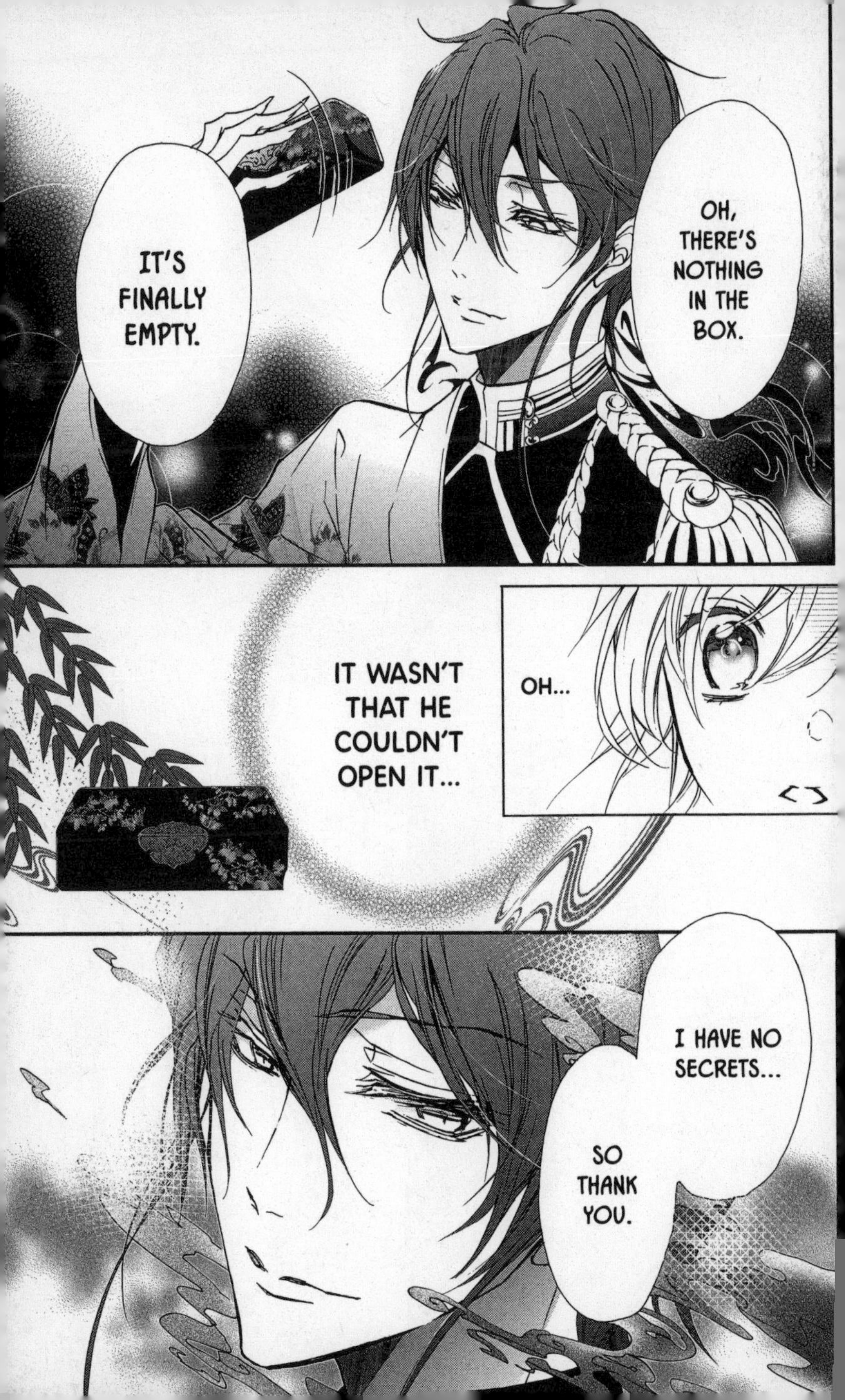
OH, THERE'S NOTHING IN THE BOX.
IT'S FINALLY EMPTY.
OH...
IT WASN'T THAT HE COULDN'T OPEN IT...
I HAVE NO SECRETS...
SO THANK YOU.

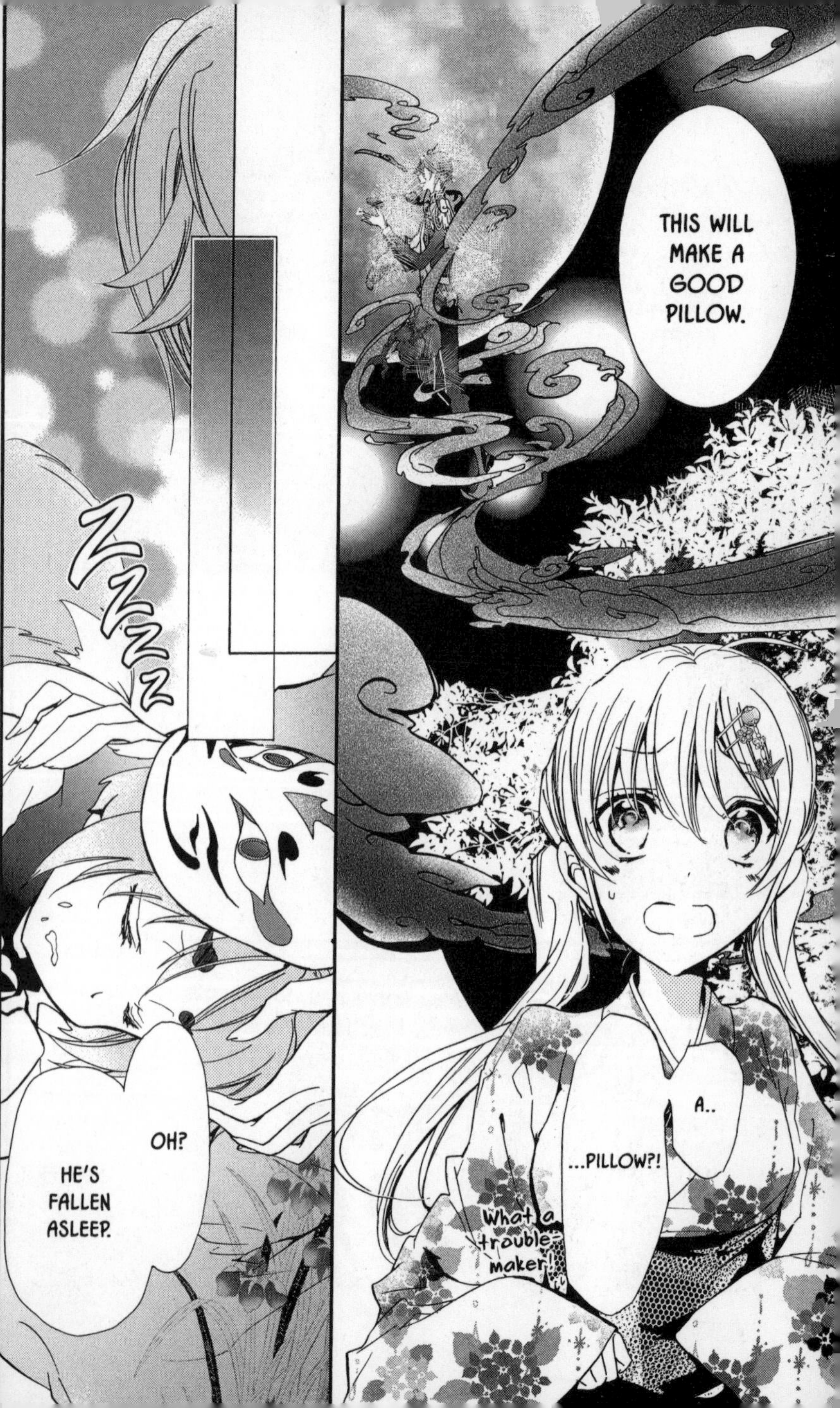
THIS WILL MAKE A GOOD PILLOW.
A..
...PILLOW?!
What a trouble-maker!
ZZZZZ
OH?
HE'S FALLEN ASLEEP.

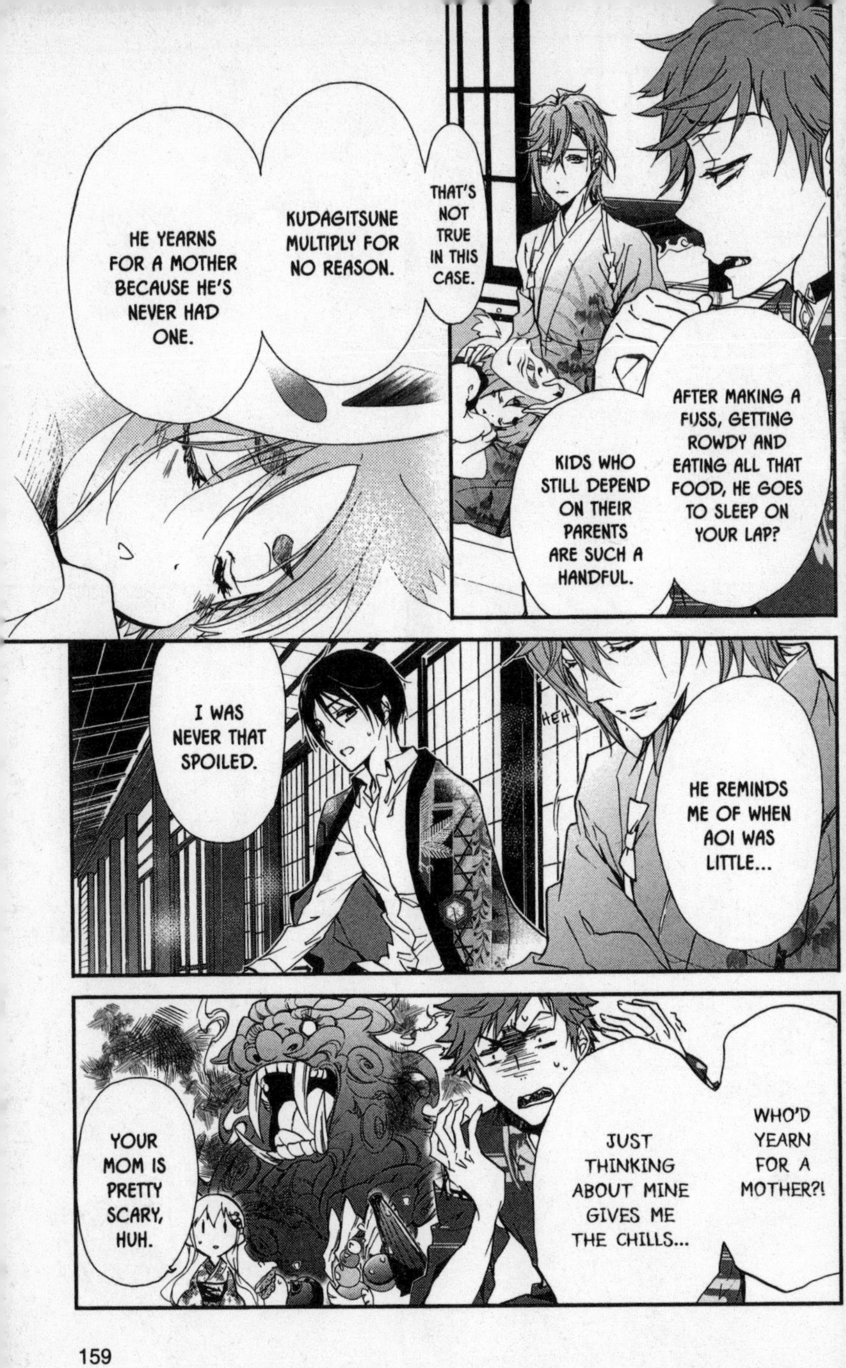

AFTER MAKING A FUSS, GETTING ROWDY AND EATING ALL THAT FOOD, HE GOES TO SLEEP ON YOUR LAP?
KIDS WHO STILL DEPEND ON THEIR PARENTS ARE SUCH A HANDFUL.
THAT'S NOT TRUE IN THIS CASE.
KUDAGITSUNE MULTIPLY FOR NO REASON.
HE YEARNS FOR A MOTHER BECAUSE HE'S NEVER HAD ONE.
HE REMINDS ME OF WHEN AOI WAS LITTLE...
HEH
I WAS NEVER THAT SPOILED.
WHO'D YEARN FOR A MOTHER?!
JUST THINKING ABOUT MINE GIVES ME THE CHILLS...
YOUR MOM IS PRETTY SCARY, HUH.

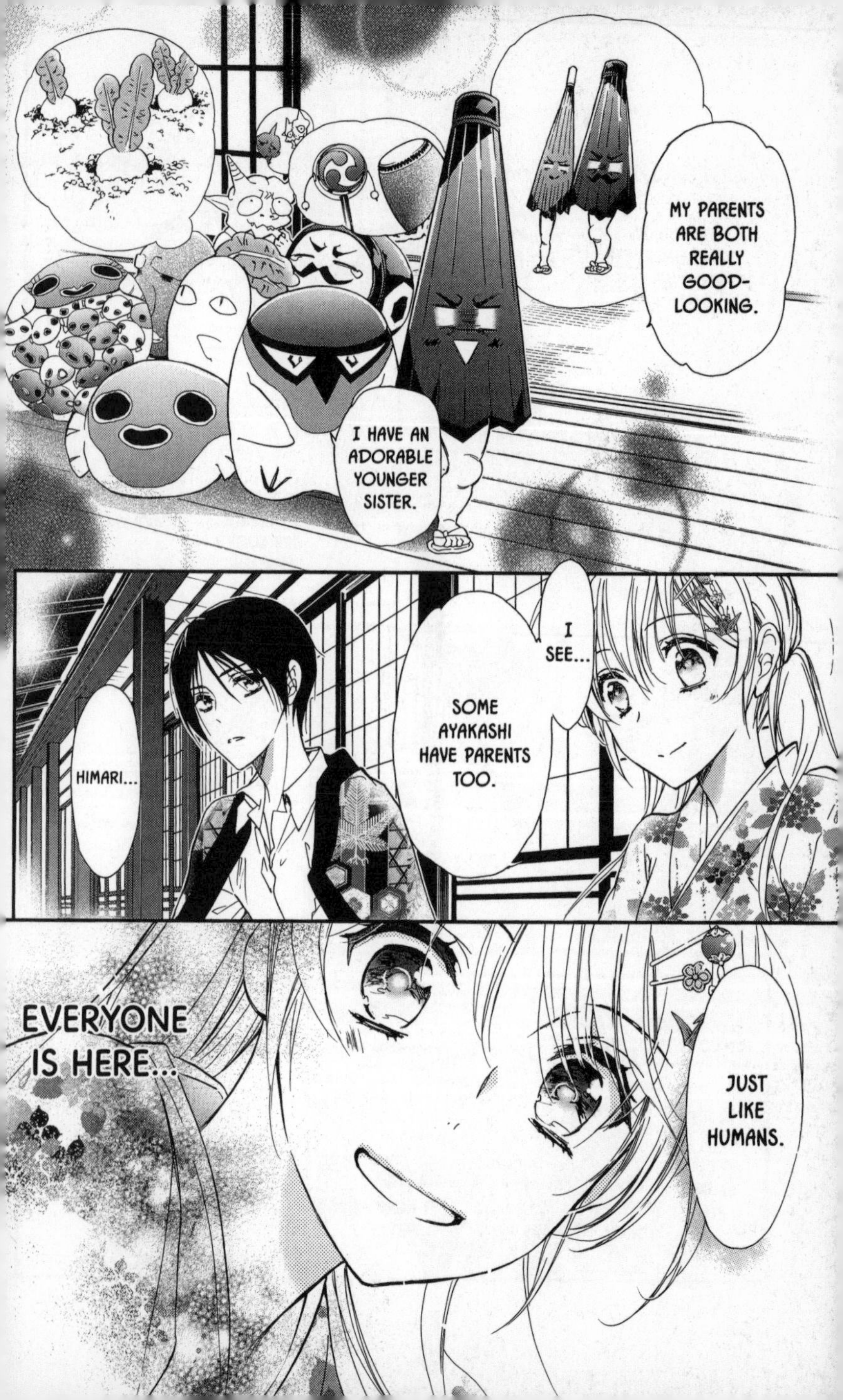
MY PARENTS ARE BOTH REALLY GOOD-LOOKING.
I HAVE AN ADORABLE YOUNGER SISTER.
I SEE...
SOME AYAKASHI HAVE PARENTS TOO.
HIMARI...
JUST LIKE HUMANS.
EVERYONE IS HERE...

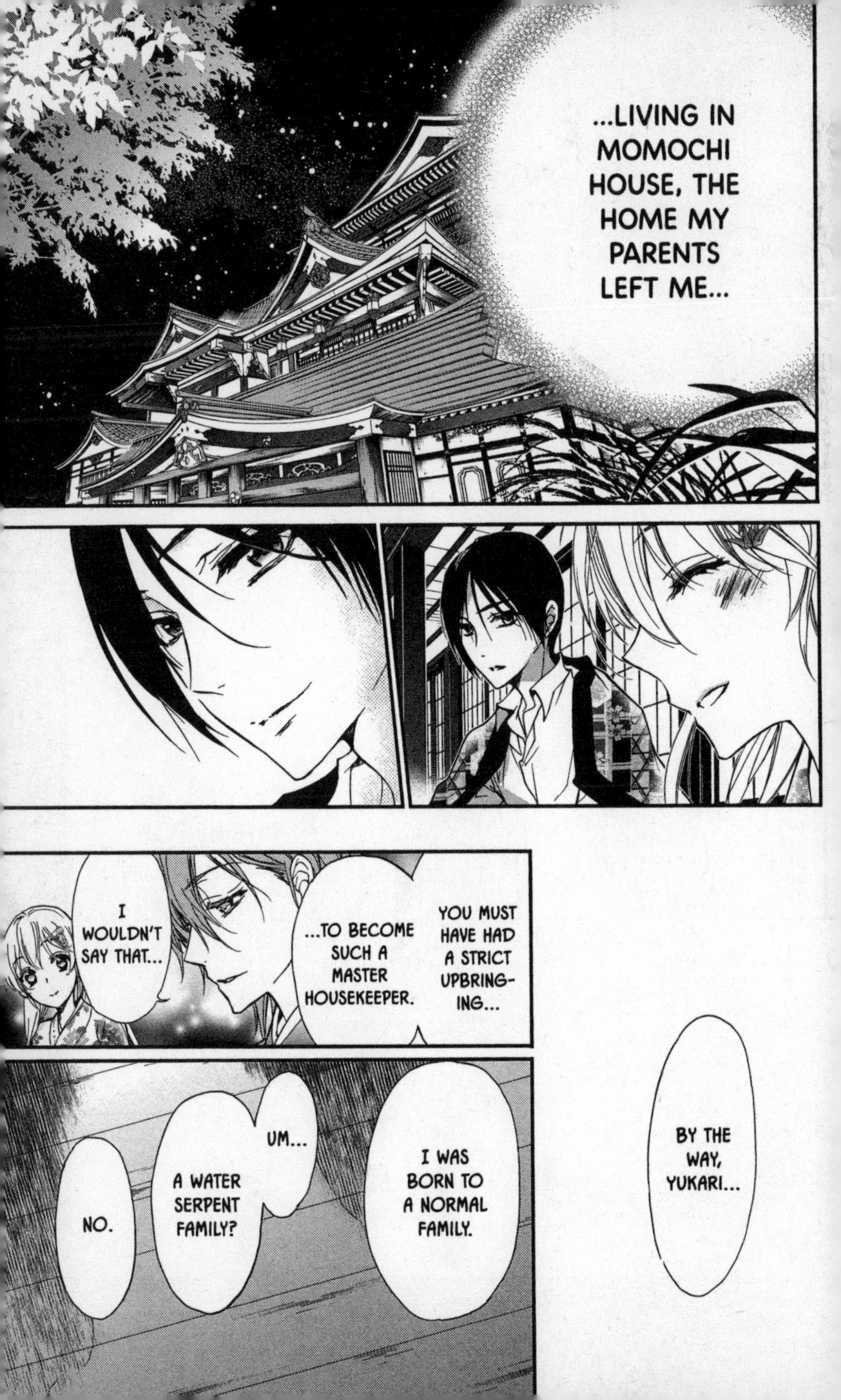

...LIVING IN MOMOCHI HOUSE, THE HOME MY PARENTS LEFT ME...
YOU MUST HAVE HAD A STRICT UPBRING-ING...
...TO BECOME SUCH A MASTER HOUSEKEEPER.
I WOULDN'T SAY THAT...
BY THE WAY, YUKARI...
I WAS BORN TO A NORMAL FAMILY.
UM...
A WATER SERPENT FAMILY?
NO.

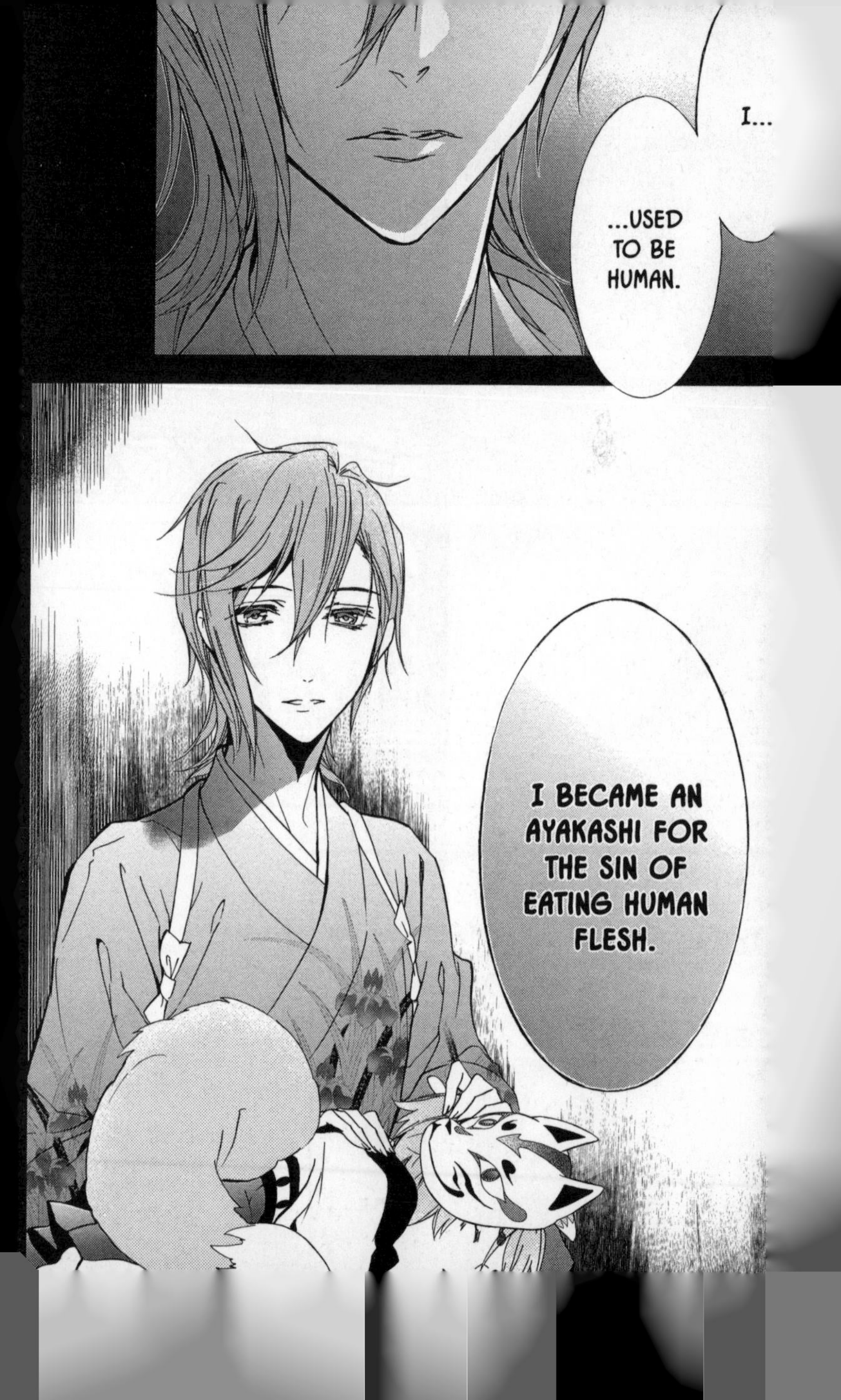
I...
...USED TO BE HUMAN.
I BECAME AN AYAKASHI FOR THE SIN OF EATING HUMAN FLESH.

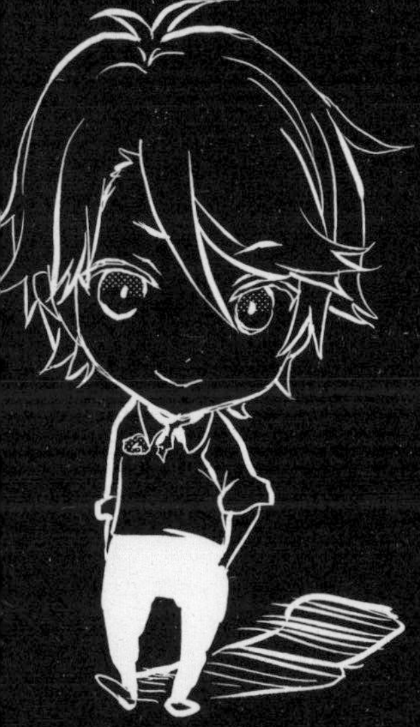

Momochi has reached volume 4. I've wanted to write the Hidaka storyline since the very start. I'm thrilled that I've finally done it. Whenever I see the sunset, I remember my childhood. I'm more likely to see the sunrise, though...

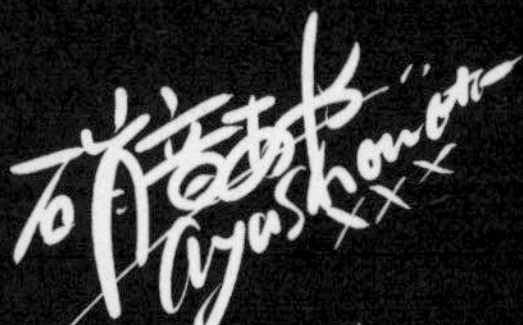

Aya Shouto

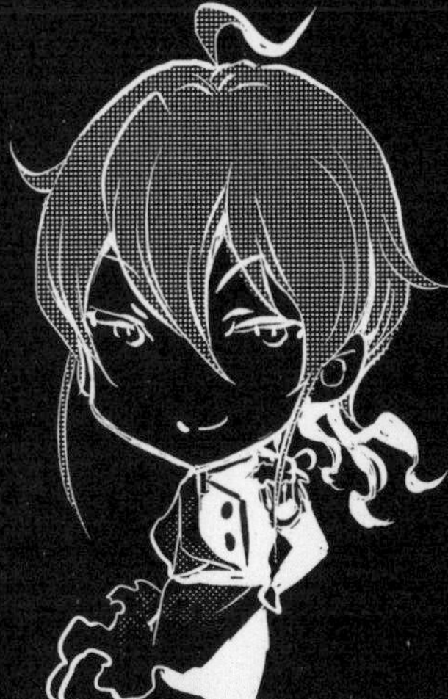

The DEMON PRINCE of MOMOCHI HOUSE

In summer when the sun is bright, I like how white fabric almost looks light purple in the shade. I think the two characters on the cover would look good in the rain, but I chose to depict them on an early summer afternoon.

-Aya Shouoto

Aya Shouoto was born on December 25. Her hobbies are traveling, staying at hotels, sewing and daydreaming. She currently lives in Tokyo and enjoys listening to J-pop anime theme songs while she works.

The Demon Prince of Momochi House

Volume 4
Shojo Beat Edition

Story and Art by **Aya Shouoto**

Translation JN Productions
Touch-Up Art & Lettering Inori Fukuda Trant
Design Fawn Lau
Editor Nancy Thistlethwaite

MOMOCHISANCHI NO AYAKASHI OUJI Volume 4
© Aya SHOUOTO 2014
Edited by KADOKAWA SHOTEN
First published in Japan in 2014 by KADOKAWA CORPORATION, Tokyo.
English translation rights arranged with KADOKAWA CORPORATION, Tokyo.

Printed in the U.S.A.

Published by VIZ Media, LLC
P.O. Box 77010
San Francisco, CA 94107

10 9 8 7 6 5 4 3 2 1
First printing, April 2016

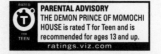
PARENTAL ADVISORY
THE DEMON PRINCE OF MOMOCHI
HOUSE is rated T for Teen and is
recommended for ages 13 and up.
ratings.viz.com

www.viz.com

www.shojobeat.com

Natsume's BOOK of FRIENDS

STORY and ART by
Yuki Midorikawa

Make Some Unusual New Friends

The power to see hidden spirits has always felt like a curse to troubled high schooler Takashi Natsume. But he's about to discover he inherited a lot more than just the Sight from his mysterious grandmother!

Natsume's BOOK of FRIENDS
STORY and ART by
Yuki Midorikawa
1

Available at your local bookstore or comic store.

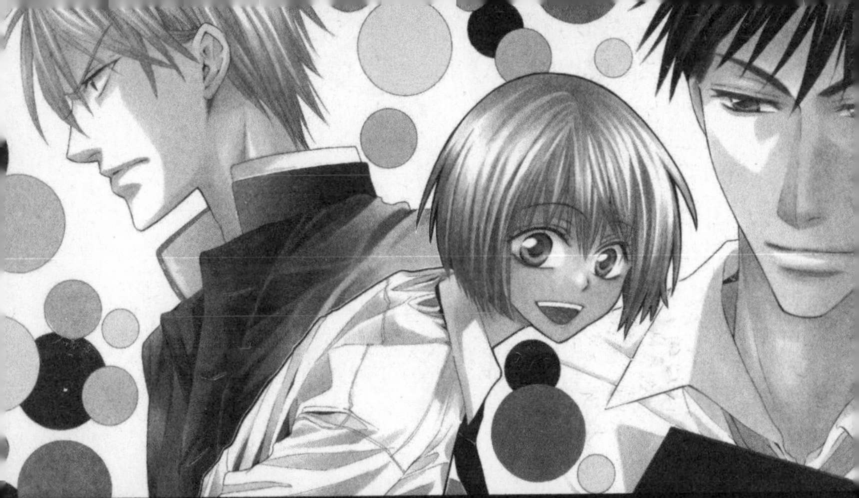

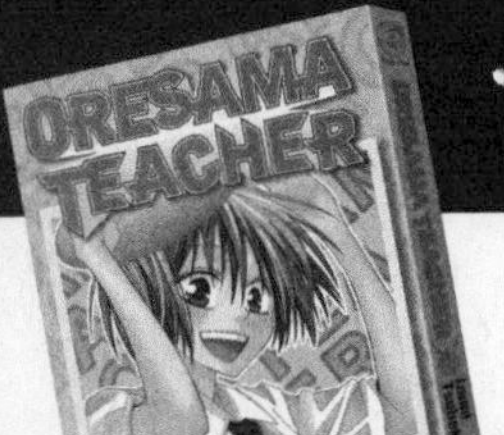
ORESAMA TEACHER
1
Izumi Tsubaki

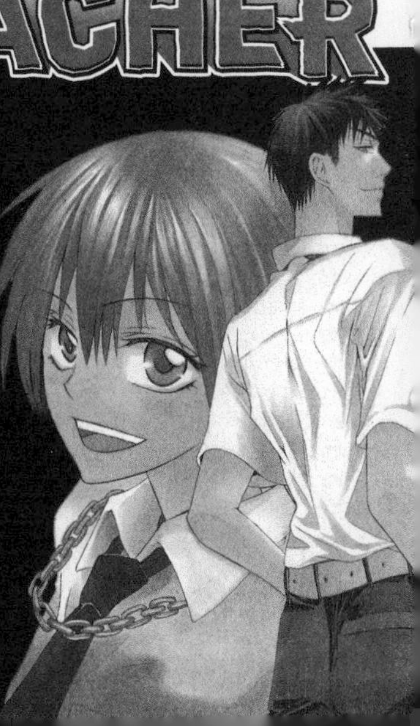

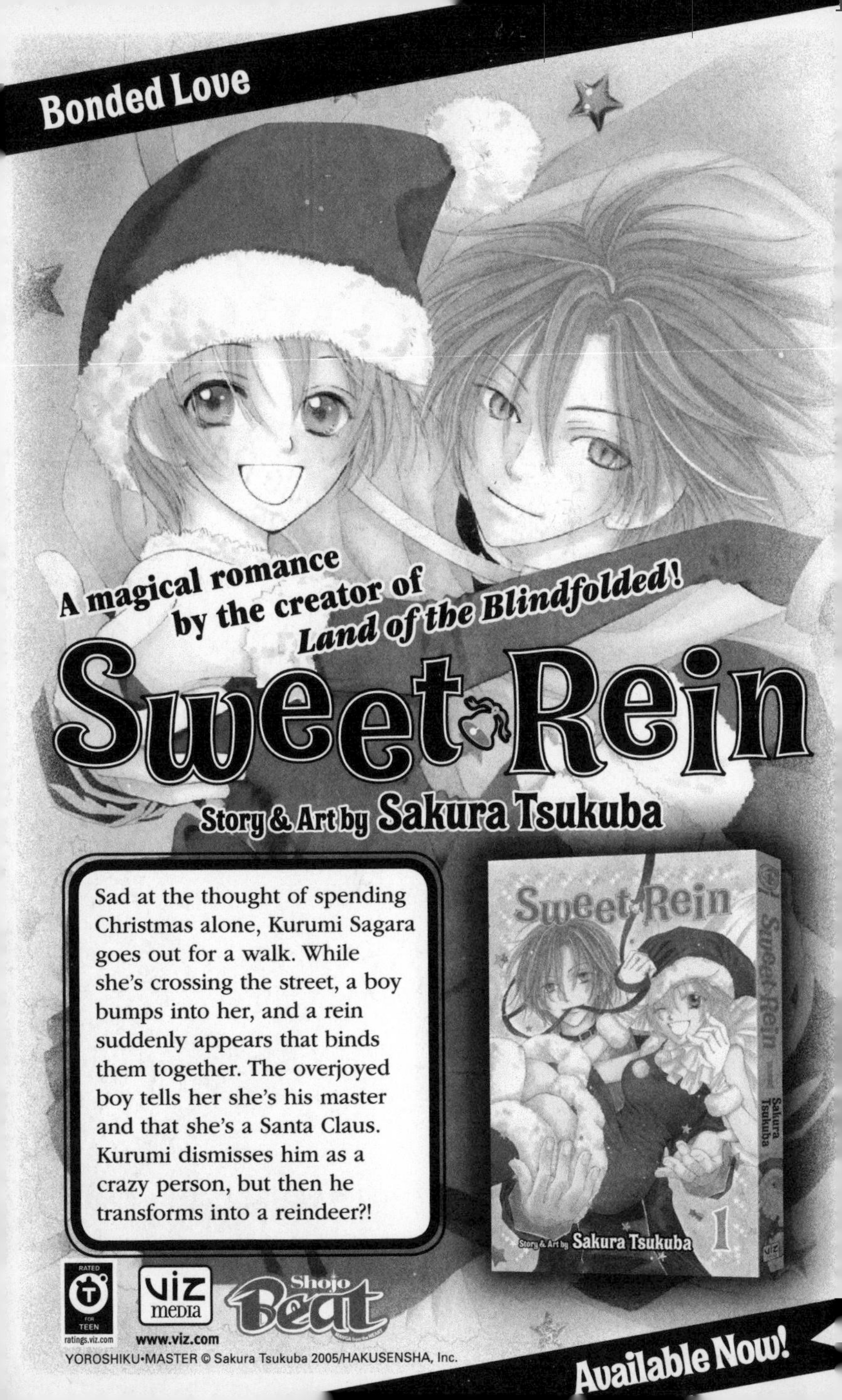

Bonded Love
A magical romance by the creator of Land of the Blindfolded!
Sweet Rein
Story & Art by Sakura Tsukuba
Sad at the thought of spending Christmas alone, Kurumi Sagara goes out for a walk. While she's crossing the street, a boy bumps into her, and a rein suddenly appears that binds them together. The overjoyed boy tells her she's his master and that she's a Santa Claus. Kurumi dismisses him as a crazy person, but then he transforms into a reindeer?!
Sweet Rein
Story & Art by Sakura Tsukuba
1
RATED T FOR TEEN
ratings.viz.com
VIZ media
www.viz.com
Shojo Beat
YOROSHIKU•MASTER © Sakura Tsukuba 2005/HAKUSENSHA, Inc.
Available Now!

You may be reading the
WRONG WAY!!

IT'S TRUE: In keeping with the original Japanese comics format, this book reads from right to left—so action, sound effects and word balloons are completely reversed. This preserves the orientation of the original artwork—plus, it's fun! Check out the diagram shown here to get the hang of things, and then turn to the other side of the book to get started!